Preface

Everyone has an opinion about brands. Planners and creatives at advertising agencies talk of conveying the personality, essence, soul and DNA of brands to consumers. These same agencies encourage existing buyers and users to spread the word about brands through Facebook, YouTube, Twitter and even good old-fashioned face-to-face conversation. It is a process that relies on exchange, interaction, viral infection, word of mouth, buzz and sometimes myth-making. Designers are proud to share examples of how pack redesign has helped to reposition an ailing product or how a new logo has brought consistency to an otherwise messy portfolio of brands, lines, and product variants. The legal fraternity see the importance of brands and trademarks as properties – properties to be protected, policed and, when threatened, defended through the judicial system. Accountants talk of goodwill, describing brands as intangible assets that are to be valued, bought and sold.

Then there are the brand owners, e.g. Unilever, Haier, Kao, Henkel, Nestle, LÓreal, Ford, Toyota, Microsoft and Google. The tendency is to focus attention on the most highly-valued global assets – the 'supermodels' of branding such as Coca-Cola, Pepsi, Chanel, Nike and Reebok. But beyond the supermodels there is considerable variation – services brands, people brands, place brands, upstart brands and dying brands. Even the anti-branding book, *No Logo*, became a potent brand for those who saw malevolence in the rise and rise of global brands. Into this world of brands and branding a niche sector of specialist agencies has arisen to offer advice, whether the problem is how to name a brand, design a logo or tagline, value intangible assets, register a trademark, or engage in the strategic repositioning of brands.

In light of these developments, it isn't surprising to find that much has been written about brand management. The challenges facing brands feature routinely and prominently in business magazines: *Fortune, Business Week,* the *Wall Street Journal* and *The Economist* – all impressive mastheads in their own right. In the research community, publications such as the *Journal of Marketing* and *Journal of Advertising Research* have carried brand-related articles for decades, and now the field is also served by specialists such as the *Journal of Brand Management* and the *Journal of Product & Brand Management*. Also in this mix are numerous books – 'how-to' books for aspiring brand managers, textbooks to meet the needs of tertiary students, lavish 'coffee table' books that offer beautiful visual displays of logos and packs, through to blogs from 'brand community' members and the sites of anti-brand agitators.

Absent, however, are books that acknowledge this complex reality of differing perspectives within and across the varied disciplines that are engaged in the process of brand management. *Perspectives on Brand Management* fills the gap. To achieve this goal, several distinct features are incorporated into the book:

1. *Different perspectives* are presented. This has been brought about consciously and deliberately in the belief that we can only begin to gain a complete picture of contemporary brand management by looking at the subject through different lenses. These lenses may appear to conflict with one another and some may seem contradictory. In some instances the apparent conflicts and

contradictions can be resolved. Debate around 'consumer-based brand equity' versus 'finance-based brand equity' is a case in point.

2. *Recent research* is assembled to inform the discussion. This is a dynamic field. Brand management, like other aspects of business, is being challenged and re-shaped by digital technologies, interactive communications, globalisation, transnational movements, consumer savvy, and many other forces of change. To explore issues, trends and challenges in the dynamic field of brand management, it is important to be abreast of current research, whilst also acknowledging the legacies of the past.

3. Throughout, the tone is *critical and questioning*. Readers are encouraged to think critically about the different perspectives: what is the weight of evidence, how reliable are the sources, is the evidence valid, do the interpretations help to move our thinking forward? Despite all the talk about brand personality and essence, for instance, there is considerable evidence to show that many consumers much of the time simply treat brands as brands – these consumers have a matter-of-fact view of the brands they buy and use. This viewpoint sits uncomfortably with the desire of brand owners to create purposeful engagement with consumers, or with the aspirations of advertising agencies to work with consumers to create meaning-rich brand myths.

4. The *multi-disciplinary* character of brand management is fully recognised. Business themes lie at the core of the book, but to achieve business success we must draw upon the understanding and insights offered by disciplines as varied as marketing, advertising, design, law, accounting, statistics, social psychology, cultural studies, and more.

5. Coverage is *global*. Examples are drawn from around the world. More importantly, the principles discussed here are as likely to resonate with audiences in any one nation as any other – notwithstanding the fact that contexts vary. The infrastructure supporting brand management is global; indeed, the growth of marketing departments, retail chains, advertising and market research agencies has been phenomenal in recent years in markets like China, India and Brazil. Consumers are connected and talking to each other about the brands they buy. Listen in and we hear about a 'good-buy' for Australian consumers if they shop online, a contamination scare in New Zealand, a new product launch in India, a highly creative campaign from China – these conversations are taking place concurrently across the globe.

To achieve the goals of *Perspectives on Brand Management*, twenty-five leading researchers have contributed, drawn from the USA, the UK, Australia, New Zealand, Malaysia and Japan. Their perspectives are varied. Their views are challenging. With such a large group of contributors, it is no surprise to find differences of opinion. This speaks to the distinct features of the book, especially that of being critical and questioning. At times this may be frustrating. Sometimes we want to be told the one recipe for success, however this emphatically is not a standard 'how to' book on brand management. To be sure, many of the authors offer advice, but it is for the reader to assess this advice in the light of supporting, or conflicting, advice from other authors and other research.

Chapters are written as research monographs and, accordingly, chapters have been peer reviewed. The whole collection of chapters should prove to be invaluable for researchers working in the field of brand management. In particular, they should find it handy to have recent material brought together, and this is intended to stimulate further research and enquiry. It is also expected the collection will offer information and stimulation to those studying the subject as part of a business degree – students of marketing should find all chapters of relevance, whereas students in accounting, law and other specific disciplines may wish to cherry-pick.

This project would not have been possible without the enthusiasm, commitment and perseverance of Rick Ryan, ably supported by Sally Keohane, both of TUP. Also, profound thanks to my wife Kathryn and sons Robert and Ewan for their unflinching support.

Mark D Uncles
November 2010, Sydney, Australia

About the editor

Mark D Uncles is Professor of Marketing and Associate Dean Undergraduate at the Australian School of Business, University of New South Wales. Prior to joining UNSW he held the position of Heinz Professor of Brand Management at Bradford Management Centre, and before that was an Assistant Professor at London Business School. Periods of sabbatical leave were undertaken at the Australian Graduate School of Management and the Judge Business School, University of Cambridge.

His research interests include brand management, employer branding, buyer behaviour, brand loyalty, store patronage and retail analysis. Publications have appeared in *Marketing Science, International Journal of Research in Marketing, Journal of Retailing, Journal of Service Research, Journal of Business Research, European Journal of Marketing, Journal of Advertising Research, Journal of Marketing Management, Sloan Management Review,* amongst others. He is on the editorial board of seven journals, including the *Journal of Product & Brand Management* and the *Journal of Brand Management.*

He has taught at all levels of tertiary education, including bachelor, specialist masters and MBA programs, doctoral programs, non-degree certificate courses, open executive programs and company-specific executive courses.

Contact: Professor Mark D Uncles, Professor of Marketing, School of Marketing, Australian School of Business, University of New South Wales, Sydney NSW 2052; P +61-2-9385-3510; F +61-2-9663-1985; E m.uncles@unsw.edu.au.

Contents

Part I: Brand Perspectives

A number of big-picture themes are presented in Part I.

In an attempt to answer three simple questions, the complexity of contemporary brand management is laid bare (Chapter 1). For even the most basic question – what is meant by 'the brand'? – potentially confusing answers are provided by different commentators and researchers. However, by taking into account a number of contingent factors, it is possible to reconcile many (if not all) aspects of the differing perspectives. How best to manage brands proves to be another question fraught with challenges, but acknowledgement of the multi-disciplinary nature of brand management helps to provide answers. At the same time as requiring functionally-based expertise, there is also a need for integration across disciplines. [Contributions to Part II build on this theme.] The third question looks to the future and invites the reader to ponder emerging challenges – once again there are complexities. [This final theme is considered in greater depth in Part III.]

There follows a review and synthesis of thinking on brand equity (Chapter 2). The tendency is for brand equity to be seen in *either* financial terms ('finance-based brand equity') *or* customer terms ('customer-based brand equity'). Both are considered here, but the important contribution of this chapter is to argue that the two should be linked and that they ought to feed into an integrated marketing balance sheet. Such a balance sheet turns concepts that are seen by some as nebulous (such as brand image, relationships, attachment and loyalty) into concrete, cash-generating assets – or processes resulting in the creation of assets – that require investment in the same way as any of the firm's tangible assets such as factories and furnishings. Measurement is central to this endeavour (consumer-based metrics are discussed further in Chapters 5 and 6).

The notion of brand equity is refined even more in the next chapter (Chapter 3). Distinctions are drawn in terms of 'value to whom' (customer and company) and 'type of value' (embodied value and exchange value). Building on these distinctions, the concept of the brand manifold is introduced, explained and illustrated. There are two key dimensions to the brand manifold: the temporal ('past brand meaning' and 'future brand meaning') and the socio-cultural ('internal brand meaning' and 'external brand meaning'). The brand manifold highlights the fact that brands do not remain static, but change and evolve over time (a theme re-visited in Chapter 12). Nor are brands unitary and monolithic, rather they are multiple-diverse socially-constructed entities (something that reappears as a point of debate in Chapter 16.

Chapter 1

Perspectives and paradigms in brand management

MARK D UNCLES

ABSTRACT

What are brands? How should brands be managed? What is the outlook for brands and brand management? These are simple questions but their simplicity is deceptive. There exist very different perspectives, controversies, contradictions, imponderables and uncertainties. Nevertheless, through the fog it is possible to identify consistent themes and insights. A distinction is drawn between 'price marks', 'trust marks' and 'love marks'. Most brands, most of the time, for most consumers are trust marks. However, the branding landscape cannot be fully understood without appreciating the variations that exist across and within products and consumers. For management, the task is how to thrive, or even simply survive, when faced with such variety. Typically, management looks to marketing communications for answers, but this is too limited a view of the task. Effective brand management must be multi-disciplinary, harnessing financial management, legal protection, design, consumer insights and employee engagement as well as marketing communications. The task is challenging and the future is uncertain – brand institutions are evolving, consumers are transforming. But the goal for brand managers may be as basic as being simply better – having more people, more of the time, trust one mark over another because it consistently and reliably delivers on its promise.

KEYWORDS

brands; brand management; price marks; trust marks; love marks; brand loyalty; consumer heterogeneity; brand futures

Introduction[1]

You are at the Yerba Buena Centre for the Arts, San Francisco. Apple CEO Steve Jobs has just arrived on stage to unveil a new tablet-style computer. The device allows users to access email, photos, ebooks, games and the web. It is hailed as a new way to read newspapers, books and reports by integrating print and digital content. With WiFi, Bluetooth and 3G options, this device offers state-of-the art levels of connectivity, and the long battery life renders it ideal for users on the move. The iPad has arrived.

In this scenario, the iPad, Apple, Steve Jobs, or co-branded combinations like 'iPad with Bluetooth' could be seen as 'the brand'. So what exactly is the brand, how is it being managed, how should it be managed, and what of the future? It turns out these are seemingly simple questions with quite perplexing answers.

What are brands?

The brand presented to potential buyers is the 'iPad'; it is the mark that identifies a particular tablet-style computer and helps consumers distinguish it from other products in the same or related markets. The mark means the iPad is not confused with, say, the Lenovo IdeaPad or the Camangi WebStation. The idea that a brand is a mark to identify one provider's product from another's is as close as we can get to a straight-forward dictionary definition, but consult any of the authoritative texts on brand management and they will all explain how 'the brand' is typically seen as embodying much more than simple identification marks (Dall'Olmo Riley 2010; deChernatony, McDonald & Wallace 2011; Kapferer 2008; Keller 2008). Our awareness of the iPad is helped immensely by the fact that the iPhone and iPod already exist – undoubtedly this is one reason why Apple chose the name, rather than call their new product 'ePad' or 'eTablet'. This suggests we cannot fully understand the distinctiveness of the iPad name without an appreciation of precursor names such as iPhone and iPod.

And what of the corporate brand name that lies behind this new gadget – Apple? You eat an apple. 'You are the apple of my eye'. For the Greek goddess Eris, the apple was the fruit of discord. Eve, one fateful day, gave Adam the forbidden fruit – possibly an apple. Newton, on a more auspicious day, was inspired by a falling apple. Such vivid associations swirl around our minds and, to an extent, are appropriated by the corporate brand – thereby adding associations, vividness, memories, personality and meaning to something that might otherwise have been regarded as bland and faceless. Apple, the corporation, took a bite (or byte?) out of the apple. So, the brand in question isn't simply the iPad, it is the 'Apple iPad', an extension of the now well-established Apple iPhone and Apple iPod brought to us by founder and saviour of Apple, Steve Jobs.

---

[1] Discussion of the iPad story draws on an editorial published in the *Journal of Brand Management* (Uncles 2010).

Stepping back from the Apple/iPad example for a moment, three perspectives in answer to the question of what is meant by 'the brand' can be identified. One response is to describe what a brand is *not* – to juxtapose brands with unbranded products. Another response is to describe brands as they are, giving a straight-forward and unembellished perspective on brands that is grounded in a realistic assessment of what is achievable in highly competitive markets. A third response is to focus on what brands aspire to be (or, strictly speaking, the aspirations that managers have for their brands) – the associations that might be created in the minds of consumers, the layers of meaning brands might instil in buyers and users, and the levels of engagement they foster amongst communities of consumers.

Perspective one: 'Price marks'

Products carry no names, logos or designs. Items are offered for sale in plain brown-paper bags or from hessian sacks stacked on the shop floor. Individual items may be distinctive – one fresh fish from a wet market isn't exactly the same as another fresh fish – but these distinctions, such as they are, are not marked out in any symbolic way. For stock-keeping purposes it may be handy for the wholesaler or retailer to give these items model numbers, but the numbers have little or no inherent meaning.

In brand-free landscapes, price is the dominant arbiter to equate supply and demand. This is the world of 'price marks'. Nowadays, in developed economies, it is difficult to find categories that are totally devoid of brands – rice, salt, onions, potatoes, fish, screws and bolts come to mind, but even here distinctive brands flourish. Adjacent to the shelves lined with value-packs and private label salts are branded Maldon, Halen Môn and Celtic sea salts, Himalayan crystal rock salt and Murray River salt. Even the value-packs and private labels carry the authority and imprimatur of established retailers who assiduously engage in branding in their efforts to build store traffic and maintain margins.

Nevertheless – despite the best efforts of marketers – consumers may hold such a 'lite' view of brands that they come close to seeing the world as brand-free. Consider the increasingly popular online 'BestBuy' sites where prospective buyers of appliances and equipment are invited to select from a range of products with enigmatic model numbers or bland, unmemorable names – competitors to Apple such as the Archos PC Tablet or ICD Ultra. In these circumstances, the choice of one item over another simply rests on a price-based evaluation of the product attributes. Price and price-related attributes (promotions, discounts, special offers, deals, coupons, warranties and so forth) are of over-riding importance.

Branding professionals like to dwell on upscale examples – Tiffany, Chanel, Gucci, Prada, Nordstrom – but many markets are heavily populated with discounters, price-beaters, bargain-basement firms and dollar-and-dime stores. Even the upscale examples indulge in special purchase sales, stock-clearance sales, not to mention facing the challenges posed by grey markets, counterfeits and fakes.

Where consumers buy on price their behaviour may appear to be promiscuous in that they simply choose the BestBuy at a particular point in time. Arguably, even this can become a form of branding, in that the everyday-low-prices offered by discounters such as Aldi, Lidl and Wal-Mart means that consumers are consistently being offered low prices. Then the question is whether any behavioural loyalty that exists in these circumstances is to the brand as such or simply a reflection of consumers' desire for low prices (i.e. is this brand loyalty or price-point loyalty?).

Perspective two: 'Trust marks'

Products are identified by their names, logos, symbols, slogans, jingles and designs, thereby helping to distinguish one provider's offering from another. Through the Apple iPad name, logo and so forth, the product is presented as a bundle of attributes that has the potential to offer (valued) benefits (utility) to prospective buyers. And, if valued, the consumer is willing to pay a price-premium. By presenting the brand in this way, the iPad is distinguished from, say, the Lenovo IdeaPad. In terms of product attributes, directly competing brands may not be vastly different from each other, but presentation of the brands differs. Thus, the look and feel of the iPad differs from the IdeaPad.

The vast majority of brands that we encounter in daily life are quite modest. Think of the cereals you buy, the grocery stores you patronise, the banks you use, the family cars you drive, or the telephony services to which you subscribe. Objectively, the bundles of attributes presented – by Vodafone, Virgin Mobile, SingTel, Telstra, AT&T, etc. – may not be vastly different from each other, but the consumer is encouraged to perceive differences. Price remains a primary attribute, along with other considerations such as quality, functionality and performance, technology and versatility, style and design, reliability and robustness, availability and service levels. Secondary attributes also may have a role to play, including country of origin/manufacture, warrantees and after sales support. If price lies at the heart of perspective one, the focus of perspective two is trust – brands as 'trust marks'.

Within categories where products are frequently bought, there is a tendency for consumers to be behaviourally loyal to a few brands – Weet-Bix *and* Kellogg's Corn Flakes, Colgate *and* Macleans, Pizza Hut *and* Burger King. Once tried and found to be satisfactory, the consumer may repeat-buy a brand. Maybe a habit forms. Over time, weak (positive) attitudes to the brand may form, underscoring the notion of brands as 'trust marks'. Typically this is not to the exclusion of all other brands in the category because the consumer may have occasionally tried some of these other brands and found them to be equally satisfactory. Indeed, faced with 2-3 equally satisfactory brands the rational course of action would be to buy on price – to buy brand A when it is on sale, brand B when it is discounted, or brand C when there is a special offer. This is not the same as the scenario in perspective one where *any* item is bought, depending on price. Here, in perspective two, the consumer has a limited repertoire of brands from which the selection is made. Polygamy is rife, not promiscuity (Dawes 2011; Ehrenberg; Uncles & Goodhardt 2004; Uncles 2011).

Perspective three: 'Love marks'

Brands are symbols that embody and convey meaning (Batey 2008). Meaning is co-created by providers (who have aspirations for 'their' brands) and consumers (who imbue 'their' brands with personal relevance). Co-creation occurs in socio-cultural space, contextualised spatially and temporally. Thus, to the extent that iPad buyers see this product as 'their' brand, it is a reflection of Apple's aspirations and of consumers' sense of personal relevance, as well as of the circumstances prevailing in the tablet-style computer market, and broader society, at a particular place and time. If perspectives one and two are about promiscuity and polygamy, the focus of perspective three is monogamy.

The language used here goes beyond describing brands as 'trust marks' to refer to 'love marks' and 'icons'. Apple is an archetypal iconic brand, a love mark[2], that knows only too well the power of marketing communications to create brands that consumers embrace passionately or, at the very least, that consumers *say* they embrace passionately. It was no accident that YouTube videos and Flickr photos appeared at the time of the iPad launch to create community interest and engagement. Through these communities, Apple stories are told and perpetuated, refined and elaborated. The immersion of the brand team (i.e. advertisers, agencies, advertising creatives) in 'populist worlds' enables stories to be co-developed which have meaning for a brand's publics (initially cultural insiders and lead-users, then cultural followers) (Holt 2004).

Such stories are constructed around myths that address contradictions in society. Stories are unlikely to be about price – in contrast to the focus of perspective one; nor are they likely to be about bundles of product attributes – in contrast to perspective two. It is the myth of Steve Jobs that reverberates through the re-telling of the Apple story, not iPad price-points, features and technologies. This speaks to the contradiction that, while consumers demand more functionality from hi-tech gadgets, they also demand user-friendliness and funky design. Technology is hidden from view, design is in the foreground. Perhaps the iPad also speaks to deeper contradictions such as our desire to stay connected in an increasingly impersonal and alienating society, or that the device has the capacity to displace the personal and render us less connected in a physical and emotional sense. This world of contradictions is creative heaven – what better way to formulate creative advertising themes than by exploring contradictions in society and shaping myths from these contradictions.

Exemplar 'love marks' tend to be high-profile, high-identity brands such as Apple, Harley-Davidson and Jeep, not brands like the Ford Focus, Opel Astra, Peugeot 307 or Volkswagen Golf in the family car market, not corporate brands like Telstra or Vodafone, Westpac or HSBC, and certainly not the humble, humdrum brands you

---

[2] As of 01 January 2011, Apple and iPod were ranked numbers 1 and 2 respectively on the Lovemarks Technology list and numbers 3 and 10 respectively on the Lovemarks Master list, see www.lovemarks.com

encounter in your local shopping mall and on supermarket shelves. As such, 'love marks' are invariably atypical of the majority of brands. Those who dwell on these examples may be accused of selection bias, wishful thinking and post-rationalisation. The attention given to Harley-Davidson is a case in point. It is an exceptional brand, with a chequered history in terms of bottom-line commercial success, where the brand myths are the stuff of romantic fiction. However, this has not stopped it from being held up as an example for others to follow if the goal is to build consumption or brand communities (Schouten & McAlexander 1995; McAlexander, Schouten & Koenig 2002).

Reconciling different perspectives: Heterogeneity in the marketplace

The three perspectives described here do not sit comfortably together. Myth-makers tend to ignore or play down price and availability, whereas realists mostly ignore myths or see them as 'mere publicity' crafted by advertising creatives. It is as if there are different paradigms, with those working within one paradigm unable or unwilling to look beyond their own boundaries. On those rare occasions when the differing groups acknowledge each other, the tone can be quite disdainful (e.g. Fournier & Yao 1997 offer a sustained critique of traditional branding concepts, whereas Sharp 2010 argues strongly for a realist viewpoint). However, it is possible to reconcile these perspectives by considering how products and consumers vary. Understanding variations, or heterogeneity, is of the upmost importance when trying to understand brands.[3]

Typically, perspective one is associated with commodities such as salt. Most consumers do not give much thought to these products and are content to base their purchasing on spot prices. There is no attitudinal brand loyalty. Some consumers might show price-point behavioural loyalty, in that they only buy when the item is below a ceiling price or within a certain price range, but again there is no attitudinal brand loyalty. However, for a minority of consumers these products will be significant purchases. Chefs will care about buying particular types of salt (e.g. table salt, sea salt, rock salt, etc.) and this might impact their brand choices (e.g. Maldon versus Halen Môn). But when dining at home, chefs may not care which brands they use. Similarly, household cooks might care about salt brands when holding a dinner party to impress a boss, but generally not be too concerned about the brands bought.

Perspective three, by contrast, is usually associated with high-identity products and iconic brands. As noted previously, Harley-Davidson is an oft-quoted example – an exceptional lifestyle brand. Most Harley owners might be expected to show exceptional levels of attitudinal and behavioural loyalty, manifest as commitment, engagement, endearment, passion and love. But for a small proportion of owners this will not be true – the possession of a Harley simply may be another 'must have' object, along with the luxury Gaggia cappuccino maker and the Magnum home

---

[3] See Heding, Knudtzen & Bjerre (2009) for an alternative framework to reconcile seemingly contradictory perspectives in brand management.

gym. Having the 'must have' object isn't about passion, it is about possession. Even where passion does exist it may wane with the passage of time; eBay dramatically illustrates how yesterday's icons become tomorrow's op shop.

Occupying the middle ground is perspective two, typically associated with middle-of-the-road 'trust marks' – frequently bought/used brands like Heinz baked beans. Here the bulk of consumers are behaviourally loyal to a few brands in each category, and these brands becoming part of a habitually bought repertoire (e.g. Heinz, Wattie's, Batchelors, Bush's, Van Camp's and SPC). Positive attitudes may form as a result of familiarity and experience with continued purchase/use. Whereas this is true for the majority of consumers, at one extreme there may be a small number who are completely indifferent about the brands they buy in these product categories ('beans are beans'), while at the other extreme are those who care passionately about particular brands (e.g. not only do they insist on buying Heinz, they collect memorabilia, subscribe to the product website, and blog about the brand). As with the other perspectives, a single person may see the brand differently depending on occasion ('am I eating alone or are friends joining me for a beans feast?') or time ('Heinz meant a lot to me as a child, but not any more').

Most brands, most of the time, for most consumers are 'trust marks'. This is so despite attempts by marketers and advertising creatives to instil consumer passion, verging on love, for particular brands. Today there is more talk than ever about securing passionate consumers, yet the best efforts of marketers are undermined by the institutional and consumer trends described later in this chapter (e.g. hyper-competition amongst directly competing brands as well as the proliferation of value-packs, private labels, me-toos, copy-cats, counterfeits and fakes).

How are brands being managed? How should they be managed?

At the launch of the Apple iPad, consumers were not only presented with a new gadget, they – and possibly you – were drawn into a carefully staged-managed marketing communications event. The event was covered with anticipation and enthusiasm by news stations and news agencies around the globe – FoxNews, the Guardian, Reuters, and many more. It was deemed important enough to feature on public broadcasting stations as well as commercial stations. The unveiling was captured on video and uploaded onto YouTube, and accompanied by live blogs and twitter. Ahead of the launch, the Yerba Buena Center for the Arts was painted in the same colours and banner designs as the press announcements and event invitations. A photographic archive of this investment in pre-event publicity was posted on Flickr and MacRumor.

The razzmatazz of the iPad launch is a well-choreographed example of the popular view of how brands are being managed in contemporary society. It displays the heavy use of marketing communications to increase brand awareness and, with luck, brand preference. Techniques have changed dramatically in recent years: more integration across multiple platforms; widespread use of interactive, digital media and search; prominence given to public relations and event management;

street-smart communicators have embraced buzz and viral word of mouth; and social media complement broadcast media. Brands are presented as 'experiences' (Brakus, Schmitt & Zarantonello 2009; Merrilees & Miller 2011). These developments have helped to keep marketing communications centre-stage as the interface between brands and their publics – irrespective of whether the focus is on existing or prospective customers, lead-users or bloggers, media commentators or fans. Marketing communications make the brand visible, audible and salient to all these publics.

This popular view of brand management not only dominates business practice, but also teaching of the subject. The iPad story is told and re-told as it migrates from MacRumor to the lecture theatres of business schools around the globe. iPad provides a script for business school instruction. Marketing communications are both channels of com-munication and the subject matter, the story and the narrative of communication. In so doing, the emphasis shifts from the iPad itself – e.g. from the facts of its screen size and battery life – to the re-telling of a quasi-evangelical launch event presided over by a semi-mythological CEO.

The iPad launch built awareness for the brand – there was considerable recall even before the product was on the shelves of electrical stores and this bode well for subsequent recognition at the point of purchase. In these tangible ways, marketing communications matters. But the advertising-centric view of brand management presents an incomplete picture. Worse, it may even distort the truth. Stories developed and perpetuated through marketing communications have the capacity to place the brand in a mythological world; myths can be very powerful, but they are also inventions born of our imagination. Brand teams need to be cautious of believing their own myths. They cannot afford to ignore the sometimes harsh realities of having to meet value/volume sales targets, of achieving margins, of product innovation, of securing legal protection, etc. Apple may be iconic, but like any other business there are financial targets to achieve. iPad is reliant on technical innovation – it would have been a non-starter without WiFi, Bluetooth, 3G, or a similar connectivity technology. Likewise, for ebooks to succeed there must be technological innovation and access to content that is worth reading. All this needs to be part of the script for thinking about the management of brands and it means going beyond the popular advertising-centric viewpoint.

A multi-disciplinary approach: Opportunities

So, how should brands be managed? Demanded is an integrated multi-disciplinary approach that gives weight to marketing communications *and* takes heed of other aspects of business: consumer psychology, consumer habit and routine, and social psychology; human resource management (HRM), organisational behaviour, and employer branding; management and financial accounting, brand valuation and brand finance, brands on and off the balance sheet, and brands in the boardroom; intellectual property, trademarks, counterfeits, and the legal aspects of branding; linguistics, signs, semiotics and symbolic meanings; graphic and product design; and so on.

By way of example, consider employer branding. It is a decade and a half since a number of trailblazing publications appeared which drew attention to trends already occurring in business practice (notably Ambler & Barrow 1996), but only in recent times can we say that employer branding has become a mainstream focus in marketing (Moroko & Uncles 2008; 2010) and HRM (Edwards 2010). Significantly, neither marketing nor HRM 'own' employer branding. Indeed, talk of 'ownership' is to miss the point. Owners possess; for successful employer branding, champions are needed – champions encourage, cajole and lead, and they may reside in either area or in a multi-disciplinary team. It is a similar message when attention turns to the interface of: branding and finance (Md Noor, Styles & Cowley 2011; Raggio & Leone 2009); brands and accounting (Sidhu & Roberts 2008); branding and trademark law (George 2006; Terry 2011); brand equity, trademarks and firm value (Krasnikov, Mishra & Orozco 2009); brands, logos and design (Wheeler 2006); and corporate strategy, corporate policy, corporate relations and corporate branding (Balmar 2010; Hatch & Schultz 2003; Ind 2007). In all these instances, there has been a shift from discipline-specific to multi-disciplinary perspectives.

None of this is easy. Coordination and integration across disciplines is required; not advertising *or* HRM, but the two disciplines working together – a multi-disciplinary approach, not a *multiple* discipline approach. Effective brand management should be seen as a silo-spanning activity, where managers are adept at making connections and linkages (Aaker 2008). 'Brand chartering' was an early attempt to facilitate this, in the belief that groups of managers needed actively to think about the multi-faceted components of branding and then consciously engage in coordinating and integrating activities (Macrae & Uncles 1997). In the absence of integrating mechanisms and activities, silo thinking is likely to prevail.

A multi-disciplinary approach: Dangers

Notwithstanding the attractions, a broader, multi-disciplinary approach presents a number of dangers: if brand management is seen as embracing everything, perhaps it becomes master of nothing; if it is subsumed within corporate management as a whole, perhaps it ceases to have any distinct identity of its own; if it is more strategic, perhaps this leaves a gap for operational specialists to enter and, in time, for them to control the territory of brand management. More specifically, is there a threat here to advertising-centric marketers and agencies? Perhaps, but it need not be so. It should be possible for them to continue in their traditional role as conductors and orchestrators – *providing* they continue to earn the right to this role. To earn this right, they will need vision to see the whole picture and exploit synergies, they will need greater mastery over a broader range of domains of knowledge, and they must be equipped with a wider set of skills than hitherto.

With imagination, dangers can be avoided and significant gains achieved. A multi-disciplinary approach should be seen as liberating and empowering for those actively engaged in brand management. It lifts branding from the realm of 'logos on business cards' to address a range of strategic themes, whilst not ignoring the operational aspects of managing brands. Re-scoping training also needs to be considered. This means helping brand managers to become boundary spanners. It means equipping them with skills and competencies that cut across traditional boundaries – for instance, showing them how to shift from a brand positioning statement (a staple of marketing courses) to the development of creative ideas and executions (which requires an advertising focus), to a much deeper consideration of graphic and product design (the traditional realm of design consultancies), to a thorough examination of name/logo/shape registration, protection and non-infringement (which puts the spotlight on legal themes).[4]

Returning to the example with which we started, the communications razzmatazz of the hyped-up launch remains a central component of the iPad story. Myth-making is also central to the story of this brand, as it was previously for Apple, Mac, iPod, and iTunes. But, in practice, the management of brands must operate across a broader platform, where external communications align with internal communications, where external brand promises to consumers align with internal brand promises to employees, where consumer-oriented myths align with employee-oriented myths, where advertising scripts align with design elements, and where all of this makes a difference in terms of brand performance – value/volume sales, premium pricing, healthy margins, competitive strength, etc. Ultimately, the iPad isn't simply about an attention-getting launch, it is about how this product, and the consumers who buy/use the product, strengthen firm value for Apple Inc. That requires multi-disciplinary thinking, practice and training.

What is the outlook for brands and brand management?[5]

What does the future hold? There are two themes to consider: institutional trends (e.g. the behaviours and actions of firms, the restructuring and redefinition of markets, the growth and significance of online vendors and intermediaries, and the opening up of new markets); and consumer trends (e.g. savvy, critical and assertive consumers, networked consumers, growing numbers of consumers who are expressing concerns about sustainable and ethical consumption, recycling and reusing, free trade and fair trade). For convenience, we will examine these themes separately, but the future lies in the complex and nuanced interplay of the two. As an example, 'brand meaning' is not chiselled onto the minds of consumers by omnipotent firms, but nor do consumers construct meaning in isolation from the intentions of brand managers and the structures of brand management; instead, meaning comes from consumers gaining value from brands and managers creating brands that they believe will offer value.

---

[4] This echoes sentiments in Aaker (2008), especially chapter 2, where the necessity to upgrade the skills of marketing staff is discussed.

[5] Discussion of the outlook for brands draw on an editorial published in the *Journal of Brand Management* (Uncles 2008).

Institutional trends in brand management

It is sobering to realise that the super-brands of today might not be the super-brands of tomorrow or, if they are, it may be for totally different areas of capability than now. Apple was founded in 1976 and Microsoft a year earlier, the biggest name in computing at the time was 'Big Blue' IBM, along with Burroughs, Control Data Corporation, Honeywell, NCR and UNIVAC. Many of the names remain, but much altered after divestitures, mergers, acquisitions, restructuring and transformations. Honeywell sold its computer division in 1990s and, like IBM, chose to emphasise its capabilities in business and technology solutions. Today the super-brands of computing are Apple and Microsoft. Symbolically, in late May 2010 Apple's market capitalisation reached US$222 billion, slightly ahead of Microsoft at US$219 billion, and second only to Exxon Mobil – valued at US$279 billion – on the New York Stock Exchange[6]. None of this was knowable back in 1976.

Changing fortunes of such magnitude have implications for brand positioning. For two decades Apple has been portrayed as an archetypal challenger brand – a minnow taking on whales, a David pitching against Goliath. This has been part of Apple's myth-making and goes some way to explain its status as an iconic brand. But does this positioning lack credibility when Apple's market capitalisation is US$222 billion? This is hardly the sum of money a David would have in his back pocket. Along with challenger positioning has been the notion that the brand is 'loved'. Is Apple now loved less as it comes to occupy a central positioning in the category? Indeed, was it ever really loved as much as is sometimes claimed? Blogs indicate some consumers display a passion for the brand, but this fails to capture all those other consumers who were never moved to contribute to a blog and those who contentedly continued (and continue) to use Microsoft products.

Ultimately, positioning is in the mind of the consumer (Ries & Trout 1986; Rossiter 2011). Consumers see a brand as central or challenging, bland or exciting, staid or innovative; nevertheless, managers have invariably tried to influence, even control, perceptions. Apple famously likes to be in control. Maybe that was realistic in the late-1970s – an era when cassette tapes were gaining traction with the mass of consumers and direct broadcast satellite was just beginning to emerge as a new communications medium. However, control over brand positioning is much less feasible in a world of near-universal online buzz and viral communications, facilitated by Facebook 'likes' and twitter. Brands are now public property. This has its upside where consumers are brand advocates, but there will be brand assassins too; ten seconds of online search takes consumers to such remarkable information

---

[6]

http://www.businessweek.com/news/2010-05-26/apple-overtakes-microsoft-in-market-capitalization-update3-.html as 'jailbreak your iPad'.[7] Realistically, between these two extremes may be a vast number of people who are reasonably indifferent to the brands with which they are presented.

In this environment, competitive intensity is a challenge for any brand, even the market leaders and innovators. At roughly the time of the iPad launch, PC World was listing 15 competing products[8] – Archos PC Tablet, Axiotron Modbook Pro, Camangi WebStation, Dell Streak, ExoPC Slate, Fusion Garage JooJoo, HP Slate, ICD Ultra, Lenovo IdeaPad, Notion Ink Adam, amongst others – this was when consumer acceptance of tablets remained unclear. The word 'hyper-competition' describes these intense levels of competition amongst directly competing brands. Advances in component technologies – enhanced HD Flash video, multi-touch screens, Blu-ray capability, camera and recording features – mean that technology-based hyper-competition continues unabated.

Then there are products that indirectly compete – e-Readers (Amazon Kindle, Aluratek Libre eBook, Barnes & Noble Nook, BeBook Neo, Entourage eDge, Foxit eSlick, iRiver Story, Jetbook, Kobo eReader, Kogan eBook Reader, Pandigital Novel, Sony Reader Touch) and laptops (Alienware Aurora, Apple MacBook, Asus Eee PC, Dell Latitude, Lenovo Thinkpad, Sony VAIO, etc), and to a lesser extent multi-media players and smart phones. A major challenge for brand managers in these circumstances is the de-differentiation of product markets (i.e. the overlapping and fuzzy boundaries that come to exist between one product category and another). Industry sees the 'tablet market' as a distinct category, but through the eyes of consumers the options might be to buy an iPad, or Amazon Kindle, or Asus Eee PC – they are not the same products, but the consumer may only spend their limited funds on buying one item, treating them all as substitutes.

Mature, non-technology markets are hardly any different. Whether attention focuses on tea or soup, there is typically a profusion of directly and indirectly competing brands: established brands and variants, value-packs and private labels, me-toos and copy-cats, counterfeits and fakes. Latest to feel the effects of intensified competition are established luxury goods retailers, as they see consumers accessing online suppliers that offer similar brands for lower prices ('BestBuy Luxury').

Consumer trends in brand management

The tenet of 'know thy consumer' is as important today as it has ever been. Astute brand managers at Apple know this, as do those at every successful firm from Microsoft to HSBC, L'Oreal to Unilever. But consumers aren't a fixed target. Consumers change: existing consumers develop new needs, change their preferences, alter their habits, and acquire new skills for engaging in purchasing

---

[7] http://www.pcworld.com/article/196415/10_great_ways_to_get_more_from_your_ipad.html

[8] http://www.pcworld.com/article/192496/slate_wars_15_tablets_that_could_rival_apples_ipad.html

and consumption; fresh consumers come into new and established markets, with their own needs, preferences and skills. Pundits talk of contemporary consumers as better informed and connected, more marketing literate and savvier than in the past, and as being more empowered. Some commentators even describe this as a new economic order – an era of consumer-centric commerce (Mitchell 2004). Assuming the pundits are correct, it would be surprising if these momentous changes didn't have implications for the way consumers think about brands and the way brands will be managed in future.

At the heart of consumer-centric commerce is the savvy consumer – someone who combines areas of competency with empowerment (Macdonald & Uncles 2007). Competency refers to practical skills and acquired knowledge to respond to a constantly changing environment. It is seen in the technological sophistication of consumers: they are ready and willing to adopt new technologies (embracing everything from 3D movies to interactive, participatory iCinema) and they are comfortable multi-tasking with their technological toolkit (seamlessly moving between word-processing to website navigation, sending SMS messages, retrieving emails from their BlackBerry and iPhone, and being guided by GPS navigation devices). Competency is also seen in the way consumers make use of their networks: the capacity to harness a network of useful personal contacts (to acquire up-to-date product information, receive word-of-mouth recommendations, and make more informed choices) and to tap into the online mega-net (with bulletin boards, chat-rooms, blogs, multi-player gaming sites, social networks, virtual communities, and word-of-web information exchange). Competency is further manifest through marketing/advertising literacy – the fact that consumers are familiar with the ideas, objectives and methods of brand management, advertising and marketing communications. This is evident in the way branding terminology is understood and used, the way consumers closely follow developments in the media business, their capacity to deconstruct and reconstruct marketing communications, and their readiness to offer judgments about products, attributes, value and levels of service. Added to which is their willingness to criticise, subvert and poke fun at business, as with the irreverent YouTube spoofs of iconic ad campaigns and more sustained attacks that are to be found on AdBuster-style anti-branding sites (Aitken 2011; Holt 2002). Such sophisticated literacy gives consumers greater control over what they see, hear and read, especially when control is combined with enabling technologies.

Empowered by access to information, but time-poor, consumers are driven by value-seeking – not just the value that accrues from consuming brands, but also value in terms of quality interactions with the organisation behind the brands. As such, they seek value-for-time, value-for-attention, and value-for-access to their personal information (Lawer & Knox 2004). The democratisation of access to information means that consumers have enhanced self-confidence in their ability to perform behaviours related to consumption – just think of the aptitude and astuteness of consumers when they engage in online grocery shopping, online travel booking, and online gift-giving. Self-confidence is in many cases fully justified – compared to conventional technologies, user-directed ones give consumers remarkable levels of control. Web users, for instance, decide which websites to visit, bookmark and revisit; they choose whether to navigate thoroughly or fleetingly; they determine if interaction should occur, how often, on what terms and for what purpose. Consumers, in short, have the ability and the confidence to 'call the shots'.

The impact on brand management of changing consumers is evident in various ways. Not least is the willingness of consumers to adopt new technologies, creating staggering opportunities for certain players to become mega-brands – from online stars like Google to gaming brands Nintendo and JagX, to re-packaged, re-invigorated, hybrid off/online businesses such as the BBC and National Geographic. In parallel is the stellar growth of comparative newcomers such as social networking sites Facebook and MySpace. This phenomenon is not entirely new – there were plenty of technological stars in the dot.com era, but these mostly proved to be shooting stars. By contrast, the mega-brands of today are committing to the long-haul – as far as that is feasible in intensely open and competitive markets.

Novel brand attributes come into play: consumers of an online social network site want to share content, communicate easily, interact in real-time, and profile themselves. Ease of use, speed and interactivity are valued attributes. Any brand that cannot match consumer expectations in terms of these attributes is likely to find its future very bleak. Information diffusion about brands is rapid through offline and online word-of-mouth communication, and through marketer-controlled and uncontrolled buzz and viral communications. Positive news travels fast, but so too does negative news. Deceits and lies are uncovered, blogged and publicised – consult MacRumors, MacBytes, iPodGear and iPodHacks. Exposure in cyberspace is full-frontal.

More and more opportunities exist for consumers to engage with brands – through brand communities, product sites, forums and blogs. But, simultaneously, there may be less and less reason to engage – why should a consumer go to the trouble of engaging when perhaps all that is wanted is a value-for-money product that will perform satisfactorily? Technological sophistication and network competency combine to reduce information asymmetry which has traditionally been biased toward the firm, giving the upper hand to consumers. This conundrum isn't fully appreciated by the brand management community. Indeed, there is a tendency to dwell on the upside rather than recognise and acknowledge there might be a downside. Businesses that over-estimate the desire of their consumers for engagement at the expense of offering basic value-for-money face a wake-up call (recollect the earlier discussion of 'price marks' and 'trust marks' versus 'love marks').

Reconciling different futures: Differentially savvy consumers

Important as all these impacts are, arguably the biggest challenge for brand managers is how to contend with differences among consumers. Consumers change, but not all at the same pace. Not all consumers are equally savvy. Not all are equally empowered. Some consumers may display competence in one area but not in another – the skilled computer operator might be inept at, or indifferent to, smart-phone usage. The new technological mega-brands appeal to the needs and aspirations of some consumers more than others. Novel attributes are more important to certain consumers than others. Online, there are consumers who fear for their privacy, whereas others flagrantly disregard their privacy and the privacy of others. Information diffuses faster through some groups than others. Engagement is desired by some and shunned by others.

In part this is generational. The under-thirties 'are more savvy, more materialistic, more media-saturated and more impatient than any generation that's preceded them' (Mackay 2007). Gen Y – the so-called options generation – wants the freedom to exercise choice. Almost all Gen Ys in developed economies own a mobile phone and computer, most will own an MP3 player, XBox or equivalent, they will use the internet daily and will routinely download music and movies (illegally as well as legally). Evidence, if evidence is needed, that these consumers are exercising choice. Further down the generational ladder, teens, tweens and Gen M know nothing but the exercise of choice, particularly when it comes to new technologies. In high school playgrounds, the brands that dominate conversation are not necessarily old-timers like Disney; rather, they are the purveyors of smart devices – Nokia N8, iPhone, iPod Touch, Windows Phone 7 – and the names behind interactive, multi-player, adventure and fantasy games – RuneScape, World of Warcraft, Call of Duty and Maple Story.

But the picture is more complicated than this: it isn't simply that the young are savvy and the old aren't. Indeed, many in the older generations are savvy and technologically sophisticated. Moreover, older consumers are striving to be younger. 'Sixty is the new 50, they want to assure us, because it reinforces the conviction that they are much younger than their parents were at the same age: they eat younger, dress younger, act younger, think younger, feel younger' (Mackay 2007). Perhaps the real difference between the generations is Gen Y and Gen M take digital, interactive technologies for granted – they are cyberspace natives – whereas older generations are immigrants who have, at differing rates and with differing abilities, had to learn about this brave new world (Lankshear & Knobel 2006). Superimposed on these generational differences are variations in gender, socio-economic status, access to technology, educational attainment and ability – all the components that go to create, on the one hand, digital communities and, on the other hand, digital divides.

Reconciling different futures: Differentially responsive brand management

One view of these differences among consumers is that they coalesce into neat segments which can be served by niche 'love mark' brands. Marketers have in mind an engagement model where brands are seen as highly customised – and therefore highly relevant – to particular groups of consumers, where there is an emotional connection or bond between consumers and brands, accompanied by strong socio-emotional relationships in physical and virtual space. Relationships are at the core of this engagement model. The gamut of marketing communications then follows from the existence of these relationships, not the other way round. 'Brand engagement drives directly to what the marketer is trying to do – get the customer involved with the brand' (Schultz 2007). However, reality may be far less comforting for those in brand management; there exists a fragile, fractured and fragmented landscape, where it is increasingly difficult for brands to be neatly aligned with well-defined, identifiable and stable groups of consumers. Even the same consumer may display heterogeneous behaviour from occasion to occasion. It is not uncommon to see 'approach-avoidance' behaviour, with the same consumer alternately drawn to new brands/technologies and repelled by them.

In this landscape it is imperative for brand managers to 'know thy consumer'. They must be attuned and alert. Their branding plans and strategies must be formulated on a multi-disciplinary platform. Everything must be done well – the razzmatazz of external communications will not work if not supported by internal communications and backroom operations. 'What separates winners from losers', write Barwise & Meehan (2004), 'is usually not their strategies but their differing ability to execute those strategies'. This calls for brand implementation that is simply better than the competition. Is the iPad simply better? Perhaps Apple's success comes down to this basic question.

Summary

In this chapter three deceptively simple questions have been examined. Key points to emerge are:

- 'The brand' can be viewed very differently, depending on whether it is seen as just one step up from a model number (as is the case with 'price marks') or as the embodiment of rich and nuanced meanings shaped and re-shaped in the socio-cultural spaces occupied by consumers and brand owners (which is where 'love marks' tend to be located). Occupying the middle ground, and arguably the most commonplace, are 'trust marks'. An appreciation of product and consumer heterogeneity helps to make sense of these seemingly contradictory portrayals of the brand.

- Brand management must be seen as a multi-disciplinary activity, with a primary focus on building successful 'trust marks'. In addition to the obvious importance of marketing communications, attention should be given to: consumer psychology, consumer habit and routine, and social psychology; human resource management, organisational behaviour, and employer branding; management and financial accounting, brand valuation and brand finance, brands on and off the balance sheet, and brands in the boardroom; intellectual property, trademarks, counterfeits, and the legal aspects of branding; linguistics, signs, semiotics and symbolic meanings; and graphic and product design. This is a long, but not exhaustive, list. Integrating mechanisms and activities are required if silo thinking is to be avoided.

- The future will be no less challenging than the past. Momentous institutional changes are matched by equally dramatic changes amongst consumers. Savvy consumers are challenging the traditional authority of brands – these consumers are competent, informed, networked, empowered and assertive, but not all consumers are equally savvy and there are digital divides as well as digital communities. An appreciation of product and consumer heterogeneity helps to make sense of emerging trends.

References

Aaker, DA 1996, *Building Strong Brands,* New York: Free Press.

Aaker, DA 2008, *Spanning Silos: The New CMO Imperative,* Harvard, MA: Harvard Business Press.

Aitken, R 2011, 'Shifting brands: Reception, resistance and revision', Chapter 17, this volume.

Ambler, T & Barrow, S 1996, 'The employer brand', *Journal of Brand Management*, 4 (3), 185-206.

Balmer, JMT 2010, 'Explicating corporate brands and their management: Reflections and directions from 1995', *Journal of Brand Management*, 18 (3), 180-196.

Batey, M 2008, *Brand Meaning,* Abingdon, UK: Routledge/Taylor & Francis.

Barwise, PT & Meehan, S 2004, *Simply Better,* Harvard MA: Harvard Business Press.

deChernatony, L, McDonald, M & Wallace E, 2011, *Creating Powerful Brands,* 4th edn, Oxford, UK: Butterworth-Heinemann.

Dall'Olmo Riley, F (ed) 2010, *Brand Management,* London: Sage Library in Marketing.

Dawes, J 2011 'Predictable patterns in buyer behaviour and brand metrics: Implications for brand managers', Chapter 6, this volume

Edwards, MR 2010, 'An integrative review of employer branding and OB theory', *Personnel Review* (forthcoming).

Ehrenberg, ASC, Uncles, MD & Goodhardt, GJ 2004, 'Understanding brand performance measures: Using Dirichlet benchmarks', *Journal of Business Research*, 57 (12), 1307-25.

Fournier, S & Yao, JL 1997, 'Reviving brand loyalty: A reconceptualization within the framework of consumer-brand relationships', *International Journal of Research in Marketing*, 14 (5), 451-472.

George, A 2006, 'Brands : Interdisciplinary perspectives on trade marks and branding', *Journal of Brand Management*, 13 (3), 175-177.

Hatch, MJ & Schultz, M 2003, 'Bringing the corporation into corporate branding', *European Journal of Marketing*, 37 (7-8), 1041-1064.

Heding, T, Knudtzen CF & Bjerre M 2009, *Brand Management: Research, Theory and Practice,* Abingdon, UK: Routledge/Taylor & Francis.

Holt, D 2002, 'Why do brands cause trouble? A dialectical theory of consumer culture and branding', *Journal of Consumer Research*, 29 (1), 70-90.

Holt, D 2004, *How Brands Become Icons: The Principles of Cultural Branding*, Harvard MA: Harvard Business Press.

Ind, N 2007, *The Corporate Brand*, London: Kogan Page.

Kapferer, J-N 2008, *The New Strategic Brand Management: Creating and Sustaining Brand Equity Long Term*, 4th edn, London: Kogan Page.

Keller, KL 2001, 'Building customer-based brand equity', *Marketing Management*, 10 (2), 14-19.

Keller, KL 1993, 'Conceptualizing, measuring, and managing customer-based brand equity', *Journal of Marketing*, 57 (January), 1-22.

Keller, KL 2008, *Strategic Brand Management: Building, Measuring and Managing Brand Equity*, 3rd edn, New Jersey: Prentice Hall.

Krasnikov, A, Mishra, S & Orozco, D 2009, 'Evaluating the financial impact of branding using trademarks: A framework and empirical evidence', *Journal of Marketing*, 73 (6), 154-166.

Lankshear, C & Knobel, M 2006, *New Literacies: Everyday Practices and Classroom Learning*, Berkshire, UK: McGraw-Hill.

Lawer, C & Knox, S 2004, 'Reverse marketing, consumer value networks and the new brand intermediaries', in Chang, Y.S. (ed.) *Value Network and ICT Symbiosis: Issues and Applications for Operational Excellence*, New York, NY: Kluwer.

McAlexander, JH, Schouten, JW & Koenig, HF 2002, 'Building brand community', *Journal of Marketing*, 66 (1), 38-54.

Macdonald, E & Uncles, MD 2007, 'Consumer savvy: Conceptualisation and measurement', *Journal of Marketing Management*, 23 (5-6), 497-517.

Mackay, H 2007, *Advance Australia ... Where?* Sydney, Australia: Hachette Australia.

Macrae, C & Uncles, MD, 1997 'Re-thinking brand management: The role of brand chartering', *Journal of Product & Brand Management*, 6 (1), 64-77.

Md Noor, S, Styles, C & Cowley, E 2011, 'Brand equity: Linking financial and customer perspectives', Chapter 2, this volume.

Mitchell, A 2004, 'The buyer-centric revolution: The rise of reverse direct', *Interactive Marketing*, 5 (4), 345-358.

Moroko, L & Uncles, MD 2009, 'Employer branding and market segmentation', *Journal of Brand Management*, 17 (3), 181-196.

Moroko, L & Uncles, MD 2011, 'Employer brands', Chapter 9, this volume.

Raggio, RD & Leone, RP 2009, 'Drivers of brand value, estimation of brand value in practice and use of brand valuation: Introduction to the special issue', *Journal of Brand Management*, 17 (1), 1-5.

Reichheld, FF & Teal, T 1996, *The loyalty effect: The hidden force behind growth, profits, and lasting value.* Boston, MA: Harvard Business School Press.

Ries, A & Trout, J 1986, *Positioning: The battle for your mind.* New York: McGraw-Hill Inc.

Rossiter, JR 2011, 'Brand positioning: The three-level positioning procedure', Chapter 4, this volume.

Schultz, D 2007, 'Focus on brand changes rules of engagement', *Marketing News*, 15 August, 7.

Sharp, B 2010, *How Brands Grow*, Melbourne, Australia: Oxford University Press.

Schouten, JW & McAlexander, JH 1995, 'Subcultures of consumption: An ethnography of the new bikers', *Journal of Consumer Research*, 22 (June), 43-61.

Sidhu, B & Roberts, JH 2008, 'The marketing accounting interface – lessons and limitations', *Journal of Marketing Management*, 24 (7-8), 669-686.

Terry, A 2011, 'Legal aspects of brand management', Chapter 11, this volume.

Uncles MD 2008, 'Editorial: Know thy changing consumer', *Journal of Brand Management*, 15 (4), 227-231.

Uncles MD 2010, 'Editorial: Broadening the scope of brand management', *Journal of Brand Management*, 17 (6), 395-398.

Uncles MD 2011, 'Understanding brand performance measures', Chapter 5, this volume.

Wheeler, A 2006, *Designing brand identity*, 2nd edn, New Jersey: Wiley.

Author biography

Mark D Uncles is Professor of Marketing and Associate Dean Undergraduate at the Australian School of Business, University of New South Wales. Prior to joining UNSW he held the position of Heinz Professor of Brand Management at Bradford Management Centre, and before that was an Assistant Professor at London Business School. Periods of sabbatical leave were undertaken at the Australian Graduate School of Management and the Judge Business School, University of Cambridge.

His research interests include brand management, employer branding, buyer behaviour, brand loyalty, store patronage and retail analysis. Publications have appeared in *Marketing Science, International Journal of Research in Marketing, Journal of Retailing, Journal of Service Research, Journal of Business Research, European Journal of Marketing, Journal of Advertising Research, Journal of Marketing Management, Sloan Management Review,* amongst others. He is on the editorial board of seven journals, including the *Journal of Product & Brand Management* and the *Journal of Brand Management*.

He has taught at all levels of tertiary education, including bachelor, specialist masters and MBA programs, doctoral programs, non-degree certificate courses, open executive programs and company-specific executive courses.

Contact: Professor Mark D Uncles, Professor of Marketing, School of Marketing, Australian School of Business, University of New South Wales, Sydney NSW 2052; P +61-2-9385-3510; F +61-2-9663-1985; E m.uncles@unsw.edu.au.

Chapter 2

Brand equity: Linking financial and customer perspectives

SHUHAIDA MD NOOR, CHRIS STYLES AND ELIZABETH COWLEY

ABSTRACT

A distinction is drawn between consumer-based brand equity (CBBE) and financial-based brand equity (FBBE). The development of brand equity from both the CBBE and FBBE perspectives is described and conceptual distinctions between these two are delineated. Then a framework is presented of the relationship between the two concepts to assist those managing, assessing, and investing in brands. A marketing balance sheet reporting both FBBE and CBBE is proposed at the end of the chapter.

KEYWORDS

brand equity; intangible assets; customer-based brand equity; financial-based brand equity; marketing balance sheet

Introduction

Tight economic conditions place increasing pressure on marketers to be accountable for their marketing investments. This follows repeated calls for the development of robust marketing metrics over the past decade. Indeed, marketing accountability has been one of the Marketing Science Institute's (MSI) top research priorities from 1998 to the present.

The Australian Marketing Institute (AMI) embarked on its Marketing Metrics Project in 2004, culminating in an extensive website of metrics that went online in 2008 (www.ami.org). Being at the centre of marketing activities, brands have become a particular focal point for measurement, leading to increasing attention to brand equity. However, the use of the term 'brand equity', while widespread, has not had uniform meaning. It has been used interchangeably to refer to the value of brands to customers (customer-based brand equity—CBBE) on the one hand and to the financial value of brands to firms (financial-based brand equity—FBBE) on the other. The former measures the impact of marketing activity on consumers while the latter is a measure of business performance. The challenge for marketers is not only to measure both forms of brand equity but also to understand the link between the two.

In this chapter, we clarify the conceptual meaning of both types of brand equity and explain how they are measured. We then present a framework of the relationship between the two concepts to assist those managing, assessing, and investing in brands. We begin by tracing the development of brand equity from both the CBBE and FBBE perspectives.

History of brand equity

The idea that brands are a source of value to firms can be traced to the 1950s when marketing practitioners discussed brand images. It was not until the 1980s, however, that the term 'brand equity' was coined to reflect the economic value of brands (Feldwick 1996).

Heightened interest in evaluating the economic value of brands to firms was observed in the early 1980s when brands were traded for substantial fortunes. Firms were paying sums in excess of the target firm's balance sheet valuations in takeover bids, with the difference being attributed to brand equity (Feldwick 1996).

Unlike other assets, the value of the brands was not explicitly reflected in the balance sheets when the firm was traded; rather was included simply as part of the firm's goodwill (Haigh 1999). In order to account explicitly for the true value of brands on the balance sheet and to avoid undervaluing brands, a more accurate brand valuation method was needed.

Financial-based brand equity

To capture the net financial worth of brands as separable assets, various methods of measuring FBBE have been developed.

For example, Simon and Sullivan (1993) introduced a technique based on financial market estimates of brand-related profits. They defined FBBE as the incremental cash flows that accrue to branded products over unbranded products. Brand equity is based on the market value of the firm that, in turn, is assumed to reflect the value of the firm's tangible and intangible assets or goodwill.

An important element of this valuation method is that brand equity reflects the expected value of future returns, as it is assumed that the stock price fully reflects all available information on expected future cash flows to stockholders. To calculate brand equity, the value of intangible assets is first estimated by subtracting the replacement cost of tangible assets from a firm's market capitalisation. The value of the intangible assets is then apportioned into:

- the value of brand equity,
- the value of non-brand factors that reduce the firm's cost relative to competitors such as R&D and patents, and
- the value of industry-wide factors that permit monopoly profits such as regulation.

The brand equity component is further divided into a demand-enhancing component influenced by factors such as advertising and positive experiences and a cost-saving component attributed to promoting branded products. These two components represent the impact of marketing activities on consumers' differential responses towards the brand.

Perhaps the most widely recognised commercial brand valuation method is that developed by Interbrand Ltd, a brand valuation consulting firm that has produced an annual list of the most valued brands in the world since 1992.

Brand value is calculated by multiplying the brand's average profitability by a price/earnings multiplier (Kamakura & Russell 1993; Barth *et al.* 1998; Kerin & Sethuraman 1998).

First, the brand's average profitability is estimated by subtracting what could be earned on a basic non-branded version of the product from the brand's after-tax operating income. The operating income of the brand is estimated through extensive discussions with market analysts and Interbrand's own analysis of the firm's financial statements, including segment disclosures.

Earnings of the non-branded version of the product are estimated by gauging the amount of capital required to generate the brand's sales and assuming that a generic version of the product would generate a 5% net pre-tax return on that capital.

Next, a measure of brand strength is calculated based on seven components:

1. leadership—the brand's ability to influence its market (maximum 25 points),

2. stability—the ability of a brand to survive (maximum 15 points),

3. market—the brand's trading environment (maximum 10 points),

4. internationality—the ability of the brand to cross geographic and cultural borders (maximum 25 points),

5. trend—the ongoing direction of the brand's importance to its industry (maximum 10 points),

6. support—the effectiveness of the brand's communications (maximum 10 points), and

7. protection—the brand owner's legal title (maximum 5 points).

The component points are added together to derive the measure of brand strength (the 'multiplier'). Brand value is then calculated by multiplying the after-tax operating income by the brand strength multiplier.

Interbrand's brand valuation method considers various possible factors that would contribute to the brand's strength in earning future cash flow, some of which are not behaviourally based—e.g. its trading environment (e.g. technological changes) and legal protection. Thus, this valuation method captures more than the strength of customer's franchise because it includes all of the firm's intangible assets related to the brand.

A survey-based brand equity evaluation method is proposed by Srinivasan *et al.* (2005) to estimate the incremental choice probabilities at the individual customer level.

They define brand equity as the incremental (dollar) contribution per year obtained by the brand in comparison with the underlying product (or service) with no brand-building efforts. They conceptualise brand equity as arising from

- increased brand awareness,

- incremental preference due to enhanced attribute perceptions, and

- incremental non-attribute preference.

The financial measure of brand equity is calculated by multiplying the incremental choice probabilities across customers by the corresponding category-level purchase quantities and the brand's contribution margin. Unlike the other two techniques which make only indirect references to individual consumer responses, this approach integrates individual consumer-response measurements with financially based measurements.

The three examples above illustrate different views on how FBBE should be measured. The first method is based on a firm's share price by estimating the proportion of a firm's future cash flow that can be attributed to its brand. The second method uses measures of market performance to estimate the value of the brand. The third method views brand value as the direct result of consumers' differential responses towards the brand compared with its unbranded equivalent and was designed specifically to capture the consumer component. Note that the strength of the consumer franchise is included in all methods. Although different views exist on how to measure FBBE, its focus is to present brand equity as a dollar value that can be viewed as the sale or replacement value of the brand (Raggio & Leone 2007, 2009a).

The recognition that brands can bring substantial monetary value to firms has triggered important theoretical questions. What is the source of this value? How is it generated? Marketing managers are concerned with how their activities generate greater awareness, interest, and responses with respect to the brands they manage, and thus to the strength of a brand's consumer franchise. While FBBE may be the ultimate bottom-line brand measure, marketing managers need explicit measures relating to the customer impact of their investments. This is the domain of the customer-based perspective on brand equity.

Customer-based brand equity

From this perspective, brand equity is viewed as the value of a brand to consumers.

CBBE is shaped by the need of marketers for a theoretical framework to explain consumers' differential responses to brands and as a way of objectively measuring the effectiveness of branding. The conceptual framework in this perspective has guided the development of several brand equity metrics such as Ambler's (2003) consumer metrics, Young and Rubicam's BrandAsset Valuator, and Total Research's EquiTrend.

Farquhar (1990) was among the first to develop a conceptual framework for customer-based brand equity. He discusses the evaluation of brands from both firm and consumer perspectives. The firm perspective refers to the incremental cash flow due to association of a brand with a product. From the consumers' perspective, brand value is said to come from:

- positive brand evaluation,
- strong, accessible, and positive customer attitudes, and
- a consistent brand image.

While both perspectives are discussed, Farquhar indicates that consumer dimensions are a major source of a brand's added value. Farquhar's constructs are important starting points for the conceptualisation of CBBE.

Similarly, Aaker (1991) and Kapferer (1997) adopt a customer-based perspective. Although both view brand equity as the result of consumers' thoughts about brands, each proposes a different set of dimensions.

Aaker's perspective

Aaker (1991) lists:

- brand loyalty,
- brand awareness,
- perceived quality,
- brand association and
- other proprietary brand assets (or liabilities) such as patents and trademarks.

Proprietary brand assets that have more firm-based than consumer value are included, reflecting the 'goodwill' view of brand equity of that time.

Kapferer's perspective

Kapferer's (1997) list includes:

- brand identity,
- brand awareness,
- perceived quality,
- level of confidence,
- significance,
- empathy, and
- liking.

Interestingly, Kapferer (1997) urges marketers to focus on brand identity (i.e. the identity elements created by marketers) instead of brand image (i.e. how consumers perceive the brand). To him, brands that are more concerned about image will lead to confusion because of the rise and fall of social and cultural fads. Brand identity, on the other hand, is decided by brand managers. He believes that brands that retain their identity will ensure consistency in the image that is projected to consumers.

Brand identity v brand image

Arguably, focus on brand identity may result in a conflict between what managers want and what consumers see in a brand. Aaker's (1991) brand image approach can be viewed as more consumer-centric than Kapferer's (1997) brand identity approach. Both, however, retain aspects of the firm's value in their brand equity dimensions – Aaker with the inclusion of proprietary assets and Kapferer with the focus on brand identity.

Realising marketers' needs for diagnostic tools for individual consumer responses, Keller (1993; 1998) goes a step further by employing the associative network model of memory to explain consumer responses. Although Aaker (1991) refers to the same model, his work focuses on listing types of associations in the network, rather than explaining how the network works.

Keller proposes CBBE as 'the differential effect that brand knowledge has on consumer response to the marketing of a brand' (Keller 1993, p. 2). There are three essential elements in the definition.

- First, the brand has equity only when it makes a difference to the consumer's response.

- Second, brand equity arises from consumers' brand knowledge, which consists of brand image and brand awareness.

- Third, differences in the responses of consumers are reflected in all aspects of their perceptions, preferences and behaviour related to the marketing of the brand, such as in their brand choice, recall of messages in advertisements, and their response to sales promotions.

Unlike the other customer-based conceptual frameworks which focus on the strength of brands at the aggregate level, Keller focuses on explaining individual consumer responses.

Although different dimensions have been proposed, there are common factors among the customer-based conceptual frameworks in the areas of brand image and awareness. Indeed, the history of brand equity takes brand image as its starting point and, from the memory perspective, brand awareness is influenced by the brand image that consumers remember. In summary, the CBBE perspective views brand value as arising from, as Ambler puts it, 'what is in people's head about the brand' (Ambler 2003, p. 46). Therefore, put simply, quantifying CBBE involves measuring what people think, feel, and buy today.

A summary of the FBBE and CBBE perspectives is presented in Table 2.1. The idea of brands providing added value is evident in both perspectives—a product's value changes when it is associated with a brand name. The difference lies in whether the added value is viewed from the perspective of consumers or a firm.

Within each perspective, there are different methods of evaluation that provide different monetary numbers in the FBBE perspective and different consumer-based measurements, such as attitude and loyalty, in the CBBE perspective. However, in both perspectives, the added value of a brand, indicated by the italics in the third column of Table 2.1, is viewed as having an effect on the firm's future cash flow. Consequently, it is imperative that brand managers understand how the two perspectives relate to each other and affect the firm's cash flow, particularly in view of marketing accountability towards the firm's profit.

Table 2.1 Summary of brand equity definitions and dimensions

Perspective	Authors	Definitions	Dimensions
Finance-based	Simon & Sullivan (1993)	The *incremental* cash flows that accrue to branded products over unbranded products. (The value of brand equity is estimated by subtracting the replacement cost of tangible assets from the firm's market capitalisation.)	• The technique extracts the value of brand equity from the value of the firm's other assets. • Brand equity is viewed as part of a brand's intangible assets. • Brand equity is composed of a demand-enhancing component influenced by factors such as advertising and positive experiences, and a cost-saving component attributed to promoting branded products.
	Interbrand Ltd. (Barth *et al.* *1998*)	Brands as a financial asset. (Brand equity is calculated by applying an earnings multiplier based on seven factors of brand strength, to the brand's profitability.)	• Leadership. • Brand stability. • Market. • International presence. • Long-term trend and stability of the product category. • Advertising and promotion support. • Trademark protection.
	Srinivasan *et al.* (2005)	The *incremental* ($) contribution* per year obtained by the brand compared with the underlying product (or service) with no brand-building efforts.)	• Increased brand awareness. • Incremental preference because of enhanced attribute perceptions. • Incremental non-attribute preference.
Customer-based	Farquhar (1990)	The *added value* that a brand endows a product.	• Positive brand evaluation. • Accessible attitude. • Consistent brand image.
	Aaker (1991)	A set of brand assets and liabilities linked to a brand, its name, and symbol that *add to or subtract from* the value to a firm and/or to that firm's customers.	• Brand loyalty. • Brand awareness. • Perceived quality. • Brand association. • Other proprietary brand assets (e.g. patents, trademarks, channel relationships).

* Incremental contribution is defined as the incremental dollar sales minus the incremental variable costs.

Perspective	Authors	Definitions	Dimensions
	Kapferer (1997) (also 2008)	Financial value of the *brand assets minus the cost* of branding and invested capital.	• Brand identity. • Brand awareness. • Perceived quality. • Level of confidence, significance, empathy, and liking.

	Keller (1993, 1998) (also 2008)	The *differential effect* that brand knowledge has on consumer response to the marketing of the brand.	• Brand awareness
			  - Brand recall
			  - Brand recognition.
			• Brand image/brand associations
			  - Strength
			  - Favourability.
			• Uniqueness.

Relationship between CBBE and FBBE

The examples above illustrate that the term 'brand equity' can be used to refer to two different things.

1. FBBE refers to the monetary value of a brand's intangible assets, such as the strength of its consumer franchise and legal protections.

2. CBBE refers specifically to consumers' brand knowledge as an asset to the brand.

That FBBE and CBBE are two different constructs is exemplified in the following scenarios provided by Raggio and Leone (2007).

• In a case where there are two different potential buyers for a brand, the brand owner and the two potential buyers may have different FBBE assessments based on how they think available resources may be used to leverage or increase the value of the brand. The value of the brand to the consumers, however, does not immediately increase by the transfer of ownership. Awareness of ownership may increase or decrease CBBE depending on whether consumers hold positive or negative views of the new owner.

• Snapple was bought by Quaker Oats for $1.7bn in 1994. Problems in the distribution of Snapple by Quaker Oats, whose strength rested in supermarkets and pharmacies rather than smaller convenience stores and gas stations that constituted most of Snapple's sales, resulted in a drop in sales. Quaker Oats was forced to sell Snapple for a mere $300m. Hence,

FBBE decreased for Snapple but CBBE may have remained the same or even increased due to exposure in supermarkets and pharmacies.

- When Lee Jeans decided to sell its products at Wal-Mart, it was expected that Lee Jeans would be able to increase its brand value because of the huge distribution gains. However, the brand equity of Lee Jeans decreased among some segments of its consumers because of the image of selling its jeans in a discount store.

While the financial value of the brand is attributed to all sources of profit including whether or not they are directly related to customers, customer-based brand equity is attributed only to customer-related contributions (Raggio and Leone 2009b). A brand's financial value may increase or decrease due to brand activities at the industry and firm-level, such as brand distribution, R&D activities, patent acquisitions and/or activities at the customer level such as advertising and brand loyalty programs. Consequently, CBBE can be viewed as a component of FBBE (Raggio and Leone 2009b).

Arguably, most of the financial value of the brand is derived from what consumers know, believe, feel, and ultimately how they behave toward the brand (Ambler 2003; Haigh 2003).

Ambler (2003) argues that customer equity (in which he includes all the stakeholders of a firm) is important because it guarantees cash flow to support all other activities of a firm. Comparing customer equity to a reservoir of cash flow, he further argues that the reservoir of customer equity has to be topped up every so often if the cash flow is to be maintained at a constant or increasing rate (Ambler 2003).

Marketing is identified as the driver of this cash flow to the firm. Its activities are geared towards generating wealth by influencing consumers' mental states so that they are likely to purchase the brand (Ambler 2003; Rust *et al.* 2004). The relationship between marketing activities, CBBE, and FBBE is presented in Figure 2.1.

Brand-related activities

Brand-related activities in Figure 2.1 denote the various actions of a firm related to its brand. At the industry level, actions pertaining to channel distribution and legal protection are geared towards overall industry-level competitiveness such as expanding availability and the pursuit of monopolistic advantages. These competitive advantages allow the brand to generate financial rewards for the firm in terms of profitability and cash flow.

Figure 2.1 An integrated framework of CBBE and FBBE

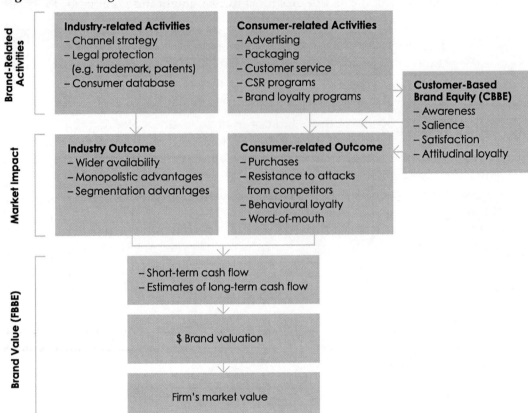

Consumer-related activities

Consumer-related activities, as shown in Figure 2.1, are those activities undertaken by the firm that relate directly to the consumer experience. These activities influence consumers' mental processes about the brand and in turn affect their responses towards the brand.

Keller (1998) explained that CBBE is essentially driven by brand knowledge, represented by the various associations linked to a brand node in memory. Positive brand equity is said to occur when the consumer is aware of the brand and holds some strong, favourable, and unique brand associations in memory. For example, the Nintendo Wii gaming console is associated with ideas of 'physical activity' and 'high interactivity' enabled by its wireless controller, which detects movements in three dimensions allowing physical experiences of games such as tennis, car racing, and bowling. The marketing role, therefore, is to ensure that target consumers perceive these associations as not only favourable but also unique compared to competing gaming consoles. Promotional activities such as advertisements can be used to constantly remind and highlight these positive associations in the hope that consumers will respond positively towards the brand.

Other brand-relationship marketing activities such as brand loyalty programs and corporate social responsibility programs (CSR) might also be used to create favourable and unique associations. Some of the differential responses to these activities (i.e. consumer-related outcomes) that can be observed in the short term include purchases that consumers make today and customer endorsement of the products to others. These actions would have an immediate impact on cash flow from higher sales and perhaps premium pricing.

CBBE a reservoir of future cash flow

There are also benefits that can accrue for the future. For example, a consumer may view a car brand as unique and favourable now, but will wait until the next purchase cycle before actually purchasing the brand. Thus, CBBE can be viewed as a reservoir of future cash flow to the firm because it will translate into revenue at a future date. CBBE, therefore, represents the brand's future value to the firm.

The perforated line in Figure 2.1 shows that existing CBBE can have a positive influence on the effectiveness of future marketing activities. For example, research shows that consumers with high brand loyalty are likely to increase purchases when brand advertising increases (Raj 1982). Furthermore, well-known brands have been shown to be more successful in brand extensions than lesser-known brands (Aaker & Keller 1990; Bottomley & Doyle 1996). Studies also demonstrate that brand leaders have better price advantages than lesser-known brands (Sethuraman 1996; Sivakumar & Raj 1997).

Development of FBBE

As demonstrated in Figure 2.1, outcomes of the various industry-based and consumer-based activities contribute to the ultimate development of FBBE by impacting short-term cash flow and estimates of long-term cash flow. This in turn impacts the monetary value of the brand, which is itself often a substantial component of overall market value. Additionally, Figure 2.1 demonstrates that the effectiveness of marketing activities to the development of FBBE is measurable, based on their level of brand recall or recognition, satisfaction, attitude, and loyalty.

FBBE and CBBE applications

FBBE and CBBE serve different functions. When an estimate of the financial value of the brand is required, FBBE is the appropriate perspective. When an evaluation of the impact of marketing investment on customer responses is required, CBBE is more helpful to a marketing manager.

Measurements from the FBBE perspective estimate the replacement value of a brand, thus providing an estimate of the financial impact of a brand and facilitating inclusion of the brand in financial calculations. Haigh (1999) identified a number of applications of brand valuation.

Although the value of a brand has yet to be included in balance sheets other than for those brands recently acquired, the financial value of a brand can appear in annual reports discussing the contribution of the brand to different segments of the market, and long- and short-term forecasts of brand performance.

Brand valuations have also been used to explain performance and as a form of motivation for the firm's internal customers (e.g. domestic and foreign operations) by explaining how the brand that they have been working with has contributed to the firm's performance.

In addition, quantitative data from brand valuations assists in budgeting decisions by providing a more systematic basis for decision making, such as allocating a budget for different brands within the firm.

Another important application of brand valuation is the involvement of brands in mergers and acquisitions. Brand valuation provides the basis for the price being paid and is also used to provide hard numbers in substantiating investments. In licensing or franchising, brand valuation provides a guide to the setting of charges to reflect the value of the asset being licensed. Brands have also been increasingly used to back borrowing, as Disney, for example, has done.

In addition, brand valuation techniques have frequently been used in legal cases to defend brand value, such as those involving the deceptive or misleading use of a brand name. Measurement, in the FBBE perspective, provides a summary in financial terms of a brand's performance; however, it does not provide specific information on the source of brand value — the customers.

Measurements from the CBBE perspective allow marketers to understand if and how marketing actions have impacted the mental state of consumers to result in differential responses towards the brand.

Proxy measures

A persistent problem for marketers is that the mental states of consumers, represented by associative nodes in their memories, are difficult to quantify (Ambler 2003). As a result, proxy measures such as:

- consumers' brand awareness,
- image,
- attitude,
- loyalty,
- satisfaction,
- commitment,
- attachment,
- relationship, and
- resonance

are commonly employed. The effectiveness of specific tactical marketing actions is measured by whether they result in an intended change in mental state. For example, advertising may be used to increase brand awareness, customer support services aim to enhance customer satisfaction, corporate social responsibility programs aspire to enhance brand image, and customer loyalty programs endeavour to boost brand loyalty.

Brand health

Marketers are also interested in the overall performance or the health of a brand to ensure that it will continue to contribute to the cash flow of the firm. To that end, customer measures are often included in brand metrics or dashboards. For example, Ambler's (2003) general brand equity metrics included:

- familiarity,
- penetration,
- consumers' opinions about brands,
- consumers' feelings about the brand,
- loyalty, and
- availability.

Keller (2001) proposed brand salience, brand performance, brand imagery, consumer judgments, consumer feelings, and consumer brand resonance in building strong brands. PepsiCo uses its own brand equity model, Equitrak, which includes measures of awareness, intellectual perception, perceived uniqueness, perceived popularity, and emotional attachment (Kish, Riskey & Kerin 2001).

In summary, in the FBBE perspective brand equity is viewed as an asset that can be the subject of a transaction. In contrast, in the CBBE perspective, brand equity is viewed as a means of reaching the bottom line. While the FBBE does not directly address wealth creation, the CBBE approach does not inform stakeholders about the returns on their investment or financial accountability. Clearly, the two perspectives need to be considered together.

The marketing balance sheet

Since 2004, new international financial reporting standards (IFRS) have been introduced globally. Previously, intangible assets (such as brands) were combined under 'goodwill'. Now, however, goodwill is separated into measurable and identifiable intangible assets such as brands, copyrights, and patents. However, this only applies to acquired brands.

Constraints of the IFRS

Internally generated brands can be valued, but not put on the balance sheet. Unfortunately, it seems the legislative framework governing the most valued asset generated by marketers is determined by the accounting profession, with little input from the professional and academic marketing community.

In many cases, the valuation of brands, when it does occur, takes place in isolation from those who develop and manage the asset. Perhaps to some extent marketers have themselves to blame for traditionally not being able to speak the FBBE language. Although this is changing, the IFRS rules still apply.

Need for a marketing balance sheet

It may well be time for the marketing profession, supported by the academic community, to devise a marketing balance sheet to supplement existing reporting requirements. Such a balance sheet could report both FBBE and CBBE, showing the relationship between the two. The benefits would be manifold.

First, it would force marketers to become involved in both the FBBE and CBBE perspectives, providing them and those to whom they are accountable with a more holistic set of tools and metrics with which they can construct more effective and efficient marketing investment plans and business cases.

It would also promote a more disciplined and analytical approach that draws upon both consumer psychology as well as finance to help marketers and others better understand cause and effect. There would be value in this approach to senior management, company boards, market analysts, and ultimately shareholders, as it would provide a more transparent link between investment, immediate cash flow generation, and asset building for the future.

There are already numerous metrics and dashboards, and so the task would seem now to be to present these in a coherent manner with equal status to the mandated (and not always obviously transparent) financial statements. The pressure for this type of reporting may come 'bottom up' from marketers, but perhaps it may come more effectively 'top down' from investors and analysts. Whatever the case, the marketing profession needs to take the lead rather than, as in the case of IFRS, being on the receiving end.

Conclusion

Our framework in Figure 2.1 shows that CBBE and FBBE are linked, despite the two perspectives often being considered separately. Thus, we advocate a more holistic view of brand equity measurement and reporting.

The challenge for marketers is to change the dominant view that marketing is more of an art form than a science—each marketing action should be linked to the outcome, from both the consumer and financial perspectives.

The financial performance measures provide the hard numbers to establish (or not) marketing's important contribution to a firm's performance. Speaking the language of finance is important for credibility with both financial and senior level executives responsible for resource allocation and accountability. However, presenting a single financial number does not provide adequate diagnostics of cause and effect with respect to marketing investments. This is where CBBE comes into play.

A major step forward is to link CBBE to FBBE. This would connect what some may see as somewhat nebulous concepts such as brand images, relationships, attachments, and loyalty into concrete, cash-generating assets that require investment in the same way as any of the firm's tangible assets such as factories, furniture, and IT systems. The memory nodes of consumers should be as valued as a database. Better measurement leads to better management.

References

Aaker, DA 1991, *Managing Brand Equity*. New York: The Free Press.

Aaker, DA & Keller KL 1990, 'Consumer Evaluations of Brand Extensions', *Journal of Marketing*, 54 (1), 27–41.

Aaker, JL 1997, 'Dimensions of Brand Personality', *Journal of Marketing Research*, 34(August), 347–56.

Ambler, T 2003, *Marketing and the Bottom Line* (2nd edition). London: Prentice Hall.

Barth, ME, Clement MB, Foster G & Kasznik R 1998, 'Brand Values and Capital Market Valuation', *Review of Accounting Studies*, 3 (1–2), 41–68.

Bottomley, PA & Doyle JR 1996, 'The Formation of Attitudes towards Brand Extensions: Testing and Generalising Aaker and Keller's Model', *International Journal of Research in Marketing*, 13 (4), 365–377.

Farquhar, PH 1990, 'Managing Brand Equity', *Journal of Advertising Research*, 30 (August), RC-7-RC-12.

Feldwick, P 1996, 'What is Brand Equity Anyway, How Do You Measure It?', *Journal of the Market Research Society*, 38 (April), 85–102.

Haigh, D 1999, 'Understanding the Financial Value of Brands', A report prepared for the *European Association of Advertising Agencies*.

Haigh, D 2003, 'An Introduction to Brand Equity: How to Understand and Appreciate Brand Value and the Economic Impact of Brand Investment', *Interactive Marketing*, 5 (1), 21–32.

Kamakura, WA & Russell GJ 1993, 'Measuring Brand Value With Scanner Data', *International Journal of Research in Marketing*, 10 (March), 9–22.

Kapferer, J-N 1997, *Strategic Brand Management: Creating and Sustaining Brand Equity Long Term* (2nd edition). London: Kogan Page.

Kapferer, J-N 2008, *The New Strategic Brand Management: Creating and Sustaining Brand Equity Long Term* (4th edition). London: Kogan Page.

Keller, KL 1993, 'Conceptualizing, Measuring and Managing Customer-based Brand Equity', *Journal of Marketing*, 57 (January), 1–22.

Keller, KL 1998, *Strategic Brand Management: Building, Measuring and Managing Brand Equity*. New Jersey: Prentice Hall.

Keller, KL 2008, *Strategic Brand Management: Building, Measuring and Managing Brand Equity* (3rd edition). New Jersey: Prentice Hall.

Kerin, RA & Sethuraman R 1998, 'Exploring the Brand Value-Shareholder Value Nexus for Consumer Goods Companies', *Journal of Academy of Marketing Science*, 26 (4), 260–273.

Kish, P, Riskey DR & Kerin RA 2001, 'Measurement and Tracking of Brand Equity in the Global Marketplace: The PepsiCo Experience', *International Marketing Review*, 18 (1), 91–96.

Raggio, LD & Leone RP 2007, 'The Theoretical Separation of Brand Equity and Brand Value: Managerial Implications for Strategic Planning', *Journal of Brand Management*, 14(5), 380–395.

Raggio, LD & Leone RP 2009a, 'Drivers of Brand Value, Estimation of Brand Value in Practice and Use of Brand Valuation', *Journal of Brand Management*, 17 (1), 1-5.

Raggio, LD & Leone RP 2009b, 'Chasing Brand Value: Fully Leveraging Brand Equity to Maximise Brand Value', *Journal of Brand Management*, 16 (4), 248-263.

Raj, SP 1982, 'The Effects of Advertising on High and Low Loyalty Consumer Segments', *Journal of Consumer Research*, 9 (June), 77–89.

Rust, RT, Ambler T, Carpenter GS, Kumar V & Srivastava RK 2004, 'Measuring Marketing Productivity: Current Knowledge and Future Directions', *Journal of Marketing*, 68 (October), 76–89.

Sethuraman, R 1996, 'A Model of How Discounting High-Priced Brands Affects the Sales of Low-Priced Brands', *Journal of Marketing Research*, 33 (November), 399–409.

Simon, CJ & Sullivan MW 1993, 'The Measurement and Determinants of Brand Equity: A Financial Approach', *Marketing Science*, 12 (1), 28–52.

Sivakumar, K & Raj, SP 1997, 'Quality Tier Competition: How Price Change Influences Brand Choice and Category Choice', *Journal of Marketing*, 61 (July), 71–84.

Srinivasan, V, Park Chan Su, & Chang Dae Ryun 2005, 'An Approach to the Measurement, Analysis, and Prediction of Brand Equity and its Sources', *Management Science*, 51 (9), 1433-48.

Author biographies

Shuhaida Md Noor is a lecturer at the School of Communication, Universiti Sains Malaysia. She has an MA (Communication) from the Universiti Sains Malaysia, and a BSc in Commerce from the University of Virgina. She previously worked in the corporate communications department of a microelectronic systems institute in Malaysia, and subsequently in a public relations company. She completed her doctorate at the University of Sydney in 2009. Her research focuses on the effects of self representations on consumers' responses to brands.

Contact: Dr Shuhaida Md Noor, School of Communication, Universiti Sains Malaysia, 11800 Minden, Penang, Malaysia; P +604-653-5281; E shuhaidamdnoor @yahoo.com.

Chris Styles is Professor of Marketing and Associate Dean at the Faculty of Economics and Business, University of Sydney. His research on exporting, international alliances, international entrepreneurship and brand management has been published in the *Journal of International Business Studies*, the *Journal of World Business*, the *Journal of International Marketing*, the *International Marketing Review*, the *International Journal of Research in Marketing*, and the *Journal of Product and Brand Management*, among others. He also sits on five editorial boards, including those of the *Journal of International Marketing*, the *International Marketing Review*, and the *British Journal of Management*. Chris was formerly a marketing manager with Procter

& Gamble and a market research consultant. He has a PhD from the London Business School.

Contact: Professor Chris Styles, Associate Dean (Executive Education) and Professor of Marketing, Faculty of Economics and Business, Institute Building (H03), The University of Sydney, NSW 2006; P +61-2-9036-5334; F 61 2 9036 7190, E c.styles@econ.usyd.edu.au.

Elizabeth Cowley is a Professor of Marketing in the Faculty of Economics and Business, University of Sydney. She has an MBA from McGill University in Montreal. After graduating, Elizabeth worked for several years in the marketing and marketing planning departments of the largest integrated oil company in Canada. Her doctorate was completed at the University of Toronto in 1997. Her research interests are consumer memory and decision making. Elizabeth's memory research focuses on how the organisation of memory affects the retrieval of brand information and the conditions under which memory is distorted during retrieval. Her research has been published in the *Journal of Consumer Research,* the *Journal of Consumer Psychology,* the *International Journal of Research in Marketing,* the *Academy of Marketing Science,* the *Journal of Advertising,* and the *Journal of Business Research.*

Contact: Professor Elizabeth Cowley, Faculty of Economics and Business, Institute Building (H03), The University of Sydney, NSW 206, P +61-2-9351-6433; F +61-2-9351-6732; E e.cowley@econ.usyd.edu.au.

Chapter 3

Brand manifold: Managing the temporal and socio-cultural dimensions of brands

PIERRE BERTHON, MORRIS B HOLBROOK, JAMES M HULBERT & LEYLAND F PITT

ABSTRACT

The debate on the role of brands in the changing marketplace has reached new heights in the past decade. Perspectives range from 'radical' to 'business as usual'. However, escalating competition and a changing marketplace portend more than the typically forecasted evolution; they suggest a need for a considered reappraisal of branding concepts and concomitant approaches at an overall strategic management rather than a mere operational marketing level. We begin by developing two vital distinctions in branding. First, we contrast various perspectives on brands, and then introduce Popper's Three Worlds model as a device to consider brand interaction. Next, we distinguish between the perceptions of a brand (brand equity) and the monetary value of those perceptions (value of the brand equity) and offer a representation that integrates the distinctions. We then enlarge the customer and company dimensions to external and internal aspects, respectively, and introduce a temporal dimension. A schema called the brand manifold is then developed in some detail to provide a comprehensive theoretical framework that can guide the proactive management of brands over time and over multiple audiences. We examine both the static and dynamic implications of this framework in ways that highlight how the role of brands will change in the new millennium.

KEYWORDS

brands; brand management; brand manifold; temporal dimensions; cultural dimensions

Introduction

During the 19th and for much of the 20th century, the value of the firm, notionally represented by the net book value of assets on the balance sheet, was heavily dependent on so-called hard assets such as plant and equipment. However, in more recent years the gap between market capitalisation and net book value has increased to enormous proportions – driven largely by the importance of so-called intangible or 'soft' assets (Lev 2004; Teece 1998). Key elements of these intangible assets are the brands of a firm and the customer- and other relationships imbedded therein. Indeed, research suggests that both price premiums and market share are associated with brand equity (Aaker 1996; Chaudhuri & Holbrook 2001). Observers of financial markets are often intrigued that the ratios of market capitalisation to revenues can range from as high as 20 to one for firms like Microsoft, Nokia and Louis Vuitton, to as low as 0.6 to one for firms such as Ford, Volkswagen and Hertz. They suspect that this may be due in part to the way these firms manage their brands.

There has been vigorous debate on the role of brands in the changing marketplace, giving vent to perspectives that range from the radical (The Economist 1994) to the refining (Morris 1996). However, escalating competition and a changing business environment portend more than the typically forecasted change. They mandate a careful rethinking of business strategies. These forces also make the management of brands an overall strategic issue that impacts on the future of the firm as a whole, rather than merely a source of focus for marketing decision-makers. Indeed, branding may have become too important to be left to marketers, for brands are no longer simply a marketing issue.

Brands are symbols around which social actors – including firms, suppliers, supplementary organisations, the public, and indeed customers – construct identities. Branding is obviously a critical issue for marketing because brands facilitate the repeat purchases on which sellers rely to enhance corporate financial performance. Brands also facilitate the introduction of new products and assist promotional efforts by giving the firm something to identify and a name on which to focus. This enables premium pricing, as well as the market segmentation that makes it possible to communicate a coherent message to a target customer group. Marketers are rightfully obsessed with brand loyalty, particularly important in product categories in which repeated purchasing is a feature of buying behaviour. However, today brands and their management have far wider ramifications for organisations large and small, both for those with a profit motive and for those without.

Brands are about finance

On 'Marlboro Friday', April 2nd 1993, Philip Morris cut prices on its premium brand of cigarettes by 20%. The company's stock fell by 23%, obliterating more than $13Bn in shareholder wealth. The shares in other branded consumer goods companies also suffered double digit declines on that same day, and the Dow Jones Industrial Average dropped 69 points. Brands are a crucial financial issue.

Brands are about human resources

Cynics and 'old school' marketers may well accuse consulting firms such as Accenture of 'advertising wastage' when their commercials air on television. After all, why broadcast a message to the entire North American population when your primary 'target market' is the top four executives in Fortune 1000 companies? Other observers might suspect that future and current employees are the real target of these ads, and that they represent an attempt by the firm to deal with the consequences of a permanent shortage of knowledge workers. Brands are a crucial human resources issue.

Brands are about strategy (and strategy is about brands)

An ingrained and thorough understanding of the firm's nucleus brand has enabled the Marriott corporation to grow its business from fast food restaurants, through airline catering and cruise ships to a wide range of hotels and resorts. JW Marriott Jr, son of the founder and chief executive officer of Marriott International, sees brands as a strategic issue: 'Expansion beyond our core brand was one of the single most important strategic decisions that allowed us to grow' (Gregersen & Black 2002). Moreover, it seems that it is not only marketers who make branding decisions in the firm. JW Marriott Jr tells interviewers: 'our strategy planning people came in and said, "You know, maybe we ought to develop a new brand of limited service hotels".' Brands are a crucial issue in corporate strategy.

Not everyone loves brands

Contrary to popular marketing rhetoric and management-speak, the whole world doesn't love brands. Not everyone is excited that brands have become more recognised in most countries than religious symbols. There is today an anti-branding movement (Klein 2000), coupled to anti-globalisation (cf. Greider 1997) and a resistance in many instances to the offerings of large corporations. The challenges posed to firms by a changing business environment, one in which brands are no longer marketing's sole prerogative, are likely to require the refinement and extension of the ideas by which brands are conceptualised and managed.

The brand manifold

We develop a schema that deals with these challenges. The framework incorporates both a temporal focus and a representation of the multiple constituencies that characterise the 21st century management quandary. We proceed as follows. First, we draw on the work of Popper (1994) to emphasise three important aspects of brands that highlight the multiplicity and equivocal nature of brand meanings. Second, based on these insights, we make two important distinctions in brand equity: *value to whom* and *type of value*. Third, we develop a simple framework that highlights the *multiple constituent* and *temporally dynamic* nature of brand meaning. Fourth, we illustrate the framework's application to a variety of 'real world' examples and conclude with suggestions for adaptations in managerial thinking.

Relationships among organisations, products, people and brands

To understand the evolving marketplace, it is essential to capture the full dimensionality of the inter-relationships among organisations, people, products and brands. Popper's *three-worlds hypothesis* (Popper 1979; Popper & Eccles 1979), provides an excellent means of doing so. Popper originally developed his three-worlds trichotomy as a conceptual tool to explore the mind-body problem in philosophy. He then employed it in a wide range of contexts, arguing that it was useful in distinguishing three different realms:

1. World 1, the realm of physical objects, states and systems;

2. World 2, the realm of subjective experience involving thoughts, emotions, perceptions, and so on; and

3. World 3, the world of 'culture' rooted in objective knowledge, science, language, literature, et cetera.

In the current context, the three realms of relevance are:

- manifest goods and services (World 1);

- individual thoughts, emotions, needs, wants and perceptions (World 2); and

- collective knowledge and images concerning brands (World 3).

The three worlds are related in the manner depicted by the diagram in Figure 3.1.

Figure 3.1 The relationship of products, brands and culture

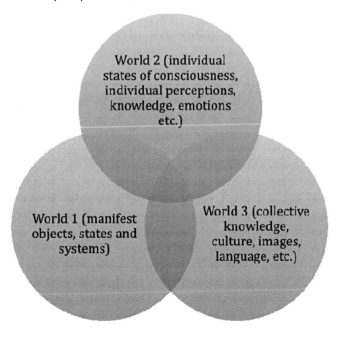

Popper's three-worlds trichotomy is useful on a number of levels:

1. It highlights the fact that, to understand the phenomenon of brands, one must understand the relationships between the three worlds. In this context, the three worlds map onto the distinctions between (1) products, (2) individuals, and (3) brands.

2. It shows that the effect of a manifest product in World 1 (e.g. an Apple computer with its familiar logo) on the collective knowledge of the brand in World 3 (e.g. the brand name 'Apple', Apple's share price, its product specifications, its documented history, etc.) is always mediated by, and thus a function of, intervening responses by individual subjects (World 2).

3. It indicates (a) that attempts to modify Worlds 1 and 3 (e.g. changing or repositioning a brand by a company) will always implicate the subjective worlds of the individuals managing and involved in the process, customers and other stakeholders (i.e. World 2), and (b) that these changes can never entirely determine one individual's World 2 (i.e., the meaning attributed to the brand by a specific customer). Here, we suggest that an individual's brand meaning and experience can never be entirely determined by another individual's or group's conscious intention or volition.

Thus, from (1) above, we derive the notion that brands are always part *manifest* (World 1) and part *abstract* (Worlds 2 and 3). Furthermore, we derive the notion that products and brands are not synonymous. From (2) above, we see that – to a greater or lesser extent – individuals attach meanings to brands and that such meanings can range from the primarily *functional* (in the sense of what the branded offering can *do* in World 1) to the primarily *enacted* (in the sense of what the branded offering can *mean* in World 3). From (3) above, we infer that the meanings associated with a brand in World 3 are always multiple and equivocal, for such meanings always reflect individual differences in World 2. At the simplest level, what the brand means to the organisation and its members may be different from what it means to its target customers – and also to other stakeholders, including the public at large.

The brand Lonsdale illustrates the 3 Worlds model, as well as the fact that the same brand can have multiple meanings to different stakeholders. The long established British brand of sports apparel (it was at one stage the number one manufacturer of boxing gloves, shorts, boots and so forth); the *product* (World 1, the physical) became the *brand* (World 3, the abstract) with very different meanings to *different stakeholders* (World 2, the individuals). To management, the brand represented apparel and was originally targeted at sportsmen and athletes. To most customers, it represented a classic brand of sports apparel. To some of the customers who purchased it in Germany (mainly the ultra-right and skinheads), however, it represented a jarring, attention-grabbing fashion statement. They realised that by wearing a cardigan or zippered track suit top over a Lonsdale sweater they could hide the L and the O on the right, and the L and the E on the left, leaving only the middle four letters NSDA visible – the German abbreviation for the National Socialist German Workers party (or simply, the Nazi party). To the public at large, the brand came to embody a nonconformist symbol of rebellion against accepted norms, and the entrenchment of racist and bigoted values (wearing it was even banned in certain Dutch and Belgian schools). Lonsdale was forced to take a number of counter-steps – including sponsoring multi-cultural events and gay pride rallies – to once again try to tip the brand toward decency.

Refining brand equity: Key dimensions

Perhaps the most important contribution of Figure 3.1 lies in motivating us to reconsider the basic role of brands in the eyes of all stakeholders. Too often, brands have been seen solely from an instrumental perspective (i.e. brands are 'owned', are 'managed', and are 'instruments' of management) – a perspective that leaves the proponent dangerously exposed to the risks posed by the changing consumption, technological and competitive environments. This simplistic but very prevalent view in organisations means that managers, especially marketing and brand managers, believe that they own the brands and that these brands are tools which, if managed properly, can help the organisation attain its objectives. Brands have, in some instances, become ends in themselves – or at least ends for the people who manage them, overlooking the fact that their critical role is as a means. In the often evangelistic focus on brands, not only customers but also the organisation's members and other stakeholders have at times been overlooked. What Levitt (1960; 1975) called 'marketing myopia' (a narrow definition of business focused on what the firm produces) has been augmented or indeed replaced by *branding myopia* (the brand becomes an end in itself)!

The three-worlds hypothesis highlights the fact that the role of a brand involves an imbrication of all three worlds. Thus, brands can never be understood in and of themselves. They are not simply 'created', 'owned', or 'used' by management. Rather, they have a life and meaning beyond and, to some extent, independent of that intended by their initiators. For example, Muniz and Schau (2005) describe the grassroots brand community currently centred on the defunct Apple Newton, a product abandoned by the company in the late 1990s.

These considerations complicate our current conceptualisations of brand equity; at the simplest level, brand equity has to do with the value of a brand. Two main existing perspectives are a financial one on the one hand, and a behavioural one on the other. The financial view on brand equity attempts to place a monetary value on a brand, typically championed by consulting firms such as Interbrand, resulting in press reports that, for example, claim that 'Coke is the world's most valuable brand, worth X billion dollars' (cf. Khermouch & Brady 2003). The behavioural view on brand equity typically uses surveys to determine what a particular brand means to customers, how valuable it is to them (cf. Ha 1996), and how this compares to other brands. Typically, these two perspectives are combined into a definition of brand equity as 'customers' willingness to pay a differential for one product over another when they are basically identical' (Kotler 2003).

The current pre-occupation with brand equity is often traced back to the takeover of UK firm Rowntree by Nestlé in the late 1980s (cf. Ellert, Hyde and Killing 2002). The focus on brands resulted from a realisation among financial analysts and journalists that part of the motivation in many company takeovers was the acquisition of brands that had been built up by the company under siege and which the attacking company realised would take them years to replicate as well as vast sums of money to develop and nurture. This shift in emphasis from physical assets (such as plant and machinery) to brands represents a swing from World 1 (the physical) to World 3 (the abstract).

Equity and value

From the previous discussion, therefore, 'equity' pertains to the perceptions of a brand, while 'value of the equity' is the monetary value of the brand to the firm. We term these two aspects 'embodied value' and 'exchange value'. Drawing on these two distinctions – *value to whom* and *type of value* – an integrative representation of brand equity appears in Figure 3.2

Figure 3.2 Refining brand equity

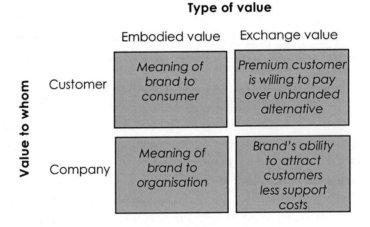

The embodied value to the company describes the perceptions and values the organisation's members see encapsulated in the brand. Of course, there is heterogeneity in these perceptions, which may not correspond to those of external groups and may or may not reflect those embodied in the brand's formal communications. Employees' perspectives may vary by function and are not necessarily consonant with management or, indeed, with the firm's advertising agency. Managers and employees alike are urged to manifest or 'live the brand'.

Other external audiences besides customers have their own sets of associations or embodied values, similarly comprising perceptions and expectations. The expectations of suppliers or consumer activists about a brand of automobile or fast food may differ significantly from those of brand-loyal customers. The expectations of legislators or regulators may well be influenced by such groups, as well as by the company that owns the brand in question.

In sum, the exchange value of *company brand equity* depends on cash-flow streams resulting from the firm's ability to acquire and retain customers for a brand. This view is not constrained by current products nor, indeed, by current customers. For many firms (e.g. an internet firm like Amazon.com), large proportions of the value are attributable to the anticipation of future customers and products. By contrast, the exchange value of *customer brand equity* hinges on the individual customer's willingness to pay for the equity associated with a branded good or service above and beyond that for an unbranded version of the same product.

The exchange value of customer brand equity – reflecting an individual customer's willingness to pay a price more than some benchmark for the branded product – in turn rests upon that individual's embodied brand value (World 2). In contrast, the exchange value of company brand equity depends also on the number of customers willing to pay a particular price and the number of units sold at that price (World 3). For example, a bottle of Chateau Margaux in the US for $500 to $1000 per bottle (cf. Deighton *et al*. 2006) can be said to have high *customer* exchange value for some customers who are willing to buy at the high offering price. In contrast, *company* exchange value would be low, because relatively *few* customers are willing to pay such a price, resulting in a low volume of sales. Conversely, a mass market wine such as Australian company Casella's Yellowtail has low *customer* embodied and exchange value (with customers unwilling to pay more than its relatively modest price), but *company* exchange value is high (because of extremely high overall sales volume).

We may develop this distinction further by contrasting the impact of high/low organisational/customer exchange value, as depicted by the typology shown in Figure 3.3. Yellowtail would clearly fall in the top right-hand corner among the mass-market brands along with many well-known brands such as Tide, Lipton and Heinz. By contrast, Ferrari, Porsche, Perrier and Grolsch are solid bottom left-hand specialty performers. Meanwhile, many brands that have traditionally fallen in the top left-hand corner – with all the disadvantages that parity status entails – have worked hard to extricate themselves. Examples of such repositioning strategies include the battles to differentiate vinegar and olive oil, or the struggle to brand bananas. Indeed, the Arm and Hammer brand of the privately-owned chemical company Dwight and Church demonstrates vividly that all is not lost even when your product is as unremarkable as baking soda. Thus, many firms seek the desirable bottom right-hand 'iconic' position exemplified by Microsoft, Coca-Cola, Starbucks and Nike in recent years. Of course, there is the danger that as former specialty brands attempt to become iconic – or are deemed so by a significant number of stakeholders – their customer-embodied value deteriorates and they become mass market brands. The once-coveted von Furstenberg and Pierre Cardin brands have suffered such a fate (Reddy *et al*. 2009), while Martha Stewart and Tommy Hilfiger appear to be headed in the same direction (Rozhon 2003).

Figure 3.3 A typology of exchange values

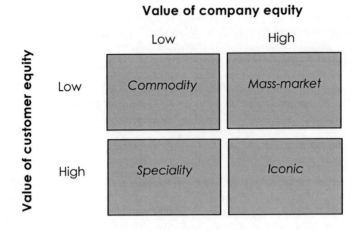

Introducing the brand manifold

Temporal factors

Within a given cultural context, language and meaning are enmeshed in a continual process of evolution. Given that language and meaning continually change, so inevitably will the signification of a brand. Brands are of course rooted in this broader context, taking their embodied meanings from discourses with their relevant stakeholders. This simple insight carries some important implications. First, the meaning of a brand can never be static. Second, brand signification is never unilaterally created, but always arises in relation to a wider linguistic and cultural community composed of various participants. Thus, companies cannot so much manage a stable brand image as *negotiate* an evolving one. This emphasis on dialogue and change thereby assumes central importance in the management of brand meanings. Such meanings are temporal in two senses – (1) the sense in which they are dynamic and (2) the sense in which their creation is a process of longitudinal negotiation, with present (future) meaning always rooted in the past (present). Thus, the management of a brand focuses both on the brand's relationship with its past and on evolving new meanings for the brand as it moves into its future.

Stakeholder assessments of the brand depend on mediated perceptions and on direct experience – that is, information *about* a brand (brand communications) and direct interactions *with* a brand (brand embodiments). Brand communications comprise information from the company, customers and other stakeholders. Brand embodiments constitute the brand as intertwined with products, employees, suppliers, channels, other third parties and consumers. If we distinguish between factors that are and are not directly under the organisation's control – designated internal and external, respectively – we see that stakeholder perceptions of the brand depend on both internal and external communications and embodiments. Managers must therefore understand and manage perceptions (meanings) of the brand among both internal and external stakeholders.

Thus, the managerial problem of brand evolution – essentially a temporal issue – revolves around the evolution of meaning through time. The existing pattern of associations with a brand constitutes its heritage, with the meaning of these associations contributing to the customer's view of equity that we developed earlier. To manage brand evolution successfully requires that the brand not lose its roots in the past. Rather, management must find ways to reinterpret the past in terms of the future or, in a complementary manner, to interpret the future in terms of the past. An example from the automobile industry appears in the famous series of advertisements for Mercedes-Benz, which evoked both the origins and the continuity of their brand (cf. www.mercedes-benz.com). In launching their new Maybach automobile, Daimler-Benz has followed a similar approach – with a lavish publication lauding the history of Wilhelm Maybach and his creations – using both German and English, on opposing pages, to strengthen the etiology of the long-dormant brand. That 'Everything Old is New Again' is as visible in BMW's ad for its 'grand touring tradition' from the 1980s, as is Porsche's new claims for its Model 968 as 'the next evolution'. Jaguar went even further with the introduction of its 'XK' Type, using its 1960's E-Type in the launch advertisements and incorporating many classic styling cues in the new car – right down to the shape of its radiator, as shown in Figure 3.4.

Figure 3.4 Jaguar XK advertisement

Multiple constituencies

In spatial terms, the orientation of brand meanings toward the past versus the future constitutes the first dimension of our evolving brand manifold. We employ the term 'manifold' to stress two aspects of brands: first, that brands have multiple aspects or dimensions; and second, that these aspects or dimensions can be thought of as delineating a topology in space and time. In mathematics and in engineering, manifold means a topological space or surface, and in physics the term is used to talk about the space-time continuum. The second dimension requires that we recognise the multi-constituency nature of the firm. In doing so, we must expand upon our earlier organisation-customer distinction to encompass a variety of external and internal stakeholders. Today, companies market almost as avidly to the investment community, to government regulators and legislators, to suppliers and to present and potential employees as they do to their intermediary and final customers. In expanding 'customer' to 'external' (subsuming a variety of external constituencies or stakeholders) and 'organisational' to 'internal' (similarly subsuming a variety of alternatives), we recognise the vastly more complicated task of managing brands in the 21st century. These various stakeholders have differing perceptions, values and expectations. Of course, customers must usually remain paramount among external audiences, but to ignore the role of other constituencies – such as shareholders, regulators, legislators or interest groups – would be naïve and would fail to deploy Popper's theory appropriately. Further, as companies rationalise their brand portfolios, they are leveraging their remaining brands (including the corporate brand) ever more widely. Rather than mediating a dialogue between firm and customer, the brands must be seen as pivotal in an expanded 'multilogue'.

The brand manifold

These two dimensions are depicted graphically in Figure 3.5 The launch of the Morgan Aero 8 (Webster 2003) provides a good example of applying this concept of the brand manifold. Charles Morgan, CEO of a very traditional specialist auto manufacturer, faced the challenge of convincing employees of the need to develop a radically new design. The relevant manufacturing techniques were also new, and finding ways to embody the brand's heritage into the design of the new physical product posed a daunting challenge. Yet, clearly, product-related information and imagery play a key role in focusing and guiding the consumer in such a high-involvement category as a specialty automobile.

Figure 3.5 The brand manifold

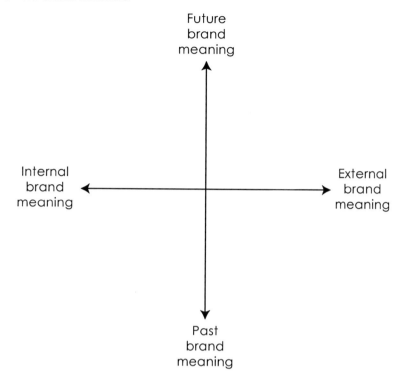

The elaborated brand manifold shown in Figure 3.6 depicts this situation and describes the challenge facing management in more detail. As an example of internal anchoring (lower left-hand corner), consider the case of an offering whose designers consciously draw on relevant brand-related meanings inherited from the past, as in the case of the much-celebrated, resurrected Mini by BMW. Where such meanings exemplify a more external anchoring (lower right), we find associations with the past that thrive primarily by virtue of the impression they make on customers, as in the case of Chrysler's retro-designed PT Cruiser and Ford's retro-styled Mustang. A more innovative form of internal evolution (upper left) would occur, for example, when a brand such as Porsche's Cayenne SUV offers advanced features that are perhaps best appreciated by the company's engineers, its skilled workers, or other automotive experts. If such features can be successfully communicated to customers, the firm achieves external evolution (upper right), as in the case of General Motors' military-evolved Hummer vehicles.

Figure 3.6 Exploring the brand manifold

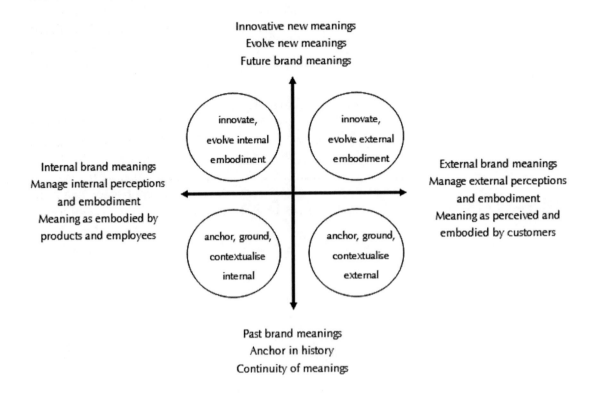

Innovative new meanings
Evolve new meanings
Future brand meanings

innovate, evolve internal embodiment

innovate, evolve external embodiment

Internal brand meanings
Manage internal perceptions and embodiment
Meaning as embodied by products and employees

External brand meanings
Manage external perceptions and embodiment
Meaning as perceived and embodied by customers

anchor, ground, contextualise internal

anchor, ground, contextualise external

Past brand meanings
Anchor in history
Continuity of meanings

Managing manifold worlds

In semiotics, an abstract concept is known as the *signified*, and the physical sound, symbol or image denoting that concept is known as the *signifier*. This is analogous to Popper's World 3 and World 1. With the diminishing importance of the signifier-signified dichotomy and the analogous disappearance of the product-brand distinction, products are becoming symbols in themselves. The signifier has become the signified for products as varied as the soft-coated Wheaton Terrier and the Coke bottle. Indeed, UK survey data suggest that the same phenomenon has occurred with Richard Branson and Virgin (Klein 2000). Rather than just personifying the values of the brand, Branson has himself become the brand. Further, brands are becoming products in themselves. At a store for aviation buffs in Carmel, one of the authors found authentic first- and business-class PanAm travel bags on sale years after the original airline's demise. Indeed, today everything is both a product (a thing in itself) and a symbol (a status marker, a sign of prestige, a representation, embodying a set of values via its associations in the consumer's mind) (cf. Baudrillard 1988).

If indeterminacy has infected the signifier-signified relationship, it has also begun to impact on the producer-consumer dichotomy. In many cases, brand owners have become at best co-owners, for customers now also own the brand. Examples of this at a lower level are the brand communities built around brands such as Harley

Davidson (McAlexander, Schouten & Koeninand 2002; Schouten & McAlexander 1995) and the Apple Newton (Ha 1996), and more recently by social network brands such as Facebook (Barnard 2009). Here the customers believe that, as co-producers of the brand, they own the brand and have a say in its future. At a higher level are open source brands such as JBoss and Linux (Benkler 2002). Here, customers co-produce both the brand and the product, so they *do* own the brand and do have a real say in its future.

Serious pitfalls are often encountered when branding resides exclusively in the marketing department. At the department level, strategic vision tends to be lost in the 'brand myopia' of day-to-day, short-term operational issues – for example, brand extension decisions, customer research, packaging design and promotional tactics. Branding decisions confined to the marketing department can all too often cause the organisation to become vulnerable at a strategic level – for example, branding decisions made in World 3 can have major strategic implications for Worlds 1 & 2. This has three corollaries:

1. marketing executives need to consider the strategic implications of branding decisions;

2. functional managers in areas such as finance, human resources and operations need to consider the impact of their actions on the organisation's brands; and

3. top management requires a deeper understanding of branding issues and how these are quintessential to the strategic trajectory of the organisation.

In this article we address these problems by offering a series of models that can help integrate branding and strategy.

The frameworks developed here reflect this debate on the role of brands in the new millennium. They highlight the fact that brands do not remain static but, rather, change and evolve over time – often in unpredictable ways. Concomitantly, brands are not unitary monoliths, but multiply-diverse socially-constructed entities. They are embodied by products and enacted by customers and by other participants in a process over which managers exert only partial control. The brand is protean and polyphonic. Ranging across its brand manifold, it plays and sings a potential symphony of meaning – for those willing to listen.

References

Aaker, DA 1996, 'Measuring Brand Equity Across Products and Markets,' *California Management Review*, vol. 38, spring, pp. 102 – 120.

Barnard, L 2009, 'Facebook Caves To User Outrage and Google Adds Semantic Search', *PC World*, vol. 27, March, retrieved on March 31, 2009 from http://www.pcworld.com/article/162132/facebook_caves_to_user_outrage_and_google_adds_semantic_search_on_pc_world_podcast_episode_22.html.

Baudrillard, J 1998, *Selected Writings*, ed. M. Poster, Stanford University Press, Stanford.

Benkler, Y 2002, 'Coase's Penguin, or, Linux and the Nature of the Firm' *The Yale Law Journal*, vol. 112, no. 3, pp. 369-446.

Chaudhuri, A & Holbrook, MB 2001, 'The Chain of Effects from Brand Trust and Brand Affect to Brand Performance: The Role of Brand Loyalty,' *Journal of Marketing*, vol. 65, April, pp. 81.

'Death of the Brand Manager', *The Economist*, (April 9, 1994), pp. 67–68.

Deighton, J, Pitt, LF, Dessain, V, Beyersdorfer, D, & Sjöman, A 2006, 'Marketing Chateau Margaux', Harvard Business School Case Study, 507033, Harvard Business School Publishing, Harvard.

Ellert, JC & Hyde, DG & Killing JP 2002, 'Nestle-Rowntree (A)', *IMD - International Institute for Management Development*, IMD Case 0111.

Gregersen, HB & Black, SJ 2002, 'W. Marriott, Jr., on growing the legacy', *Academy of Management Executive*, vol.16, no. 2, pp. 33-39.

Greider, W 1997, *One World Ready Or Not: The Manic Logic Of Global Capitalism*, Simon and Schuster, New York.

Ha, L 1996, 'Advertising Clutter in Consumer Magazines', *Journal of Advertising Research*, vol. 36 July/August, pp. 76-84.

Khermouch, G & Brady, D 2003, 'The Best Global Brands', *Business Week*, vol. August 19, 2003, pp. 69.

Klein, N 2000, *No Logo*, Picador, New York.

Kotler, P 2003, *Marketing Management,* 11th edn, Prentice-Hall, Englewood Cliffs, p. 422.

Lev, B 2004, 'Sharpening the Intangibles Edge', *Harvard Business Review*, vol. 82, June pp. 109 – 116.

Levitt, T 1960, 'Marketing Myopia 1960,' *Harvard Business Review*, July-August, pp. 45-56.

Levitt, T 1975, 'Marketing Myopia (with retrospective comment),' *Harvard Business Review*, September-October, pp. 26-48.

Morris, B 1996, 'The Brand's the Thing,' *Fortune*, (March 4, 1996): 28–38.

Muniz Jr., AM & Schau, HJ 2005, 'Religiosity in the Abandoned Apple Newton Brand Community', *Journal of Consumer Research*, vol. 31, no. 4, pp. 737-747.

Popper, KR 1979, *Objective Knowledge: An Evolutionary Approach,*" Oxford University Press, Oxford.

Popper, KR & Eccles, JC 1979, *The Self and Its Brain*, Springer International, New York.

Popper, KR 1994, *Knowledge and the Body-Mind Problem: In Defense of Interaction*, ed. Nottumo MA, Routledge, London.

Reddy, M, Terblanche, NS, Pitt, LF & Parent, M 2009, 'How Far Can Luxury Brands Travel? Avoiding The Pitfalls Of Luxury Brand Extension' *Business Horizons*, vol. 52, no. 2, pp. 187-197.

Rozhon, T 2003, 'Men Ask: Who Needs to Buy Clothes,' *New York Times*, vol. June, 2003, no.3, pp.1.

Teece, DJ 1998, 'Capturing Value from Knowledge Assets: The New Economy, Markets for Know-how, and Intangible Assets', *California Management Review*, vol. 40, no. 3, pp. 55–80

Webster, L 2003, 'The Morgan Aero 8,' *Car and Driver*, vol. November, pp. 23–27.

Author biographies

Pierre Berthon holds the Clifford F Youse Chair of Marketing and Strategy at Bentley University. He has held academic positions at Columbia University, Henley Management College, Cardiff University and the University of Bath. He has also taught at Rotterdam School of Management, Copenhagen Business School, Norwegian School of Economics and Management, University of Cape Town and Athens Laboratory of Business Administration. His research focuses on the interaction of technology, corporate strategy and consumer behaviour, and has appeared in journals such as *Sloan Management Review, California Management Review, Information Systems Research, Technological Forecasting and Social Change, Journal of the Academy of Marketing Science, Journal of International Marketing, Business Horizons, Journal of Interactive Marketing, Journal of Business Ethics* and others.

Contact: pberthon@bentley.edu.

Morris B Holbrook is the recently-retired WT Dillard Professor Emeritus of Marketing in the Graduate School of Business at Columbia University where he taught courses in such areas as marketing strategy, consumer behaviour, and commercial communication in the culture of consumption. His research has covered a wide variety of topics with a special focus on issues related to communication in general and to aesthetics, semiotics, hermeneutics, art, entertainment, music, jazz, motion pictures, nostalgia and stereography in particular. His books and monographs include *Daytime Television Game Shows and the Celebration of Merchandise: The Price Is Right*, 1993; *The Semiotics of Consumption*, 1993; *Consumer Research*, 1995; *Consumer Value*, 1999; and *Playing the Changes on the Jazz Metaphor: An Expanded Conceptualization of Music-, Management-, and Marketing-Related Themes*, 2008.

Contact: mbh3@columbia.edu.

James M Hulbert is RC Kopf Professor Emeritus, Columbia Business School (where he also served as Vice Dean and Chair of the Marketing Department) and Visiting Professor, Guanghua School of Management, Peking University in China. Hailed as a 'Marketing Whiz' by *Business Week*, he has taught in executive development programs on all the continents, serving for many years as Faculty Director of Columbia's highly regarded sales management and strategic marketing programs. He has written over one hundred academic papers, appearing in such journals as the *Journal of Marketing, Management Science, Strategic Management Journal, Journal of Marketing Research, Journal of International Business Studies, Sloan Management Review, Long Range Planning, Industrial Marketing Management, Journal of Advertising Research, Decision Sciences, California Management Review, Journal of Interactive Marketing, Business Horizons* and others.

Contact: jmh10@columbia.edu.

Leyland F Pitt is the Dennis Culver Executive MBA Professor of Marketing, Segal Graduate School of Business, Simon Fraser University, Vancouver, Canada, and Senior Research Fellow, Leeds University Business School in the UK. He has also taught on executive and MBA programs at schools such as the Graham School of Continuing Studies (University of Chicago), Columbia University Graduate School of Business, Rotterdam School of Management, and London Business School. His work has been accepted for publication by such journals as *Information Systems Research, Journal of the Academy of Marketing Science, Sloan Management Review, California Management Review, Communications of the ACM,* and *MIS Quarterly* (which he also served as Associate Editor).

Contact: Segal Graduate School of Business, Simon Fraser University, 500 Granville Street,Vancouver, BC V6C 1W6, Canada; P +1 778 7827712; E lpitt@sfu.ca.

Part II: Brand Management

The nuts and bolts of brand management are considered in the nine chapters that form Part II.

Brands are positioned in order to 'sell more' and 'sell better' than would be the case if they were offered to potential buyers with no advertising support and with only limited on-pack information (Chapter 4). Building on this idea, a positioning procedure is described which requires managers to think about their customers and their brands at three levels (macro, meso and micro). At the core of this procedure is the positioning statement which describes the target customer and explains how the brand meets category need by best delivering a particular benefit or combination of benefits.

Once launched into an established product category, the performance of a brand can be assessed using measures of brand size, loyalty and switching (Chapter 5). These measures are based on analysis of the revealed behaviour of buyers – not what buyers say they might think or do, but their actual purchases. This is the business end of brand management, in the sense that revenue from actual purchases pays the bills incurred by the marketing department. It is shown how these measures can be used to describe the performance of brands in an existing market, study the effect of the demographic profile of buyers on the structure of a market, and make predictions for a new brand in an established market.

An understanding of brand performance measures is used again in the next chapter to examine three important issues in brand management – the route to brand growth, the idea that brands should be uniquely differentiated, and the building and maintenance of brand equity (Chapter 6). Evidence is presented to show that customer acquisition is central to brand growth; brands need to attract new customers, and therefore cannot solely rely on loyalty-building initiatives. Directly competing brands tend not to be strongly differentiated, despite attempts by brand owners to position their brands distinctively in the minds of buyers (as described in Chapter 4). One reason is copy-cat behaviour by competitors, which means that it is tough for a brand to 'best deliver' a particular benefit or combination of benefits in a unique way for any prolonged period of time. To acquire more customers when competing brands are not seen as strongly differentiated, the task is to build brand associations across a wide population group and to not depend on customers having strong emotional connections or attachment to the brand (in contrast to some of the reasoning in Chapters 14 and 16).

To achieve the performance and sales goals discussed in the two previous chapters, brands must be prominent. Prominence, or top-of-mind awareness, gives rise to the concept of 'brand salience' (Chapter 7). Brand salience is seen as a major influence on purchase likelihood and ultimately purchase. It has such influence because of the way salience determines whether a brand is in a consumer's consideration set. For a brand to be included in a consideration set, consumers must have knowledge and awareness of the brand (which might range from low-level familiarity to well-grounded experience). Brand image and media consumption also contribute to brand salience by building exposure and links to the brand in memory.

Earlier chapters in Part II have mainly looked at discrete brands, but use is frequently made of various forms of co-branding, such as physical product integration (Adidas shoes with Goodyear soles), complementary use (Coca-Cola and NutraSweet), and ingredient branding (IBM and Intel) (Chapter 8). Reasons for co-branding include the desire to influence (positively) consumers' perceptions of the composite brand and constituent brands, the provision of extra cues to signal product quality to consumers, and the capacity to enhance perceptions of lesser known partner brands. Organisation co-branding is a growing trend, including sponsorship arrangements like those between Adidas and the New Zealand Rugby Union. An outcome of this trend is to give traditional product brands such as Adidas an 'experiential edge' through participation in a sporting activity like New Zealand Rugby Union (a theme to which we return in Chapter 15).

Consumers and customers are the most obvious groups to reach out to with branding. But prospective and current employees are also in the sights of those responsible for branding (Chapter 9). The argument is that, by better positioning a brand in the minds of employees, there are gains externally (in terms of employee recruitment, the servicing of customers, and the ability to meet customer expectations), internally (such as employee retention and staff engagement), and at the intersection of the two (in that employees are able accurately and consistently to represent the organisation if they fully understand the employer brand). A more holistic, process-based view of employer branding requires the active involvement of multiple divisions within an organisation, notably human resource management and marketing.

For many brands, a substantial part of their revenue comes from business-to-business (B2B) markets – think of GE, IBM, Cisco, Oracle and Accenture (Chapter

10). Even consumer brands need to be 'sold in to' the trade – the immediate customers of Chanel and L'Oreal are Bloomingdale's and Printemps, not final consumers. The question here is the extent to which branding matters to organisational buyers in B2B markets and, where it matters, does it operate differently from consumer markets? The value of branding is not as obvious in business markets; for instance, trust is likely to be inter-personal (between sellers and buyers who are known to each other), rather than something conveyed to a mass audience through the mechanisms of branding. Alternative frameworks that focus on the value of a B2B brand as a resource are discussed. These frameworks see brands as market-based resources, or assets, which are important in maintaining long-term inter-organisational relationships.

Preceding chapters show that brand management not only involves an understanding of traditional marketing themes (with a focus on final consumers) but also organisational management, human resource management and resource-based theories of the firm. Hugely important too are the legal aspects of brand management (Chapter 11). The utility and value of brands is built on their legal recognition and protection. The registered trademark regime is the primary means of brand protection. This protection is supplemented by the common law passing off action and the prohibition of misleading conduct. While the focus here is on Australian law, legal recognition and protection is a universal challenge, especially if we recognise that all leading brands operate in an increasingly open global business environment.

It is appropriate to end Part II with a discussion of brand evolution and demise (Chapter 12). Managers might put considerable effort into repositioning and rejuvenating their brands, or stretching and extending their brands. Such actions might help to prolong the lifespan of certain brands, but the unsettling thought is that, sooner or later, failure and death awaits all brands. Biological metaphors are called upon to support the claim that brand death is inevitable. Also noted is the over-emphasis on success. The representative brands of the dot.com era are not Microsoft, Apple and Google, but the long-dead shooting stars who were fleetingly salient (if at all) and of which we now have no recall or recollection. Indeed, even the expression 'dot.com' now seems quaint and dated.

Chapter 4

Brand positioning: The three-level positioning procedure

JOHN R ROSSITER

ABSTRACT

Brand positioning is conceptualised as a management decision process that consists of three levels. The first and broadest level is 'macro-positioning' whereby, using the T-C-B model, the manager must position the brand to appeal to a particular type of target customer (T) so as to meet a specific category need (C) by offering a perceptually distinct key benefit (B). At the second, middle or 'meso-positioning' level, using the I-D-U model, the brand manager must expand on the B factor by identifying a key benefit, or key benefit combination, for the brand that is important (I) to the target customer, believably deliverable (D) by the brand, and seen as relatively unique (U) and preemptive for the brand. The final level is 'micro-positioning' using the a-b-e model in which the key benefit is positioned as and made into a key benefit claim that will be seen or heard in the ad. The brand manager should decide the brand's micro-positioning, and the a-b-e micro-model of positioning provides guidelines for whether the brand's communicated positioning should focus on its objective technical attributes (a), or on its subjective benefit or benefits (b), or on the newly popular emotional (e) positioning. This chapter provides a comprehensive theoretical framework for brand positioning.

KEYWORDS

brand positioning; macro-positioning (T-C-B model); meso-positioning (I-D-U model); micro-positioning (a-b-e model)

Introduction

Most introductory textbooks in brand management and marketing communications emphasise the importance of positioning. Practitioners frequently talk about positioning and many have been exposed to simplistic treatments of the subject. Typically, simple rules for positioning are presented (see especially Ries & Trout 1971). By contrast, the viewpoint presented here is that positioning – of either a brand overall or a particular product or service marketed as a sub-brand – is a multilevel concept that requires a complex procedure. Presented in this chapter is a detailed three-level procedure (see Figure 4.1) for brand positioning, which is a distillation of ideas previously developed in two marketing communications textbooks by Rossiter and Percy (1997) and Rossiter and Bellman (2005). Some new aspects are added and new examples are used to illustrate the procedure.

Figure 4.1 The three levels of brand positioning and associated positioning models

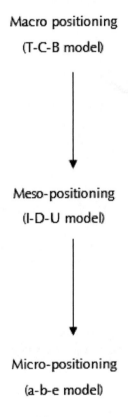

Macro positioning

(T-C-B model)

Meso-positioning

(I-D-U model)

Micro-positioning

(a-b-e model)

To define brand positioning, one first has to articulate its purpose. The purpose of positioning a brand, superficially considered, is to 'sell more' of it than would be sold if the brand were not positioned but rather just offered to potential buyers with no advertising support and the barest on-pack information. However, the deeper and more sophisticated purpose of brand positioning is to enable the brand to 'sell better'. The enablement is to create and increase two vital communication effects, which are mental responses to the brand established in the minds of the target audience. These two communication effects are brand awareness and brand attitude (see Figure 4.2). The first communication effect, *brand awareness*, requires the establishment of a two-way linkage between another communication effect, called *category need*, and the *brand identifier*. The brand identifier is the consumer's mental representation of the brand-object in the temporal lobes of the brain (see Martin 2007 for the brain location of object representations). The representation has to be the brand's package or logo (for brand recognition) or the brand name (for brand recall). The second communication effect, *brand attitude*, requires establishing a one-way linkage between the brand identifier and either one or several *benefits* – more precisely, as we shall see later, attributes, benefits or emotions – or a multiple benefit combination. It is the dual communication effects of *brand awareness*, necessary in the first place otherwise the prospective buyer cannot find the brand let alone choose it, and then *brand attitude*, both absolute and relative to other brands, that sell the brand 'mentally' by making the target audience more likely to choose it.

Figure 4.2 T-C-B macro-model of positioning and how positioning relates to three communication effects: category need, brand awareness (brand recognition and brand recall), and brand attitude

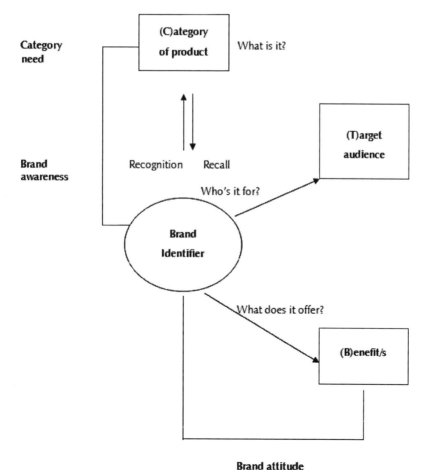

Brand positioning can therefore be defined as: 'To target customers (T), BRAND BLANK is a brand that meets category need (C), by best delivering a particular benefit or combination of benefits (B)'. This is the format for the *positioning statement* that the manager should write for every brand and brand-item (specific product or service) marketed by the company or organisation. It also describes the first or 'macro' level of the overall positioning *procedure*, which is represented by the T-C-B model (see Rossiter & Bellman 2005 and note that this is the new name for the X-YZ model in Rossiter & Percy 1997).

The overall positioning procedure consists of two further levels (and models) which are an expansion of the benefits (B) factor in the T-C-B model and are necessary to execute and achieve brand positioning. The model at the middle or 'meso' level of positioning is the I-D-U model, which says that the brand should be positioned on a benefit or combination of benefits that is important (I) to the target audience, deliverable (D) by the brand, and unique (U) in the category. At the final, 'micro' level of the positioning procedure is the a-b-e model (lower case to emphasise its micro focus) which is used – by the brand manager or often (implicitly) by the brand's advertising agency – to select specific attributes, benefits or emotions to be included in the brand's marketing communications.

The format of this chapter on brand positioning follows the procedural order of T-C-B positioning, I-D-U positioning, and a-b-e positioning.

T-C-B positioning

The first level of positioning is T-C-B positioning, in which the manager must choose:

- the target audience (T) for the brand;
- the product category (C), which may be literal or more psychological in the sense of a category *need* into which the brand is to be positioned; and
- the key benefit (B) for the brand.

The T, C, and B each involve major decisions, as explained next.

The target audience (T) decision

The target audience for the brand answers the basic question of: 'Who is it for?' The options for the target audience positioning decision are given in Table 4.1. This decision is based on the premise that not all potential buyers are good prospects for generating sales of the brand. Early in the product *category* life cycle – think digital-reception TV sets, for example, or portable music players – the best prospects will be (potential) *new category users*, abbreviated NCU. Selection of an NCU target audience for the brand automatically has implications for the C and B decisions in T-C-B positioning because the brand must inform or educate, and indeed *sell* NCUs on the new category (C) to which the brand is positioned to belong as well as convey *two* sets of benefits (B) – one set for the product or service category to establish the category need communication effect, and another set for the brand itself as the reason or reasons for the target audience acquiring a favourable, and preferably preferential, brand attitude communication effect (see also Howard's 1977 theory of extensive problem-solving).

Table 4.1 The target audience (T) decision at the macro (T-C-B) level

Stage in product category life cycle	Target audience
Introduction	New category users
Growth	New category users and Favourable brand switchers
Maturity	Favourable brand switchers and Other-brand switchers
Decline	Brand loyals

If the brand is in, or is newly being launched in, the *growth* phase of the product category life cycle, then two target audience groups will often need to be selected. One is NCUs, because there will still be potential new users entering the category. The other is *favourable brand-switchers*, FBSs, who are defined as consumers who are *already favourable* toward the brand (they have acquired a positive – if tentative – brand attitude) even though they may not yet have tried it. A good example is the favourable attitude most consumers had toward the Apple brand when the iPod was launched. This definition of FBSs thus accommodates the case of consumer durables – such as annual models of new cars – because the consumer is 'not yet' a switcher, or 'in-switcher', but is likely to become one because of his or her favourable attitude. For fast-moving consumer goods (fmcg) products or services, on the other hand, most FBSs are already actually switching between brands and including our brand in their 'repertoire' of purchases.

If the brand is in the *maturity* phase of the product category life cycle – the usual situation facing brand managers for most of their brands – there are also two target audiences that represent the best prospects for positioning the brand. These are FBSs, who are also targeted during the growth phase, and secondly *other-brand switchers*, OBSs. Other-brand switchers are consumers who switch between several brands that do not include our brand but their switching behaviour suggests that they may be persuaded to 'switch in' to our brand. This competitive focus represented by the second target audience, OBSs, is quite normal in the mature phase of the life cycle where the brand's sales can only increase by taking sales – or market share – away from competitors. It is important to note that for consumer durables, OBSs, just like FBSs, are defined in terms of their brand predispositions with respect to the *next* purchase rather than in terms of their past actual switching behaviour.

Not mentioned for the maturity phase is another potential target audience – which is the fifth and exhausts all possibilities – called other-brand loyals, or OBLs. There are some products and services characterised by weak or spurious loyalty which may make OBLs a viable target for increasing our brand's sales in maturity. According to extensive research by Ehrenberg (1987), many fmcg products are characterised by weak loyalty which would make OBLs a viable target audience.

If the brand is in a product category that is in the *decline* phase – and nearly all products or product subtypes with the apparent exceptions of a few perennials such as Scotch whisky (or Irish *whiskey*) and babies' diapers will eventually decline – then the target audience focus narrows down to the brand's own *brand loyals*. Usually, no advertising or just very brief reminder advertising – most often at the point-of-purchase – is used to support the brand in the decline phase. Brand loyals, BLs, are usually identified behaviourally as those buyers who devote their majority 'share of requirements' to our brand, although there is no universal cutoff for 'majority' because some product categories (e.g. cigarettes, medicines, makeup) inspire much higher behavioural loyalty to brands than do the more commodity types of products (e.g. household paper products and, surprisingly, beer, due to the regular flood of new brands into the market).

Brand loyals are also a secondary target audience in all phases of the product category life cycle. Fortunately, marketing communications directed at the other target audience groups will automatically work on BLs. However, in tracking the sales results of the brand's marketing (and positioning) efforts, sales to BLs should be identified in the analysis, as should the sales going to the primary target audience group or groups. If this is not done, then the manager will never know whether the target audience positioning decision was correct. For instance, supermarket 'loyalty programs' are targeted at FBSs, but a recent study (Meyer-Warden & Benavent 2009) reveals that they mainly influence the purchase behaviour of the store's own BLs, and then only a small amount over about a 6- to 9-month 'honeymoon' period.

The category (C) decision

The very first question that the consumer asks upon encountering a new brand – in a new TV commercial, for instance – is: 'What is it?' The most typical first question asked by consumers in advertising pretests, for instance, is: 'What are they advertising?' and, with the postmodern style of advertising in vogue today, this question may never be answered in most consumers' minds – or not until the consumer has seen or heard the advertising a large number of times. This means that the manager must position the brand as clearly belonging to a particular product category (which can be most easily done by including the product category name with the brand name) and, more precisely, as meeting a particular *category need*. The category need can be flagged by the brand name (e.g. Diet Coke) or else it has to be brought out in the brand's marketing communications and advertising (the latter was the case for Coke Zero, where it was not clear initially what the product was or what 'Zero' meant). The requirement to position a new brand into a product category or category need is the main reason for the 'brand architecture' procedure of *sub-branding* via a compound brand name (such as Coke *and* Zero).

Older sub-brands in Coca-Cola's diet brand architecture are Tab, which did not use a compound name and has all but died, and Diet Coke.

The present approach to the category positioning decision takes the decision further by calling for the manager to decide *how* it will be positioned into the category or category need, as shown in Table 4.2. There are really only two choices. The brand can be positioned as a *central* brand in the category, which means that it must *imply* that it offers *all the main benefits* of products in that category. (This means that the C decision has automatic implications for the benefit, B, positioning decision.) The pioneer or (subsequent) market leader brand would naturally adopt central category positioning. So too would (later entering) 'me-too' brands, which are brands that claim to offer the same benefits as the market leader but with a large (easily discernible) price saving. All other brands – which should mean most brands – adopt a *differentiated* position within the category (thus following, although they wouldn't know it, Chamberlin's 1933 theory of monopolistic competition and, for recent experimental confirmation, see Cunha & Laran 2008).

It may be noted that most marketing textbooks recommend differentiated positioning for *all* brands, but this is incorrect. Market leader or me-too brands should seize the central position. A market-leader brand can seize central positioning by tying itself to the entire product category or category need. A good example of this is the key benefit claim chosen to reposition Australia's market-leading beer brand, Victoria Bitter (known by consumers as 'VB'): 'The drinking beer'. Initially criticised by marketing journalists as being too generic, as *all* beers are 'for drinking', this is actually a brilliant decision that epitomises central positioning, because 'drinking' is the category-need trigger or cue for nominating a brand. It could be argued philosophically that the centrality of market-leader and me-too brands *is* their differentiation, or point of difference, from sharply differentiated, specialised brands. In practice, many brands that *should* adopt a differentiated position within the category fail to do so and are seen by consumers as me-too brands. An example in the Australian beer category is Carlton Draught, which is trailing VB by a long way.

Table 4.2 The category (C) positioning decision at the macro (T-C-B) level

Status of brand	Category positioning
Pioneer or market leader	Central
Me-too (benefits match leader's, with large price saving)	Central
All other brands	Differentiated

The benefit (B) positioning decision

At the macro (T-C-B) level, the benefit positioning decision involves an important choice between two options, as shown in Table 4.3. In the brand's marketing communications, the manager has to decide whether to make the *user* the hero or main focus, or whether to make the *product* the main focus, which is what most managers tend to want to do – especially those from an engineering or an accounting background.

Table 4.3 The benefit (B) positioning decision at the macro (T-C-B) level

Type of product (or service)	Macro-benefit positioning
Technical product with 'novice' target audience	User-as-hero
Social approval product	User-as-hero
All other products	Product-as-hero

As indicated in the table, there are two situations in which the main 'selling point' is the user, not the product or service itself. One situation for 'user-as-hero' positioning is for a brand of a technical product aimed at a 'novice' target audience. With truly 'new to the world' innovations, there is usually only a small proportion of potential buyers who will become knowledgeable experts, and most of the buyers will thus fall into the novices group. The same situation applies to major innovations within an older product category such as computers and other high-tech electronic products and also, these days, new pharmaceutical products including new illicit drugs. It is almost impossible to teach novice users about the technical attributes of the product, and often they are not interested anyway. By positioning the product as suitable for a particular type of user – by using an *expert endorser* approach – the need for technical education can be avoided with a novice target audience. Financial advisory services are an example.

The second situation in which 'user-as-hero' positioning is recommended is for social approval products. The reason is that brands of these products are primarily differentiated by the ideal type of person who uses them. The presenter should be an *admired user* (frequently a celebrity). Well-known examples for luxury wristwatch brands (see the study by Praxmarer & Rossiter 2009) are Brad Pitt for Tag Heuer men's watches and Uma Thurman for Tag Heuer women's watches.

If neither of these situations applies, then the manager should adopt *product-as-hero* positioning at this macro level. Emphasis in product-as-hero ads is on the branded product and its particular benefits.

I-D-U positioning

The second level of positioning is I-D-U positioning which, as mentioned at the beginning of this chapter, is an expansion of the benefit, B, decision of macro-positioning. I-D-U positioning consists of an overall I-D-U positioning rule (actually three rules) and a number of strategies that the manager must choose between to implement the first rule, that of benefit *emphasis*. The rules and the strategies were derived from *multiattribute theory*, which has a long history in consumer behaviour research (see especially the review in the consumer behaviour textbook by East, Wright & Vanhuele 2008, chapter 6). The term 'multiattribute' introduces an important realisation that applies to the I-D-U model and also the model at the final level of positioning, called the a-b-e model, and this is that the term 'attribute' as well as the term 'benefit' refers to three distinct types of product (or service) characteristics: attributes, benefits, and emotions. These terms will be defined in conjunction with the a-b-e model in the next section of this chapter. For now, the generic term 'benefits' will be used.

Table 4.4 I-D-U meso-model of positioning: the I-D-U positioning rule and benefit emphasis strategies

I-D-U positioning rule
1. *Emphasise* the brand's important (I) and unique (U) benefit or benefit combination – the 'key' benefit.
2. *Mention* its important (I) but equal 'entry-ticket' benefits.
3. *Trade off* any important (I) benefit on which the brand has inferior delivery (D).
Benefit emphasis strategies
1A. Increase or maintain the uniqueness (U) of the brand's perceived delivery (D) on an important benefit (I) or combination of benefits.
1B. Increase the importance (I) of a benefit on which the brand will be seen as delivering uniquely (D,U).
1C. Weaken a competitor's perceived delivery (D_{comp}) on an important benefit (I) to eliminate a unique competitive advantage (U_{comp}).
1D. Add a new benefit unique to the brand (D,U) and of at least moderate importance (I).
1E. Alter the consumer's choice rule to favour the brand (equivalent to changing the benefits' importance weights, the Is).

I-D-U positioning rule

The I-D-U rule is a sequence of three rules (see Table 4.4). To implement these rules, the manager has to conduct intensive consumer research (preferably large-scale qualitative research) with *each* target audience – or at least with the primary and secondary target audiences. This is because the importance of the benefit (the I factor in I-D-U) may differ between target audiences or may have changed over time. For example, in the early 1990s, Unilever's Uvistat suncare lotion made a switch to 'tanning', an emerging important consumer benefit; unfortunately, its original key benefit, 'skin protection', became the most important benefit by the turn of the century. Uvistat couldn't successfully switch back as it had lost its unique earlier positioning, and the brand slipped to a 2.2% market share (Admap 2005). The manager has to determine what the brand's most unique (U) benefit – or *key* benefit – will be from among the target audience-defined important (I) benefits in the product category. As noted in the rule, the key benefit may be a unique *combination* of benefits, which is what a 'central' brand offers, without any particular benefit being uniquely offered as would be the case with a 'differentiated' brand.

The second rule is that the brand's marketing communications must mention *entry-ticket* benefits. This is especially important when the target audience is new to the brand. This means a target audience of NCUs, OBLs, OBSs, or FBSs, excluding only BLs, the brand's own brand loyals. Entry-ticket benefits are important (I) benefits that it is necessary to be offered at a sufficient level so that the brand is seen as a legitimate 'player' in the product category. Some examples are: new cars that must state they have airbags (now typically multiple airbags), ABS brakes and a central-locking device, although other previous entry-ticket benefits such as power steering, power windows and seat belts have become so standard that there is no longer any need to mention them; new TV sets, in which it has to be stated that the digital recorder, previously a 'set-top box', is built in; and fruit juices, for which it is now almost mandatory to state 'no added sugar'. In many product categories – particularly insurance, alcoholic beverages and pharmaceuticals – there are often legally mandated 'entry-ticket' benefits which must be mentioned in the brand's communications (and in its positioning statement). A recent experiment by Gunasti and Ross (2008) demonstrated that, if an otherwise attractive brand omitted information on an important entry-ticket benefit, then about 40% of consumers would 'walk away' (defer a choice) from the entire product category and that the others, of course, would be much less likely to choose that brand (about 10% versus about 40% who would choose it had the information been offered). In food products, the benefit 'organic' threatens to become an entry-ticket benefit despite the vagueness of this attribute.

The third rule is trickier and more strategic. If the brand has any important (I) benefits on which the brand is perceived by the target audience to have inferior delivery (D) and if the brand is *not* going to improve this delivery in its new positioning, then this benefit must be explicitly (openly) *traded off* against one of the brand's important and unique (U) benefits. Typically, thank goodness, any given brand has only one important inferior benefit. A common example of tradeoffs are long waiting times against superior cuisine or superior social prestige in restaurants; a lack of 'extra' technical features in electronic products which are traded off against a lower price; and the perennial trade-off in food products, which is usually hidden rather than explicit (although well known to the consumer), of taste versus salt or sugar content.

Benefit emphasis strategies

Benefit emphasis strategies get into the most interesting and difficult aspect of brand positioning (although the other aspects are all equally necessary). The benefit emphasis strategies are listed in the lower part of Table 4.4 (earlier). These strategies should be considered by the manager, for the brand's I-D-U positioning, in *descending* order because the five strategies are progressively more difficult to implement.

By far the easiest and most common benefit emphasis strategy is 1A: to increase – or maintain if most of the target audience believe that the brand already has it – the brand's uniqueness of perceived delivery on an important benefit or an important combination of benefits. The vast majority of advertisements for brands follow this *unique selling proposition* or USP strategy.

By carrying out a *simulated* I-D-U test among managers (see Rossiter & Percy 1997 or Rossiter & Bellman 2005), it is possible to make a reasonably good estimate of whether one of the other benefit emphasis strategies might be more advantageous for the brand. The most likely of these alternative strategies is 1B, which is to increase the importance of the to-be-emphasised benefit. In a $280 million dollar gamble on this strategy, Unilever is pushing the idea that 'Dirt is good' for its stain-remover laundry detergent brands globally (Wentz 2005). Via the I-D-U model's I term, this will increase brand attitude – one of the essential communication effects discussed earlier.

Strategy 1C is to attack a major competitor's brand, usually the market leader, which is the strategy implemented in comparative advertising. Explicit comparative advertising is common in the US, and also seems to be spreading to other western markets or product categories that are in the mature stage of the life cycle (category sales are flat and so the only way to grow the brand is to take share from one or more competitors). Explicit comparative advertising is, however, outlawed in some countries, notably European Union countries; also, it can backfire badly and result in lawsuits (e.g. BMW versus Volvo in the US market over Volvo's advertising claim that Volvo's station wagon accelerated faster than a similar engine capacity BMW sedan, which Volvo won).

Strategy 1D is the 'product innovation' strategy and, whereas this is often technically difficult and very expensive, it can also be very effective because, for a short time at least (longer if patent protection can be achieved), the brand has a unique advantage on at least a moderately important benefit which, via the multiattribute model, can result in a big boost to the brand's brand attitude rating. An example is Nike's innovation of 'air cushion' sports shoes – endorsed by basketball star Michael 'Air' Jordan – which gave Nike a couple of years of boosted sales.

The last and most difficult strategy, 1E, is to try to persuade consumers that they should make their brand choice in a different manner – using a different choice rule. As noted, this is the equivalent to changing the importance weights (the Is) of the benefits, which is a major undertaking in a relatively well-established or mature product category, such that the importance weight of a benefit on which the brand delivers uniquely becomes 1.0 and the importance weights of the other benefits are driven to zeroes. Luxury wristwatches provide a good example of this in that the only benefit that they seem to want the consumer to consider is prestige value (using a celebrity user-as-hero approach). Diet sodas partly follow this strategy by promoting the benefit of 'no sugar' or 'few calories' – but only partly because they want to maintain the main benefit of taste. Pepsi Max is an example, as is Coke Zero.

A-b-e positioning

The final level of brand positioning, a-b-e positioning, is deliberately in lower case to highlight that it is 'micro'. It pertains to the core content of the brand's marketing communications – the so-called 'consumer insight' – and is a decision that is often delegated to, or simply left to, the brand's advertising agency. However, this is the only level of positioning that the target audience will actually see (in its ads or on the pack) and so this decision should be made – ultimately anyway – by the brand manager. (T-C-B positioning and, though very difficult, I-D-U positioning can only be seen by reverse engineering competitors' ads and packages, as well as one's own, and it is recommended that this be done as part of background 'desk research' for developing a positioning strategy. However, you cannot do this without first having a *framework* for this content analysis exercise, and the T-C-B model and the I-D-U model provide the necessary two frameworks.) It should be pointed out that the a-b-e stage of positioning is where otherwise sensible positioning efforts most often fail.

In the brand's marketing communications, the manager has to decide that the message content emphasis should be on *attributes* (objective technical features of the product or service), *benefits* (subjective characteristics that consumers 'want' from attributes), or *emotions* (subjective feelings associated with the brand that can be entirely free-standing and not connected to either attributes or benefits, and can be positive *or* negative). As shown in Table 4.5, there are also several two-step sequences of a's, b's, and e's to be considered for micro positioning.

Table 4.5 a-b-e micro-model of positioning: six micro-positioning tactics

When to use	a-b-e tactic
Expert target audience	Attribute/s only (a)
When a highly rational, 'reason why' message is needed – new or hostile target audience	Attribute/s to benefit/s (a → b)
Informational (problem-solving, problem-prevention, and conflict-resolving) products – introduction and growth stages	Negative emotion-shift to benefit ($e^- \to b$)
Transformational (sensory gratification, intellectual stimulation, or social approval) products – introduction and growth stages	Benefit to positive emotion ($b \to e^+$)
Informational products in maturity stage	Benefit/s only (b)
Transformational products in maturity stage	Emotion/s only (e^+)

Two of the tactics involve attributes. The first is the *attribute/s only* tactic, which is used when the brand is to be positioned to an expert target audience. Experts *know* what the benefits are and it would be 'talking down' to them to spell them out. The second attribute-based tactic is an *attribute/s-to-benefit/s* 'chain' that underpins the 'reason why' approach to advertising. This approach is most often used for 'high-risk informational' products or services aimed at a new – or hostile – target audience. The new audience situation would cover the case of a technical product being advertised to a nonexpert or 'novice' target audience where it is necessary to spell out what benefits the attributes lead to. The hostile audience situation also calls for a → b chaining because 'evidence-supported' arguments are the most convincing. The Australian consumer audience, for instance, turned hostile when a cream cheese formulation of Vegemite was unconvincingly named iSnack 2.0 when its attributes were a combination of two very old ones.

The third and fourth tactics focus on benefits, but with 'emotional support'. So-called *informational* products begin with some sort of problem, portrayed with a negative emotion (e^-), and the benefit (b) that follows constitutes a 'negatively reinforcing' emotion shift. The end-state following reception of the benefit is usually one of emotional neutrality (e.g. relief) rather than a decidedly positive emotional state. This is the classic 'problem-solution' approach pioneered by Procter & Gamble and still used today (e.g. 'Tide detergent gets out tough stains'). On the other hand, with *transformational* products, a highly positive emotional end-state follows receipt of the benefit (b → e^+). Special K cereal commercials, for instance, end with how 'fit' you'll feel. The informational and transformational tactics, which are quite elaborate to execute in marketing communications, are required mainly in the introduction and growth stages of the product category life cycle.

In the maturity stage of the product category life cycle, both informational products and transformational products (and, as always, services can be included here) require only a single focus because the respective sequential 'arguments' or 'chains' will be well known to consumers. Thus, informational products in the maturity stage need only emphasise the brand's unique benefit (e.g. 'Tide cleans best') or unique combination of benefits. And transformational products in the maturity stage need only to emphasise the brand's unique positive emotional association (e.g. 'Coke adds life', a positive emotional claim that could, if the brand manager were pressed, be traced back to a supporting attribute, namely that it contains caffein). 'Pure emotion' micro-positioning – always using a positive emotion, hence e^+ – is very popular with ad agencies at present, but a new study by Rossiter and Bellman (forthcoming) reveals that this is a risky approach that has been successful for very few brands. Benefit-focus is the tried-and-true a-b-e tactic for established brands.

Identification of the conditions of use of the micro-positioning tactics are a unique contribution of the present chapter (and the associated textbooks) that will be found in no other source. The two positioning frameworks for macro-positioning and meso-positioning do have some original forerunners (notably Howard 1977), but have never been stated as concisely as they have here. To actually use the three-level positioning procedure, however, readers are encouraged to seek the further detail in the author's two textbooks.

References

Admap 2005, 'Research is dangerous', September, p. 9.

Chamberlin, EH 1933, *The Theory of Monopolistic Competition – A Reorientation of the Theory of Value.* Cambridge, England: Cambridge University Press.

Cunha, M, Jr. & Laran, J 2008, 'Asymmetries in the sequential learning of brand associations: implications for the early entrant advantage'. *Journal of Consumer Research*, 35 (4), 788-799.

East, R, Wright, M & Vanhuele, M 2008, *Consumer Behaviour: Applications in Marketing.* Los Angeles: Sage.

Ehrenberg, ASC 1987, *Repeat-Buying: Theory and Applications.* London: Griffin.

Gunasti, K & Ross, WT, Jr. 2008, 'How inferences about missing attributes decrease the tendency to defer choice and increase purchase probability'. *Journal of Consumer Research*, 35 (4), 823-837.

Howard, JA 1977, *Consumer Behavior: Application of Theory.* New York: McGraw-Hill.

Martin, A 2007, 'The representation of object concepts in the brain'. *Annual Review of Psychology*, 58, 25-45.

Meyer-Warden, L & Benavent, C 2009, 'Grocery retail loyalty program effects: self-selection or behavior change?', *Journal of the Academy of Marketing Science*, 37 (3), 345-358.

Praxmarer, S & Rossiter, JR 2009, 'Physically attractive presenters and persuasion'. Paper presented at the International Conference on Research in Advertising, Klagenfurt, Austria, June 25-27.

Ries, A & Trout, J 1971, *Positioning: The Battle for Your Mind.* New York: McGraw-Hill.

Rossiter, JR & Bellman, S (forthcoming), 'Emotional branding: fad or fortune?', *Journal of Advertising Research*, accepted for publication.

Rossiter, JR & Bellman, S 2005, *Marketing Communications: Theory and Applications.* Frenchs Forest, Australia: Pearson Prentice Hall.

Rossiter, JR & Percy, L 1997, *Advertising Communications and Promotion Management*, 2nd edn. New York: McGraw-Hill.

Wentz, L 2005, 'Talking dirty for detergents leads executive to 'brand conversation', *Advertising Age*, October 17, p. 42.

Author biography

John R Rossiter is Research Professor of Marketing in the Faculty of Commerce, University of Wollongong, Australia, where he is co-director of the Marketing Research Innovation Centre, and is Visiting Professor of Marketing at Bergische Universität Wuppertal, Germany. John Rossiter is the principal author of a worldwide textbook on advertising and promotion, and of a broader textbook on marketing communications. The theory in this chapter is based on these two textbooks. He is also a marketing consultant to many government organisations and commercial companies.

Contact: jrossite@uow.edu.au.

Chapter 5

Understanding brand performance measures

MARK D UNCLES

ABSTRACT

The focus of this chapter is brand performance measures (BPMs); specifically brand size measures (market share and penetration), loyalty-related measures (average purchase frequencies, frequency of purchase distributions, product rates of buying and share of category requirements), and switching-related measures (duplicate buying). With an example, it is demonstrated how brand managers can use BPMs to: (a) describe the performance of brands in an existing market, (b) study the effect of the demographic profile of buyers on the structure of a market, and (c) make predictions for a new brand in an established market. These uses are greatly helped by the fact that BPMs meaningfully describe patterns of buyer behaviour and structures of markets to such an extent that these patterns and structures are predictable using models (the NBD and Dirichlet). Further applications are noted, as are several broader implications. Despite the predictability of the patterns associated with BPMs, there is plenty of scope for brand managers to make a difference (in the example, market shares range from 1% to 21%, which suggests quite different brand management tactics are being used even amongst directly competing brands).

KEYWORDS

brand performance measures; brand metrics; brand choice; brand loyalty; brand duplication; private labels; product variants; NBD model; Dirichlet model.

Introduction

Jill Klein is the manager responsible for a brand of fully-coated biscuit bar in the UK market owned by one of the major multinational manufacturers – Mars, Nestle, Kraft Foods, United Biscuits and Arnott's[9]. Jill wants answers to questions such as: (a) what patterns of loyalty and competition are there in her market, (b) what effect, if any, does the demographic profile of buyers have on the structure of the market, and (c) what does this imply for the introduction of a new brand into this market? Typically, Jill has access to considerable amounts of market research – especially survey and consumer panel data from agencies such as Nielsen, TNS and GfK – but simply having the data is not the same as being able to interpret the numbers in a meaningful way. The purpose of this chapter is to show how insights can be drawn from the data, giving managers like Jill an understanding of their market and helping them to make more informed decisions.

In answer to question (a), there are well-established patterns, and these are easily seen if the data are presented clearly and if there is a purposeful search for norms. Absolute differences in measures of brand performance are evident when we look at demographic profiles. However – in answer to (b) – the structure of the market is largely unaltered. That is, the same patterns of loyalty and competition are found regardless of the demographic profile. Familiarity with an existing market, especially when we know there are patterns, helps the manager to think about the introduction of a new brand. What we have is a solid basis for answering (c) – for having a set of reasonable expectations about the buying of the new brand once it has settled down after the initial launch.

Having considered Jill's case in detail, the discussion is widened to consider the role of brand performance audits, growing existing brands, product variants, different geographical contexts and different product categories, as well as broader implications for brand management. From the outset it is important to note that, despite the existence of well-established patterns, there is plenty of scope for brand managers to make a difference.

Description of an existing market

Inspection of consumer panel data for the fully-coated biscuit market ('FC Countlines'[10]) shows there are many regularities with respect to a range of brand

---

[9] Data in Tables 5.1 to 5.10 are drawn from an unpublished Aske Research report written by M.D. Uncles & A.S.C. Ehrenberg. To preserve confidentiality, brand names, dates and locations are suppressed. Jill is an entirely fictitious character.

[10] The product category is formally defined as 'FC Countlines', comprising fully-coated biscuits/confectionery sold individually, in twin packs or in multi-packs, including brands such as Tim Tams, Penguin, KitKat, and Snickers, and supplied to the market by manufacturers like Mars, Nestle, Kraft Foods, United Biscuits and Arnott's. Brands on the market vary from country to country, although some are very widely available – KitKat is a prime example.

performance measures (BPMs). Here we consider penetration and average purchase frequencies for brands and for individual multi-packs, also frequency of purchase distributions, product rates of buying, share of category requirements, and duplication of purchasing between brands and between multi-packs. These BPMs illustrate how a market may be described – this list is not exhaustive[11]. Research shows these regularities, or patterns, are described using theoretical norms based on the NBD and Dirichlet models (summarised in Ehrenberg 1988). These tried and tested models of buyer behaviour have been found to apply in many other product categories and under varied conditions[12]. We note that the Dirichlet model offers norms for stationary, unsegmented markets – assumptions which can be examined (empirically) and which appear to hold true for the market under consideration (at least in the short-to-medium term).

Penetration and average purchase frequencies: Brands

Table 5.1 shows the market shares, annual penetrations and average purchase frequencies per buyer for 12 leading national brands (NBs) and five leading private labels (PLs). Observed data (O) and Dirichlet predictions (D) are reported. Purchase frequencies are given in terms of the number of weeks in which the brands were bought at least once (which is fairly close to the unit of analysis used in the definition of the theoretical models, namely the 'purchase occasion')[13].

The dominant factor in the market shares is the number of buyers (penetration) – a brand size measure. This number varies greatly between brands. In contrast, there is relatively little difference in purchase frequencies per buyer – a loyalty-related measure. Such differences as there are relate to the Double Jeopardy effect: that small brands tend to suffer in two ways – they have fewer buyers who buy the brand less often than larger brands. Thus, NB-12 has far fewer buyers and somewhat lower average purchase frequencies than NB-01. This tendency for small brands to be 'punished twice' just for being small is very commonly observed and is explained as a statistical selection effect (McPhee 1963; Ehrenberg, Goodhardt & Barwise 1990).

Another division of Jill's firm produces a private label (e.g. for a retail giant such as Tesco or Sainsbury) and naturally she is interested in how BPMs for her brand

---

[11] Other BPMs include measures of repeat purchase (e.g. the incidence of repeat buyers and their average purchase frequencies) and measures of conditional purchasing (e.g. repeat buying by heavy/light buyers) (see Ehrenberg 1988).

[12] Technical aspects of the NBD and Dirichlet models are not presented here – the interested reader is directed to Goodhardt, Ehrenberg & Chatfield (1984) and the summaries provided in Ehrenberg (1988). Of considerable importance to us is the ability of the model to describe various patterns in the BPMs and to do consistently, using quite simple inputs for estimation purposes and a few well-based assumptions.

[13] Table 5.1 also shows that of the 75% of the consumer panel buying FC Countlines, they buy 14.6 times on average. The market share in this table is 93% (not 100%) because brands of cereal bars are excluded from the calculations.

compare with those for this and other private labels in the product category. The figures show that, given their market shares, private labels have significantly higher purchase frequencies: their buyers, although fewer in number, tend to buy somewhat more often than is the case for brands with the same shares or penetrations. Possible reasons have to do with the 'population at risk' and the regional strengths of retail chains, both of which have proved to be important in other product categories (Ellis 1989; Ellis & Uncles 1991; Bound & Ehrenberg 1997). This means that the penetrations of private labels are low rather than their loyalty being high.

From Table 5.1 it is apparent that the observed results (including the Double Jeopardy effect) are mostly well predicted by the Dirichlet model, using the brands' market shares as the only brand-specific input (compare the figures in the O and D columns). The relatively high purchase frequencies for private labels is shown very clearly by comparing observed figures with the predictions. In terms of purchase weeks, for example, the average national brand at 4.0 is fractionally *below* the predicted frequency of 4.2, whereas the average private label at 4.1 is well *above* the predicted frequency of 3.7.

One or two other deviations from the predicted norms may also be meaningful. An example is NB-01 which, in terms of its purchase frequency in the previous year, was slightly more of a brand leader than its market share warranted – this is now replicated one year later. Such an effect among market leaders has also been observed in some other product fields, to the extent that it has been dubbed 'the excess loyalty premium' (Fader & Schmittlein 1993). A reason for this effect is that leading brands are more likely to be kept in stock by both national chains and independents. Another deviation is the low observed purchase frequency for smaller brands and especially NB-11. This latter case appears to be a one-off deviation – it wasn't seen in data for the previous year so, perhaps, there was an exceptional non-stationarity here (e.g. a major stock-out for a couple months of the year).

Penetration and average purchase frequencies: Multi-packs

A distinguishing feature of this market is that bars can be bought individually or as twin packs, but many are bought as multi-packs from grocery outlets. Table 5.2 gives the corresponding penetration and average purchase frequencies for different pack sizes. Again, the dominant factor in sales is the number of buyers, and not so much their rates of buying. Relatively high purchase frequencies, such as for NB-01 6-pack, NB-02 5-pack and NB-03 7-pack, tend to align with high penetrations.

At the bottom of the table are compared the purchasing frequencies for multi-packs with those for total brands. On average, the multi-packs have much lower frequencies. This is explained at least in part by the Double Jeopardy effect in that the multi-packs have lower market shares. This is confirmed by the fact that the Dirichlet model gives a generally close fit to the individual multi-packs, just as if they were well-differentiated brands with the same market shares. Their lower average purchase frequencies are not because they are specific multi-packs but because of their lower penetrations. This is exactly the same as was found for the preceding year – a consistent finding[14].

Frequency of purchase distributions

Table 5.3 shows the frequencies with which individuals buy each brand (shown here for just five of the leading brands). This BPM can be thought of as the scatter about the average purchasing frequencies in Table 5.1. Of the 43% of the population who bought NB-01, about a quarter bought it only once in a year, almost half bought it one to three times, and roughly 10% bought it every week or more often. For smaller brands, the incidence of once-only buyers is even higher and very few people buy even as much as once a month. This is in line with the Double Jeopardy trend for the average purchase frequencies.

The distributions are heavily skewed (with the average purchase frequencies seldom being at all typical). This is usual. The observed figures are in fact closely predicted by the theoretical Dirichlet model.

Table 5.4 gives the corresponding results for four of the NB-01 multi-pack sizes. The incidence of once-only buyers is even higher, in line with the generally lower average purchase rates. Thus, for NB-01 6-pack a third buy just once, and for NB-01 8-pack this rises to a half. Again, there is nothing abnormal about this in that the model offers very close predictions. For NB-01 18-pack the number of once-only buyers is even higher than might be expected given the Double Jeopardy effect. A similar 'under-prediction' was seen the previous year as well, so it is a consistent deviation[15].

Product category rates of buying

Table 5.5 shows the average rates at which the buyers of each brand buy the total product category (i.e. *any* fully-coated biscuit bars). The rates of product category buying tend to increase slightly for smaller brands. It is seen, for example, by comparing the figure of 19 purchases made by NB-01 buyers with the 24 among the NB-12 buyers. This is also a normal pattern, again predicted by the Dirichlet model. It has been called 'Natural Monopoly' to reflect that large brands have a natural tendency to attract lighter buyers (if a light buyer is going to buy the product at all s/he will tend to buy a major brand, although typically the tendency is only slight) (McPhee 1963).

The Dirichlet under-predicts the product buying rate in a number of cases. This may be because the formal definition of the model is in terms of purchase

---

[14] Also, a number of different flavours are sold – plain, milk, orange, almond, even sunflower seed and caramel. Exactly the same conclusions are drawn with regard to these flavour variants as are drawn for the multi-pack variants.

[15] An important factor here may be the consistently small sample size – when working with data for smaller brands it is always wise to discount sample size effects before offering more substantive (and possibly wrong) interpretations.

occasions, whereas the data here relate to purchase weeks. In view of this, perhaps it is surprising how well the model predicts the product category purchase rates.

Private labels show no difference from national brands with the same market shares. They are not bought by particularly heavy, or light, buyers.

The last column of Table 5.5 gives the share of category requirements met by each brand – another useful loyalty-related BPM. Generally the share is low – under 20% for the average brand – but somewhat larger for major brands like NB-01 and NB-02. This pattern reflects both Double Jeopardy in the numerator and Natural Monopoly in the denominator[16].

Duplication of purchase

A further BPM concerns duplication of purchase (also called a switching or cross-purchasing measure)[17] – that is, the proportion of buyers buying one brand who also buy another brand within some stipulated observation period such as a year. Table 5.6 sets out the annual duplication of purchase between the leading brands of FC Countlines. The normal pattern, which recurs here, is that the findings in each column are generally fairly similar, and mostly close to their average. This means that in the first column, NB-01 was bought in the year by about 72% of the annual buyers of each of the other brands, with the variation going from 65% to 79%. For brands arranged in order of declining market shares, the average duplication will fall. Thus, following NB-01 at 72% comes NB-02 at 60%, and so on, down to NB-12 with an average figure of 6%.

The tendency to duplicate is proportional to the penetration of the brands (the 'Duplication of Purchase Law') (Ehrenberg 1988). This is close to the average Dirichlet predictions (as shown here), although the Dirichlet model implies somewhat lower duplications than those we observe.

There is no evidence of substantial clusters (which might indicate a partitioned market) or large exceptions (which would suggest an excess or deficit of duplication). It is *not* as if all brands owned by a single firm form a distinct cluster, or that duplication between private labels is very low (relative to their market shares).

---

[16] Broadly, the message is the same for Dirichlet predictions of product category rates of buying by buyers of specific multi-packs (NB-01 6-pack, NB-02 5-pack, etc.). The main result is the uniformity and predictability of the product buying rates from item to item, although the rates again show a predictable Natural Monopoly trend (buyers of small items buying fractionally more of the product category).

[17] Cross-purchasing tables can be analysed in various ways. Just how many ways is apparent from the Car Challenge – this was an exercise where three dozen marketing analysts and statisticians were challenged to analyse six sets of two-period duplication tables. Some analysts examined duplication, along the lines described here, but many alternative approaches were pursued (Colombo, Ehrenberg & Sabavala 2000). The exercise also showed the importance of arranging data in meaningful ways (e.g. arranging brands by market share, not alphabetical order).

Table 5.7 gives the comparable figures for specific multi-packs. Here the same general pattern applies, except there is somewhat higher duplication between the different sizes of each brand, as shown in bold and summarised near the bottom of the table. Within NB-01 multi-packs, duplicate buying of NB-01 6-pack is 79%, compared to 62% across other multi-packs. In general, the within-brand duplication is under-predicted and the between-brand duplication is over-predicted; the predictions themselves being based on the Duplication of Purchase Law.

There is little variation in each column in terms of annual rates of buying by these duplicate buyers (in purchase weeks). The table of results is not shown here, nevertheless we note that duplicate buyers of NB-01 bought it on average 11 times in the year, almost irrespective of which other brand they bought as well, whereas for NB-12 the figure was three times. All these rates were roughly 50% higher than those at which *all* buyers of a brand bought it (i.e. duplicate buyers are heavier buyers).

Demographic analyses

A further question for Jill is whether the patterns associated with BPMs (as described above) are affected systematically by differences among buyers. What effect does the demographic profile have on the structure of the market? This question concerns segmentation, something that is of keen interest to most brand managers.

Data for the FC Countline market show that absolute differences occur, depending on the nature of the household (e.g. bigger households buy more). But the relative positions are mainly the same and so is the structure of the market. This finding is illustrated in the following tables where reference is made to the impact of the presence of children and household size on patterns of buyer behaviour.

Descriptive patterns

In Table 5.8 market shares are tabulated for the whole consumer panel, for households with and without children, and for five household sizes. It is noticeable that the brands are ranked in a similar way almost irrespective of the demographic group. NB-01 is always the leading brand. PL-3, PL-4 and PL-5 only ever achieve 1-2% of the market. Some brands, like NB-01 and NB-02, swap places in certain demographic groups but not in any dramatic way. For many of the brands, market shares are also quite stable across the groups. This is borne out by the market shares of the 'average brand' or 'average private label' which hardly vary from 6% and 2% respectively.

However, at a more detailed level, there are differences (e.g. NB-01's share is definitely higher among smaller households than among larger ones). These second-order differences may be of interest to the marketer who is looking for gaps in the market or who is attempting to diagnose the finer details of market behaviour.

Market shares depend on how many households buy and how often they do so – the BPMs of penetration and average purchase frequency that we encountered above. These components are shown in Tables 5.9 and 5.10 for our selection of demographic groups. The main pattern is that brands with higher shares have higher penetrations and higher average purchase frequencies. This Double Jeopardy effect – which we noticed for the whole market in Table 5.1 – is replicated here for *every* sub-group.

A larger proportion of those in households with children will buy brands of FC Countlines, and they will do so more often than those without children. Likewise, among larger households the proportion buying and their rates of buying exceed smaller households. These differences apply to *every* brand – it is not as if NB-01 is unusually popular among larger households, but rather that NB-01 through to NB-12 are all bought by more people and bought more often as household sizes increases.

Generally, there is systematic empirical evidence that the buyer profiles of directly competing (and therefore substitutable) brands seldom differ (Hammond, Ehrenberg & Goodhardt 1996; Kennedy & Ehrenberg 2001). In other words, the buyers of similar brands are very similar, as would tend to follow if so many of them use several of these brands. Despite this lack of segmentation between brands, there can be strong segmentation at the category or sub-category level: cat food buyers have cats and dog food buyers have dogs (of course, some buyers have both cats and dogs), buyers of luxury cars tend to have greater wealth than the typical buyer of an economy car (although some luxury car buyers may buy an economy as a second car), pre-sweetened cereals are eaten more by children (but some adults will eat these too and some children will eat un-sweetened cereals – though only after adding sugar!).

Predicted patterns

If the patterns of buying are essentially the same across different demographic profiles, it should be possible to predict behaviour knowing only the brand shares and purchasing distributions for the product category as a whole. In general, this is the case and the same Double Jeopardy pattern is predicted for each sub-group using the Dirichlet model. Jill should expect other aspects of buying – sole buying and share of requirements, switching and duplication – to be predictable too. A further theoretical twist is that, given a sufficiently long time period, small households or those without children would buy as often as larger ones do in the observation period here.

A caveat should be kept in mind – private labels have higher than expected purchase frequencies (as noted in relation to Table 5.1). Their market shares rarely exceed 4%, but their average purchase rates are as high as those brands with shares over 8%. This shows up by comparing the observed and predicted averages for brands and private labels in Tables 5.9 and 5.10. The explanation, as previously stated, is that a private label's penetration (and hence market share) is 'artificially' restricted by its limited distribution. Allowing for this, its average purchase rate would then probably be normal. Empirically, Jill could test for this in two ways. One option is to combine all private labels to create a 'superbrand' – in which case the problem of limited distribution is likely to disappear. The other option is to work with data for brands and private labels within specific outlets (Tesco, Sainsbury, etc.) – such data are not available here but might be easily obtained by a manager in Jill's position.

Predictions for Brand X

Numerous specific applications and general implications arise from a better understanding of BPMs (Ehrenberg, Uncles & Goodhardt 2004[18]). To show how the descriptive findings associated with BPMs might be used to address a specific managerial issue, consider the case of Jill being responsible for the launch of a new brand, Brand X, in the FC Countline market. Initially, she is confronted by a number of perplexing questions. Should the advertising spend and promotional budget be directed at a few loyal buyers or at the mass market? What purchase frequency should she expect from buyers of Brand X: twice on average or ten times? Once the brand starts to settle down, should the pricing policy be designed to keep existing buyers buying more, or would it be better to get Brand X into the repertoire of as many buyers as possible (given that buyers tend to switch brands a lot)?

Answers to these questions will give a better idea of how well Brand X might perform relative to other brands managed by the firm and its competitors. The first step is to set targets for sales and market shares at the estimated breakeven point and for various levels of profit impact. Given these targets, Jill can learn how buyers are most likely to behave, and from market research or trials in test markets she can see whether this offers a viable way forward (e.g. whether she can afford the promotional expenses needed to reach the requisite number of buyers).

Achieving the sales target for Brand X

Let us assume the breakeven point for Brand X is 55 purchases per 100 households (a 5% share of the FC Countline market[19]). The best-case outcome might be 110 purchases per 100 (a 10% share). At the other extreme, only 28 purchases per 100 (a 2.5% share) might require a full-scale reappraisal of the project. Each of these targets – whatever their precise values – can be achieved in several ways in buyer terms. For the breakeven target of 55 purchases per 100 households, 1% might buy 55 times, or 55% might buy once, or some other combination which multiplies to 55. This is a simple arithmetic exercise, but very different implications follow:

---

[18] The practical applications and broader implications listed in this chapter draw heavily on Ehrenberg, Uncles & Goodhardt (2004). A critical assessment of this work is provided in a commentary by Kannan (2004), prompting a reply by Uncles, Ehrenberg and Goodhardt (2004).

[19] The shares reported here relate to the FC Countline market (75% buy 14.6 times giving a total market of 1095 per 100 buyers). Therefore the figures are slightly higher than those in Table 5.1, which are based on shares of the whole Countline market (coated and fully-coated).

(a) If 1% buys 55 times, the brand fills a niche; there is a keen but small group of very frequent buyers. It would make sense to reach these with a carefully targeted campaign, and perhaps encourage them to repeat-buy (e.g. by offering '5% off the price of the next purchase' or 'buy five family packs and get one free').

(b) If, on the other hand, 55% buy once, then Jill is dealing with an occasional choice; the brand is in the repertoire of many buyers, but for few of them is it all that important. The approach here must be to reach many potential buyers (e.g. offering say free samples, or showing how eating Brand X will add a little variety).

However, because there are patterns in the existing market and because these have been described, there is a solid basis for predicting the consumer uptake of Brand X. For the 12 brands and five private labels shown in Table 5.1, we know that the per cent buying varies closely with market share and that there is a clear Double Jeopardy effect. All this is also predictable using the Dirichlet model.

This is extremely useful. Rather than worry whether 1% buy 55 times or whether 55% buy once, Jill can be sure that Brand X will be bought in much the same way as the other brands – after it has settled down. At breakeven point it will look similar to NB-08 (14 x 3.7 = 52 purchases). The Dirichlet model gives the more specific prediction that Brand X will be bought by about 14% of households on average 3.9 times, at the breakeven point of 55 purchases.

For the existing brands, downward adjustments must be made to their market shares once Brand X has settled down (by definition, shares cannot sum to more than 100%). The market structure implies pro rata adjustment, but spread over the different brands the numerical effect will be small. Only if the existing market was partitioned, or if it grew, would more complex adjustments be needed.

BPMs for Brand X

All other BPMs also can be predicted for Brand X at breakeven; buyers of Brand X will make 22 purchases of the product category, the new brand will meet 17% of its buyers requirements, and so forth. Exactly the same principles apply when predictions are made for other levels of profit impact – at 28 purchases per 100 households (2.5% market share) or at 110 purchases (10% market share) – BPMs can be predicted for these too.

All the predictions shown so far have been for a 12-month period. Most of the statements, therefore, ought to have the suffix '... in a year'. But there is no difficulty in making predictions for the breakeven target market share of 5% over different length time periods: one week, one month, six months and 24 months, as well as the base period of 12 months. For instance, Jill should expect 10% of households to buy Brand X in a six-month period, 14% in a year and 18 over two years.

We can also say something about which other brands will be bought. At its simplest, all we need do is read-off the duplication of purchase figures at the breakeven point of 55 purchases per 100 households (i.e. for a 5% market share). This can be done by interpolation (using Table 5.6) or, more precisely, with the Duplication of Purchase Law or the Dirichlet model. Thus, roughly 70% of buyers of Brand X will also buy NB-01, whereas less than 10% will buy a small brand like NB-12 or PL-03; which other brands 'your buyers' select mostly depends on the market shares of direct competitors.

Other practical applications

The example of making BPM predictions for Brand X shows the potential for application in a brand management context. An actual case of analysing a successful new brand launch, Shield, is presented by Wellan & Ehrenberg (1988), and potential cannibalisation effects of new brand launches and line extensions are reported by Lomax et al. (1997) and Lomax & McWilliam (2001).

Other applications that a manager like Jill might envisage include the following:

(a) *Brand performance audits.* BPMs for single brands tell the manager very little – these are simply isolated, hard-to-interpret facts (e.g. Jill would have difficulty knowing whether any of the figures observed for her brand are high, low or normal, or good, bad or indifferent). Whereas the fact that BPMs are associated with patterns of buyer behaviour equips managers with a tool for undertaking audits (now there are norms against which Jill can assess figures for her own brand).

(b) *Growing existing brands.* One route to growth is for a brand to gain more sales by finding new/lapsed buyers, and another is to secure more sales from existing buyers. The latter option has become popular, spurred on by heavy investments in CRM systems and loyalty/rewards programs, but the type of analysis illustrated here shows the importance of the first route to growth – the need to gain new/lapsed buyers (Dawes 2010; Sharp 2010). Additionally, the implications for loyalty programs have been investigated (Sharp & Sharp 1997; Meyer-Waarden & Benavent 2006).

(c) *SKU-related product variants.* Product variants are functionally highly differentiated (e.g. small/large pack sizes, strawberry/avocado flavours, economy/luxury versions) and, as a result, they can attract very different loyalty levels. We saw this earlier with the study of multi-packs in the FC Countline market. However, analysis shows these different loyalty levels are closely related to big differences in the market shares (and, therefore, penetrations) of variants (refer back to Table 5.2). In general, higher loyalty predictably goes hand-in-hand with higher sales (Singh, Ehrenberg & Goodhardt 2008, see also Fader & Hardie 1996).

(d) *Different geographical contexts.* What if Jill is posted to China – would any of her understanding of BPMs be of use to her? Many aspects of life in China are different from the UK – not least, people speak a different language, live at higher densities, eat more rice, and are more likely to use a bicycle. These are obvious and stereotypical differences. On the other hand, similarities are emerging – not only are Snickers manufactured in China, the brand now sells in that market, and Tesco and Wal-Mart private labels are on the shelves of retail outlets in China (through joint-venture partnering). Given these facts, perhaps it isn't so surprising to find similar patterns of buyer behaviour as in other parts of the world and, therefore, to see a need for understanding of BPMs in emerging markets as much as mature ones (Uncles, Wang & Kwok 2010).

(e) *Different product categories.* Job rotation dictates that Jill is unlikely to remain working as a brand manager in the FC Countline market for more than two to three years. Rather, within the multi-divisional structure of the firm, she may find herself subsequently having responsibility for brands of mineral water, or laundry detergent, or insect repellent. Once again, her in-depth knowledge of BPMs in one category should give her a good basis for considering other categories, especially other packaged-goods categories where items are frequently bought from a selection of directly competing brands. One such study involved the systematic analysis of 34 product categories to see if BPMs for P&G brands were as expected, given Dirichlet norms (Uncles *et al.* 1994). Some of Jill's marketing peers work in seemingly vary different sectors – ranging from consumer electronics to state lottery products – but, even in these markets, the type of BPMs presented here are often of interest and may reveal patterns (e.g. studies of television brand buying [Bennett 2008] and state lottery products and gambling purchases [Mizerski *et al.* 2004; Lam & Mizerski 2009]). To varying degrees, both repertoire and subscription markets are amenable to the form of analysis described here (Wright, Sharp & Goodhardt 2002).

It is evident that there are many practical applications. Of course, there are limits to the scope of the BPM patterns. We wouldn't expect the same conclusions to be drawn for pre-competitive markets where there is a monopoly provider, or where the product is so new that brands in the conventional sense have yet to be established (e.g. nascent nanotechnology products). Highly turbulent situations are not necessarily a limit; indeed, general competitive turbulence (e.g. price promotions, couponing activity, minor packaging changes, interest-free periods, etc.) is to be expected, and this is captured by the notion of dynamic equilibrium. Structural turbulence, however, will mean it is hard to make well-informed predictions (whatever form of modelling is used) – thus, the opening up of online retailing gave rise to a period of considerable uncertainty, several false-starts and many false-predictions, but that is now in the past and there is every reason to believe BPM patterns exist in virtual spaces as much as offline spaces (Danaher, Wilson & Davis 2003)[20].

---

[20] Another consideration is that the BPMs are based on 'purchase occasions' (or equivalents such as 'purchase weeks'). Additional analyses are required to reflect volume and value variations across purchase occasions. The examination of multi-packs begins to address this theme, but it is only a start. Furthermore, in none of these analyses is any allowance made for differing cost structures and the impact this might have on brand margins and profits (e.g. hypothetically, Mars

Broader implications

Understanding brands

The BPM modelling reported here treats brands as (approximately) identical, in that no differentiating attributes need to be specified except for the brand names and market shares. This is often so in practice, since sales-effective product advantages and innovations are usually soon copied (e.g. Ehrenberg, Barnard & Scriven 1997; Romaniuk & Gaillard 2007; Romaniuk, Sharp & Ehrenberg 2007). Even early-mover advantages tend not to last. It seems that *sustainable* product differentiation of a major kind seldom occurs between directly competitive brands.

However, functional differentiation does exist, but usually *within* brands, as SKU-related product variants: different multi-pack sizes and flavours of FC Countlines; shampoos for oily, dry and even normal hair; interest rates varying by withdrawal notice (immediate access, one month notice, three months notice, etc.); mobile phones with a great variety of different technical specifications and applications; and so on. Buyers may spend more time, effort and money choosing between functional specifications than between brands as such. But competitive brands in a category tend to have much the same range of product variants. In this sense, nearly all brands are umbrella brands and similar to each other as brands.

In many product categories, some functionally distinct sub-markets or partitions have been deliberately created (e.g. chocolate-coated and non-chocolate-coated confectionery, decaffeinated and regular coffee, hybrid and electric cars). Typically, direct competitors will then each launch product-variants into these sub-markets. Sometimes these product-variants are given distinct brand names, possibly with the same house-name (such as Kellogg's or Heinz for all of the variants), but not always (for Unilever, Procter & Gamble, Kao, Henkel and Reckitt Benckiser brands, buyers in many countries will hardly know from which corporation the product brands and variants come).

Brand management

The universality of the BPM patterns, together with markets often being more or less steady in the short-to-medium run, could lead managers like Jill to have doubts about the role of marketing. For example, are marketing inputs such as advertising worth it if they do not soon lead to extra sales? Perhaps CFOs have a point when they see marketing as a discretionary cost rather than as an ongoing investment. In practice, however, there is plenty of scope for marketing, since market shares differ greatly. The leading FC Countline in Table 5.1 had a market share of 21%, compared to NB-12 with a 1% share. However, such scope exists also for competitors – managers responsible for NB-12 will be trying to protect and build share, as will managers of NB-01. The outcome is, therefore, often competitive

---

may derive higher profits from its FC Countlines than Nestle because it has been more successful in controlling costs, rather than because of anything to do with buyer behaviour).

equilibrium rather than actual big gains or losses, at least in the short-to-medium term. This calls for maintenance of sales and retention of split-loyalty buyers (both consumer and trade). In this sense, competition first and foremost means running hard to stand still and, in those circumstances where lasting gains are secured, it is about being 'simply better' (e.g. being somewhat smarter when setting prices, securing better distribution and on-shelf display, reminding experienced buyers in more creative ways, etc.) (Barwise & Meehan 2004).

Summary

Three key points are worth emphasising by way of conclusion:

- There are clear BPM patterns, summarised for instance by the Double Jeopardy effect and the Duplication of Purchase Law. In general, the patterns of buyer behaviour associated with different brands are very similar, except for the effects of market share.

- Absolute levels of purchasing vary from one demographic sub-group to another, but the underlying market structure – as illustrated by the Double Jeopardy effect – is unaltered. The data examined here show that brands are bought in ways which vary little from sub-group to sub-group.

- Given the existence of patterns and relationships, the NBD and Dirichlet models of buyer behaviour can be used to simulate the way a new brand is likely to be bought, should it be introduced into an existing market. This is one of many practical applications that can be envisaged.

The main ways to build brands usually require working within these constraints, rather than seeking to cash in on non-systematic irregularities.

Table 5.1 Penetration & average purchase frequencies: Brands & private labels

Annual data	Market share (in weeks)	Penetration		Average purchases per buyer (in weeks)	
	O%	O%	D%	O	D
FC Countlines	**93**	**75**	-	**14.6**	-
Brands					
NB-01	21	43	*51*	7.5	*6.3*
NB-02	11	33	*34*	4.9	*4.8*
NB-03	9	35	*32*	4.4	*4.8*
NB-04	4	22	*22*	4.3	*4.2*
NB-05	3	18	*16*	3.5	*4.0*
NB-06	3	17	*16*	3.7	*4.0*
NB-07	3	17	*15*	3.4	*3.9*
NB-08	2	14	*13*	3.7	*3.9*
NB-09	2	15	*13*	3.3	*3.8*
NB-10	2	11	*10*	3.4	*3.8*
NB-11	2	14	*9*	2.6	*3.7*
NB-12	1	3	*2*	2.9	*3.5*
Ave NB	**5**	**20**	*19*	**4.0**	*4.2*
Private labels					
PL-01	3	10	*12*	4.6	*3.8*
PL-02	2	7	*9*	4.8	*3.7*
PL-03	1	5	*6*	4.3	*3.6*
PL-04	1	5	*5*	4.1	*3.6*
PL-05	1	6	*5*	2.9	*3.6*
Ave PL	**2**	**7**	*7*	**4.1**	*3.7*

National brand is 'NB' and private label is 'PL'; observed is 'O' and Dirichlet norms is 'D'.

Table 5.2 Penetration & average purchase frequencies: Multi-packs

Annual data	Market share (in weeks)	Penetration		Average purchases per buyer (in weeks)	
	O%	O%	D%	O	D
FC Countlines	93	75	-	14.6	-
Multi-packs					
NB-01 6-pack	10	33	40	5.0	4.1
NB-03 5-pack	9	35	39	4.4	4.0
NB-01 7-pack	8	31	32	3.7	3.6
NB-02 7-pack	7	27	31	4.0	3.5
NB-01 8-pack	3	19	14	2.0	2.8
NB-05 5-pack	2	14	15	3.1	2.9
NB-01 8-pack	1	9	6	1.6	2.6
NB-01 14-pack	1	6	5	2.0	2.6
NB-05 7-pack	1	6	5	1.9	2.6
NB-01 18-pack	1	2	1	1.5	2.5
Ave multi-pack	4	18	19	2.9	3.1
Ave NB	5	20	19	4.0	4.2

National brand is 'NB'; observed is 'O' and Dirichlet norms is 'D'.

Table 5.3 Frequency distributions of purchases: Leading brands

Annual data		Number of purchase weeks							
		1	2	3	4	5	6	7-20	21+
FC Countlines	O%	12	9	6	6	4	4	31	28
	D%	13	9	7	6	5	4	33	23
Leading brands									
NB-01	O%	23	14	9	7	6	5	26	10
	D%	28	16	10	8	6	5	21	6
NB-02	O%	33	18	10	7	7	4	17	4
	D%	36	17	11	7	5	4	16	4
NB-03	O%	36	17	11	6	6	5	17	2
	D%	36	17	11	7	5	4	16	4
NB-04	O%	40	20	10	8	5	3	12	1
	D%	42	18	10	7	5	3	13	2
NB-06	O%	41	15	11	6	6	4	15	2
	D%	42	18	10	7	5	3	13	2
Ave brand	O%	35	17	10	7	6	4	17	4
	D%	37	17	10	7	5	4	16	4

National brand is 'NB'; observed is 'O' and Dirichlet norms is 'D'.

Table 5.4 Frequency distributions of purchases: Multi-packs

Annual data		Number of purchase weeks							
		1	2	3	4	5	6	7-20	21+
Total NB-01	O%	23	14	9	7	6	5	26	10
	D%	28	16	10	8	6	5	21	6
Multi-packs									
NB-01 6-pack	O%	31	17	10	7	6	4	21	4
	D%	37	18	11	8	5	4	15	2
NB-01 7-pack	O%	32	19	14	9	7	4	15	0
	D%	41	19	11	7	5	4	12	1
NB-01 8-pack	O%	53	23	13	6	3	1	1	0
	D%	50	19	10	6	4	3	8	0
NB-01 18-pack	O%	74	19	3	1	0	0	2	0
	D%	55	18	9	5	3	2	8	0
Ave NB-01	O%	48	20	10	6	4	2	10	1
	D%	46	19	10	7	4	3	10	1

National brand is 'NB'; observed is 'O' and Dirichlet norms is 'D'.

Table 5.5 Average Purchases of product category & share of requirements:
Brands & private labels

Annual data	Market share (in weeks)	Average purchases of product category per buyer of brands (in weeks)		Share of requirements (in weeks)	
	O%	O	D	O%	D%
FC Countlines	93	15	15	100	100
Brands					
NB-01	21	19	18	39	34
NB-02	11	20	21	25	24
NB-03	9	20	21	22	23
NB-04	4	22	22	20	20
NB-05	3	25	22	14	18
NB-06	3	25	22	15	18
NB-07	3	23	22	15	18
NB-08	2	26	22	14	17
NB-09	2	25	23	13	17
NB-10	2	23	23	15	17
NB-11	2	23	23	11	16
NB-12	1	24	23	12	15
Ave NB	5	23	22	17	20
Private labels					
PL-01	3	20	23	23	17
PL-02	2	24	23	20	16
PL-03	1	25	23	17	16
PL-04	1	23	23	18	16
PL-05	1	20	23	15	16
Ave PL	2	22	23	19	16

National brand is 'NB' and private label is 'PL'; observed is 'O' and Dirichlet norms is 'D'; data
for average purchases of the product category and share of requirements include cereal bars.

Table 5.6 Duplication of purchase: FC Countline brands

Annual data	Percentage who also bought											
Of those who bought:	NB 01	NB 02	NB 03	NB 04	NB 05	NB 06	NB 07	NB 08	NB 09	NB 10	NB 11	NB 12
NB-01	-	53	54	36	32	30	29	24	25	17	21	5
NB-02	68	-	58	34	34	34	30	27	29	22	22	5
NB-03	66	55	-	38	36	36	31	27	30	21	24	5
NB-04	71	52	60	-	37	34	34	30	31	22	35	5
NB-05	79	63	72	45	-	47	44	40	42	25	30	6
NB-06	77	67	75	45	50	-	38	41	44	28	34	7
NB-07	72	59	64	44	46	37	-	36	35	23	24	4
NB-08	76	65	70	48	51	50	44	-	42	26	34	7
NB-09	72	66	72	46	50	50	40	39	-	28	30	6
NB-10	65	66	66	43	40	43	35	33	37	-	31	6
NB-11	68	55	62	55	39	41	30	34	33	25	-	6
NB-12	74	61	62	38	43	41	27	34	33	25	31	-
Average	72	60	65	43	42	40	35	33	35	24	29	6
Prediction	*72*	*50*	*48*	*33*	*24*	*24*	*22*	*20*	*19*	*15*	*14*	*4*
Penetration	43	33	35	22	18	17	17	14	15	11	14	3

National brand is 'NB'; prediction is the average from the Dirichlet model.

Table 5.7 Duplication of purchase: FC Countline multi-packs

Annual \data	Percentage who also bought										
Of those who bought:	NB 01 6-P	NB 01 7-P	NB 01 8-P	NB 01 18-P	NB 02 7-P	NB 02 8-P	NB 02 14-P	NB 05 5-P	NB 05 7-P	NB 07 5-P	NB 07 7-P
NB-01 6-pack	-	**70**	**45**	**6**	46	17	8	27	13	26	11
NB-01 7-pack	**76**	-	**50**	**6**	48	18	10	28	14	26	12
NB-01 8-pack	**78**	**80**	-	**8**	54	20	11	30	17	25	13
NB-01 18-pack	**84**	**83**	**65**	-	58	24	26	34	20	19	15
NB-02 7-pack	56	54	38	5	-	**26**	**16**	27	14	24	11
NB-02 8-pack	60	59	42	6	**78**	-	**22**	28	18	22	10
NB-02 14-pack	49	53	37	10	**77**	**36**	-	23	18	19	12
NB-05 5-pack	66	62	42	6	54	19	10	-	**27**	37	15
NB-05 7-pack	70	71	53	7	62	27	17	**61**	-	37	25
NB-07 5-pack	65	59	37	3	50	15	8	38	17	-	**27**
NB-07 7-pack	69	66	44	6	57	17	12	38	28	**64**	-
Average											
- within brand	**79**	**78**	**53**	**7**	**78**	**31**	**19**	**61**	**27**	**64**	**27**
- between brands	62	61	42	6	54	20	13	30	18	26	14
Prediction	*75*	*70*	*43*	*5*	*61*	*20*	*14*	*32*	*14*	*29*	*14*
Penetration	33	31	19	2	27	9	6	14	6	13	6

National brand is 'NB'; data for 'within brand duplication' are shown in bold; prediction is the average from the Dirichlet model.

Table 5.8 Demographics: Market shares: Brands & private labels

Annual data	Total panel	Presence of children		Household size				
		Without	With	1	2	3	4	5+
	%	%	%	%	%	%	%	%
FC Countlines	93	94	93	96	93	95	93	93
Brands								
NB-01	21	25	18	28	24	34	18	18
NB-02	11	10	13	9	8	10	13	13
NB-03	9	10	8	11	11	8	9	7
NB-04	4	6	3	6	6	5	4	3
NB-05	3	3	4	3	3	3	3	4
NB-06	3	2	4	2	2	3	4	4
NB-07	3	4	2	6	4	3	2	2
NB-08	2	2	3	2	3	3	3	3
NB-09	2	2	3	3	2	2	3	3
NB-10	2	3	3	2	3	2	3	2
NB-11	2	2	2	2	1	2	2	2
NB-12	1	2	1	2	2	2	2	1
Ave NB	5	6	5	6	6	6	6	5
Private labels								
PL-01	3	2	4	2	2	3	4	5
PL-02	2	2	3	1	1	3	3	3
PL-03	1	1	2	0	1	2	2	2
PL-04	1	1	2	1	1	2	2	1
PL-05	1	2	1	1	2	2	1	0
Ave PL	2	2	2	1	1	2	2	2

National brand is 'NB' and private label is 'PL'.

Table 5.9 Demographics: Penetration: Brands & private labels

Annual data	Total panel	Presence of children		Household size				
		Without	With	1	2	3	4	5+
	%	%	%	%	%	%	%	%
FC Countlines	74	68	87	63	68	82	85	89
Brands								
NB-01	43	37	56	32	37	50	55	57
NB-02	33	24	55	17	23	41	56	56
NB-03	35	30	47	25	30	40	48	46
NB-04	22	20	26	15	19	29	25	28
NB-05	18	12	30	8	12	22	29	32
NB-06	17	10	34	6	10	21	31	36
NB-07	17	15	22	11	14	22	22	25
NB-08	13	10	22	7	10	17	20	22
NB-09	15	10	25	6	10	18	25	27
NB-10	14	9	25	6	8	16	25	27
NB-11	11	7	19	4	7	15	19	20
NB-12	14	11	20	6	10	21	19	21
Ave NB	21	16	32	12	16	26	31	33
Prediction	*20*	*16*	*29*	*12*	*16*	*24*	*29*	*31*
Private labels								
PL-01	10	8	15	5	8	11	15	19
PL-02	7	5	13	3	5	8	12	14
PL-03	5	3	10	1	3	7	10	10
PL-04	5	3	8	2	3	6	8	9
PL-05	6	6	6	4	7	8	6	5
Ave PL	7	5	10	3	5	8	10	11
Prediction	*9*	*6*	*17*	*3*	*6*	*13*	*16*	*17*

National brand is 'NB' and private label is 'PL'; penetrations are calculated somewhat differently here which explains why the total panel data differ from figures shown in Table 5.1; prediction is the average from the Dirichlet model.

Table 5.10 Demographics: Average purchase frequencies: Brands & private labels

Annual data	Total panel	Presence of children		Household size				
		Without	With	1	2	3	4	5+
	%	%	%	%	%	%	%	%
FC Countlines	159	120	234	76	106	186	239	272
Brands								
NB-01	63	58	71	44	52	73	73	81
NB-02	43	35	51	26	28	41	52	60
NB-03	32	29	36	22	28	31	40	38
NB-04	26	25	27	19	24	29	30	26
NB-05	23	20	25	17	20	19	24	34
NB-06	24	20	28	12	17	24	31	27
NB-07	23	25	20	26	21	25	22	23
NB-08	27	22	34	15	23	25	33	40
NB-09	22	20	23	22	16	20	24	26
NB-10	23	25	22	16	25	23	25	23
NB-11	18	19	18	22	14	16	20	21
NB-12	14	15	14	14	13	16	17	11
Ave NB	28	26	31	21	23	29	33	34
Prediction	*31*	*28*	*34*	*22*	*25*	*31*	*36*	*37*
Private labels								
PL-01	41	26	61	20	18	39	58	74
PL-02	41	34	47	21	24	54	49	48
PL-03	34	26	40	7	21	37	40	41
PL-04	38	31	46	30	32	40	46	34
PL-05	23	23	22	14	22	36	21	11
Ave PL	35	28	43	18	23	41	43	42
Prediction	*26*	*24*	*28*	*19*	*22*	*26*	*29*	*31*

National brand is 'NB' and private label is 'PL'; average purchase frequencies are calculated somewhat differently here which explains why the total panel data differ from figures shown in Table 5.1; prediction is the average from the Dirichlet model.

References

Barwise, PT & Meehan, S 2004, *Simply Better,* Boston MA: Harvard Business Press.

Bennett, D 2008, 'Brand loyalty dynamics – China's television brands come of age', *Australasian Marketing Journal,* 16 (2), 39-50.

Bound, J & Ehrenberg, ASC 1997, 'Private label purchasing', *Admap,* 32 (7), 17-19.

Colombo, R, Ehrenberg, ASC & Sabavala, D 2000, 'Diversity in analyzing brand-switching tables: The car challenge', *Canadian Journal of Marketing Research,* 19, 23-36.

Danahar, PJ, Wilson, IW & Davis, RA 2003, 'A comparison of online and offline consumer brand loyalty', *Marketing Science,* 22 (4), 461-476.

Dawes, J 2010, 'Predictable patterns in buyer behaviour and brand metrics: Implications for brand managers', Chapter 6, this volume.

Ehrenberg, ASC 1988, *Repeat-Buying: Facts, Theory and Applications,* 2nd edn, New York: Oxford University Press [Reprinted in the Journal of Empirical Generalisations in Marketing Science, 2000, 5, 392-770, available: www.empgens.com].

Ehrenberg, ASC, Barnard, N & Scriven, JA 1997, 'Differentiation or salience', *Journal of Advertising Research,* 37 (6), 7-14.

Ehrenberg, ASC, Goodhardt, GJ & Barwise, PT 1990, 'Double Jeopardy revisited', *Journal of Marketing,* 54 (July), 82-91.

Ehrenberg, ASC, Uncles, MD & Goodhardt, GJ 2004, 'Understanding brand performance measures: Using Dirichlet benchmarks', *Journal of Business Research,* 57 (12), 1307-25.

Ellis, K 1989, 'Private label buyer behaviour', PhD thesis, London: London Business School.

Ellis, K & Uncles, MD 1990, 'How private labels affect consumer choice', *British Food Journal,* 93 (9), 41-49.

Fader, PS & Hardie, BG 1996, 'Modeling consumer choice among SKUs', *Journal of Marketing Research,* 33 (November), 442-452.

Fader, PS & Schmittlein, D 1993, 'Excess behavioural loyalty for high-share brands: Deviations from the Dirichlet model for repeat-buying', *Journal of Marketing Research,* 30 (November), 478-493.

Goodhardt, GJ, Ehrenberg, ASC & Chatfield, C 1984, 'The Dirichlet: A comprehensive model of buying behaviour', *Journal of the Royal Statistical Society,* 147 (5), 621-55 (with discussion).

Hammond, K, Ehrenberg, ASC & Goodhardt, GJ 1996, 'Market segmentation for competitive brands', *European Journal of Marketing,* 30 (12), 39-49.

Kannan, PK 2004, 'Commentary on "Understanding brand performance measures: Using Dirichlet benchmarks"', *Journal of Business Research,* 57 (12), 1326-1328.

Kennedy, R & Ehrenberg, ASC 2001, 'There is no brand segmentation', *Marketing Insights, Marketing Research,* 13 (1), 4-7.

Lam, D, Mizerski, R 2009, 'An investigation into gambling purchases using the NBD and NBD-Dirichlet models', *Marketing Letters,* 20, 263-276.

Lomax, W, McWilliam, G 2001, 'Consumer response to line extensions: trial and cannibalisation effects', *Journal of Marketing Management*, 17 (3-4), 391-406.

Lomax, W, Hammond, K, East, R & Clemente, M 1997, 'The measurement of cannibalization', *Journal of Product & Brand Management*, 6 (1), 27-39.

McPhee, WN 1963, *Formal Theories of Mass Behavior*, Glencoe, NY: Free Press.

Meyer-Waarden, L, Benavent, C 2006, 'The impact of loyalty programmes on repeat purchase behaviour', *Journal of Marketing Management*, 22, 61-88.

Mizerski, R, Miller, R, Mizerski, K & Lam, D 2004, 'The stochastic nature of purchasing a state's lottery products', *Australasian Marketing Journal*, 12 (3), 56-69.

Romaniuk, J & Gaillard, E 2007, 'The relationship between unique brand associations, brand usage and brand performance: Analysis across eight categories', *Journal of Marketing Management*, 23 (3), 267-84.

Romaniuk, J, Sharp, B & Ehrenberg, ASC 2007, 'Evidence concerning the importance of perceived brand differentiation', *Australasian Marketing Journal*, 15 (2), 42-54.

Sharp, B 2010, *How Brands Grow*, Melbourne, Australia: Oxford University Press.

Sharp, B & Sharp, A 1997, 'Loyalty programs and their impact on repeat-purchase loyalty patterns', *International Journal of Research in Marketing*, 14 (5), 473-486.

Singh, J, Ehrenberg, ASC & Goodhardt, GJ 2008, 'Measuring customer loyalty to product variants', *International Journal of Market Research*, 50 (4), 513-532.

Uncles, MD, Hammond, K, Ehrenberg, ASC & Davis, RE 1994, 'A replication study of two brand-loyalty measures', *European Journal of Operational Research*, 76, 375-384.

Uncles, MD, Ehrenberg, ASC & Goodhardt, GJ 2004, 'Reply to commentary on "Understanding brand performance measures: Using Dirichlet benchmarks"', *Journal of Business Research*, 57 (12), 1329-1330.

Uncles, MD, Wang, C & Kwok, S 2010, 'A temporal analysis of behavioural brand loyalty among urban Chinese consumers', *Journal of Marketing Management*, 26 (9/10), 921-942.

Wellan, DM & Ehrenberg, ASC 1988, 'A successful new brand: Shield', *Journal of the Marketing Research Society*, 30 (1), 35-44.

Wright, M, Sharp, B & Goodhardt, GJ 2002, 'Purchase loyalty is polarised into either repertoire or subscription patterns', *Australasian Marketing Journal*, 10 (3), 7-20.

Author biography

Mark D Uncles is Professor of Marketing and Associate Dean Undergraduate at the Australian School of Business, University of New South Wales. Prior to joining UNSW he held the position of Heinz Professor of Brand Management at Bradford Management Centre, and before that was an Assistant Professor at London Business School. Periods of sabbatical leave were undertaken at the Australian Graduate School of Management and the Judge Business School, University of Cambridge.

His research interests include brand management, employer branding, buyer behaviour, brand loyalty, store patronage and retail analysis. Publications have appeared in *Marketing Science, International Journal of Research in Marketing, Journal of Retailing, Journal of Service Research, Journal of Business Research, European Journal of Marketing, Journal of Advertising Research, Journal of Marketing Management, Sloan Management Review,* amongst others. He is on the editorial board of seven journals, including the *Journal of Product & Brand Management* and the *Journal of Brand Management.*

He has taught at all levels of tertiary education, including bachelor, specialist masters and MBA programs, doctoral programs, non-degree certificate courses, open executive programs and company-specific executive courses.

Contact: Professor Mark D Uncles, Professor of Marketing, School of Marketing, Australian School of Business, University of New South Wales, Sydney NSW 2052; P +61-2-9385-3510; F +61-2-9663-1985; E m.uncles@unsw.edu.au.

Chapter 6

Predictable patterns in buyer behaviour and brand metrics: Implications for brand managers

JOHN DAWES

ABSTRACT

This chapter examines three important issues in brand management – the route to brand growth, the idea that brands should be uniquely differentiated, and the building and maintenance of brand equity. The chapter presents evidence from numerous studies to show that: (1) the route to brand growth must focus on customer acquisition; (2) brands tend not to have strong, differentiated positioning, but this lack of differentiation does not stop them being successful; and (3) brand-equity endeavours should focus on building the prevalence of brand associations across a wide population group, and focus less on the extent to which customers have strong emotional connections or attachment to the brand.

KEYWORDS

brand loyalty; brand equity; positioning; brand performance metrics

Introduction

Managers usually want to grow their brand. A growth strategy often involves trying to construct a differentiated brand positioning and building brand equity. This chapter discusses these three topical issues – the route to growth, positioning and brand equity – and shows how knowledge of generalised patterns in buyer behaviour can help managers make better decisions about such issues. The generalised patterns that are referred to originate from the work of Ehrenberg and colleagues (e.g. Ehrenberg *et al*. 2004, see also Uncles 2010). The three issues of growth, brand equity and positioning are now discussed.

The route to growth

Most brand managers have objectives to grow the market share of their brand. But what are the alternative growth paths? In theory, there are two routes to growth: more sales from finding new customers/non-buyers, or more sales from existing buyers (a loyalty strategy). The loyalty strategy is in vogue based on the writings of Reichheld (1990; 1996) who extols the financial efficiency of customer retention and boosting loyalty, compared to the apparently expensive route of finding new customers. However, Reichheld's prescription is inconsistent with decades of research studying consumer purchasing behaviour. That research, which led to the development of the NBD-Dirichlet model (Goodhardt *et al*. 1984), says that only one course of action for brand growth is realistic: attracting more non-buyers and very occasional buyers to buy in the time period. The reasons for this are now explained.

To understand why new buyers are so crucial, we examine the pattern of a brand's sales and the proportion of its customers who bought it once, twice, three times and so on in a period of a year. The pattern is always the same: *many* light or infrequent buyers and *far fewer* heavy, frequent buyers. Indeed, the buying pattern is quite specific and follows a known statistical distribution called the 'NBD[21]' – initially reported as far back as 1959 (Ehrenberg 1959).

The fit of consumer purchases to this statistical distribution might seem rather trivial, but turns out to be very important because it tells us about the way in which a brand must grow.

To illustrate, let us compare two brands in the US market for Hair Care: Pantene Pro-V and Garnier Fructis. Data kindly provided by Nielsen shows their market shares to be around 10 and 6 per cent of unit sales respectively (these are among the largest brands in a very fragmented market). In 2007, Pantene was bought by 17% of US households at an average rate of 1.8 times per year. By contrast, Fructis was bought by 11% of households at an average rate of 1.6 times per year. These results are in line with the 'double jeopardy' effect, with the larger brand having slightly higher loyalty. To understand the marketplace position of these brands more fully,

---

[21] *Negative Binomial Distribution*

we examine their purchase rates: how many customers bought either brand once, twice, three times and so on in a year. This is shown in histograms, in Figures 6.1 and 6.2.

Figure 6.1 Pantene

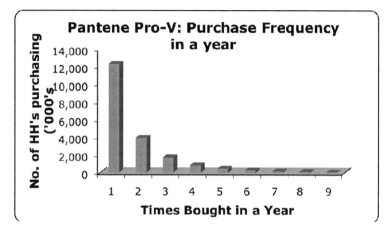

Figure 6.2 Garnier Fructis

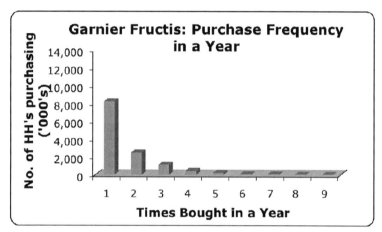

The *major* difference between the brands is that Pantene has massively more buyers, principally 1- and 2-time buyers, compared to Fructis.

These simple histograms follow the NBD[22].

The NBD pattern shown here is the same as found in dozens of other markets. The histograms show that each brand has very large numbers of 'light' or very infrequent buyers, and far fewer heavy or frequent buyers. Indeed the largest group of brand buyers, for either Pantene or Head and Shoulders, only bought the brand once in the 12-month period. Pantene was bought once by 12 million households, twice by about 4 million households, three times by 1.7 million households and so on. This pattern has a very important implication for planning

---

[22] The purchase rates are truncated at nine purchases per annum because the numbers of households buying more frequently than nine becomes too small to show.

for brand growth. To explain why, let us take the viewpoint that we are the management team of Fructis and we would like to grow our brand to be the size of Pantene. This means that we need to take our market share from around 6% to 10%. The important point is that if we were to do so, our brand *would then look like Pantene in terms of its buying pattern*. To get to Pantene's size, we would therefore need a massively larger number of buyers who buy once in a year (4 million more than currently), also many more buyers who buy two times (1.4 million extra), some more three time buyers (almost 600,000 extra) and so on. This requirement is shown in more detail in the table below.

Table 6.1 How would Fructis grow to the size of Pantene?

Purchase frequency	Number HHs buying **Fructis** in a year ('000 HHs)	Number HHs buying **Pantene** Pro-V in a year ('000 HHs)	For Fructis to grow to Pantene's size, it would need this many more buyers at each level of buying frequency ('000 HHs)
1 x per year	8,203	12,285	4,082 buying once
2 x per year	2,497	3,909	1,412 buying twice
3 x per year	1,112	1,707	595 buying three times
4 x per year	429	823	394 buying four times
5 x per year	210	449	239 buying five times
6 x per year	59	232	173 buying six times
7 x per year	80	140	60 buying seven times
8 x per year	25	94	69 buying eight times
9 x per year	19	49	30 buying nine times

Very large numbers of 1-time and 2-time buyers are needed, comparatively fewer extra 3-time, 4-time buyers and so on are needed for Fructis to grow to the size of Pantene.

The main task for brand growth in this case is, therefore, to attract massive numbers of additional customers, *most* of whom will buy the brand once or perhaps twice in the period of a year. We would also need more 2-time, 3-time and 4-time buyers, but the biggest numbers needed are the one and two-time buyers. We could not grow Fructis by deciding to somehow selectively boost the number of highly loyal or 'heavy' brand buyers. Management could try this but it will not work because to do that would result in an entirely different distribution of brand purchases, and brands have *consistently* been found to follow an NBD distribution of purchase frequency.

The reader might at this point be thinking that brands surely don't *always* follow the NBD distribution. To add more evidence, let us briefly consider another product category. This time we look at the US butter market. This product category is bought around 5 times per year on average, slightly more than shampoo which has an average purchase rate of around 3-4 times per year. The two brands we look at now are Land O Lakes and Challenge. Land O Lakes is a market leader with a 21% market share, while Challenge has a 5% market share. Despite this, they have rather similar loyalty levels: 2.6 purchases per year for Land O Lakes compared to 2.3 for Challenge. We see the NBD distribution again in Figures 6.3 and 6.4. The main difference between the brands is, again, the massively higher number of 1-time and 2-time buyers for Land O Lakes. For either of these brands, the route to growth is the same: growth will come from getting many more people to buy in the period – more of every type of buyer but with the biggest increases in customer numbers being among the 1-time and 2-time buyers[23].

At this point one might ask, since Land O Lakes is the market leader, where can these one-time buyers come from? The answer is: there are plenty of non-buyers. Even for the market leader Land O Lakes, of the 68 million households who bought butter, 40 million did not buy Land O Lakes at all in the 12-month period.

Figure 6.3 Land O Lakes

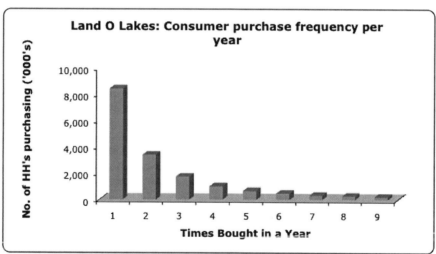

---

[23] Of course, a buyer who buys many times in the year accounts for more sales than a buyer who buys only once. But the point is that the brand cannot selectively attract just heavy brand buyers – if it is to grow it must attract large numbers of light or infrequent buyers. The numbers of heavier buyers will also increase, but in a proportion that retains the shape of the NBD distribution.

Figure 6.4 Challenge

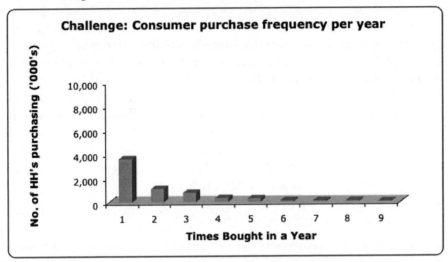

The major difference between the brands is that Land O Lakes has massively more buyers than Challenge, most noticeably in the numbers of 1- and 2-time buyers.

How do we attract these large numbers of new buyers? There are two main ways. The first is to find new distribution points – that is, make the brand available in places where people cannot currently buy it. This extra presence could be in terms of new accounts, new types of distribution channels or new locations, as well as pushing on the quality of distribution presence, e.g. in-store placement and visibility. The second tool for growth is marketing communication to reach people who are non-buyers at the present time. Communicating to those who already buy the brand is not enough, simply because they already buy and therefore the scope to increase their purchase rates is very limited. This also means that relying principally on in-store communications for the brand is inadequate – that approach tends to unduly hit current brand buyers. Likewise for services companies, a reliance on mailings and newsletters to current buyers is also not enough. Brand growth must involve growing the size of the customer base.

Now that we have established the path to growth, we consider another issue that is said to distinguish successful from unsuccessful brands: building and monitoring brand equity.

Building and monitoring brand equity

Most managers recognise that their market share at the present time is due to two factors: the marketing mix currently employed, and consumer-based *brand equity* – that is, the time-lagged effect of past marketing activity and brand usage.

Since brand equity is apparently linked to long-term marketplace success, managers are interested in building and monitoring it. However, there is a wide array of terms and definitions surrounding the concept. Some of the terms used to describe and measure brand equity can lead to marketers worrying about the wrong things. This section identifies some of the language used to discuss brand equity that is either prone to misunderstanding or that is actually counterproductive. It then outlines a more useful way of thinking about the brand equity concept, and presents empirical evidence about the composition of certain brand performance measures that are commonly used to measure brand equity. This empirical evidence shows that brand equity is very largely a reflection of brand size, and that among the users of competing brands, brand equity is at similar levels. The management implications of these well-established facts are then laid out.

To begin with, this discussion excludes dollar valuation of brands; this is sometimes discussed under the title of brand equity but is really to do with brand valuation. We focus on the narrower issue of consumer-based brand equity. In many cases, brand equity is described as a composite of brand awareness and brand perceptions or associations (Keller 1993) – what can be called 'market-based assets' (Sharp 1995). Loyalty and price premiums are also often incorporated into the definition (Aaker 1996), although some authors point out shortcomings with these (e.g. Feldwick 1996) (see also Md Noor, Styles & Cowley 2010).

There are quite a few instances where the gamut of brand equity is expanded to include concepts that are perhaps more appropriately applied to interpersonal relationships. Feldwick (1996) noted that one of the common uses of the term brand equity included brand strength – that is, the strength of consumer attachment to the brand. Keller, who wrote one of the defining papers on brand equity (Keller 1993), stated that brand equity includes resonance – the 'depth of the psychological bond customers have with the brand' (Keller 2001). Young and Rubicam's Brand Asset Valuator (BAV), one of the world's largest brand equity monitors, has a four-component view of brand equity – one of which is knowledge. Knowledge, in the BAV, comprises the level of *intimacy* consumers have with the brand (see, for example, www.brandassetconsulting.com).

The language used in some of these descriptions of brand equity implies that consumers think, feel or act towards brands in a way that may not reflect reality. While brands unquestionably provide benefits to consumers that go beyond the merely functional, the use of words such as 'resonance', 'attachment', 'bond', 'strength[24]' and 'intimacy' seem to signify that consumers have strong feelings about – and are emotionally attached to – brands. Or, that perhaps such feelings on the part of consumers are necessary for a brand to be successful.

Furthermore, these descriptions of brand equity or its indicators can be interpreted as implying that the typical consumer will actively think about brands in positive terms and will reflect on the relationship or attachment they feel they have with brands on a reasonably regular basis. A moment of introspection will reveal this is

---

[24] As with many words, 'strong' has multiple interpretations. A consumer may clearly or easily link a brand to certain cues or attributes – in this sense there is strength of association. The critique here is more about the idea that consumers do, or should, strongly hold evaluative beliefs about brands.

hardly likely for most buyers or for most brands. There are simply too many brands used by any individual, and too many other life events for people to think about, to reflect much about any particular brand from one time period to the next. Indeed, many consumers have little idea of what brands they even use at present. What brand of ice cream is in the reader's freezer at present, or indeed what brand of refrigerator is the ice cream in? What brand of tyre is on one's car, or what brand of vitamins is in the cupboard? Many readers simply will not know. So, while consumers know about brands, recognise them when they see them, like them and like using them, they do not think *about* them much. It is therefore hard to justify the idea of brand intimacy or attachment in the absence of much conscious thought on the part of the consumer.

The empirical reality is that most consumers exhibit 'split-brand' loyalty over time, coupled with fairly low levels of brand evaluation. Ehrenberg and colleagues documented over many years that consumers typically exhibit multi-brand buying (e.g. Ehrenberg & Goodhardt 1970), with the usual scenario being that the buyers of any particular brand *A* bought other brands as much or more as they bought *A*. In terms of evaluating brands, evidence shows that consumers typically engage in little pre-purchase evaluation of packaged goods, exhibiting quick purchase selection and rather imprecise recall of information such as price paid straight after purchase (Dickson & Sawyer 1990). The situation is similar for higher-priced or more complex purchases: 'consideration sets' of one car brand are fairly common (Lapersonne *et al.* 1995), and often only one bank or insurance company is considered in financial services purchasing (Dawes *et al.* 2009). Coupled with that, multi-brand buying is quite common in financial services (Mundt *et al.* 2006), and around 50% of consumers buy a different car brand over consecutive purchases (Colombo *et al.* 2000). The combination of split-brand loyalty and somewhat low levels of evaluation casts doubt about the extent to which brands 'resonate' with or are 'attached strongly' to buyers. The evidence suggests that consideration or active evaluation of brands is something that consumers want to get out of the way quickly so they can get back to their busy lives.

The second issue with some of the representations of brand equity mentioned above lies in what they imply management's priority should be. If brand equity is needed for success, and brand equity is said to comprise, in part at least, strong brand associations (in the sense of associations being intensely held) and psychological attachment, logic says the brand manager therefore needs to build stronger and more favourable associations and deeper consumer attachment to the brand. Unfortunately, this produces a misguided focus on strengthening brand equity at the level of the individual consumer – that is, going from *strong* to *stronger*. This focus is misguided because the key factor that distinguishes brands with high brand equity scores from those with low brand equity scores is the number of consumers who have *any* mental associations with the brand at all, not the depth of their positive disposition towards the brand. Supporting empirical evidence for this can be found in two studies. The first is by Barnard and Ehrenberg (1998) and is based on a typical brand equity monitor whereby respondents are asked to state which brands possess certain attributes. In this case the product is toothpaste, with attributes such as 'promotes strong healthy teeth', 'fights bad breath' and so on. Table 6.2 reports the extent to which these attributes are linked to each brand – in the population overall, and by the regular buyers of each brand. For instance in column 3 we see that on average, 42% of consumers agreed that Colgate DC possesses certain positive attributes over a sequence of questions, 30% for Macleans and so on.

Table 6.2 Stated beliefs about brand attributes

Brand	% of population who buy this brand	Average % of people stating this brand possesses certain attributes*: a measure of 'brand equity'	Average % of **regular brand buyers** who state this brand possesses such attributes
Colgate DC	37	42	62
Macleans	18	30	60
Crest	18	31	61
Colgate BMG	14	26	55
Aquafresh	10	23	50
Gibbs SR	8	22	51
Mentadent P	8	22	56
Ultrabrite	7	21	52
Average toothpaste brand	**15**	**27**	**56**

The 'brand equity' score correlates highly with brand size (columns 2 and 3). Brand users have similar levels of positive sentiment about their brands (column 4).

* Attributes such as 'promotes strong healthy teeth' and so on.

Colgate DC, Macleans and Crest have more 'brand equity' in the sense they capture more of the positive brand associations among the public. Gibbs, Mentadent and Sensodyne have less brand equity. However, the variation in brand equity is closely in line with the numbers of consumers using the brand (r=0.99). The bigger brands get higher brand equity scores because they have more users, and brand users are twice as likely to state a brand possesses a positive attribute than non-users[25] (e.g. Bird *et al.* 1970). So a brand with more users *will always* get higher overall scores in a perceptions-based brand equity survey such as this.

---

[25] This pattern applies to evaluative attributes, that a consumer would need to have bought the brand to know about. It applies less so to descriptive attributes such as 'comes in a red can' or those that simply reflect advertising messages ('A glass and a half in every half pound') that do not require brand purchase or use for the consumer to know about.

The other important point is that when we look at the sentiment that exists *among* the users of each brand, it is about as positive for each brand as any other – we can see this in the rightmost column. On average, 56% of the users of any of these brands will respond that it has a particular attribute of the type asked about in a brand equity monitor. The variation around the average is quite small. The proportion is a bit higher for the larger brands – another manifestation of the double jeopardy effect (Ehrenberg *et al.* 1990). So the 'brand equity' (in the sense of the depth or extent of positive sentiment) for brand A among its users is about the same as the brand equity for brand B among *its* users - the overall *difference* in brand equity scores between the brands lies primarily in the numbers of users of each brand.

Corroborating evidence for the idea that brand equity is accounted for principally by the brand's market share[26] is contained in a study by Romaniuk and Sharp (2008), who examined the composition of brand knowledge across the population of buyers. Brand knowledge is a very closely related concept to consumer-based brand equity as it comprises the sum total of all perceptual associations held by consumers about the brand. Brand knowledge is explained using a simple example: suppose the brand perceptions of 10,000 consumers are elicited using a battery of ten questions using the typical 'pick any' approach, whereby consumers match attributes ('tastes good', 'good value', 'a high quality brand') to brands. A certain brand elicits 15,000 responses – it is linked to certain brand attributes 15,000 times in the survey. This total is the sum of brand knowledge for that brand in the survey. Plainly, the total number of attributes attached to the brand across a sample of consumers corresponds closely with the brand equity concept. Romaniuk and Sharp calculated the extent to which this brand knowledge is spread across the brand's customer base using data for 28 product categories and 208 brands. They found that about half of brand knowledge is concentrated among 20% of buyers, and the remainder is spread is thinly across the remaining 80% of buyers. Moreover, this percentage split was the same for both big and small brands. That is, the spread of brand knowledge was the same for brands with high equity scores as it was for brands with low equity scores. The *difference* in scores between the brands lay in their number of users. There were no brands with small user bases that displayed an especially rich or strong level of perceptual associations for that brand.

What this finding suggests is that for a brand to grow its brand equity scores, it needs massively larger numbers of people who exhibit quite low levels of knowledge or depth of association for the brand, and far fewer extra people who know a lot about it or who hold a deep or extensive breadth of association for the brand. Brand equity is built in bits, across masses of people.

---

26 This is not a new idea. Ehrenberg sparked a vigorous debate on the topic of brand equity in the 1990s. See Dyson *et al.* 1997, Ehrenberg 1993 a, 1993 b, Feldwick 1993.

Brand positioning

Since brands are often similar in functional terms, it is considered to be important for marketers to create a 'position' for the brand in the mind of the consumer. As with many marketing terms, there is no single or 'right' definition for brand positioning, but we can turn to some prominent authors to get a sense of what is meant by the term.

> *Positioning a brand means emphasising the characteristics that make it different from its competitors and appealing to the public. ... indicate what the brand's essential difference and raison d'etre is in comparison to the other products and brands of that category. ... identify and take possession of a strong purchasing rationale that gives us a real or perceived advantage. ... For the consumer, it [positioning] should result in: 'only brand X will do this for me' (Kapferer 2004, pp. 99-100, pp. 102-103).*

> *Brand position ... demonstrates an advantage over competing brands. ... develop a point of advantage that resonates with the customer ... provide a point of difference with respect to competitive offerings (Aaker 1996, p. 176, p. 182).*

> *The essence of brand positioning is that the brand has a sustainable competitive advantage or 'unique selling proposition' that gives consumers a compelling reason for buying that particular brand (Keller 1993, p. 6).*

Not all authors who write about positioning emphasise the idea that it involves a strong selling benefit. Ries and Trout, in their book on positioning (1986), did not claim that positioning necessarily provided a rational benefit to buyers. However, they did state that a brand must occupy a particular 'niche' in the consumer's mind and be perceived as unique on a key perceptual attribute.

The idea of brand positioning as portrayed by many writers appears to be strongly influenced by traditional buyer behaviour models that emphasise the role of active evaluation of alternatives in consumer purchase. A buyer could have bought *A*, *B*, *C*, or *D* – why did they buy brand *A*? The answer, logically, is that the buyer perceived that brand *A* was superior on some attribute that was important to them. In other words, it had the correct *positioning* for this buyer. However, there are four empirical facts that appear to rebut the idea that brands *do* generally occupy distinct perceptual positions in consumers' minds; they also rebut the idea that brands *need* to occupy such positions. The evidence relates to:

1. widespread repertoire buying;
2. brands sharing perceived attributes rather than being differentiated by them;
3. lack of perceived uniqueness of brands on the part of consumers; and finally
4. consumers giving different responses about brand positioning attributes when re-interviewed.

Repertoire buying

The *raison d'etre* of positioning, as Kapferer put it, is that consumers see an important difference in the brand and that difference gives them a reason to buy the brand. If this is true, it is reasonable to think that if the buyer buys brand *Y* because of its 'positioning' on one occasion, then they should buy it again the next time they buy from that product category. Obviously, this might not be always the case because consumers actively seek variety in some product categories and because their circumstances can change over time, which might alter their purchase habits. But generally, if a brand is bought *because* the consumer believes that brand possesses specific attributes to a much greater extent than any other brand, surely the logical outcome is very high levels of repeat-purchase loyalty to that brand. Yet, as we talked about earlier, one of the most fundamental outcomes of empirical studies of brand buying is that consumers buy from *repertoires* of brands – in other words they are 'polygamous' or 'split-brand' loyal. Indeed, the buyers of any brand tend to buy *other* brands about in line with the market share of those other brands – called the 'Duplication of Purchase law' (Goodhardt *et al.* 1984). This empirical pattern is illustrated in the table below, based on purchasing data for toothpaste courtesy of TNS, where many buyers of Aquafresh, Macleans and Sensodyne also bought Colgate. About a third of the buyers of Colgate, Macleans and Sensodyne also bought Aquafresh, and so on. Fewer again bought Sensodyne, in line with it being a smaller brand. It seems difficult to think these brands are bought due to special or enduring brand positions when their customers freely buy competitor brands as well.

Table 6.3 Cross-purchasing of brands

Brand	% buying once or more in 12 months	% who also bought ...			
		Colgate	Aquafresh	Macleans	Sensodyne
Colgate	49	-	30	23	12
Aquafresh	26	57	-	27	10
Macleans	20	58	37	-	12
Sensodyne	12	47	22	19	-
Average		**54**	**30**	**23**	**11**

On average, the buyers of each of these brands bought other brands in line with the overall market share of those other brands. Data courtesy of TNS UK.

Positioning attributes are shared across brands

Keller, cited above in the introduction to this section, points out that brands tend to share associations with other brands (Keller 1993, p.6). That is, many people could believe brand A is a high tech brand, for example, but it will not be the only brand considered to have this attribute. However, the literature on positioning primarily emphasises points of differentiation and uniqueness, and underplays the idea of competing brands possessing common or shared attributes. The emphasis on *difference* leads to the conclusion for the marketing manager that they must obtain sustainable perceived differentiation from competitors. This is misguided, because the empirical research shows that brands *share* perceived attributes with competitors more so than they exhibit marked *differences* in perceived attributes compared to those competitors. This attribute sharing is illustrated with an extract of results from a typical brand tracking survey, in this case for banking services (see Table 6.4). A large (n >1,000) sample of consumers was asked to nominate which bank brands possessed certain attributes such as: *safe and secure, good for home loans, good to get financial advice, trustworthy* and *local*. These are exactly the type of attributes that banks try to position on. The results are tabulated below for five large banks in a state of Australia. The brands are arranged in market share order. There are two main take-outs from this table. First, the brands share attributes much more so than being distinguished by them. Second, while one of the brands does appear to be particularly known for an attribute, the other brands do still possess it as well.

Table 6.4 Brand performance on positioning attributes

Bank brand (in descending size order)	Per cent of responses given to each bank brand for these positioning attributes (columns sum to 100)							
	Safe and secure	Ongoing financial advice	Good for home loans	Low fees	Trust-worthy	Would look after me	Local	**Average**
B	21	22	26	24	24	25	31	**25**
C	24	25	23	23	23	24	21	**23**
A	21	22	19	23	21	20	19	**21**
Ad	16	15	17	17	17	16	18	**17**
W	18	17	15	13	15	14	11	**15**
Total	**100**	**100**	**100**	**100**	**100**	**100**	**100**	

Key take-out: brands that score well on any one attribute tend to score roughly the same on the others, reflecting their brand share.

To show the similarity in 'positioning' among the brands on most of these attributes, we can look at the proportion of responses each banks gets for each of these attributes. For example, for the *safe and secure* attribute, bank C scores 24 per cent of all the mentions for *safe and secure*. This score is good; it is the highest for that attribute and 3 points above the next best performers brand B and brand A. However, bank C scores an average of 23 per cent for *any* of the attributes – more than A, Ad and W – because it is a bigger brand than them. If we look across the rows for any of the brands, most of their scores on these attributes are quite similar. The bigger brands score highly on all attributes, and the smaller brands score lower on all attributes.

Now we look at a difference between the brands. There does appear to be one brand that is particularly known for being *local* – brand B. It received 31% of all responses for *local*, which is more than it obtained for any of the other attributes (21% to 26%). However, we can hardly say brand B is uniquely positioned on *local*, because the other brands score on it roughly in-line with their size (although brand W scores worse on *local* than any other attribute).

This table reinforces the idea that brands share positioning attributes with each other to a very great extent. Brands can be known for particular attributes, but this does not mean they 'own' the attribute[27].

Lack of perceived uniqueness

Related to the idea of brands sharing perceived attributes is the surprising finding that few consumers think particular brands are different or unique. Romaniuk, Sharp and Ehrenberg (2007) analysed brand uniqueness using survey data across 17 product categories. In the surveys, consumers were provided a list of brands and asked to nominate which brands, if any, they believed were different or unique. The study found that only about one in ten people see brands (such as Coke, Pepsi; or KFC, McDonalds) as different or unique. There were some product categories in which the result was higher - in particular spirits, supermarkets and skin care – but even in these categories the average brand was seen as different or unique by only up to 14%, or 1 in 7 consumers. This finding dampens the idea that brands can be uniquely positioned.

Further evidence as to the general lack of strong, differentiated brand positioning comes from a further study that examined how many consumers attach a positioning attribute to only one particular brand. Romaniuk and Gaillard (2007) examined this issue using data from the Young & Rubicam BAV surveys. They examined the extent to which consumers stated that a particular brand, and *only* that brand, possessed a positioning or image attribute (the terms are similar enough

---

[27] More distinct positioning differences will probably emerge if brands from various sub-categories are analysed together, or if one brand really *does* have a functional difference – a cholesterol lowering margarine, a hybrid fuel car, or a markedly different quality level to competitors are examples. But functional differences with marketplace appeal are usually quickly copied by competitors.

to be used interchangeably). For example, for the pour-in sauce category, the question posed was how many consumers, when asked which brands were healthy, *only* said Heinz or *only* said Dolmio and so on. Romaniuk and Gaillard tabulated results across eight product categories and 130 brands using dozens of different image attributes. The main result was that only 2 per cent, on average, of consumers allocated an image attribute uniquely to one brand. This strongly suggests consumers do not see brands as possessing unique attributes. The authors concluded that consumers do not need to perceive a brand as having a unique attribute in order to purchase it. The rationale was that, since the vast majority of buyers of these brands did not allocate them a unique positioning/image attribute, having one can hardly be an important success factor. This finding implies that imparting *any* attributes for the brand is the key to brand success, rather than endeavouring to create uniquely held attributes.

Consumers give different answers about brands in different surveys

The general way that a brand's image or positioning is determined is by asking consumers whether the brand possesses certain attributes. A market research interviewer will typically read out a list of brands to the respondent and then administer an image battery. For example: 'Which of those brands do you think is *good value*? … Which of those brands do you think is *modern*?' and so on. If many respondents state that brand Y is *modern* compared to other brands, or compared to other brand attributes, we conclude that brand Y is positioned as a modern brand. Leaving aside the fact that brands tend to share such attributes to a considerable extent, research has also shown that many consumers who said brand Y had an attribute like *modern* in one survey will not say it is *modern* in a second survey a week or a month later! This fact also seems to dampen the idea that brands are strongly positioned in people's minds. Research on this topic has been reported in a number of studies, including Castleberry *et al.* (1994), Dall'Olmo Riley *et al.* (1997), Sharp (2002) and Rungie *et al.* (2005). The consistency across multiple studies suggests this is a robust phenomenon.

Why might consumers give different responses about brands when asked the same question at different times? Possible reasons were suggested by Dolnicar and Rossiter (2008) including respondent fatigue, respondent guessing (although surveys such as Young and Rubicam's BAV do not instruct respondents to guess), and lack of familiarity with certain brands. Dolnicar and Rossiter (2008) examined the impact of these factors in an empirical study. They reported an overall level of brand response instability of about 50%. They also found that this level of instability could be reduced through the use of shorter questionnaires and the inclusion of only familiar brands, although even with these factors there was still very marked instability of responses. It may simply be that the process by which consumers link brands to attributes is *probabilistic* - just as brand choice appears to be. In simple terms, this means that a consumer may have certain memory links between brand *A* and attributes such as *modern* or *tastes nice* or *high quality*, but whether the link between brand *A* and any of those particular attributes is actually recalled – either in a purchase situation or in a market research interview – there is an element of chance, even after controlling for the limitations inherent in whatever survey method is employed.

This section has presented a case that competing brands are not, by and large, 'positioned' such that consumers believe they are uniquely differentiated from other brands. Brands can be known for some attributes more than others, but this does not mean competitors are unknown for that attribute. The achievement of true 'points of difference' (Keller 2003) seems elusive.

Where does this leave the brand manager and the advertising agency? The findings presented here suggest that less emphasis needs to be placed on finding the exactly right proposition, selling point or unique positioning attribute. Rather, the brand manager should be endeavouring to build memory links between their brand and *multiple* attributes or buying cues, not just a solitary positioning attribute. If the link between any *one* attribute and the brand is probabilistic, creating *multiple* links to the brand seems a more sure way of heightening the chance that the brand will be retrieved from memory during a buying situation.

Let us then briefly re-iterate the key points made and summarise the managerial recommendations.

Summary

This chapter has outlined three topical issues for brand management, assessed pertinent evidence, and then applied some knowledge from repeated empirical studies on these topics. The key points are:

- The big difference between big and small brands is primarily their number of buyers and, in particular, big brands have massively greater numbers of light or infrequent buyers compared to smaller brands. Therefore, to grow the brand one needs to attract many new buyers – more infrequent buyers as well as more heavy buyers, but massively more of the former compared to the latter. The emphasis should not be on grooming existing buyers to buy more.

- Brand equity is said to be crucial for long-term success. The most useful way for managers to think about it is in terms of the prevalence of brand knowledge or associations across the population, not the depth or strength it exhibits in individuals. Half of a brand's user-based brand equity, in the sense of the collective sum of all mental associations about the brand among its buyers, is spread thinly across 80% of the brand's user base. And this spread does not vary much across brands, small brands have half their collective brand knowledge spread thinly across 80% of their users, the same as big brands. Marketing communication should therefore focus on moving consumers from nearly zero levels of association about the brand to some small, non-zero level. Communication should not try to build deep and meaningful attachments with buyers. Moreover, brand managers must bolster this level of association regularly through advertising, since brand memories and associations will decay back down to very low levels over time because of the weight of competitor activity and because of the fact that consumers have so many more interesting things to think about.

- Brands tend not to be uniquely positioned or differentiated in the sense of being imbued with special qualities that competing brands do not possess. Rather, brands tend to share perceived attributes, and many consumers will allocate different positioning attributes to brands when asked about them on separate occasions. Therefore, it makes little sense to spend the company's money trying to build a unique brand position. Indeed, emphasising positioning attributes for the brand can de-emphasise the brand itself in communication. Instead, managers should focus less on exactly *what* consumers think about the brand, and instead focus more on building *any* sort of relevant memory links to the brand. To do this, they need to ensure that the content of marketing communication is primarily *about* the brand - not primarily about a creative idea, and not primarily about a selling message. The purpose of marketing communication is to publicise the brand (Ehrenberg *et al.* 2002), remind people it exists, and link the brand to pertinent cues – in a clever way that catches consumer attention, of course. This strategy works without creating a differentiated brand position by bolstering the brand in memory – that is, simply helping the brand to come to mind more easily. Brands don't compete by being thought of as unique or superior; rather, they compete just by being thought of at all, and by as many people as possible.

References

Aaker, DA 1996, *Building strong brands*. New York: Free Press.

Barnard, N & Ehrenberg ASC 1998, 'Advertising and brand attitudes', in Report 3 for Corporate Members. Adelaide: Ehrenberg-Bass Institute for Marketing Science.

Bird, M., Channon C & Ehrenberg ASC 1970, 'Brand image and brand usage', *Journal of Marketing Research*, 7 (3), 307-14.

Castleberry, SB, Barnard NR, Barwise TP, Ehrenberg ASC & Dall'Olmo RF 1994, 'Individual Attitude Variations Over Time', *Journal of Marketing Management*, 10 (1-3), 153-62.

Colombo, R, Ehrenberg ASC & Sabavala D 2000, 'Diversity in analyzing brand-switching tables: The car challenge', *Canadian Journal of Marketing Research*, 19, 23-36.

Dall'Olmo RF, Ehrenberg ASC, Castleberry SB, Barwise TP & Barnard NR 1997, 'The Variability of Attitudinal Repeat-Rates', *International Journal of Research in Marketing*, 14 (No. 5), 437-50.

Dawes, J, Mundt K & Sharp B 2009, 'Consideration Sets for Financial Services brands', forthcoming in *Journal of Financial Services Marketing*.

Dickson, PR & Sawyer AG 1990, 'The Price Knowledge and Search of Supermarket Shoppers', *Journal of Marketing*, 54 (July), 42-53.

Dolnicar, S & Rossiter JR 2008, 'The low stability of brand-attitude associations is partly due to market research methodology', *International Journal of Research in Marketing*, 21 (2), 104-08.

Dyson, P, Farr A & Hollis N 1997, 'What Does the Marketing Team Need, Description or Prescription? A Response to Comments by Andrew Ehrenberg', *Journal of Advertising Research*, 37 (1, January/February), 13-17.

Ehrenberg, ASC 1993a, 'If You're So Strong, Why Aren't You Bigger?', *Admap* (October), 13-14.

Ehrenberg, ASC 1993b, 'No Need for the Brand Equity Crutch?', *Admap* (December), 18.

Ehrenberg, ASC 1959, 'The Pattern of Consumer Purchases', *Applied Statistics*, 8 (1), 26-41.

Ehrenberg, ASC & Goodhardt GJ 1970, 'A model of multi-brand buying', *Journal of Marketing Research*, 7 (February), 77-84.

Ehrenberg, ASC, Barnard N, Kennedy R & Bloom H 2002, 'Brand advertising as creative publicity', *Journal of Advertising Research*, 42 (4), 7-18.

Ehrenberg, ASC, Goodhardt GJ & Barwise TP 1990, 'Double Jeopardy revisited', *Journal of Marketing*, 54 (July), 82-91.

Ehrenberg, ASC, Uncles MD & Goodhardt GJ 2004, 'Understanding brand performance measures: Using Dirichlet benchmarks', *Journal of Business Research*, 57 (12), 1307-25.

Feldwick, P 1993, 'Big and Strong Brands: A Comment', *Admap* (December), 17.

Feldwick, P 1996, 'What Is Brand Equity Anyway, and How Do You Measure It?', *Journal of the Market Research Society*, 38 (No. 2, April), 85-104.

Goodhardt, GJ, Ehrenberg ASC & Chatfield C 1984, 'The Dirichlet: A comprehensive model of buying behaviour', *Journal of the Royal Statistical Society*, 147 (5), 621-55.

Kapferer, J-E 2004, *The new strategic brand management: Creating and sustaining brand equity long term*. London: Kogan Page.

Keller, KL 2001, 'Building customer-based brand equity', *Marketing Management*, 10 (2), 14-19.

Keller, KL 1993, 'Conceptualizing, measuring, and managing customer-based brand equity', *Journal of Marketing*, 57 (January), 1-22.

Keller, KL 2003, *Strategic Brand Management*, 2nd edn, New Jersey: Prentice Hall.

Lapersonne, E, Laurent G & Le Goff, JJ 1995, 'Consideration Sets of Size One: An Empirical Investigation of Automobile Purchases', *International Journal of Research in Marketing*, 12, 55-66.

Md Noor, S, Styles, C & Cowley, E 2010, 'Brand equity: Linking financial and customer perspectives', Chapter 2, this volume.

Mundt, K, Dawes J & Sharp B 2006, 'Can a brand outperform competitors on cross-category loyalty? An examination of cross-selling metrics in two financial services markets', *Journal of Consumer Marketing*, Vol. 23.

Reichheld, FF & Sasser, WE Jr. 1990, 'Zero Defections: Quality Comes to Services', *Harvard Business Review*, 68 (5, September-October), 105-11.

Reichheld, FF & Teal T 1996, *The Loyalty Effect: The Hidden Force Behind Growth, Profits, and Lasting Value*. Boston, Massachusetts: Harvard Business School Press.

Ries, A & Trout J 1986, *Positioning: The Battle For Your Mind*. New York: McGraw-Hill Inc.

Romaniuk, J & Gaillard E 2007, 'The relationship between unique brand associations, brand usage and brand performance: Analysis across eight categories', *Journal of Marketing Management*, 23 (3), 267-84.

Romaniuk, J & Sharp B 2008, 'Where knowledge of your brand resides: the pareto share of brand knowledge', in Report 44 for Corporate Sponsors. Adelaide: Ehrenberg-Bass Institute for Marketing Science.

Romaniuk, J, Sharp, B & Ehrenberg ASC 2007, 'Evidence concerning the importance of perceived brand differentiation', *Australasian Marketing Journal*, 15 (2), 42-54.

Rungie, C, Laurent G, Dall'Olmo RF, Morrison DG & Roy T 2005, 'Measuring and modeling the (limited) reliability of free choice attitude questions', *International Journal of Research in Marketing*, 22 (3), 309-18.

Sharp, A 2002, 'Searching for boundary conditions for an empirical generalisation concerning the temporal stability of individual's perceptual responses', Unpublished PhD thesis, University of South Australia.

Sharp, B 1995, 'Brand Equity and Market-Based Assets of Professional Service Firms', *Journal of Professional Services Marketing*, 13 (1), 3-13.

Uncles, MD 2010, 'Understanding Brand Performance Measures', Chapter 5, this volume.

Author biography

John Dawes is a Senior Researcher with the Ehrenberg-Bass Institute at the University of South Australia. His research interests are brand performance metrics and the impact of price promotions. He regularly conducts industry-funded research projects analysing retailer sales data and consumer purchase panel data. John has a keen interest in developing empirically-based, useful knowledge for marketing managers.

Contact: Associate Professor John Dawes, Ehrenberg-Bass Institute for Marketing Science, University of South Australia, GPO Box 2471 Adelaide, South Australia 5001; E john.dawes@marketingscience.info.

Chapter 7

A model of brand salience

JULIAN VIECELI & ROBIN N SHAW

ABSTRACT

Brand salience relates to brand prominence or top-of-mind awareness. Salient brands are more accessible to consumers. These brands have a higher likelihood of being recalled early and included in a consumer's consideration set. Salient brands have a higher likelihood of being purchased by consumers. A multi-attribute model of brand salience has been proposed and discussed in this chapter. The model of brand salience takes into account the antecedents to, and the outcomes of, brand salience. In addition, the construct of brand salience has been discussed with regard to the model of brand equity. The antecedents to brand salience include brand knowledge, brand associations, media consumption and brand awareness. The outcomes for a salient brand are purchase likelihood and purchase. Brand managers should build brand knowledge and the depth and breadth of brand associations to enable consumers to access the brand name under a variety of circumstances.

KEYWORDS

brand salience; brand equity; brand associations; brand awareness; brand image

Introduction

Brand salience has been defined as 'the prominence or level of activation of a brand in memory' (Alba & Chattopadhyay 1986, p. 363). It has been shown that more accessible brands tend to lead to consumer choice (Hauser & Wernerfelt 1990). In addition, salient brands tend to be recalled to the exclusion of other competing brands. When a consumer recalls a brand name, this brand is highlighted and then replaced in memory, available for further recall. The act of recall, however, makes the brand more accessible (salient). Thus, the salient brand has a higher chance of recall to the exclusion of competing brands (Alba & Chattopadhyay 1986). This chapter discusses the definitions of brand salience, proffers a model of brand salience, and discusses the antecedents to brand salience and the role of brand salience within the larger model of brand equity.

Over the past two decades, there has been a large amount of research dedicated to the area of branding, and in particular brand equity. Much of the work on brand equity has dealt with the measurement of the consequences (outcomes) of brand equity (see Crimmins 2000). This work has dealt with the important area of measuring the monetary value of the brand to the company. However, less research has been conducted into the sources of, or inputs to, brand equity (see Aaker 1991; Keller 1993; 2003; Romaniuk & Sharp 2004).

This chapter concentrates on the sources of brand equity, and in particular, the role of brand salience in providing a building block for further understanding of the activities of an organisation's customers, especially in regard to formulating further branding strategy. If an organisation can build the salience of a brand, that brand may be recalled earlier by the consumer and this may lead to greater purchase likelihood.

The concept of brand salience has been discussed in the literature, and a variety of definitions of brand salience have been offered (see Table 7.1). Ehrenberg *et al.* (1997) indicated that while great confusion exists over the understanding of differentiation in product lines across many fast-moving consumer good categories (e.g., laundry detergent), there was a marked effect for the salience of a brand. Ehrenberg *et al.* (1997) noted that brand salience was broader than mere awareness, and although awareness is a necessary pre-requisite to brand salience it was not itself an adequate measure to capture the salience of a brand.

Background

The brand has been viewed as residing in the mind of the consumer (Ehrenberg *et al.* 1997), and the value and position of the brand have been said to be the sole domain of the consumer (Bullmore 2001). These views, whilst taking a narrow focus, do stress that unless the consumer is aware of the brand it does not have a chance of being recalled, and has a diminished chance of being selected. Proponents of branding have taken the view that the success or failure of a brand is influenced by the knowledge and awareness (Keller 2003) – and processing time (Ambler *et al.* 2004) – that a consumer allocates to a brand.

Models of brand salience

Sutherland and Galloway (1981) proposed a model of brand salience that is based on the prominence of a brand in the media. In this model media prominence caused salience, which then leads to behavioural outcomes. It is likely that for low-involvement decision areas (e.g. buying soft drinks), salience also influences choice (behavioural outcomes) by determining or constraining the consideration set, or the set of brands considered by a consumer when making a choice decision (Sutherland & Galloway 1981). Salient brands may be influenced heavily by the stimulus situation (e.g. observing brands on supermarket shelves), but memory and alternatives obtained by memory evocation (using brand recall) will also have an influence. That is, consumers may see a brand on a supermarket shelf, but it is proposed that consumers use memory-based decision-making at the same time. This means that, although the consumer sees the brand on the shelf, he or she may still run a quick check of memory to scan for alternatives and to review positive or negative associations with the brand. This may explain why price promotions do work, but brands that are not on price promotion continue to gain sales as consumers still choose brands that are salient to them.

The brand salience construct

The concept of brand salience is a combination of views, investigating which brands customers think about, and what they think of these brands. Fazio *et al.* (1992) stated that brands earn a differential advantage in memory, and have a greater likelihood of being activated from memory upon product category consideration (e.g. brands of shampoo), if they are top-of-mind – which is a function of associative strength between the product category and the brand. This consists of how early a brand is named when a customer is directed to list all members of a product category, and the delay involved in identifying a brand name as correctly belonging to a product category, which is correlated highly with recall position. For example, how soon will a consumer recall the brand Head and Shoulders when directed to recall all brands of shampoo that they can recall?

Brand salience is an indication that customers not only have brand knowledge, but also have higher order awareness and a richness of information associated with each brand in their consideration set (Keller 2003). This allows consumers to access brands early and under a variety of conditions. The section following discusses definitions of brand salience from the literature, and offers an alternative definition of brand salience.

Definitions of brand salience

There are many definitions of brand salience. These definitions include: accessibility of the brand in memory as evidenced by recall (Nedungadi & Hutchinson 1985), associative strength (Fazio, Powell & Williams 1989), recall position (Miller & Berry 1998), the position in the customer's consideration set (Ehrenberg, Barnard & Scrivens 1997), and prominence (Alba & Chattopadhyay 1986).

There has also been debate about the difference between brand awareness and brand salience based on recognition versus recall. This is related to stimulus-based (Lynch & Srull 1982) versus memory-based evocation. Memory-based evocation refers to top-of-mind awareness or salience (Nedungadi & Hutchinson 1985). Further, Alba and Chattopadhyay (1986) refer to absolute awareness (brands that are known or recognisable) and situational awareness (brands recalled at a particular time). Arguably, increased salience, or top-of-mind awareness, is important for a brand in order to increase the retrieval probability of that brand when customers make a choice decision. Research has indicated that consumers use the information most salient to them when problem solving, for example, making a purchase decision (Domke, Shah & Wackman 1998), which may be in part due to the reduced information processing effort required on the part of the consumers (Pryor & Kriss 1977). Further, it has been shown that salient information gains disproportionate amounts of attention, is recalled in disproportionate amounts (Alba, Hutchinson & Lynch 1991), and will determine if the brand is recalled at a key time in the purchasing process (Aaker 1991). Thus, a salient brand will dominate in the consumer's mind when he or she attempts to recall other brands.

Table 7.1 contains a range of the definitions of brand salience from current literature. The definitions have been placed in order based on the key component of the definition. The majority of definitions fall into the categories of prominence, familiarity, accessibility, order and associations.

Table 7.1 Definitions of brand salience from the literature

Definition	Reference
Prominence	
Brand salience has been defined as the prominence or level of activation of a brand in memory.	Alba & Chattopadhyay 1986.
Salience is seen to be prominence.	Eastman & Newton 1998; Johnstone & Dodd 2000.
Salience is seen as top-of-mind awareness.	Nedungadi & Hutchinson 1985; Sutherland & Galloway 1981.
Salience is information at the forefront of conscious thought that is prompted by the immediate situation in which they find themselves. Salience is composed of natural prominence and comparative distinctiveness.	Higgins 1996.
Brand salience — the extent to which a brand stands out visually from competitors.	Van der Lans, Pieters & Wedel 2008.

Definition	Reference
Salience of a construct depends upon both its prominence (quality of its attributes) and distinctiveness (uniqueness of attributes and monopoly of taxonomic level of inclusiveness).	Higgins & King 1981.
Accessibility	
Salience refers to accessibility of information. All information is available in memory. Salience refers to the information that is accessible.	Pryor & Kriss 1977.
Cognitive psychologists define salience as the accessibility or ease of activation of certain memory content. Psychological salience is the accessibility or easiness of activation of certain memory content.	Gluck & Indurkhya 2001.
Associations	
Brand salience is the presence and richness of memory traces that result in the brand coming to mind in relevant choice situations. Brand salience has been defined as much more than mere awareness of the brand in the product category.	Romaniuk & Sharp 2003.
Brand salience is the common factor in how many people are aware of the brand (by any measure), have it in their consideration sets, regard it as value-for-money (sic.), buy it, or use it, and so on.	Ehrenberg, Barnard & Scrivens 1997.
Order	
Salience, or presence, is the degree to which a given brand comes to consumers' minds in the context of a particular purchase occasion or consumption occasion, entering the consumers' evoked set.	Moran 1990.
Brand salience is the propensity of the brand to be noticed, or thought of, in buying situations.	Romaniuk & Sharp 2004.
Brand salience refers to the order in which brands come to mind. It refers not to what consumers think about brands but to which ones they think about.	Miller & Berry 1998.
Familiarity	
Salience concerns the 'size' of the brand in one's mind, and all of the memory structures that allow the brand to come forward for the wide range of recall cues that can occur in purchase occasions. Salience has been defined as awareness and memory traces, plus familiarity, plus assurance.	Ehrenberg, Barnard, Kennedy & Bloom 2002.
Salience has been defined as familiarity relative to other brands in the consideration set.	Ambler 2003.

There are a variety of definitions of brand salience drawn from of fields such as psychology, advertising and politics. Common themes that emerge are brand prominence in the memory of the consumer, accessibility of information, familiarity with the brand, brand associations and order of recall.

Brand salience is defined in this chapter as the probability that a brand will be recalled early in a consumer's consideration set, under a variety of situations and via a variety of stimuli, to the exclusion of competing brands.

Brand salience not only influences the propensity of a brand to be recalled due to consumer knowledge and awareness of the brand, but it may also influence when the brand is recalled. Romaniuk and Sharp (2004) indicated that a model of brand salience should contain a representative range of attributes or cues, measures of recall relative to competitors, and should focus on whether the brand is thought of rather than seeking how favourably the brand is judged. The model of brand salience is expected to have higher correlations with measures of brand familiarity than attitude, a higher correlation with long-term rather than single use brands, and stability over time (Romaniuk & Sharp 2004). Factors such as media consumption and brand associations (positive versus negative, and unique brand associations) also influence the salience of the brand. Taking these factors into account, a model of brand salience incorporating the antecedents and outcomes for brand salience is shown in Figure 7.1, in which b_n refers to brand n, a particular brand recalled by a respondent.

Figure 7.1 shows that brand salience is proposed as a multi-attribute construct, with brand knowledge as the precursor to brand salience. Without brand knowledge, brand awareness does not exist, and brand knowledge and brand awareness are key antecedents to a brand being recalled. For a brand to be included in the consideration set, consumers must have knowledge and awareness of the brand. Brand image (measured via brand associations) and media consumption also contribute to brand salience by building exposure and links to the brand (associations) in memory. In turn, brand salience will influence purchase likelihood for a brand, and eventually brand purchase. The components for the model of brand salience and their relationship with the model in Figure 7.1 are discussed in the sections following.

Figure 7.1 A proposed model of brand salience, its antecedents and outcomes

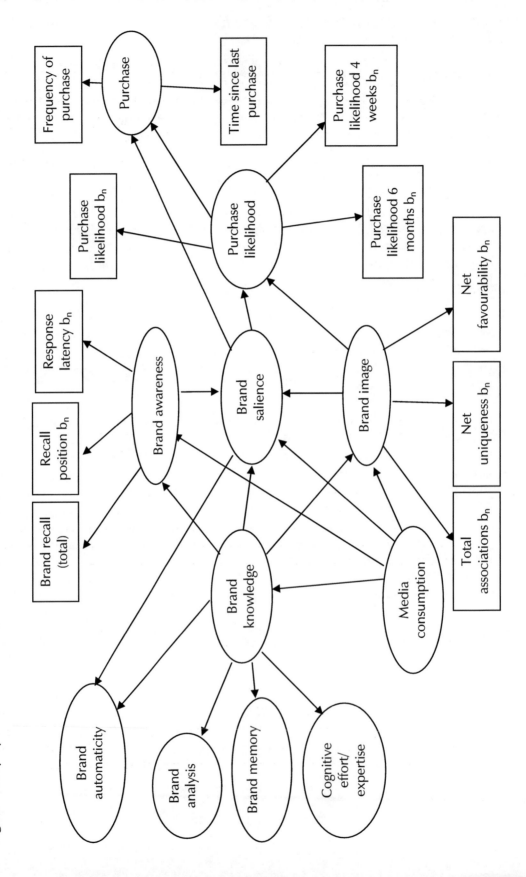

Awareness and brand salience

For a brand to be effective, it needs to be known not just by its immediate target market, but also by those people outside of the target market (Bullmore 2001). The recognition of the brand by non-users increases the value of the brand in the minds of the brand's current users. For example, the Ferrari brand with be devalued if the only people who recognised the brand were those who owned or drove the cars.

Ambler (2003) argued that brand awareness is not likely to be a driving force of purchase intent, but brand salience, as indicated by relative familiarity, indicates purchase intent and so applies to new and mature brands. The effectiveness of brand awareness is thought to decline with the maturity of the brand. Without understanding the processing of brand information in the mind of the customer and the actions that take place with the storage and retrieval of brand information, an organisation's brand actions may be ineffectual.

It can be concluded that mere awareness (recall) is not enough when looking at the space that a brand occupies in a customer's mind (Ehrenberg et al. 1997; Keller 2003). Mere awareness does not indicate the richness of the information, associations and usage situations that a measure of brand salience provides. The concept of brand salience used in this chapter synthesises a range of views, from the brands customers think about to what they think of these brands. This may also be seen as a synthesis between the North American views (Aaker 1991; Keller 2003) and the European view (Ehrenberg et al. 1997). Ehrenberg et al. (1997) indicated that brand salience is responsible for leading customers to purchase, especially in categories where differentiation is becoming harder to clearly demonstrate (e.g. breakfast cereals).

Advertising and brand salience

In established brand categories, advertising works primarily because it improves – or maintains – brand salience, or it increases slightly or 'nudges' brand salience (Barnard & Ehrenberg 1997; Miller & Berry 1998). This view is more in line with the brands about which the customers think, and not what they think about the brands.

Brand salience may influence a brand's sales and market share because of two reasons. Firstly, brands that come to mind on an unaided basis are likely to be the brands in a consumer's consideration set, and thus have a higher probability of being purchased (Miller & Berry 1998). Salience of the brand changes with changes in advertising exposure levels. This change is related to changes in the consideration set, which arguably does not expand continuously, but does change composition in response to advertising and in response to a communications activity such as a brand promotion. Brands may be dropped from or included in a consideration set (e.g. Coke Zero may replace Tab). Secondly, advertising weight and brand salience are cues to customers indicating which brands are popular. Customers tend to buy popular brands, thus there is said to be a connection between brand salience and sales for the brand (Ehrenberg 1997).

The section following outlines the antecedents to brand salience and the outcomes of brand salience. Brand salience is posited to have contributions from consumer brand knowledge, brand image, brand associations, and brand awareness. The media consumption of consumers has been taken into account as an antecedent to brand salience and brand awareness. In addition, brand salience has been linked to the behavioural outcomes of purchase and to the purchase likelihood on the part of the consumer. The concept of brand salience has been linked to the larger, broader concept of brand equity, of which the more recent models have brand salience as a foundation to the development of brand equity (Keller 2003) and as a precursor to customer choice (Hauser & Wernerfelt 1990).

Brand salience and brand equity

Over the past 20 years, there has been a substantial increase in the amount of research into brand equity. In particular, the research has focussed on theorising on the value of brands and the measurement of marketing effects that have occurred as a result of a product's brand name. The seminal work on brand equity by Aaker (1991) outlined the contributors to brand equity. Keller (1993; 2003) developed a framework that refined a range of contributing factors to customer-based brand equity. These fall into the broad categories of brand awareness and brand image. Within the framework of brand equity reside brand awareness and the concept of brand salience (see Keller 2003).

The two predominant views of brand equity are the accounting viewpoint and the customer-based view (Bristow *et al.* 2002). The customer-based view of brand equity, which aligns more to the sources of brand equity, is discussed in the section following. Brand salience is an input to brand equity, and this chapter focuses on the customer-based model of brand equity.

Customer-based brand equity

The Keller (1993) model of brand equity utilised the spreading activation theory of memory. The spreading activation theory suggested that memory is organised into a series of nodes and linkages (Collins & Loftus 1975), where the brand name would be the node and the linkages would be the brand associations. When the brand is activated, in many cases by an external cue such as an advertisement or the product itself, associated nodes are also activated through the series of linkages that are in place. Brand names are considered sequentially, and may be part of several different sequences depending on which path was activated. The implications of this model lie with the types of brand associations formed in memory by the marketing mix. These associations are cue dependent and may be weakened by competitive activity and decay over time.

This section following discusses the sources of brand equity, and in particular brand salience. A better understanding of the sources of brand equity may enable clearer tracking and targeting of product performance and of activities that build brand equity. Once the sources of brand equity are understood, corrective actions or maintenance actions may be outlined more easily.

'Customer-based brand equity is the differential effect of brand knowledge on customer response to marketing of the brand' (Keller 1993, p. 2). According to this definition, the key component of brand equity is customer brand knowledge, which Keller (1993) defined as being composed of brand awareness and brand image. According to Keller (2003), the causes of customer-based brand equity occur when the customer has a high-level awareness of, and familiarity with, the brand and holds some strong, favourable and unique brand associations in memory. If the brand has a salient and unique association, then the customer response may differ to that of other brands within the category.

Brand equity, brand salience and brand awareness

Residing within the framework of brand equity (Keller 1993; 2003) is the concept of brand salience, which has been defined as 'aspects of the awareness of the brand, e.g. how often and easily is the brand evoked under various situations and circumstances [and] to what extent is the brand top-of-mind and easily recalled or recognised.' (Keller 2003, p. 76). Another view point states the importance of brand salience as '… much more than mere awareness of a brand in a product category and [that it] is vital for a brand to remain in one's consideration set' (Ehrenberg, Barnard, Kennedy & Bloom 2002, p. 8). Further, it has been suggested that brand salience goes beyond awareness, or even the strength of such awareness (first recall), but is said to concern the 'size' of the brand in a customer's mind (Romaniuk and Sharp 2004).

For a brand to be considered salient it must have not only brand awareness, but also be accessible and have prominence in the mind of the consumer.

Brand awareness

Brand awareness refers to the customer's ability to recall and recognise that a brand is a member of a certain category (Aaker 1991). A salient brand, one with heightened or top-of-mind awareness (Alba & Chattopadhyay 1986), must have both depth and breadth of brand awareness. It is important for salience that a brand be recalled (depth); but of equal importance is the breadth, or when and where the brand is recalled (Keller 2003).

Brand awareness can be represented by recognition (prompted by showing consumers the brand names) or spontaneous recall (prompted by some definition of the product field), with a further refinement being collecting the first name.

Brand awareness can assist a brand by acting as an anchor to brand associations, and by creating familiarity – which for low involvement products such as fast-moving consumer goods (e.g. soft drink) may lead to purchase. For durable goods (e.g. whitegoods, cars), brand awareness is a signal of substance and commitment. Overall, brand awareness allows a brand to be considered and to enter the consumer's considerations set (Aaker 1991).

One method of increasing awareness and brand salience is via advertising, which may allow consumers to form more links to a brand in memory, which increases the chance of a consumer recalling that brand under a variety of different situations – and ahead of competing brands. Increasing the salience of a brand may move the brand further up in the customer's consideration set, to the first two or three brands recalled, increasing the brand's chance of being chosen – especially for fast-moving consumer goods (Alba & Chattopadhyay 1986).

One of the key reasons to increase the salience of a brand is that, for some product categories, it has been indicated that customers tend to process information and make brand choices for fast-moving consumer goods in less than one second (Ambler *et al.* 2004). Decisions that are made quickly by consumers may rely on a heuristic such as the first brand recalled (e.g. Coke) or the brand that is most salient visually (Van der Lans, Pieters & Wedel 2008). Therefore, as consumers become more aware of a brand, their level of brand familiarity increases.

Brand familiarity

Recognition of a brand provides a sense of familiarity, and people tend to like and trust the familiar. As such, brand familiarity is the most rudimentary form of consumer knowledge. Awareness of a brand or product will help in reducing the risk for customers as their sense of familiarity is increased, which makes the decision easier for customers. Ehrenberg *et al.* (1990) indicated that popular brands are bought by more people more often. Conversely, fewer people buy the less popular brands, and they buy them less often.

Brand knowledge

Brand knowledge captures both the aspects of the interest in the brand and the consumer's previous experience level with the brand, suggesting that more knowledgeable consumers are more engaged with the brand (Algesheimer, Dholakia & Herrmann 2005). Conversely, novice consumers are more likely to be in the learning process about the brands, and forming relationships with the brand. The more consumers know about the brand, the more confident they are expressing their (positive or negative) opinions about the brand.

Brand knowledge may be created in many ways. Any point of contact or potential encounter with a brand may change the consumer's knowledge of the brand, and of the product category. Once consumers know about a brand, they must be able to recall the brand and brand information to utilise this information for brand choice.

Salience effects and expertise

Brand salience is also likely to affect different customers to different extents. Experts should tend to remember non-salient information more readily, whereas novices should tend to find it harder to challenge advertisers' claims, and they will recall salient information preferentially (Alba & Chattopadhyay 1986).

Brand recall and brand salience

The role of brand recall, and even more importantly, brand salience, is crucial for frequently purchased products such as coffee, detergent and headache tablets, where brand decisions may be made usually before going to the store (Aaker 1991). This decision may be made via the use of an external memory aid, such as a shopping list, in which case consumers might use brand salience to assist in compiling the brands for the list. In some categories, such as cereal, there are so many choices that customers may be overwhelmed, and brand salience may play an important role here as consumers may purchase the brand that they recall first, which may be affected by prior use, recency of use, media exposure, brand image, brand awareness, and prior brand knowledge. This is supported by the theory of selective hypothesis testing, which refers to the tendency of individuals to evaluate competing hypotheses one at a time and to not consider a large set of competing options prior to choice (Hsee, Lowenstein, Blount & Bazerman 1999). If one option (brand) is more salient than the others, then this brand is chosen ahead of alternatives.

Brand awareness, although important to a brand, may not generate sales by itself. Other factors, such as liking, uniqueness and valence may need to be present for customers to take the next step. Valence is the positive or negative value attached to a brand, and is usually measured via brand association research. For example, Keller (2003) indicated that a market leader in a category could increase market share by getting customers to think of using the brand in a variety of different situations. However, a brand with more negative than positive brand associations, whilst it may be recalled early, might be recalled to the set of brands that would not be considered for purchase (rejected set), rather than the consideration set. Arguably, a brand with higher equity will be more salient, with more associations and stronger links between associations, allowing greater accessibility.

The relationship between brand salience, consideration sets, and purchase likelihood

Brand salience may affect consideration set composition because a salient brand inhibits the recall of competing brands (Alba & Chattopadhyay 1986). In addition, brand salience has been linked to purchase likelihood (Domke, Shah & Wackman 1998). Consumers also use the information that is most accessible when making a purchase decision. Brand salience has been shown to affect product choice and the purchase behaviour of customers (Ambler 2003; Ambler *et al.* 2004).

Customer choice

Due to the limited nature of processing in human memory, customers make their choice decisions typically from a small set of alternatives (Hauser & Wernfelt 1990). Arguably, all customer decisions rely on some memory component, which depends heavily on the accessibility of information from memory. Schindler and Berbaum (1983) found that customers tend to choose the most salient (accessible) of all alternatives, even if the outcomes of the choice are unrelated to the features that cause the salient alternatives to stand out. Salience was found to be an attribute to which customers were loyal, especially in the case of perceptual salience of product attributes. Salient facts may be recalled continually and unavoidably during attempts to retrieve information, despite effortful attempts to recall other information (Schindler & Berbaum 1983; Van der Lans *et al.* 2008).

Alba and Chattopadhyay (1986) suggested that advertising might alter the perception of a product subtly by increasing the salience of particular attributes. If a product possesses several attributes, presentation of a subset of these at the point of attitude formation may inhibit the recall and, therefore, consideration of remaining attributes and brands.

Ehrenberg *et al.* (1997) treat brand salience as being influenced by and, in turn, having an influence on many variables. Brand salience is seen to be not merely awareness but also associations with a brand, the external cues for a brand, and breadth of knowledge. In addition, media and media consumption are seen to have an influence on brand salience.

Managerial implications

A salient brand is a brand that is recalled more easily by consumers, has a high chance of being included in the consideration set, and is likely to lead to brand choice. In order to build brand salience, managers must work on building brand knowledge and brand awareness in a variety of situations and with a variety of cues. The greater the number of positive brand associations, the number of situations in which a consumer can recall brand information and the higher the chance that the brand will be salient and recalled to the consumer's consideration set. In addition, building the salience of a brand attribute may inhibit the recall of other brand attributes.

Methods to increase the salience of a brand include advertising the brand to a broad range of consumers, and using a broad range of situations within the advertising. Increasing the salience of a brand may also decrease the ability of the consumer to recall competing brands, offering a brand equity advantage to the organisation which owns the brand.

Conclusion

Brand salience is a complex, multi-attribute construct. The salience of a brand will influence the accessibility of information and the position in which the brand is recalled by the consumer. A more salient brand will be recalled earlier in a recall process by consumers, and this will then influence purchase intention and may influence purchase of the brand. In order to influence brand salience, marketers should build consumers' brand knowledge, and embed numerous brand associations under a variety of circumstances. A salient brand has both depth and breadth of awareness, and can be accessed by consumers under numerous situations.

References

Aaker, DA 1991, *Managing Brand Equity: Capitalising on the Value of a Brand Name*, The Free Press, New York.

Alba, J & Chattopadhyay, A 1986, 'Salience effects in brand recall', *Journal of Marketing Research*, vol. 23 (4), pp. 363-369.

Alba, J, Hutchinson, JW & Lynch, JG 1991, 'Memory and Decision Making', in HH Kassarjian, & T S Robertson (eds.) *Handbook of Consumer Theory and Research*, Prentice Hall, Englewood Cliffs, New Jersey.

Algesheimer, R, Dholakia, UM & Herrmann, A 2005, 'The social influence of brand community: Evidence from European car clubs', *Journal of Marketing*, vol. 69 (3), pp. 19-34.

Ambler, T 2003, *Marketing and the Bottom Line: The Marketing Metrics to Pump up Cash Flow*, 2nd edn, Pearson Education Limited, London.

Ambler, T, Braeutigam, S, Stins, J, Rose, S & Swithenby, S 2004, 'Salience and choice: Neural correlates of shopping decisions', *Psychology and Marketing*, vol. 21 (4), pp. 247-261.

Barnard, NR & Ehrenberg, ASC 1997, 'Advertising: Strongly persuasive or nudging?' *Journal of Advertising Research*, vol. 37 (1), pp. 21-31.

Bristow, DN, Schneider, KC & Schuler, DK 2002, 'The brand dependence scale: Measuring consumers' use of brand name to differentiate among product alternatives', *Journal of Product and Brand Management*, vol. 11 (6), pp. 434-456.

Bullmore, J 2001, 'Posh Spice and Persil', Inaugural Lecture to the British Brands Group (BBG), London, December, <http://ww2.wpp.com/Marketing/Marketing_1_1_Article_PoshSpice_06_02.html>.

Collins, AM & Loftus, EF 1975, 'A spreading activation theory of semantic processing', *Psychological Review*, vol. 82 (6), pp. 407-428.

Crimmins, JC 2000, 'Better measurement and management of brand value', *Journal of Advertising Research*, vol. 40 (6), pp. 136-144.

Domke, D, Shah, DV & Wackman, DB 1998, 'Media priming effects: Accessibility, association and activation', *International Journal of Public Opinion Research*, vol. 10 (1), pp. 51-75.

Eastman, ST & Newton, GD 1998, 'The impact of structural salience within on-air promotion', *Journal of Broadcasting and Electronic Media*, vol. 42 (1), pp. 50-79.

Ehrenberg, ASC 1997, 'Description and prescription', *Journal of Advertising Research*, vol. 37 (6), pp. 17-22.

Ehrenberg, ASC, Barnard, N, Kennedy, R & Bloom, H 2002, 'Brand advertising as creative publicity', *Journal of Advertising Research*, vol. 42 (4), pp. 7-18.

Ehrenberg, ASC, Barnard, N & Scriven, J 1997, 'Differentiation or salience', *Journal of Advertising Research*, vol. 37 (6), pp. 7-14.

Ehrenberg, ASC, Goodhardt, GJ and Barwise, TP 1990, 'Double jeopardy revisited', *Journal of Marketing*, vol. 54 (3), pp. 82-91.

Fazio, RH, Herr, PM & Powell, MC 1992, 'On the development and strength of category-brand associations in memory: The case of mystery ads', *Journal of Consumer Psychology*, vol. 1 (1), pp. 1-13.

Fazio, RH, Powell, MC & Williams, CJ 1989, 'The role of attitude accessibility in the attitude-to-behaviour process', *Journal of Consumer Research*, vol. 16 (3), pp. 280-288.

Gluck, J & Indurkhya, A 2001, 'Assessing changes in the longitudinal salience of items within constructs', *Journal of Adolescent Research*, vol. 16 (2), pp. 169-187.

Hauser, JR & Wernfelt, B 1990, 'An evaluation cost model of consideration sets', *Journal of Consumer Research*, vol. 16 (4), pp. 393-408.

Higgins, ET 1996, 'Knowledge activation: Accessibility, applicability, and salience', in ET Higgins & AW Kruglanski (eds.) *Social Psychology: Handbook of Basic Principles*, Guilford, New York, pp. 239-270.

Higgins, ET & King, G 1981, 'Accessibility of social constructs: Information-processing consequences of individual and context variability', in N Cantor & JF Kihlstrom (eds.) *Personality, Cognition and Social Interaction*, Lawrence Erlbaum Associates, Hillsdale, New Jersey, pp. 69-121.

Hsee, CK, Loewenstein, GF, Blount, S & Bazerman, MH 1999, 'Preference reversals between joint and separate evaluations of options: A review and theoretical analysis', *Psychological Bulletin*, vol. 125 (5), pp. 576-590.

Johnstone, E & Dodd, CA 2000, 'Placements as mediators of brand salience within a UK cinema audience', *Journal of Marketing Communications*, vol. 6 (3), pp. 141-158.

Keller, KL 1993, 'Conceptualizing, measuring, and managing customer-based brand equity', *Journal of Marketing*, vol. 57 (1), pp. 1-22.

Keller, KL 2003, *Strategic Brand Management: Building, Measuring and Managing Brand Equity*, 2nd Edition, Pearson Education Inc., Upper Saddle River, New Jersey.

Lynch, JG & Srull, TK 1982, 'Memory and attentional factors in consumer choice: Concepts and research methods', *Journal of Consumer Research*, vol. 9 (1), pp. 18-37.

Miller, S & Berry, L 1998, 'Brand salience versus brand image: Two theories of advertising effectiveness', *Journal of Advertising Research*, vol. 38 (5), pp. 83-88.

Moran, W T 1990, 'Brand presence and the perceptual frame', *Journal of Advertising Research*, vol. 30 (5), pp. 9-15.

Nedungadi, P & Hutchinson, JW 1985, 'The prototypicality of brands: Relationships with brand awareness, preference and usage', in E Hirschman & M Holbrook (eds.) *Advances in Consumer Research*, Association for Consumer Research, Provo, Utah, vol. 12, pp. 498-503.

Pryor, JB & Kriss, M 1977, 'The cognitive dynamics of salience in the attribution process', *Journal of Personality and Social Psychology*, vol. 35 (1), pp. 49-55.

Romaniuk, J & Sharp, B 2003, 'Brand salience and customer defection in subscription markets', *Journal of Marketing Management*, vol. 19 (1/2), pp. 25-44.

Romaniuk, J & Sharp, B 2004, 'Conceptualizing and measuring brand salience', *Marketing Theory*, vol. 4 (4), pp. 327-342.

Schindler, RH & Berbaum, M 1983, 'The influence of salience on choice', in RP Bagozzi & AM Tybout (eds.) *Advances in Consumer Research*, Association for Consumer Research, San Francisco, California, vol. 10, pp. 416-418.

Sutherland, M & Galloway, J 1981, 'Role of advertising: Persuasion or agenda setting?' *Journal of Advertising Research*, vol. 21 (5), pp. 25-29.

Van der Lans, R, Pieters, R & Wedel, M 2008 'Competitive brand salience', *Marketing Science*, vol. 27 (5), pp. 922-931.

Author biographies

Julian Vieceli is Senior Lecturer in Marketing at the Deakin Business School, Deakin University, Melbourne, Australia. His research interests include branding, brand associations, brand knowledge and consumer behaviour. His research has been published in national and international journals and conferences.

Contact: Julian Vieceli, Deakin Business School, Faculty of Business and Law, Deakin University, 221 Burwood Highway, Burwood, Victoria, Australia, 3125; P +61 3 92445541; E julian.vieceli@deakin.edu.au.

Robin N Shaw is the Foundation Professor of Marketing at the Deakin Business School, Deakin University, Melbourne, Australia. His PhD is from Cornell University. His research has been published in the *Journal of Service Research*, *Industrial Marketing Management*, the *Journal of Travel Research*, *Tourism Management*, and the *Journal of Travel and Tourism Marketing*, among others. He has received several grants from the Australian Research Council in recent years to support his research into the consumer behaviour of people paying to go to places for emotional experiences, whether that is to the opera or a football game.

Contact: robin.shaw@deakin.edu.au.

Chapter 8

Co-branding: When mixing images and metaphors can deliver better results

PASCALE QUESTER

ABSTRACT

This chapter explores both the general issue of co-branding as well as the more specific case of event marketing and sport sponsorship where co-branding has been more frequently observed in recent years. The chapter starts by a literature review of the concept of co-branding, providing a definition of what it is – and what it is not. The chapter then moves on to identify a number of issues and variables relevant to the discussion of co-branding. Finally, it provides a review of the specific context of sport sponsorship and event marketing in order to illustrate some of the specific aspects of co-branding that may be of interest to academics and practitioners alike. Implications and directions for future research conclude the chapter.

KEYWORDS

co-branding; product branding; corporate branding; brand extension; branding strategy; sponsorship

Introduction

Branding, and for that matter marketing as a whole, is all about setting a brand apart. By building specific associations and images and by linking them quite specifically to one brand and its visual identity, marketers have aimed to secure a privileged space, both within consumers' mind and in the marketplace. By endowing their brand with exclusive meanings, brand managers aim to differentiate it from the universe of all competing brands.

The notion of co-branding, therefore, may appear initially counter-productive, linking as it does *two* (or more) brands, their intrinsic equity and distinct meanings. Yet, co-branding has demonstrated, especially in the global context, a capacity to deliver for the brands involved a greater performance than either one might have achieved on its own. A particularly visible context for co-branding has been the area of event marketing and sponsorship. In such instances, the brand of an event (e.g. the Olympic Games) and that of a product or service (e.g. VISA or Samsung) have been intricately linked for the purpose of advancing both.

This chapter explores both the general issue of co-branding as well as the more specific case of event marketing and sport sponsorship where co-branding has been more frequently observed in recent years. The chapter starts by a literature review of the concept of co-branding, providing a definition of what it is – and what it is not. The chapter then moves on to identify a number of issues and variables relevant to the discussion of co-branding. Finally, it provides a review of the specific context of sport sponsorship and event marketing in order to illustrate some of the specific aspects of co-branding that may be of interest to academics and practitioners alike. Implications and directions for future research conclude the chapter.

Co-branding defined

In recent years, researchers have paid considerable attention to the 'growing and pervasive phenomenon' of co-branding as a viable method for improving brand value (Simonin & Ruth 1998, p.30; Walchli 2007). This concept is referred in the literature by a variety of terms, including brand-alliances, ingredient branding, joint promotions, cross-promotions, joint branding and symbolic marketing to name but a few (Helmig, Huber & Leeflang 2008; Simonin & Ruth 1998). Furthermore, co-branding strategies have been employed for both short- and long-term associations as well as both vertical and horizontal expansion (Helmig, Huber & Leeflang 2008; Walchli 2007). As well as corporate co-branding, retailer co-branding such as the agreement between McDonalds and McCafe has emerged as a recent trend (Wright, Frazer & Merilees 2007).

Co-branding occurs when two (or more) brands (constitute brands) are presented to consumers in conjunction with each other to form a new independent brand or product (composite brand) of mutual benefit (Washurn, Till & Priluck 2000) Specifically, it may be defined as 'the short- or long-term association or combination of two or more individual brands, products, and/or other distinctive proprietary assets' (Bluemelhuber, Carter, Lambe 2007, p. 428; Simonin & Ruth 1998, p. 30). Marketplace examples include Diet Coke and NutraSweet as well as Intel 'inside' IBM and Compaq computers (Rao, Qu & Ruekert 1999; Rao & Ruekert 1994; Simonin & Ruth 1998). Furthermore, many different forms of co-branding exist, including joint advertising, celebrity product endorsement and physical product integration (d'Astous, Colbert & Fournier 2007; Seno & Lukas 2007; Washburn, Till & Priluck 2000). Although co-branding can be viewed by some as a substitute to traditional brand extension strategies (Walchli 2007), the two concepts are conceptually different: in a typical brand extension scenario only one brand exists (Simonin & Ruth 1998). Figure 8.1 provides a conceptual framework differentiating these concepts and Table 8.1 provides key definitions and references.

Figure 8.1 Co-branding and brand extension

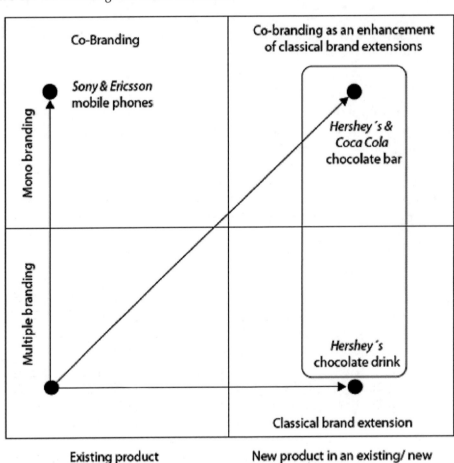

Source: Helmig, B, Huber, JA & Leeflang, PSH 2008, 'Co-branding: The state of the art', *Schmalenbach Business Review*, 60, pp. 359-377.

Table 8.1 Co-branding definitions

Term	Definition	Example	References
Brand extension	Extension of a brand in either existing or new product categories.	Unilever's Dove brand extending from soap and body lotion into hair shampoo product categories.	Helmig, Huber & Leeflang (2008)
Co-branding	A situation in which two (or more) brands are presented to consumers in conjunction with each other in order to form a new independent brand or product of mutual benefit. Co-branding may take two forms: *Physical product integration:* one brand cannot be used or separated from another brand. *Complementary us:* either brand forming the alliance may be used without the other.	*Co-branding:* Betty Crocker Brownie Mix in combination with Hershey's chocolate sauce. *Physical product integration:* Adidas shoes with Goodyear soles. *Complementary use:* Coca-Cola and NutraSweet.	Rao *et al.* (1999) Rao & Ruekert (1994) Simonin & Ruth (1998) Washurn, Till & Priluck (2000) James (2006)
Horizontal co-branding	Horizontal co-branding can be defined as both the production and distribution of a co-branded product by producers at the same level in the value chain.	Sony and Ericsson mobile phones.	Helmig, Huber & Leeflang (2008)
Vertical co-branding	Vertical co-branding also often referred to as ingredient branding refers to the vertical integration of products to form one product by producers at different levels of the value chain.	IBM and Intel.	Helmig, Huber & Leeflang (2008)
Sponsorship co-branding	When the brand of an event or property is associated with that of the sponsor.	Nike sponsoring Tiger Woods to endorse products. VISA and the Olympics Games	Motion, Leitch & Brodie (2003) Seno & Lukas (2007)

...nefits of co-branding

Multiple variables have been identified as determinants of consumers' attitudes towards co-branded products (d'Astous, Colbert & Fournier 2007). Once viewed by consumers as an unrealistic strategy, co-branding has been found to:

- enhance brand equity,

- improve consumer quality evaluations of brand combinations,

- yield spillover effects for individual brands,

- achieve transfer of consumer affect between brands,

- foster favourable images for lesser known partner brands, and

- generate improvements in consumer quality perceptions of the intangible product attributes of a partner brand.

(Levin, Davis & Levin 1996; Park, Jun & Shocker 1996; Rao & Ruekert 1994; Simonin & Ruth 1995; Washburn, Till & Priluck 2004.)

Influence of co-branding on brand equity

Consumers use brand equity as a decision-making cue to form perceptions of products and their respective attributes and to make judgments in the absence of alternative informational cues (Washburn *et al.* 2004). Brand equity can be defined as 'a set of brand assets and liabilities linked to a brand, its name and symbol, that add or subtract from the value provided by a product or service to a firm and/or to that firm's customers' (Aaker 1991, p.15; Washburn, Till & Priluck 2000, p.592). Therefore equity creation is an important objective for marketers seeking to achieve a competitive advantage (Seno & Lukas 2007). This may be done through associations with other brands (co-branding).

Examining the effects of co-branding on brand equity for both constitute and composite brands was the primary aim of an investigation by Washburn *et al.* (2000). Their findings indicated co-branding effects to be beneficial for both co-branding partners, regardless of consumer's original equity perceptions of the partner brands (Washburn *et al.* 2000). Moreover, this study demonstrated that low equity brands benefited the most, although high equity brands were not adversely affected, even when paired with low equity brands (Washburn *et al.* 2000).

Washburn, Till and Priluck (2004) examined the concept of customer-based brand equity, whereby brand equity is viewed from a customer's perspective, and found high equity pairings to result in more positive evaluations of the individual constitute brands than before pairing. Further, low-equity and mixed-equity brand pairings were found to both achieve higher brand evaluations than prior to partnership (Washburn *et al.* 2004), possibly because the simple act of pairing brands may indicate lower risk and additional credibility. Overall, past research suggests that co-branding strategies may not only positively influence consumers perceptions of a composite brand but also that of the constitute brands (Washburn *et al.* 2004).

Influence of co-branding strategies on perceived quality

Extensive research in relation to co-branded strategies indicates that greater success for co-branded products may be achieved when the perceived quality of the constitute brands is high (Rao, Qu & Rueckert 1999), possibly because the brand names act as signals of unobservable quality (Rao *et al.* 1999). Hence, the perceptions of an unknown brand may be improved when paired with a high-quality partner brand which functions as a quality assurance or risk reduction device (Fang & Mishra 2002).

The literature suggests that a branded ingredient may also act as a cue to product quality (McCarthy & Norris 1999). McCarthy and Norris (1999) identified conditions in which a branded ingredient form of brand alliance may be advantageous. However, their study identified success of branded ingredient strategies (improvement in competitive position) to depend on host brand quality. Moreover, moderate-quality host brands were found to be more likely to benefit from ingredient branding strategies than higher-quality host brands (McCarthy & Norris 1999).

Variables influencing the effectiveness of co-branding

Researchers in the areas of co-branding have sought to identify a number of brand specific variables and environmental factors susceptible to enhance or hinder the effectiveness of co-branding. For example, Figure 8.2 shows the range of variables deemed to impact co-branding effectiveness.

Figure 8.2 Theoretical model of co-branded products

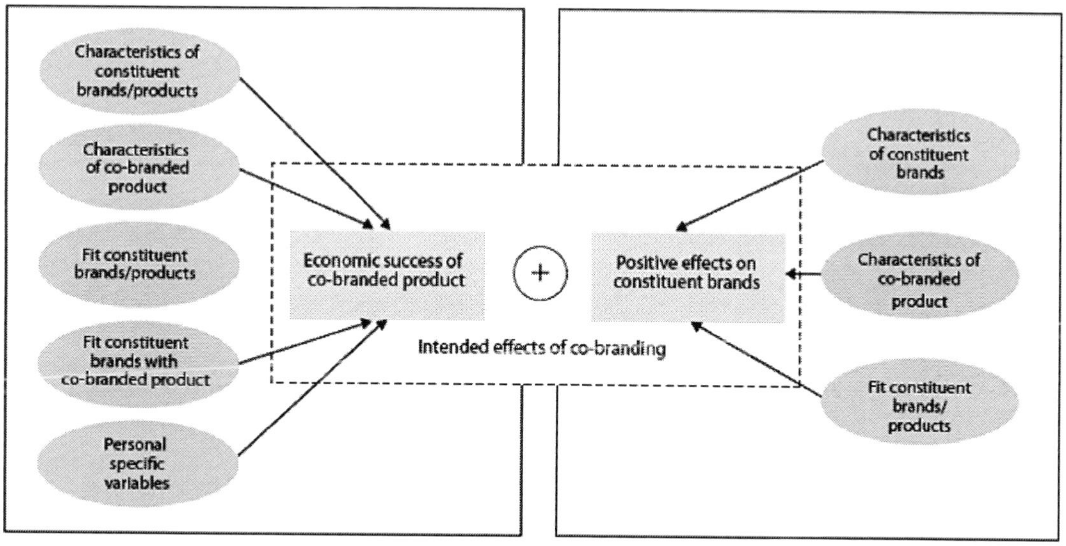

Source: Helmig, B, Huber, JA & Leeflang, PSH 2008, 'Co-branding: The state of the art', *Schmalenbach Business Review*, 60, pp. 359-377.

Fit or congruence

Research focusing on the concept of fit or congruence in co-branding strategies has traditionally focused on the match between individual brands and the formed alliance (Walchli 2007). For example, success is more likely to occur for a co-branded product when there is congruence between the brands and newly formed co-branded product (Hadjicharalambous 2001). This is because a close fit is necessary to allow brand associations to be transferred from the brands to the newly created product (d'Astous, Colbert & Fournier 2007). Indeed, Park, Jun and Shocker (1996) investigated ingredient branding and demonstrated that a combination of brands with complimentary attribute levels led to the co-branded product enjoying a better brand profile in consumers' minds than a direct extension of one of the composite brands or than an extension using highly favourable but non-complimentary brands.

An additional dimension of congruence only recently introduced in co-branding literature focuses on the evaluations of co-branded products (between-partner congruity) (Walchli 2007). This is an important concept providing significant insights into consumer's perceptions of brand partnerships and has significant implications for partner selection. Walchli's (2007) investigation showed that in conditions of high consumer involvement (or motivation to process marketing stimuli), preference (or higher value) was achieved by moderately incongruent co-branded partnerships over either more highly congruent or completely incongruent branding. These seemingly surprising results can be explained by the fact that consumers must undertake greater cognitive efforts to resolve moderately incongruent conditions. Highly congruent conditions require little or no processing efforts by consumers, whereas highly incongruent conditions may cause consumers frustration given the high processing demands placed on them (Walchli 2007).

The literature shows that the perceived 'fit' or compatibility of product categories as well as the perceived 'fit' of brands can impact on attitudes towards a marketing alliance (Simonin & Ruth 1998). However, perceived 'fit' does not moderate the contributions of constitute brands to the partnership, nor the magnitude of the spillover effects on the individual brands (Simonin & Ruth 1998). Nonetheless, a less than desirable brand still has opportunity to improve brand equity as long as a favourable fit exists between the brand and the co-branded product (Baumgarth 2003; Broniarczyk & Alba 1994; Simonin & Ruth 1998).

Furthermore, research Bluemelhuber, Carter and Lambe (2007) investigated the impact of country of origin fit (COO) and brand fit on consumer attitudes to cross-boarder or transnational co-brands (e.g. Sony Erickson). Their findings demonstrated that COO has a significant impact on transnational co-branding efforts. Moreover, COO effects were found to be stronger than that of brand fit when consumers are unfamiliar with a particular brand (Bluemelhuber, Carter & Lambe 2007). Conversely, when familiarity levels of consumers increase, brand fit plays a more significant role (Bluemelhuber, Carter & Lambe 2007).

Brand familiarity

An investigation into the extent to which evaluations of a co-branding alliance 'spill over' onto the individual constitute brands of the partnership identified level of brand familiarity as a moderating variable on the strength of an alliance relationship (Simonin & Ruth 1998). Familiarity is believed to affect the magnitude of spillover effects across partnering brands, with Simonin and Ruth (1998) indicating that spillover effects are not always felt equally by partners. Moreover, less familiar brands in a partnership have been found to exert stronger spillover effects (Simonin & Ruth 1998). Alternatively, when two highly familiar brands pair-up, the enormity of spillover effects is equal for both partners (Simonin & Ruth 1998). Additional empirical evidence from a replication study confirms these findings, with brands of low familiarity benefiting the most from co-branding (Baumgarth 2004).

As well as moderating the magnitude of the spillover effects between partners, familiarity influences the individual contribution of brands to an alliance (Simonin & Ruth 1998). Moreover, when highly familiar brands form a partnership, both make equal contributions to the alliance. Conversely, a less familiar brand within an alliance will make a smaller contribution to the partnership but gain the most from the relationship (Simonin & Ruth 1998).

Brand attitudes

Empirical evidence has suggested prior attitudes towards constitute brands impact on consumer attitudes towards a partnership (Simonin & Ruth 1998). However, the interpretation of these results can only be tentative, as a replication study testing different cultures, brands and product categories found contradictory results, suggesting attitudes towards individual brands to have a lower significance on co-branding evaluation by consumers (Baumgarth 2004).

Co-branding ingredients versus self-branded ingredients

An important issue facing managers implementing brand extensions is selecting the most appropriate label for branded ingredients of a new product (Desai & Keller 2002). Results of an experiment testing two alternative ingredient branding strategies on host brand expansions show a greater preliminary acceptance for co-branded ingredients (attributes supplied by another firm) in slot-filler expansion scenarios (Desai & Keller 2002). A slot expansion can be characterised as a modification to an existing attribute (Desai & Keller 2002). Co-branded ingredients were found to be potentially limiting in the long run. Alternatively, with new-attribute expansions (new attributes added to a product), co-branded ingredients lead to more positive evaluations by consumers regardless of the timeframe (Desai & Keller 2002). Therefore managers may benefit from selecting a co-branded ingredient for extensions into categories not directly related to the host brand.

port sponsorship and event marketing

Current observable trends in co-branding indicate a move towards organisation co-branding and away from product specific co-branding (Wright, Fraser & Merrilees 2007). A particular form of co-branding, 'sponsorship relationships' is reportedly gaining in popularity globally (Wright *et al*. 2007). Corporate brands may seek to adopt co-branding strategies and develop co-branding relationships in order to distil brand identity, reposition the brand and/or build their own brand equity (Motion, Leitch & Brodie 2003). In fact, more and more corporate brands are now developing business strategies based upon 'locking-in' competitors into business alliances and networks in order to leverage opportunities (Leitch & Richardson 2003). Co-branding offers corporate brands many benefits, including access to the brand strategies of the partner brand and opportunities to build equity through alignment of brand values, marketing communications associations, co-brand reach and access to a network of relationships (Motion *et al*. 2003).

The extant literature draws a distinction between sponsorship arrangements and co-branding (Motion *et al*. 2003). In their simplest form, sponsorships may be viewed as mere transactions where cash is offered in return for improvements in brand reputation, image and public awareness (Motion *et al*. 2003). Sponsorship, however, can also be conceptualised as a much more complex form of co-branding, whereby 'sponsorship moves from being a one-off exchange to being a long-term relationship between two or more organisations, and, as a consequence, sponsorship may be repositioned within the co-branded spectrum of the continuum' (Motion *et al*. 2003, p.1083). Indeed, research has established the relational nature of sponsorship and highlighted the need for sponsorship agreements to be market and long-term orientated (Farrelly & Quester 2005).

Corporate brands adopting such a co-branding approach to their sponsorship include Adidas and New Zealand Rugby Union (NZRU) (Motion *et al*. 2003). Adidas was the successful contenders for the New Zealand Rugby Union sponsorship after offering both money and the opportunity to move from sponsorship towards building a powerful co-branded relationship that would expose the All Blacks to the global market (Motion *et al*. 2003). In return, Adidas would gain media exposure and the chance to expand the size of the global rugby-apparel market (Motion *et al*. 2003). Importantly, the brand values of the All Blacks were closely related to those of Adidas. Moreover, Adidas's corporate vision to create the best global sports brand reflected that of the NZRU to present the All Blacks as a leading international sports brand (Motion *et al*. 2003). Such long-term strategic commitment between a sponsor and a sponsored property results in a marketing strategy firmly built on long-term sponsorship, a practice coined 'sponsorship-linked marketing' (Cornwell and Weeks 2005). Importantly, research shows that long-term, mutually trusting relationships between the sponsor and the property – the bedrock of any co-branding strategy – may provide some beneficial protection against ambush marketers and other firms seeking to derive benefits from misleadingly claiming an association with the same event. This is because genuine co-branding: builds recognition by consumers of the long-term nature of the sponsorship; builds up the legitimacy of both partners; and, in effect, offers a buffer against any 'pretenders' (Farrelly, Quester & Greyser 2005).

The literature has also established that co-branding is a source of equity for not only product-specific brands but also for corporate brands, and provides a chance to dispose of inappropriate or negative values (Motion *et al.* 2003). The investigation by Motion *et al.* (2003) demonstrated how two brands can move along the continuum from sponsorship to a successful co-branding relationship through the 'construction of a unified identify… that resulted in the formulation of successful linkages' (Motion *et al.* 2003, p.1091).

Co-branding provides access to the strategies of co-brand partners as well as the opportunity for each brand to pursue these strategies with the help and knowledge of an experienced partner brand (Motion *et al.* 2003). As such, the opportunity to co-brand with leading firms may represent one of the value-generating features of engaging in large scale global sponsorship. Leading sports properties, including the International Olympic Committee or French Tennis Open Roland Garros, are purposefully reducing the stable of their sponsors so as to enable them to work collaboratively over the long term. Indeed, managers of such leading sport events report that a valuable benefit identified by sponsors in entering the restricted club of top sponsors is precisely the capacity to leverage this elite membership in a variety of ways. In addition to the expectation of 'preferred supplier' status with a number of large organisations, sponsors hope and anticipate that their own business operations will benefit from whatever knowledge transfer is afforded by frequent and continuous interactions, be it before, at or after the event. Such 'intangibles' are sources of competitive advantage and might, ultimately, surpass the benefits delivered by the sponsorship in terms of consumer awareness or attitudes. This is one example of co-branding where up to 8 or 10 brands join in the sponsorship, each believing that the association with the remaining brands will in some way benefit their own, provided all are of similar status and the association ultimately 'makes sense' to the target audience as a group.

In the domain of sports particularly, product-celebrity endorsement is another popular form of co-branding recognised within the literature as a tool for creating both brand and celebrity equity (Seno & Lukas 2007). In fact, Nike spent around $US1.44 billion on celebrity endorsers including golf pro Tiger Woods (Seno & Lukas 2007). Similarly, the endorsement deal between Gillette and soccer star David Beckham is worth between $US30 – 50 million (Seno & Lukas 2007). However, whilst the benefits of endorsement deals may be great, research indicates that celebrity-product congruence is important for identifying potential endorsers (Seno & Lukas 2007).

Limitations and dangers of co-branding

Whilst more and more brands are engaging in co-branding arrangements globally, caution must be taken with these strategies in order to develop effective associations and to ensure that both brands leverage the most benefit out of a partnership. Given that co-branding involves linking one brand's associations with another, Grossman (1997) suggests that prior-brand associations may potentially affect co-branding possibilities. For example, Coke-Cola is renowned for its wide network of associations from celebrities endorsing the drink, music linked to it, as well as the Olympic Games which has been sponsored by Coke for over 100 years (Grossman 1997). Therefore, because of the wide-ranging links tied to Coke, it may be difficult to associate another brand with it. In order to protect brand equity and avoid erosion of brand image, brands should limit the number of alliances formed (Grossman 1997). Furthermore, co-branding may be particularly hazardous when the target brand is of low quality (Grossman 1997) or when it comes under scrutiny by consumer groups for other reasons.

Conclusion

Co-branding is not, and cannot be deemed, a panacea. Used wisely and strategically, it has the potential to deliver synergetic outcomes. But this requires a preliminary understanding of each of the constitute brands so as to ensure that brand values are aligned and can be meaningfully, from the consumers' point of view, combined. A co-branded identity is unlikely to emerge from radically incongruent brands and where quality levels, preliminary consumer attitudes or perceptions of quality are too far at odds.

When undertaken strategically, as appears to have been the case for many of the large scale sponsorship co-branding campaigns evident around events such as World Cups, Olympic Games or Tennis Opens, the opportunities to leverage the benefits of co-branding seem promising. Co-branding can therefore be expected to enjoy increasing degrees of complexity and sophistication, moving away from simplistic forms of co-branding such as product specific co-branding, to more complex organisation/retailer co-branding efforts that truly make both organisations co-dependant and equally committed to long-term mutually beneficial relationships based, as other business relationships are, on trust and a shared sense of purpose.

An intriguing area for future research lies around the notion of co-creation, whereby consumers take the initiative in determining what a brand should mean or do to continue to appeal to them. It may be that co-created co-branding strategies could be developed by merely observing, and then formalising, the fact that consumers use some brands together, for example when practicing a sport or a high involvement activity.

Acknowledgement

The author is grateful to Ms Rory Challen who provided research assistance for this project.

References

Aaker, DA, 1991, *Managing Brand Equity*, The Free Press, New York, NY.

Baumgarth, C 2004, 'Evaluations of co-brands and spill-over effects: further empirical evidence', *Journal of Marketing Communications*, 10, pp. 115-131.

Broniarczyk, SM & Alba, JW 1994, 'The Importance of Brand in Brand Extension', *Journal of Marketing Research*, 31, pp. 214-28.

Bluemelhuber, C, Carter, LL, & Lambe, CJ 2007, 'Extending the view of brand alliance effects. An integrative examination of the role of Country of Origin', *International Marketing Review*, vol. 24, no.4, pp. 427-443.

Cornwell T.B, and Weeks, CS 2005, 'Sponsorship-linked Marketing: Opening the black box'. *Journal of Advertising*, vol. 34, no 2, pp. 21-42.

d'Astous, A, Colbert, F & Fournier, M 2007, 'An experimental investigation of the use of brand extension and co-branding strategies in the art', *Journal of Service Marketing*, 21/4, pp. 231-240.

Desai, KK & Keller, KL 2002, 'The Effects of Ingredient Branding Strategies on Host Brand Extendibility', vol. 66, pp. 73-93.

Fang, X & Mishra, S 2002, 'The Effect of Brand Alliance Portfolio on the Perceived Quality of an Unknown Brand', *Advances in Consumer Research*, vol. 29, pp. 519-520.

Farrelly, F and Quester, P 2005, 'Investigating large-scale sponsorship relationships as co-marketing alliances', *Business Horizons*, 48, 55-62.

Farrelly, F, Quester, P & Greyser, SA 2005, 'Defending the Co-Branding Benefits of Sponsorship B2B Partnerships; The Case of Ambush Marketing', *Journal of Advertising Research*, September, pp. 339-348.

Grossman, RP (1997) 'Co-branding in advertising: developing effective associations', *Journal of Product and Brand Management*, vol.6, no.3, pp. 191-201.

Hadjicharlambous, C 2003, *Show Me Your Friends and I Will Tell You Who You Are: A Consumer Evaluation of Cobranding Extensions Using Structural Equation Modeling*, New York, NY.

Helmig, B, Huber, JA & Leeflang, PSH 2008, 'Co-branding: The state of the art', *Schmalenbach Business Review*, 60, pp. 359-377.

James, DO (2006) 'Extension to alliance: Aaker and Keller's model revisited', *Journal of Product and Brand Management*, 15/1, pp. 15-22.

Leitch, S & Richardson, N 2003, 'Corporate branding in the new economy', *European Journal of Marketing*, vol37, no.7/8, pp. 1065-1079.

Park, CW, Jun, SY & Shocker, AD 1996, 'Composite Branding Alliances: An Investigation of Extension and Feedback Effects', *Journal of Marketing Research*, vol.XXXIII, pp. 453-466.

McCarthy, MS & Norris, DG 1999, 'Improving competitive position using branded ingredients', *Journal of Product and Brand Management*, vol.8, no.4, pp. 267-285.

Rao, AR & Ruekert, RW 1994, 'Brand Alliances as Signals of Product Quality', *Sloan Management Review*, 36, pp. 87-97.

Rao, AR, Qu, L & Ruekert, RW 1999, 'Signaling Unobservable Product Quality Through a Brand Ally', *Journal of Marketing Research*, vol.XXXVI, pp. 258-268.

Seno, D & Lukas, B 2007, 'The equity effect of product endorsement by celebrities. A conceptual framework from a co-branding perspective,' *European Journal of Marketing*, vol.41, no.1/2, pp. 121-134.

Simonin, BL & Ruth, JA 1998, 'Is a Company Known by the Company It Keeps? Assessing the Spillover Effects of Brand Alliances on Consumer Brand Attitudes', *Journal of Market Research*, vol.XXXV, pp. 30-42.

Motion, J, Leitch, S & Brodie, RJ 2003, 'Equity in corporate co-branding. The case of Adidas and the All Blacks', *European Journal of Marketing*, vol.37, no.7/8, pp. 1080-1094.

Walchli, SB 2007, 'The Effects of Between-Partner Congruity on Consumer Evaluation of Co-Branded Products', *Psychology & Marketing*, vol.24(11), pp. 947-973.

Washburn, JH, Till, BD & Priluck, R 2000, 'Co-branding: brand equity and trial effects', *Journal of Consumer Marketing*, vol.17, no.7, pp. 591-604.

Washburn, JH, Till, BD & Priluck, R 2004, 'Brand Alliance and Customer-Based Brand-Equity Effects', *Psychology & Marketing*, vol. 21(7), pp. 487-508.

Wright, O, Frazer, L & Merrilees, B 2007, 'McCafe: The McDonald's co-branding experience', *Journal of Brand Management*, vol. 14, no. 6, pp. 442-457.

Author biography

Pascale Quester is Professor in Marketing at the University of Adelaide Business School. She holds a PhD from Massey University and an MA from Ohio State University, having completed her undergraduate studies in France. A dedicated lecturer, Pascale has authored or co-authored three leading textbooks, one on consumer behaviour and another in French. She is an active researcher with over 150 refereed publications, many in top rating journals such as *Journal of Consumer Research, Journal of Advertising Research, Psychology & Marketing, Recherche et Application en Marketing* and the *Journal of International Business Studies*. Her areas of expertise include sponsorship, country-of-origin effects and the impact of social influence on consumer choices. She is also interested in social marketing, studying the effects of anti-smoking messages and the impact of marketing on children's food choices. She is a regular invited professor at Paris I-Sorbonne and a director of FACIREM, the Franco-Australian Centre for International Research in Marketing.

Contact: Professor Pascale Quester, Executive Dean, Faculty of the Professions, The University of Adelaide, L11, Nexus10, 10 Pulteney Street, Adelaide SA 5000; P +61-8-8303-3886; E pascale.quester@adelaide.edu.au.

Chapter 9

Employer brands

LARA MOROKO & MARK D UNCLES

ABSTRACT

Employer branding is defined and the virtuous circles of employer branding are described. These comprise an outer circle (the outcomes of employer branding on the external position of firms), an inner circle (the impact on the internal capabilities of firms), and interactions (where internal and external outcomes intersect). There follows a discussion of the identification of successful and unsuccessful employer brands. Finally, a call is made for a more holistic, process-based view of employer branding.

KEYWORDS

employer branding; virtuous circles; employee recruitment; employee retention

Introduction

In the year to June 2009, the Australian Defence Force (ADF) spent AUS$34m on placing advertisements in media and a further AUS$11 on agency costs (Commonwealth of Australia 2009). This advertising spend, which was greater than that for any other Australian government agency, was not aimed at communicating the strategy and tactics at play in their current theatres of operation; it was in fact directed at attracting recruits, promoting the ADF as a desirable employer, and highlighting the career paths on offer. With a shortfall of appropriate applicants and increasing turnover, the ADF is but one of many organisations worldwide faced with the same question: 'How do we attract and retain the staff we need to meet the demands of our business?' Like its counterparts in the private sector, the ADF turned to employer branding to address this question.

Defined as 'the package of functional, economic and psychological benefits provided by employment, and identified with the employing company' (Ambler & Barrow 1996, p. 187), employer branding has become a strategic imperative, driven by both marketing and human resources departments. The increase in interest in employer branding is due, in part, to a growing understanding of the critical role that employees play in the success of consumer brands (i.e. corporate, product and service brands). Because of ongoing personal contact, employees have a great deal of influence over the way customers view firms, their products and their services. This reinforcement of brand character and attribute differentiation through interpersonal contact helps to build strong and enduring brands, particularly in the services sector.

Employer branding is seen as an effective method of recruiting and retaining employees who can consistently and positively represent the brand in interactions with customers. As such, it has been adopted by firms such as Virgin, GE, American Express, Yahoo, Procter and Gamble, Vodafone, Nokia, Google, Phillips, Reuters, easyJet, Saab, Deutsche Bank, Johnson and Johnson, and Diageo as a strategy for securing competitive advantage.

The employer brand concept draws on a broad spectrum of existing thought – such as identity/image management, brand management and differentiation, internal marketing, employee attraction, retention and motivation, and company culture – to describe the ways in which current and prospective employees interact with a firm's brand and, in particular, the firm's image as an employer.

In the next section we describe the virtuous circles of employer branding. This is followed by a discussion of the identification of successful and unsuccessful employer brands. We conclude by considering how our understanding of employer branding may be improved by taking a more holistic, process-based view.

The virtuous circles of employer branding

The focus of employer branding literature has been to define the phenomenon (Ambler & Barrow 1996; Ewing *et al.* 2002), consider its foundations (Ambler &

Barrow 1996; Backhaus & Tikoo 2004; Miles & Mangold 2004; Mosley 2007) or examine specific aspects of the process, for example, employer brand attributes, attractiveness or positioning (Ewing *et al.* 2002; Lievens & Highhouse 2003; Backhaus 2004; Berthon *et al.* 2005; Knox & Freeman 2006; Lievens *et al.* 2007; Davies 2008). In this body of work, positive outcomes are ascribed to employer branding based on a consideration of marketing, human resources and organisational behaviour principles. The practitioner-oriented literature makes similar claims about the benefits of pursuing an employer branding strategy, typically illustrated by anecdotal evidence from specific firms (e.g. Johansson 2005; Martin & Hetrick 2006; Vorster 2008; Pitcher 2009). These positive outcomes are characterised as 'virtuous circles' of employer branding which we can envisage as comprising an outer circle (the outcomes of employer branding on the external position of firms), an inner circle (the impact on the internal capabilities), and interactions (where internal and external outcomes intersect).

The outer circle: Outcomes that impact the external position of the firm

The first group of positive outcomes ascribed to employer branding impact on the firm's external position; that is, the firm's position with respect to customers, competitors, markets and the broader environment (Aaker 2007). Also of significance in the employer branding context are stakeholders and interested parties such as prospective employees, alumni, shareholders, recruiters and the media. These outcomes have the ability to impact the *performance* of the firm (e.g. through customer satisfaction, revenue and profit). They also may influence the *image* of the firm; that is, through outsiders' perceptions of the firm, and through the attributes of employees and the ways in which they represent the firm (Kapferer 2008; Hatch & Shultz 2009). These external outcomes are summarised in Figure 9.1.

Figure 9.1 Impact of employer branding outcomes on the external position of the firm

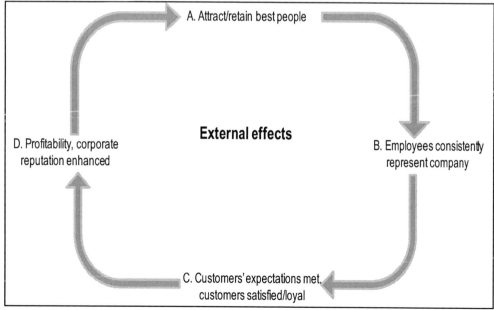

At the crux of the employer branding process, from the firm's perspective, is the attraction and retention of the best employees. In this context, 'best' refers to those employees who can add value to the firm and are able to deliver on the firm's brand promise (Backhaus & Tikoo 2004).

In defining the value proposition for employees and aligning it with the firm's brand promise, the firm may attract prospective employees with skills and personal values that allow them to deliver on the brand promise, and enable them to represent the brand and firm in a consistent way (A:B in Figure 9.1 – Ambler & Barrow 1996; Reichheld 1996; Berthon *et al*. 2005; Davies 2008). Thus, employees are able to meet or exceed the expectations of customers based on brand promise or previous encounters with the firm (B:C – Pringle & Gordon 2001; Miles & Mangold 2004; Mosley 2007). By customer expectations being exceeded (i.e. by providing positive disconfirmation) customers attain satisfaction (Woodruff *et al*. 1983), and increases in customer satisfaction can drive increases in customer loyalty (although this is not automatic) (Heskett *et al*. 1994; Anderson & Sullivan 1993; Rust & Zahorik 1993; Dowling 2001; Yeung *et al*. 2002; Lings & Greenley 2009).

This, in turn, drives revenue growth and profitability (C:D – Miles & Mangold 2004). Schultz (2004) makes a strong link between employees' alignment with the brand promise, customer satisfaction and increases in profit. By fostering conditions for profitability and a positive external corporate reputation, the employer branding process attains an aspect of self-perpetuation. Profitable firms with positive external reputations both attract (Fombrun & Shanley 1990; Ambler & Barrow 1996) and retain (Michaels *et al*. 2001) employees who want to share in and be associated with the firm's success (D:A). Sustained profitability and a positive reputation can also add to overall employer attractiveness or the 'envisioned benefits that a potential employee sees in working for a specific organisation' (Berthon *et al*. 2005, p. 156).

The inner circle: Outcomes that impact the internal capabilities of the firm

Employer branding outcomes can also impact the firm's internal capabilities; that is, the firm's strengths, weaknesses, problems, constraints and strategic options (Aaker 2007) (Figure 9.2). Positive outcomes attributed to employer branding strengthen internal capabilities through attracting, retaining and motivating staff (Davies 2008), and increase strategic flexibility through being able to efficiently attract desirable employees (Chambers *et al*. 1998). There is significant overlap in the outcomes attributed to employer branding with respect to the internal capabilities of the firm and the positive outcomes of internal marketing and internal branding (Mosley 2007).

Figure 9.2 Impact of employer branding outcomes on the internal capabilities of the firm

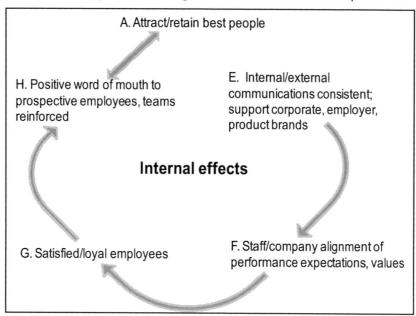

In actively managing their employer brand, firms can maintain consistency of key brand messages across stakeholder groups, a practice which may be of value (E in Figure 9.2 – Duncan & Moriarty 1998). Not only does congruence positively influence the perception of all related messages (by employees, customers and other stakeholders), it also ensures that employees are 'properly aligned' with the brand and what it represents (F – Backhaus & Tikoo 2004; Vallaster & de Chernatony 2005; Keller 2008). This allows employees to *live* the brand, delivering on the objectives of the brand/organisation, and reinforcing corporate values and performance expectations among new and existing staff (E:F – Greene *et al.* 1994; Ind 2004; Miles & Mangold 2004).

Satisfied, loyal employees are more likely to remain with the firm (Hesket *et al.* 1994) and to share good views about the firm with each other and with prospective employees (G:H – Reichheld 1996). Positive word of mouth among employees assists in building camaraderie within and across teams, engendering greater loyalty to the firm and to team members (H – Herman 1991), and thus improving staff retention. Furthermore, existing employees have a large 'signalling' impact on prospective employees (Rynes *et al.* 1991; Knox & Freeman 2006). Positive word of mouth helps contextualise the employment experience for prospective employees, attracting those with values that will fit the brand and flourish (H:A – Ambler & Barrow 1996; Chambers *et al.* 1998; Ind 2004; Miles & Mangold 2004). Positive, consistent word of mouth helps to counter information asymmetry for prospective employees, reducing perceived risks and increasing the credibility of the employing firm, thereby increasing employer attractiveness (Wilden *et al.* 2010).

The interplay between internal and external impacts of employer branding

Figure 9.3 provides a visual summary of key aspects of the internal and external effects of the employer branding process, as described in the previous sections.

Figure 9.3 Virtuous circles – Internal and external effects of the employer branding process

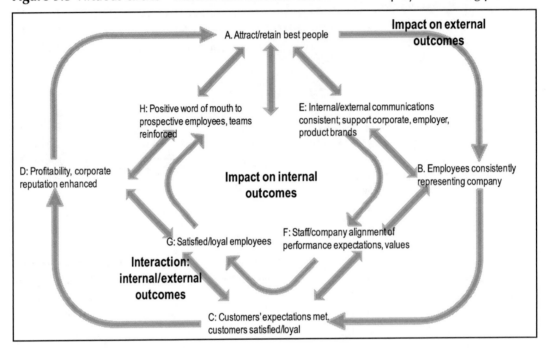

Hatch and Schultz (1997) suggest that, due to 'networking, business process re-engineering, flexible manufacturing, delayering and the new focus on customer service', the external and internal boundaries of firms are 'collapsing' (p. 356). So too are the boundaries between the outcomes of external and internal marketing. For example, Lings (2004) illustrates the relationship between the benefits of internal and external market orientation and performance; specifically, he proposes that internal market orientation (i.e. internal market research, communications and responsiveness) serves to enhance internal performance (employee satisfaction, retention and commitment), which in turn acts as an antecedent to both external market orientation and external performance (customer satisfaction/retention and profit).

Interactions between the external and internal virtuous circles of employer branding are seen as mutually reinforcing, as shown in Figure 9.3 and described in Table 9.1. For example, the link between points G and D is made as: satisfied, loyal employees support profitability through increases in productivity (Heskett *et al.* 1994; Uncles 1995; Bolino *et al.* 2002; Backhaus & Tikoo 2004); and turnover is reduced (Lings 2004) and employee citizenship behaviour is displayed. In addition to increasing profitability, the latter can enhance a firm's reputation.

Correspondingly, profitability and enhanced corporate reputation help retain satisfied, loyal employees. Identity and self-esteem of employees is partly determined by membership of social organisations, such as employees' place of work (Lievens *et al.* 2007). The external image of a firm (as construed by outsiders) serves as a mirror for employees, which they use to evaluate the value of their organisation and themselves (Dutton *et al.* 1994). A positive or prestigious corporate reputation can therefore support the positive self-identity of employees and their willingness to be associated with the firm, and can even result in higher morale (Wilden *et al.* 2010). Less esoteric, perhaps, is the impact of ongoing profitability. A profitable, successful firm is likely to offer a competitive range of benefits to employees, adding to its overall attractiveness as an employer (Berthon *et al.* 2005).

It is important to note that many of the interactions between internal and external outcomes of employer branding have been examined through the perspective of internal marketing. Conceptualisations such as the 'employee-customer-profit chain' explicitly link positive employee attitudes to positive customer attitudes and behaviours, which in turn promotes revenue growth (Rucci, *et al.* 1998). Recently, the pathways between internal marketing activity and profit growth have received increased attention. Empirical support for the relationship between the internal marketing 'mix' (strategic reward, internal communications, training and development, and senior leadership) and business performance has been established (Ahmed *et al.* 2003). Evidence for the impact of internal marketing on corporate culture, job satisfaction, service and customer orientation, and corporate brand perceptions has also been documented (Papasolomou & Vrontis 2006; Gournaris 2008).

Table 9.1 Interaction between external and internal components of the employer branding process

Reference	Nature of the interaction	Referred to in the literature by
E:B	Internal and external communications are consistent, uniformly reinforcing corporate culture and brand promise to staff.	Grönroos (1990) Gilly & Wolfinbarger (1998) Asif & Sargeant (2000) Keller (2008) Gounaris (2008)
B:F	When performance expectations and corporate values are explicit and clear, employees are given the means by which they can consistently deliver on the brand promise.	Grönroos (1990) Morrison (1994) Ind (2004) Papasolomou & Vrontis (2006)
F:C	Standards for service delivery and behaviour, based on brand promise, keep negative service surprises to a minimum. Service is delivered consistently and 'authentically', engendering customer loyalty.	Pringle & Gordon (2001) Bansal *et al.* (2001) Grayson & Martinec (2004) Miles & Mangold (2004) Papasolomou & Vrontis (2006) Mosley (2007)

Reference	Nature of the interaction	Referred to in the literature by
C:G	Satisfied employees have their needs met and are enabled/motivated to meet the needs of the customer. Loyal employees have more time to build solid relationships, acquire job-specific skills and are more likely to meet and exceed customer expectations.	Iaffaldano & Muchinsky (1985) George (1990) Shershic (1990) Berry & Parasuraman (1991) Reichheld (1996) Clark (1997) Lings (2004) Papasolomou & Vrontis (2006) Gounaris (2008) Lings & Greenley (2009)
G: D	Employee satisfaction can drive employee loyalty, which in turn drives productivity. Incremental increases in productivity lead to revenue growth and profitability. Additional incremental profit can also be derived from costs saved from reduced turnover and from employees displaying employee citizenship behaviour. Profit growth and positive reputation can help to retain existing employees.	Dutton *et al.* (1994) Heskett *et al.* (1994) Piercy (1994) Uncles (1995) Ambler & Barrow (1996) Rucci *et al.* (1998) Bolino *et al.* (2002) Bruhn (2003) Lings (2004) Berthon *et al.* (2005) Lievens *et al.* (2007) Wilden *et al.* (2010)
D:H	Employees perpetuate positive word of mouth about performance-oriented, successful companies to be identified with the success.	Michaels *et al.* (2001)
H:A	Long-term, loyal employees generate high calibre job applicants through positive word of mouth.	Reichheld (1996) Chambers *et al.* (1998)
E:A	Clear, consistent employer brand signals ensure 'employer of choice' position is understood by prospective employees, differentiating the firm from other employers and impacting on candidate preferences.	Wilden *et al.* (2010)

Identification of successful and unsuccessful employer brands

The previous discussion indicates that firms undertaking employer branding experience positive outcomes, particularly with respect to attracting and retaining desirable employees (as summarised in Figure 9.3). It is not known, however, whether there may also be neutral or negative outcomes attributable to the employer branding process. For example, Aldrich and Ruef (2006) raise what may be a potentially undesirable outcome of the process; they suggest that, when there is a high level of cultural consistency in an organisation, organisational growth may be threatened as variation to existing work practices introduced by employees is likely to be low. Organisational behaviour literature points to a similar phenomenon where employers hire employees with similar characteristics, skills and attitudes as themselves. This approach is not necessarily beneficial to the firm as it limits diversity.

Similarly, negative outcomes of the process may arise when employees find their experience of employment differs from that promised by the firm in communication of the employer brand. Rousseau (1990) describes a psychological contract as 'individual beliefs in reciprocal obligations between employers and employees' (p. 389). Brands, by definition, contain a 'promise of performance' (Feldwick 1991, p. 149) which, if unfulfilled in the eyes of the employee, may have negative consequences for the employee and firm. A sense of anger and betrayal may be felt by the employee if he/she believes that the organisation has failed to keep its promises (i.e. a violation of the psychological contract), resulting in reduced job satisfaction, reduced organisational trust and commitment, decreased job performance, and increased turnover (Robinson & Rousseau 1994; Robinson 1996; Suazo 2009).

In response to these issues, attempts recently have been made to distinguish the hallmarks of a successful or unsuccessful employer branding process (Moroko & Uncles 2008). A typology of the characteristics of successful and unsuccessful employer brands is depicted in Figure 9.4, based on data from a panel of experts. From this investigation, it is apparent that there are two key dimensions of successful/unsuccessful employer branding. One dimension is highly consistent with what is known about consumer/corporate-focused branding, in that employer brands also:

- need to be known and noticeable,

- need to be seen as relevant and resonant, and

- need to differentiate them from their direct competitors.

Collectively, these characteristics define an attractiveness dimension (attractive–unattractive). The interplay between employee attraction (to a firm) and attractiveness (of a firm) is a feature of work in human resource management as well as in marketing (Belt & Paolillo 1982; Rynes & Barber 1990).

Figure 9.4 Typology of employer brand success characteristics

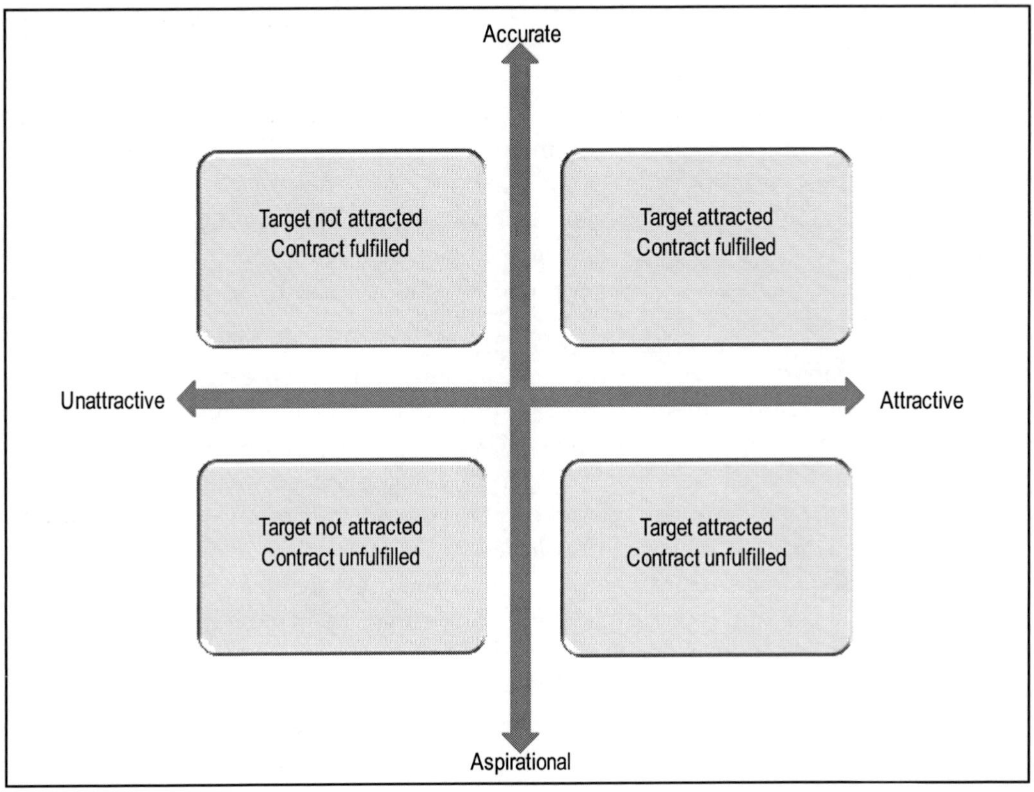

Source: Adapted from Figure 9.1, Moroko & Uncles 2008.

Additional characteristics, including fulfilling a psychological contract and the unintended appropriation of brand values, have also been uncovered. These characteristics define an accuracy dimension (accurate–aspirational). Employer brands are 'accurate' when the image the company portrays as an employer matches the employment experience of staff at the firm (i.e. the expectations of staff of their employment experience are consistently met or exceeded). Conversely, employer brands are not accurate when a gap exists between the image of the employment experience portrayed by the company (i.e. the employer brand identity) and the typical employment experience of their staff. This gap can be caused by inconsistent delivery of the employment experience (e.g. stockbrokers at a financial services firm may feel the employer brand identity is accurate, but back-office and administration staff may feel that the employer brand identity over-promises and under-delivers). It can also be caused when a company portrays an employer brand identity that their line managers are ill equipped or practically unable to deliver. Typically, companies with an inaccurate employer brand are not being purposefully misleading. Rather, they promote an identity of how they would *like* the employment experience at their company to be, and that exceeds their ability to reliably deliver on this experience (i.e. their employer brand is aspirational).

Significant managerial implications follow from both the typology itself and the implications that can be derived for each sector of the typology. Figure 9.5 provides an overview of the strategic issues that firms with employer brands in each of the sectors may face.

Figure 9.5 Managerial implications of the typology of employer brand success characteristics

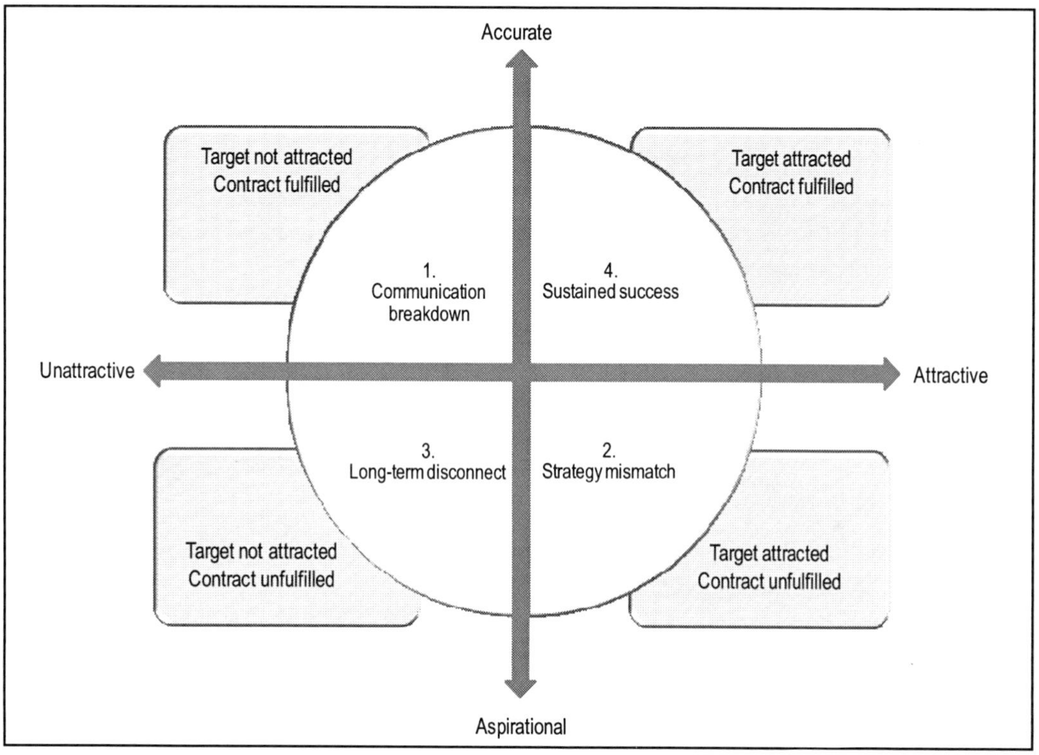

Source: Adapted from Figure 9.2, Moroko & Uncles 2008.

Sector 1: Communication breakdown

The first sector describes a firm that has an attractive employer brand but is not immediately considered by its target candidates. This may be due to a number of communications breakdowns; for example, the corporate, employer and/or consumer brands having conflicting value propositions, the misappropriation of a dominating and negative consumer brand image, the target candidates simply being unaware of the breadth of roles offered by the employer, or the employer being unable to distinguish itself from competitors. This situation may be improved by a more strategic, integrated approach to communications.

Sector 2: Strategy mismatch

The second sector describes a firm attracting the right employees but being unable to deliver on the employee value proposition for existing staff. In this firm there may be a higher than industry average level of applications for positions, matched with high turnover and/or low employee engagement, in addition to the misappropriation of a dominating and positive consumer brand image. This situation can be difficult to address as it requires managing the implied employer brand promise so that it is more realistically represented, or working on cultural and internal engagement issues to improve the employee experience.

Sector 3: Long-term disconnect

The third sector describes a precarious employer brand in which the employer is not seen as attractive, is not considered by prospective employees, and does not have an employment experience that is sufficiently robust to retain staff. In this scenario, the firm may need to re-engineer the employment product through human resources policies and procedures and, perhaps, through cultural change. Once successfully implemented, these changes then need to be communicated to the broader employment market to form the basis of a new promise. This is a truly challenging position that requires ongoing, coordinated strategy and practice renewal to resolve.

Sector 4: Sustained success

The fourth sector describes those firms that have employer branding success. Once attracted, candidates commence employment, and their experience matches or exceeds the perception they formed during the recruitment process. This is the most desirable position, as it ought to result in the firm being able to acquire and retain the best possible candidates. Furthermore, these employees are likely to be highly engaged, resulting in buoyant productivity.

It should be noted that, although a firm may find itself in any of these sectors at a given time, it cannot be assumed that the company will maintain its position over the long term. In particular, those firms believing themselves to be in Sector 3 should not despair, and those in Sector 4 need to be wary of complacency. Given the very nature of firms and employment, the perceptions of current and prospective staff will change over time:

- based on their experiences;
- due to information presented by the company;
- through other channels (the press, popular media, word-of-mouth comments, etc.); and

- due to changes in the competitiveness and desirability of the core employment experience.

There is also the impact over time of varying levels of employee knowledge, motivation and adaptive behaviour, especially in the wake of re-branding initiatives (Hankinson *et al.* 2007). Therefore, a firm's degree of success or otherwise cannot be thought of as static over time; rather, it may move towards any sector in the typology based on the strategic management (or lack thereof) of the employer brand by the firm.

Managing employer branding success

One example of the active management of employer brands over time is the way firms make use of segmentation. It is clear that various types of market segmentation are being used in employer branding practice. Look no further than the marketing of jobs in the armed forces of countries that do not have compulsory military service for instances of how the preferred product features/benefits of the target market are communicated to a broad target audience to increase overall rates of application and of job offer acceptance. This is most apparent in countries without conscription or national service – e.g. Australia, the US, the UK, and Belgium (e.g. see Lievens 2007 for a discussion of employer branding and the Belgium Army). Recall the statistic with which we opened this chapter. Similarly, high quality graduates in business, law and engineering are bombarded with multimedia campaigns promising exciting careers, promotion, travel and exceptional remuneration – called into service is everything from information evenings with cocktails to funky YouTube videos.

It is also evident that marketers and human resources managers working in this area might drive their employer branding strategies harder (and smarter) by thinking in terms of the wider range of segmentation types; for instance, by giving greater emphasis to profitability-based segmentation. The segmentation of employees based on role type and cost to the firm is an established practice in human resource management, but a small number of leading edge firms are going further than this – they are also segmenting employees and job roles based on their prospective profit contribution to the business (Lavelle 2007). Roles that are classified as 'business critical' become an employment segment targeted as a priority and as such are allocated more resources for attraction and retention programmes. While this may not seem to be a revolutionary approach to planning, in practice it differs markedly from the transactional view of recruitment in many firms (i.e. it differs from the practice of replacing an exiting employee with someone who has a similar skill set, qualifications and experience). When segmentation approaches that are typically used in consumer marketing – such as profitability, choice barrier and product (or in this instance, job) feature preference segmentation – are applied to employer branding, opportunity is created to move beyond transactional recruitment and toward workforce planning that best supports the long-term strategic objectives of firms (Moroko & Uncles 2009a, 2009b).

Future directions in employer branding

The possibilities for extending employer branding understanding and practice are significant, particularly in terms of measurement, process studies, scope of the process, temporal dynamics, and diverse contexts.

Measurement

It would be useful to develop improved measures of employer branding processes. For example, to assist in evaluating the relative success of an employer brand, in line with the typology presented in Figure 9.4, we encourage the use of human resource metrics (e.g. number of applicants per role, per cent of job offers accepted, average length of tenure, average staff turnover, level of staff engagement). An extension of this work could lie in quantitatively verifying the correlation between these metrics and employer branding success (or otherwise) across firms from different industries and contexts (e.g. privately or government owned). It would also be beneficial to develop diagnostic tools to evaluate the existence of conditions supporting or eroding success. Such tools would be useful for firms seeking to understand specific areas of process strength or weakness, as this would enable firms to construct an informed plan for change, improvement or evolution.

Process studies

The virtuous circles conceptualisation tends to highlight positive outcomes. It is inherently optimistic about the contribution of employer branding to company performance. An empirically-based understanding of how these outcomes – be they positive, neutral or negative – are achieved in practice is needed to gauge the true impact of employer branding. This gap in our current knowledge will exist until there is a robust investigation of the *process* of employer branding in practice.

Employer brands take shape through both 'the package of functional, economic and psychological benefits' provided and promoted by an employing firm and through current and prospective employees identifying benefits with the employing firm (Ambler & Barrow 1996). This interplay can be seen as the employer branding *process*, or the process by which the intended targets of an employer brand (current and prospective employees) interpret, interact with and respond to efforts made by the firm to manage the employer brand. Holistic research into the employer branding process which takes into account the perspectives of firms, and their target audiences has the potential to shed light on how employer branding occurs and on the full range of outcomes that can arise from employer branding in practice.

Scope of the process

There is a view that traditional marketing techniques are not directly applicable but should be adapted to suit the specific context of employer branding (Ambler & Barrow 1996). This raises the question: 'What other techniques/mechanisms are relevant to employer branding and how are they adapted?' The review of literature indicates that other schools of thought, in addition to marketing, may offer insight into the employer branding process. Human resources and organisational management literatures, for example, may provide mechanisms critical for the employer branding process, particularly with respect to employee and employer interactions. In order to employ a systematic approach to the examination of the process, the full scope of mechanisms that combine to create and perpetuate the employer branding process need to be identified. A focused and theoretically meaningful analysis of the process in practice can then occur, based on the presence and operation of employer branding mechanisms. Furthermore, the mechanisms will enable a systematic examination of employer brands by providing the basis for a consistent framework for comparison in order to establish substantive differences in successful and unsuccessful employer branding processes.

Temporal dynamics

Significant theory and practice development has been derived from studying processes over time; that is, from inception to maturity across contexts and firms in such areas as market orientation (e.g. Noble *et al.* 2002; Gebhardt *et al.* 2006). Longitudinal research here could extend our knowledge by illuminating: (a) the way in which employer branding processes are formed over time; (b) the way in which mechanisms identified in this research interact at different points in time to create processes; and (c) perhaps most importantly, the quantifiable benefit of pursuing an employer branding strategy.

Contexts

Employer branding has been investigated across varied conditions; however, some contexts may present barrier conditions to the employer branding process as conceptualised in the preceding sections. For example, are additional mechanisms important for international or global employer brands? Or, at the other end of the spectrum, are similar principles applicable for smaller and medium-sized firms (SMEs)? Are factors such as the personality/influence of the company founder more critical in a small firm environment? In addition to firm-level and employee-level factors, industry/sector mechanisms may also have an influence on the employer branding process. Industry or sector associations may act as a dominant force in attracting, retaining or indeed deterring employees. Positive associations of the employment experience offered by the industry/sector may influence and inform the associations of the employing firm for some employees in, say, the entertainment/music business, while negative industry associations may be seen as troublesome for recruiters and employees alike in industries such as correctional services, tobacco or gambling.

The advances in the relatively new area of employer branding in practice and theory are encouraging. Although dismissed as a fad and a buzzword in its infancy, employer branding has been embraced as a key strategic activity by leading firms for more than two decades. With the addition of robust, empirical research addressing the process as a whole and providing insight into the areas of measurement and context, employer branding is likely to continue as a field of growing interest to theorists and practitioners alike.

References

Aaker, DA 2007, *Strategic Market Management* (8th ed.). New York: Wiley.

Ahmed, P, Rafiq, M, & Saad, N 2003, 'Internal marketing and the mediating role of organisational competencies'. *European Journal of Marketing*, 37 (9), 1221-1241.

Aldrich, H & Ruef, M 2006, *Organizations Evolving* (2nd edn). Thousand Oaks: Sage.

Ambler, T, & Barrow, S 1996, 'The employer brand'. *Journal of Brand Management*, 4 (3), 185–206.

Anderson, EW, & Sullivan, M 1993, 'The antecedents and consequences of customer satisfaction for firms'. *Marketing Science,* 12 (2), 125–143.

Asif, S, & Sargeant, A 2000, 'Modeling internal communications in the financial services sector'. *European Journal of Marketing,* 34 (3/4), 299–318.

Backhaus, K 2004, 'An exploration of corporate recruitment descriptions on monster.com'. *Journal of Business Communication,* 41 (2), 115–120.

Backhaus, K, & Tikoo, S 2004, 'Conceptualizing and researching employer branding'. *Career Development International,* 9 (4/5), 501–517.

Bansal, HS, Mendelson, MB, & Sharma, B 2001, 'The impact of internal marketing activities on external marketing outcomes'. *Journal of Quality Management,* 6 (1), 61–76.

Bateman, TS, & Organ, DW 1983, 'Job satisfaction and the good soldier: the relationship between affect and employee "citizenship"', *Academy of Management Journal,* 26 (4), 587–596.

Belt , JA, & Paolillo, JGP 1982, 'The influence of corporate image and specificity of candidate qualifications on response to recruitment advertisement'. *Journal of Management,* 8 (1), 105–112.

Berry, L, & Parasuraman, A 1991, *Marketing Services: Competing through Quality*. New York: The Free Press.

Berthon, P, Ewing, M., & Hah, L. L. (2005). 'Captivating company: dimensions of attractiveness in employer branding'. *International Journal of Advertising,* 24 (2), 151–172.

Bolino, MC, Turnley, WH., & Bloodgood, JM 2002, 'Citizenship behavior and the creation of social capital in organisations'. *The Academy of Management Review,* 27 (4), 505–523.

Bruhn, M 2003, 'Internal service barometers: conceptualization and empirical results of a pilot study in Switzerland'. *European Journal of Marketing,* 37 (9), 1187-1204.

Chambers, EG, Foulon, M, Handfield-Jones, H, Hankin, SM, & Michaels, EG 1998,' The war for talent (attracting and retaining the best talents)' *The McKinsey Quarterly,* 1 (3), 44–58.

Clark, M 1997, 'Modeling the impact of customer-employee relationships on customer retention rates in a major UK retail bank'. *Management Decision,* 5 (4), 293–301.

Davies, G 2008, 'Employer branding and its influence on managers'. *European Journal of Marketing,* 42 (5/6), 667–681.

Dowling, G R 2001, *Creating Corporate Reputations: Identity, Image, and Performance*. Oxford: Oxford University Press.

Duncan, T, & Moriarty, SE 1998, 'A communication based marketing model for managing relationships'. *Journal of Marketing*, 62 (2), 1–13.

Dutton, JE, & Dukerich, JM 1991, 'Keeping an eye on the mirror: image and identity in organizations'. *Academy of Management Journal*, 34 (3), 517–555.

Ewing, MJ, Pitt, LF, de Bussy, NM, & Berthon, P 2002, 'Employment branding in the knowledge economy'. *International Journal of Advertising*, 21 (1), 3–22.

Feldwick, P 1991, 'Defining a brand'. In C Cowley (Ed.), *Understanding Brands*. London: Kogan Page.

Fombrun, C, & Shanley, M 1990, 'What's in a name? Reputation building and corporate strategy'. *Academy of Management Journal*, 33 (2), 233–258.

Gebhardt, GF, Carpenter, GS, & Sherry, JF 2006, 'Creating a market orientation: longitudinal, multi-firm, grounded analysis of cultural transformation'. *Journal of Marketing*, 70 (4), 37–55.

George, WR 1990, 'Internal marketing and organizational behavior: a partnership in developing customer conscious employees at every level'. *Journal of Business Research*, 20 (2), 63–70.

Gilly, MC, & Wolfinbarger, M 1998, 'Advertising's internal audience'. *Journal of Marketing*, 62 (1), 69–88.

Gounaris, S 2008, 'The notion of internal market orientation and employee job satisfaction: some preliminary evidence'. *The Journal of Services Marketing*, 22 (1), 68-90.

Grayson, K & Martinec, R 2004, 'Consumer perceptions of iconicity and indexicality and their influence on assessments of authentic market offerings'. *Journal of Consumer Research*, 31 (2), 296–313.

Greene, WE, Walls, GD, & Schrest, LJ 1994, 'Internal marketing: the key to external marketing success'. *The Journal of Services Marketing*, 8 (4), 5–13.

Grönroos, C 1990, *Services Management and Marketing: Managing the Moments of Truth in Service Competition*. Lexington: Lexington Books.

Hankinson, P, Lomax, W, & Hand, C 2007, 'The time factor in re-branding organizations: its effects on staff knowledge, attitudes and behaviour in UK charities'. *Journal of Product & Brand Management*, 16 (4), 236–246.

Hatch, MJ & Schultz, M 1997, 'Relations between organizational culture, identity and image'. *European Journal of Marketing*, 31 (7/8), 356–365.

Hatch, M & Schultz, M 2009, 'Of bricks and brands: from corporate to enterprise branding'. *Organizational Dynamics*, 38 (2), 117–130.

Herman, RE 1991, *Keeping Good People: Strategies for Solving the Dilemma of the Decade*. New York: McGraw-Hill.

Heskett, JL, Jones, TO, Loveman, GW, Sasser, EW, & Schlesinger, LA 1994, 'Putting the service-profit chain to work'. *Harvard Business Review*, 72 (2), 164–171.

Iaffaldano, MT, & Muchinsky, PM 1985, 'Job satisfaction and job performance: a meta analysis'. *Psychological Bulletin*, 97 (2), 251–273.

Ind, N 2004, *Living The Brand: How to Transform Every Member of Your Organization into a Brand Champion* (2nd ed.). London: Kogan Page.

Johansson, C 2005, *Employer Branding Global Best Practice*. Sweden: Universum Communications.

Kapferer, JN 2008, *The New Strategic Brand Management* (4th ed.). London: Kogan Page.

Keller, KL 2008, *Strategic Brand Management* (3rd ed.). New Jersey: Prentice Hall.

Knox, S & Freeman, C 2006, 'Measuring and managing employer brand image in the service industry'. *Journal of Marketing Management,* 22 (7/8), 695–716.

Lavelle, J 2007, 'On workforce architecture, employment relationships and lifecycles: expanding the purview of workforce planning & management'. *Public Personnel Management,* 36 (4), 371–385.

Lievens, F 2007, 'Employer branding in the Belgian Army: the importance of instrumental and symbolic beliefs for potential applicants, actual applicants, and military employees'. *Human Resource Management,* 46 (1), 51–69.

Lievens, F & Highhouse, S 2003, 'The relation of instrumental and symbolic attributes to a company's attractiveness as an employer'. *Personnel Psychology,* 56 (1), 75–103.

Lievens, F, Van Hoye, G & Anseel, F 2007, 'Organizational identity and employer image: towards a unifying framework'. *British Journal of Management,* 18 (1), 45–59.

Lings, IN 2004, 'Internal market orientation: construct and consequences'. *Journal of Business Research,* 57 (4), 405–413.

Lings, I & Greenley, G 2009, 'The impact of internal and external market orientations on firm performance'. *Journal of Strategic Marketing,* 17 (1), 41-53.

Major, DA, Kozlowski, SWJ, Chao, GT & Gardner, PD 1995, 'A longitudinal investigation of newcomer expectations, early socialization outcomes, and the moderating effects of role development factors'. *Journal of Applied Psychology,* 80 (3), 418–432.

Martin, G & Hetrick, S 2006, *Corporate Reputations, Branding and People Management: A Strategic Approach to HR*. Oxford: Butterworth Heinemann.

Mendes, A 1996, *Inspiring Commitment: How to Win Employee Loyalty in Chaotic Times*. Chicago: Irwin.

Michaels, E, Handfield-Jones, H & Axelrod, B 2001, *The War For Talent*. Boston: Harvard Business School Press.

Miles, SJ, & Mangold, G 2004, 'A conceptualization of the employee branding process'. *Journal of Relationship Marketing,* 3 (2/3), 65–87.

Moroko, L & Uncles, MD 2008, 'Characteristics of successful employer brands'. *Journal of Brand Management,* 16 (3), 160–175.

Moroko, L & Uncles, MD 2009a, *Employer branding and market segmentation. Journal of Brand Management,* 17 (2), 181-196.

Moroko, L & Uncles, MD 2009b, 'Employer branding'. *Wall Street Journal,* 23 March, 253 (67), R7-R8.

Morrison, EW 1994, 'Role definitions and organizational citizenship behavior'. *Academy of Management Journal,* 37 (6), 1543–1567.

Mosley, R 2007, 'Customer experience, organisational culture and the employer brand'. *Journal of Brand Management,* 15 (2), 123–134.

Noble, C, Sinha, R & Kumar, A 2002, 'Market orientation and alternative strategic orientations: a longitudinal assessment of performance implications'. *Journal of Marketing*, 66 (4), 25–39.

Papasolomou, I & Vrontis, D 2006, 'Building corporate branding through internal marketing: the case of the UK retail bank industry'. *Journal of Product and Brand Management*, 15 (1), 37-47.

Pitcher, G 2009, 'Get the right mix'. *Personnel Today: Your guide to employer branding (Special Issue)*, (January), 4–6.

Pringle, H & Gordon W 2001, *Brand Manners: How to Create the Self-Confident Organization to Live the Brand*. New York: John Wiley & Sons.

Reichheld, FF 1996, *The Loyalty Effect: The Hidden Force Behind Growth, Profits and Lasting Value*. Boston: Harvard Business School Press.

Robinson, SL 1996, 'Trust and breach of the psychological contract'. *Administrative Science Quarterly*, 41 (4), 574–599.

Robinson, SL & Rousseau, DM 1994, 'Violating the psychological contract: not the exception but the norm'. *Journal of Organizational Behavior*, 15, 245–259.

Rousseau, DM 1990, 'New hire perceptions of their own and their employer's obligations: a study of psychological contracts'. *Journal of Organizational Behavior*, 11 (5), 389–400.

Rucci, A, Kirn, S & Quinn, R 1998, 'The employee-customer-profit chain at Sears'. *Harvard Business Review*, 76 (1), 82-97

Rust, RT & Zahorik, AJ 1993, 'Customer satisfaction, customer retention and market share'. *Journal of Retailing*, 69 (2), 193–215.

Rynes, SL & Barber, AE 1990, 'Applicant attraction strategies: an organizational perspective'. *Academy of Management Review*, 15 (2), 286–310.

Rynes, SL, Bretz, RD Jr., & Gerhart, B 1991, 'The importance of recruitment in job choice: a different way of looking'. *Personnel Psychology*, 44 (3), 487–521.

Schultz, D 2004, 'Building an internal marketing management calculus'. *Interactive Marketing*, 6 (2), 111–129.

Suazo, M 2009, 'The mediating role of psychological contract violation on the relations between psychological contract breach and work-related attitudes and behaviors'. *Journal of Managerial Psychology*, 24 (2), 136–160.

Uncles, MD 1995, 'Viewpoint: securing competitive advantage through progressive staffing policies'. *International Journal of Retail & Distribution Management*, 23 (7), 4–6.

Vallaster, C & de Chernatony, L 2005, 'Internationalisation of services brands: the role of leadership during the internal brand building process', Journal of Marketing Management, 21 (1/2), 181–203.

Vorster, G 2008, 'Delivering results'. *Personnel Today*, 24 January, 2008, 56–58.

Wilden, R, Gudergan, S & Lings, IN 2010, 'Employer branding: strategic implications for staff recruitment'. *Journal of Marketing Management* (forthcoming).

Woodruff, RB, Cadotte, ER & Jenkins, RL 1983, 'Modeling consumer satisfaction processes using experienced based norms'. *Journal of Marketing Research*, 20 (3), 296–304.

Yeung, MCH, Lee CG & Ennew, CT 2002, 'Customer satisfaction and profitability: a reappraisal of the nature of the relationship'. *Journal of Targeting, Measurement & Analysis for Marketing*, 11 (1), 24–34.

Author biographies

Lara Moroko is a lecturer at Macquarie Graduate School of Management, Macquarie University. Her research focus is employer branding, the HR-marketing interface, and the investigation of management processes. She has a PhD from the Australian School of Business, University of New South Wales. She has held consulting positions in the field of corporate and employer branding strategy.

Contact: Dr Lara Moroko, Macquarie Graduate School of Management, Macquarie University, Sydney NSW 2109. E morokoco@gmail.com.

Mark D Uncles is Professor of Marketing and Associate Dean Undergraduate at the Australian School of Business, University of New South Wales. Prior to joining UNSW he held the position of Heinz Professor of Brand Management at Bradford Management Centre, and before that was an Assistant Professor at London Business School. Periods of sabbatical leave were undertaken at the Australian Graduate School of Management and the Judge Business School, University of Cambridge.

His research interests include brand management, employer branding, buyer behaviour, brand loyalty, store patronage and retail analysis. Publications have appeared in *Marketing Science, International Journal of Research in Marketing, Journal of Retailing, Journal of Service Research, Journal of Business Research, European Journal of Marketing, Journal of Advertising Research, Journal of Marketing Management, Sloan Management Review*, amongst others. He is on the editorial board of seven journals, including the *Journal of Product & Brand Management* and the *Journal of Brand Management*.

He has taught at all levels of tertiary education, including bachelor, specialist masters and MBA programs, doctoral programs, non-degree certificate courses, open executive programs and company-specific executive courses.

Contact: Professor Mark D Uncles, Professor of Marketing, School of Marketing, Australian School of Business, University of New South Wales, Sydney NSW 2052; P +61-2-9385-3510; F +61-2-9663-1985; E m.uncles@unsw.edu.au.

Chapter 10

Business-to-business brand management

Mark S Glynn

ABSTRACT

This chapter examines how business-to-business (B2B) brands create and maintain value for firms. Major B2B texts emphasise the differential effect of strong brands and often assume a consumer branding (B2C) perspective. However, while some of world's most valuable brands are B2B in nature, the question arises as to how important branding is in B2B marketing. In this chapter the relevance of B2C theoretical frameworks of branding to the B2B context are first discussed. Next, the B2B brand building process is examined against a background of research showing the impact of brand strategies on organisational buyers. As building strong B2B brands means considering the customer in the longer term, business-to-business relationships are important in creating and maintaining value between buyers and sellers. Thus, the extent to which B2B brands could benefit business relationships is considered.

KEYWORDS

business-to-business marketing; brands; resources; relationship management; brand management

Introduction

Many brands in the *Business Week* top 100 brand list (Helm & Arndt 2008) are B2B brands, including four of the top ten brands, namely GE, IBM, Intel and Microsoft. Looking further down this list, at least 17 other brands earn a substantial part of their revenue from B2B markets. These B2B brands include: HP, Cisco, Oracle, UPS, SAP, Siemens, Accenture, Reuters and Caterpillar. The value of these brands is, in many cases, greater than some better known consumer brands. However, brand management is more closely associated with consumer goods and services and is perceived as being less important in B2B marketing. An early study comparing brand equity by industry showed that industrial firms had less intangible asset value as a proportion of total asset value than did consumer goods firms. In some industries, such as metals, utilities and petroleum, brand equity was not important.

The *Business Week* list shows that the high asset value of these companies means that a small percentage increase in brand value can lead to a big change in B2B brand value when measured in dollar terms (Gregory & Sexton 2007). Gregory and Sexton also analysed B2B brand by industry, and one surprising finding was how the value of B2B brands varied among competing firms within an industry. This finding shows that some B2B firms may not be using their brands very effectively and would benefit from a strategic brand management approach. Many of these B2B firms are also involved in B2C markets. Therefore, the divisions between B2B and B2C are becoming blurred as firms use the brand equity created in one channel to benefit their business in another.

Despite the recognition of B2B branding's importance, many research studies apply a B2C branding lens when examining the value of branding from an organisational buying perspective. The emphasis in the organisational buying literature is on how value is created and delivered between firms. Organisation buying differs from consumer buying in that:

- the value of the transaction is much larger,
- the buying process often involves buying committees not just a purchasing manager,
- the buyer is often not the end user, and
- the purchase may be used within a firm's production process or resold to the buying firm's customers.

Some business marketing texts, including Anderson and Narus (2004), now emphasise the value of branding. Such texts show that the benefits of B2B branding for the firm in the selling process include:

- better information efficiency – particularly with complex products or services,

- an improved image benefit, and

- risk reduction.

(Kotler & Pfoertsch 2006)

Anderson and Narus (2004) maintain these benefits are underpinned by the need of the firm to create value for the organisational buyer. B2B brands create value by:

- encouraging trial and likelihood of purchase,

- reducing time to close the sale,

- receiving a larger share of the purchase requirement,

- becoming less resistant to price increases, and

- becoming less willing to trial competitive offerings.

(Anderson & Narus 2004)

In this chapter the relevance of B2C branding frameworks to B2B brands is examined by considering:

1. the nature of the B2B branding process from the firm perspective,

2. the existing research on building B2B brands, and

3. the importance of B2B brands in buyer seller relationships.

The relevance of B2C frameworks for B2B brands

For a B2B brand marketer, a key question is: how does branding benefit the firm and can the associated marketing expenditure be justified for a small group of organisational buyers? For consumer marketers, strong brands benefit the selling firm by:

- improving the efficiency of marketing spend,

- creating more loyalty,

- allowing a price premium to be charged, and

- providing a platform for further brand extensions or new lines to be introduced using that brand name.

B2B transactions are often motivated by derived demand, which means there is more of an economic focus, larger transactions, fewer customers, more emphasis on personal selling in external communication, and business partnerships. In addition, there are often buying committees comprised of decision makers who have different functional roles within the firm. Lee and colleagues investigated whether or not the existence of a brand management approach benefits business-to-business customers. Such a brand management system includes:

- the CEO's interest in the brand,

- the brand manager's power, and

- employee education and training.

(Lee, Park, Baek & Lee 2008)

Their research shows that the impact of a brand management system was stronger for B2B brands on customer preference compared to B2C brands.

Kotler and Pfoertsch (2006) use Kevin Keller's customer-based brand equity framework (Keller 2003) to explain the B2B brand building process. In this process, brand equity is the differential built by two components – brand awareness and brand image. Awareness is simply whether a customer has heard of a particular brand, whereas the brand image consists of the attributes and benefits that buyers associate with that brand. Another perspective is Erdem and Swait's model which emphasises a brand's perceived quality, perceived risk and information efficiency from an information economics perspective (Erdem & Swait 1998). Many B2B brand researchers apply these consumer-based frameworks in their research (Michell, King & Reast 2001). These studies show that many aspects of consumer branding are relevant to industrial buyers.

Some commentators, however, question the relevance of B2C frameworks with their emphasis on consumer psychology to the industrial buying process. There are subtle differences with B2B branding compared to consumer branding, including an emphasis on corporate rather than product branding and more emphasis on risk reduction (Mudambi 2002). Some researchers suggest the applicability of the emotional and self-expressive dimensions from Keller's framework, such as customer feelings towards a brand, are less relevant in the industrial purchase context (Kuhn, Alpert & Pope 2008). Mudambi (2002) considers that in consumer markets:

- products are more standardised,

- the relationship between buyer and seller is impersonal, and

- there is a reliance on mass advertising.

In contrast, with industrial markets there is more emphasis on service, customised products and personal selling. Furthermore, the emphasis in these B2C frameworks is on mass communication with the end-customer. This emphasis is not always relevant to B2B branding, as personal selling (Lynch & de Chernatony 2004) is often the principal means of communication.

Thus, the traditional branding frameworks associated with the consumer goods industry do not completely address the different marketing processes associated with the diverse industries that B2B marketers are involved in. There have been calls for more understanding of a broader process of brand management and brand equity development involving other stakeholders, not just focusing on brands and customers. Brodie and colleagues show that this wider meaning of the word equity includes relational, network (co-branding and alliances) and financial as well as customer brand equity (Brodie, Glynn & Little 2006). Anderson and Narus (2004) also propose a broader perspective which includes brand equity (brands and consumers) partnerships with other firms such as resellers (channel equity), and resellers' relationships with end-customers (reseller equity) which creates market-place equity. In a similar vein, Rust and colleagues also suggest that brand equity is part of a wider perspective which includes value and relationship equity which together create customer equity (Rust, Zeithaml & Lemon 2004). These perspectives indicate that B2B brand marketers need to consider wider processes in addition to the traditional brand-to-customer linkage.

Another useful perspective in understanding B2B branding is the resource-based view of the firm (RBV), which underlines the effects of brands in the wider marketplace. Within the RBV, resources such as brands are valuable to firms if they are valuable, rare and not able to be imitated or substituted. The framework of Srivastava and colleagues highlights the value of brands as market-based (intangible) assets. In this framework, the brand is a firm resource which influences external business relationships and thereby enhances shareholder performance (Srivastava, Shervani & Fahey 1998). There are three marketing processes through which this brand influence occurs:

- product development,

- supply chain management, and

- customer relationship management.

This framework emphasises the brand as a resource within a wider firm context such as in B2B marketing, unlike the traditional B2C frameworks which focus on the end-customer brand awareness and brand image.

The resource-based view also underpins the service dominant logic which views the brand as an operant resource (Vargo & Lusch 2004). An operant resource is one that firms can use to act on other resources. Here, the provision of goods and services are seen as a distribution mechanism for service to the customer. Furthermore, the customer, particularly the industrial buyer, often co-creates value with the seller before the purchase through the provision of purchasing specifications or supplier briefings. There is also a direct service interaction with the customer as well as an indirect interaction where the firm uses the goods or services supplied (Ballantyne & Aitken 2007). In this broader service brand context, Brodie, Glynn and Little (2006) also view the brand as a resource that facilitates and directs the relationship between its employees, company and its customers. For B2B marketers, brands function as a resource 'tie' between suppliers and customers (Ford 1998). Thus, in the brand co-creation process the early stage of brand creation involves external resources such as the marketing mix where the firm is control. However, in the later stages of brand co-creation the value of a brand is determined by customers and customer relationships (Boyle 2007).

Building the B2B brand

The first step in building brand equity is to create some brand awareness and familiarity, known as a brand identity. Several business-to-business buying studies have examined the creation of brand identity. In Gordon, Calantone and di Benedetto's (1993) research, brands were ranked fourth out of a series of six factors that influenced an electrical contractor's choice of distributors for electrical switches. In this case the firm had stopped selling direct to customers, so the task of creating brand awareness (providing sales leaflets) was left to their distributors. Other parties, such as architects and engineers, were also influential in the final decision to buy switches (Gordon, Calantone & di Benedetto 1993). As well as the differences in buying contexts and marketing approaches, there are important psychological differences between consumers and industrial buyers, including the use of experts as opposed to consumer who are more likely to refer to peer groups. Research in the office products category found that buyers were more likely to choose well-known brands where a poor decision could lead to organisational and personal failure. Industrial brands are more likely to be chosen when the purchase is more complex and when buyers are pressed for time (Hutton 1997). To create brand awareness for the B2B brand, personal selling is vital (Bendixen, Bukasa & Abratt 2004). Bendixen *et al.* (2004) found that the opinions of technical consultants and sales representatives were regarded as more important to the industrial buyer than advertising and direct mail.

Other studies examine the effect of brand awareness as a component of the overall buying decision. Davis and colleagues found that customers were willing to pay more for logistics services when service providers had a strong brand name (Davis, Golicic & Marquardt 2008). When purchasing tractors, farmers and farm contractors placed the most store on brand names – accounting for the highest proportion of the purchase decision compared to the price, dealer and service quality attributes (Walley, Custance, Taylor, Lindgreen & Hingley 2007). Yoon and Kijewski examined industrial buyer's brand attitudes and found that brand preference was relevant at certain price and volume purchasing thresholds (Yoon & Kijewski 1995). In a study of local accounting firms, the adoption of an affiliated 'big name' accounting firm led to higher fee revenue (Firth 1993). Buyers in Bendixen *et al.* (2004)'s study also ranked price and delivery as more important than the brand name in the final purchase decision. Furthermore, the impact of mass communications on industrial buyers is influenced by their personal involvement in the purchase and cognitive processing of advertising. In all these studies, B2B brand awareness is closely linked to revenue and performance outcomes.

Building brand awareness allows the formation of brand associations, which consist of attributes and benefits about a brand, which are relevant to the industrial buyer. Research into the attributes and benefits of B2B brands shows that a wide range of intangible benefits are important to buyers. Jim Shaw and colleagues found that, when complex industrial products such as mainframe computers were purchased, intangible attributes were more important than product performance attributes because of the future uncertainty about product developments in that industry (Shaw, Giglierano & Kallis 1989). These attributes and benefits create value for the buyer and the firm's reputation and encompass:

- product features such as no defects,

- distribution aspects such as just in time and reliable delivery, and

- support services such as problem-solving advice and world class expertise.

(Mudambi 2002)

In this purchasing context, the tangible and intangible attributes of the purchase as well as the corporate services associated with the brand were important. This multidimensional nature of the B2B brand involving the corporate services related to the product contrasts with consumer marketing where the focus is often on the consumer's experience with the product brand.

Other research also underscores the importance of presenting the brand as a total solution for the B2B customer and focusing on a promise-centric approach rather than on a product-centric approach. For example, suppliers of steel laser cutters focused on solving technical and logistical problems and on providing support for customers, while the brand name also reflected an overall corporate orientation to the customer. Brands also allow industrial buyers to reduce the time spent selecting alternative brands that are less risky in terms of addressing possible technical problems and resolving internal production problems (McQuiston 2004). Industrial brands also provide symbolic benefits to users; one study showed that power–tool brands enabled building tradesmen to achieve aspirational goals such as accomplishment and job satisfaction (Ringberg & Gupta 2003).

It appears that industrial buyers also have different predispositions towards branding. Mudambi (2002) found some industrial buyers were 'branding receptive', while others either had low interest in branding or were more interested in the tangible product aspects. In this research, branding was one of three important decision attributes, along with product and service, and was influenced by both buyer and purchase characteristics. Mudambi (2002) found that buyers who were branding receptive were less influenced by price.

When selecting a new supplier such as a subcontractor, the buying firm often has very little information. In one study (Blombäck & Axelsson 2007), the selection process involved sequentially moving from a situation where the customer had little tangible information about the contractor other than brand awareness through to the customer gathering all the information necessary to make a final decision. When comparing the separate effects of brand image and corporate reputation, a firm's reputation was more influential on customer loyalty and customer value than the firm's brand image (Cretu & Brodie 2007). Much research has focussed on the relevance of performance attributes to industrial buyers rather than considering the influence of brand image. One study found that supplier image was more important to industrial customers than brand awareness, while suppliers regarded brand awareness as more important than image (Davis *et al.* 2008), showing that suppliers and customers can have different perspectives of a brand.

Maintaining firm relationships with B2B brands

While the company marketing efforts are directed towards creating awareness and favourable attitudes for B2B brands and towards closing the sale, many B2B decisions involve purchasing products and services already used by the buying firm. Such B2B buying decisions can involve rebuying the B2B brand, rebuying the B2B brand with modifications, or a completely new purchase. Thus, the ongoing nature of industrial buying involves considering long-term relationships between buyers and sellers. Relationship management is considered an important outcome for buyers and sellers, and many B2B brands are regarded as being relationship builders (de Chernatony & McDonald 2003). Research shows that consumer marketers are more transactional or short-term than B2B marketers, who tend to be more relational or long-term in their approach (Coviello, Brodie, Danaher & Johnston 2002). Many business-to-business texts, however, do not address the relationship marketing advantages of B2B brands.

In consumer markets, building a strong brand results in some attachment to the brand (Keller 2003). Customer relationship processes for B2B brands enhance buyer identification with the brand, customer contact and loyalty. Customer relationships are vital for B2B marketers as these firms often rely on outside firms for resources. One study showed how sales relationships with channel partners such as chefs enabled venison marketers to build awareness and relationships in the supply chain (Beverland 2005). Some industrial firms see more benefit to their own company of having a brand name, but often consider the benefit of branding to their customers as being less important (Shipley & Howard 1993). Michell *et al.* (2001) showed that B2B brands enhance the customer's perception of the seller. However, B2B brands did not increase customer commitment to the seller or confer long-term relationship benefits. The marketing variables that generated brand loyalty were product- and service-related, while advertising and sales force relationships were secondary considerations.

Research into B2B brand relationships generally considers the value of customer loyalty to the selling firm. There is a distinction between corporate and product brand knowledge effects on customer loyalty in B2B buying (van Riel, Pahud de Mortanges & Streukens 2005). Van Riel, Pahud de Mortanges and Struekens (2005) show that the product value and distribution aspects of the purchase influence product brand equity, while components such as buyer information and company personnel influence the service component and corporate brand equity. In this study, corporate brand equity had more of an effect on customer loyalty than product-based brand equity. Cretu and Brodie (2007) found a similar result where product brand image influenced buyer ratings of the product and service features while corporate reputation influenced the more global concerns of the buyer such as customer value. In B2B marketing, the corporate brand has an important role in addition to the product brand which is usually the focus of B2C marketing.

Industrial purchasers must also be satisfied with the purchase. In addition to these product and quality considerations, the degree of cooperation with the seller and the contact salesperson was also important.

Research into distribution channels shows that brands represent a pledge or commitment to a buyer and can balance business risk, thereby contributing to relationship stability (Glynn, Motion & Brodie 2007). Glynn, Motion and Brodie (2007) demonstrated how B2B relationships with retailers enabled minor brands to better obtain supermarket listings, as these smaller brands had more flexibility in dealing with retailers. For retailers, a manufacturer's brand offers several benefits:

- financial (providing a means for profit),

- manufacturer brand support (including support of retailers' promotions),

- customer benefits (the retailer is expected to carry that brand), and

- the certainty of demand created by brand equity.

These brand benefits impact on retailer satisfaction and performance perceptions as well as on commitment to the brand. Moreover, these brand benefits enhance the retailer's trust of the manufacturer. These benefits were more evident in high value retail categories such as wine and beer (Glynn 2007).

Strong brands have been considered important to B2B relationship success (Anderson & Narus 2004). However, some authors from a distribution channels perspective suggest that this is not always the case. Relationships with B2B buyers such as retailers can mean the loss of control for retailers as manufacturers' support for their brands also benefits competing retailers. Inter-firm relationships, while creating strategic advantage, also have their costs such as the loss of firm bargaining power and exposure to opportunism. Combs and Ketchen (1999) emphasise the value of resource sharing, because together manufacturers and buyers both perform value creation functions that no one firm can complete individually (Combs & Ketchen 1999). They showed that firms with less brand equity are more likely to engage in inter-firm cooperation than firms with strong brands, as these firms had fewer resources.

Relationships make fewer resource demands in a cooperative relationship as firms do not have to provide all the resources. Resource-abundant firms only use inter-firm cooperation when it helps lower their resource costs. Han and Sung (2008) show that the supplier's competence is an important determinant of B2B brand value. This brand value leads to an improved relationship quality and performance perception (Han & Sung 2008). Other determinants of relationship quality include satisfaction and trust. The personal involvement of the buyer with the category and satisfaction with the service leads to increased B2B brand loyalty (Bennett, Hartel & McColl-Kennedy 2005). Also in B2B services, switching costs often encourage buyers to remain loyal to a brand (Yanamandram & White 2006). Trust and performance of a shopping centre brand was an important consideration for shop tenants when renewing a lease (Roberts & Merrilees 2007).

Dyer and Singh (1998) consider that sources of competitive advantage can also arise from such resource sharing within a B2B relationship. These inter-organisational sources of advantage include, with examples of manufacturer resources in brackets:

- relational specific assets (brands),
- knowledge sharing (brand market information, expertise),
- complementary resources (manufacturer marketing expenditure and service), and
- effective governance (sales force and marketing expenditure).

These sources of advantage create relational rents which are preserved through inter-organisational asset connectedness, partner scarcity, and resource indivisibility, and can be difficult to imitate by competitors. Not only are brands sources of advantage in B2B relationships, but their inherent properties allow this advantage to be maintained (Dyer & Singh 1998). An example of this advantage is with B2B co-branding alliances, where trust and brand reputation is transferred between partner firms. However, co-branding relationships do involve some risk, and in franchise relationships some firms prefer to develop their own brands to minimise this risk (Wright & Frazer 2007).

Ghosh and John (1999) highlight a value creation problem for B2B brands in firm exchanges. Once the value is created for a B2B brand, both buyers and sellers will try to minimise their stake by reducing their investment in the relationship. These authors consider that the firm resources such as technology, customer (brand equity) and supply chain (partners) give access to marketplace positions which are valued by customers and influence the governance form and short- or long-term exchanges (Ghosh & John 1999). In interfirm exchanges, firms with strong brands should build market demand, whereas firms with weaker brands are better off building relationships with B2B customers. Many B2B brands such as Microsoft Windows, Intel and Gortex are examples of B2B brands that have created market demand through an 'ingredient' branding strategy which is often useful in lowering the risk in purchases that involve greater buying complexity.

Conclusion

It has been argued that the traditional B2C frameworks of branding do not address the multidimensional nature of B2B brands in creating value between firms. This multidimensional nature stems from the different marketing processes of B2B firms which emphasise interfirm corporate relationships and not one-off transactions. Brands are an important source of value for large industrial organisations. However, this brand value is not as obvious in B2B marketing as it is in consumer markets. Alternative frameworks that focus on the value of a B2B brand as a resource have been discussed (Srivastava *et al.* 1998). The resource-based view of the firm which regards brands as a market-based asset or resource provides an alternative perspective which emphasises the brand's importance in maintaining inter-organisational relationships. While B2B firms ensure that a product meets the buyer's specification through attention to the product attributes and benefits, most transactions have a long-term relationship component. B2B purchasing within the supply chain shows how brands can enhance the customer's business, particularly when firms have complementary resources.

Some research findings suggest that brand strength may not always be advantageous where the brand does not complement the buying firm's resources. Further research should identify the potential costs of B2B brands as well as the benefits to buyers and the circumstances where brands are important or less important in interfirm relationships. Such research could examine the nature of the purchase (e.g. rebuy, modified rebuy or new purchase) and its brand equity implications. Research into product and service processes could also explore how B2B brands may reduce market acceptance and solution implementation time. The impact of B2B brands on market performance needs to be explicitly examined alongside these other-firm resources. B2B branding effects should also be considered against a wider portfolio of relationship outcomes other than customer satisfaction and loyalty. Research should also investigate the usefulness of B2B brands in acquiring customers, customer retention, customer education, price concessions and customer solutions. In addition, supply chain issues including the role of B2B brands in cost minimisation, managing channel conflict and cooperation could be further explored.

References

Anderson, J C & Narus, J A 2004, *Business Market Management: Understanding, Creating and Delivering Value* (2nd ed.), Upper Saddle River, NJ, Prentice Hall Inc.

Ballantyne, D & Aitken, R 2007, 'Branding in B2B markets: insights from the service-dominant logic of marketing', *Journal of Business & Industrial Marketing*, Vol. 22 No. 6, pp. 363-371.

Bendixen, M, Bukasa, K A & Abratt, R 2004, 'Brand equity in the business-to-business market', *Industrial Marketing Management*, Vol. 33 No. 5, pp. 371-380.

Bennett, R, Hartel, C E J & McColl-Kennedy, J R 2005, 'Experience as a moderator of involvement and satisfaction on brand loyalty in a business-to-business setting', *Industrial Marketing Management*, Vol. 34 No. 1, pp. 97-107.

Beverland, M 2005, 'Creating value for channel partners: the Cervena case', *Journal of Business & Industrial Marketing*, Vol. 20 No. 3, pp. 127-135.

Blombäck, A & Axelsson B 2007, 'The role of corporate brand image in the selection of new subcontractors', *Journal of Business & Industrial Marketing*, Vol. 22 No. 6, pp. 418-430.

Boyle, E 2007, 'A process model of brand cocreation: brand management and research implications', *Journal of Product & Brand Management*, Vol. 16 No. 2, pp. 122-131.

Brodie, R J, Glynn, M S & Little, V 2006, 'The service brand and the service-dominant logic: missing fundamental premise or the need for stronger theory?' *Marketing Theory*, Vol. 6 No. 3, pp. 363-379.

Combs, J G & Ketchen, D J, Jr. 1999, 'Explaining interfirm cooperation and performance: Toward a reconciliation of predictions from the resource-based view and organizational economics', *Strategic Management Journal*, Vol. 20 No. 9, pp. 867-888.

Coviello, N E, Brodie, R J, Danaher, P J & Johnston, W J 2002, 'How firms relate to their markets: an empirical examination of contemporary marketing practices', *Journal of Marketing*, Vol. 66 No. 3, pp. 33-46.

Cretu, A E & Brodie, R J 2007, 'The influence of brand image and company reputation where manufacturers market to small firms: A customer value perspective', *Industrial Marketing Management*, Vol. 36 No.2, pp. 230-240.

Davis, D F, Golicic, S L & Marquardt, A J 2008, 'Branding a B2B service: Does a brand differentiate a logistics service provider?' *Industrial Marketing Management*, Vol. 37 No.2, pp. 218-227.

de Chernatony, L & McDonald, M 2003, *Creating powerful brands: in consumer, service and industrial markets* (3rd ed.), Oxford, Elsevier/Butterworth-Heinemann.

Dyer, J H & Singh, H 1998, 'The relational view: cooperative strategy and sources of inter-organizational competitive advantage', *Academy of Management Review*, Vol. 23 No. 4, pp. 660-679.

Erdem, T & Swait, J 1998, 'Brand equity as a signalling phenomenon', *Journal of Consumer Psychology*, Vol. 7 No. 2, pp. 131-157.

Firth, M 1993, 'Price setting and the value of a strong brand name', *International Journal of Research in Marketing*, Vol. 10 No. 4, pp. 381-386.

Ford, D 1998, *Managing Business Relationships*, Chichester (England), Wiley.

Ghosh, M & John, G 1999, 'Governance value analysis and marketing strategy', *Journal of Marketing*, Vol. 63, Special Issue, pp. 131-145.

Glynn, M 2007, 'How retail category differences moderate retailer perceptions of manufacturer brands', *Australasian Marketing Journal*, Vol. 15 No. 2, pp. 55-67.

Glynn, M S, Motion, J M & Brodie, R J 2007, 'Sources of brand benefits in manufacturer-reseller B2B relationships', *Journal of Business & Industrial Marketing*, Vol. 22 No. 6, pp. 400-409.

Gordon, G L, Calantone, R J & Di Benedetto, C A 1993, 'Brand equity in the business-to-business sector: An exploratory study', *Journal of Product & Brand Management*, Vol. 2 No. 3, pp. 4-16.

Gregory, J R & Sexton, D E 2007, 'Hidden wealth in B2B brands', *Harvard Business Review*, Vol. 85 No. 3, p. 23.

Han, S-L & Sung, H-S 2008, 'Industrial brand value and relationship performance in business markets - A general structural equation model', *Industrial Marketing Management*, Vol. 37 No. 7, pp. 807-818.

Helm, B & Arndt, M 2008, 'Best Global Brands', *Business Week* No. 4101, p. 52.

Hutton, J G 1997, 'A study of brand equity in an organisational buying context', *Journal of Product and Brand Management*, Vol. 6 No. 6, pp. 428-439.

Keller, K L 2003, *Strategic brand management: building, measuring, and managing brand equity* (2nd ed.), Upper Saddle River, N.J., Prentice Hall.

Kotler, P & Pfoertsch, W 2006, *B2B brand management*, Berlin ; New York, Springer.

Kuhn, K L, Alpert, F & Pope, N K Ll. 2008, 'An application of Keller's brand equity model in a B2B context', *Qualitative Market Research: An International Journal*, Vol. 11 No. 1, pp. 40-58.

Lee, J, Park, S Y, Baek, I & Lee, C-S 2008, 'The impact of the brand management system on brand performance in B-B and B-C environments', *Industrial Marketing Management*, Vol. 37 No. 7, pp. 848-855.

Lynch, J & de Chernatony, L 2004, 'The power of emotion: Brand communication in business-to-business markets', *Journal of Brand Management*, Vol. 11 No. 5, pp. 403-419.

McQuiston, D H 2004, 'Successful branding of a commodity product: The case of RAEX LASER steel', *Industrial Marketing Management*, Vol. 33 No. 4, pp. 345 -354.

Michell, P, King, J & Reast, J 2001, 'Brand values related to industrial products', *Industrial Marketing Management*, Vol. 30 No. 5, pp. 415-425.

Mudambi, S 2002, 'Branding importance in business-to-business markets: Three buyer clusters', *Industrial Marketing Management*, Vol. 31 No. 6, pp. 525-533.

Ringberg, T & Gupta, S F 2003, 'The importance of understanding the symbolic world of customers in asymmetric business-to-business relationships', *Journal of Business & Industrial Marketing*, Vol. 18 No. 6/7, pp. 607-626.

Roberts, J & Merrilees, B 2007, 'Multiple roles of brands in business-to-business services', *Journal of Business & Industrial Marketing*, Vol. 22 No. 6, pp. 410-417.

Rust, R T, Zeithaml, V A & Lemon, K N 2004, 'Customer-centered brand management', *Harvard Business Review*, Vol. 82 No. 9, pp. 110-118.

Shaw, J, Giglierano, J & Kallis, J 1989, 'Marketing complex technical products: the importance of intangible attributes.' *Industrial Marketing Management*, Vol. 18 No. 1, pp. 45-53.

Shipley, D & Howard, P 1993, 'Brand-naming industrial products', *Industrial Marketing Management*, Vol. 22 No. 1, pp. 59-66.

Srivastava, R K, Shervani, T A & Fahey, L 1998, 'Market-based assets and shareholder value: A framework for analysis', *Journal of Marketing*, Vol. 62 No. 1, pp. 2-18.

Van Riel, A C R, Pahud de Mortanges, C & Streukens, S 2005, 'Marketing antecedents of industrial brand equity: An empirical investigation in specialty chemicals', *Industrial Marketing Management*, Vol. 34 No. 8, pp. 841-847.

Vargo, S L & Lusch, R F 2004, 'Evolving to a new dominant logic for marketing.' *Journal of Marketing*, Vol. 68 No. 1, pp. 1-17.

Walley, K, Custance, P, Taylor, S, Lindgreen, A & Hingley, M 2007, 'The importance of brand in the industrial purchase decision: a case study of the UK tractor market', *Journal of Business & Industrial Marketing*, Vol. 22 No. 6, pp. 383-393.

Wright, O & Frazer, L 2007, 'A multiple case analysis of franchised co-branding', *Australasian Marketing Journal*, Vol. 15 No. 2, pp. 68-80.

Yanamandram, V & White, L 2006, 'Switching barriers in business-to-business services: a qualitative study', *International Journal of Service Industry Management*, Vol. 17 No. 2, pp. 158-192.

Yoon, E & Kijewski, V 1995, 'The brand awareness-to-preference link in business markets: a study of the semiconductor manufacturing industry', *Journal of Business-to-Business Marketing*, Vol. 2 No. 4, pp. 7-36.

Author biography

Mark S Glynn is a Senior Lecturer in the Faculty of Business and Law at Auckland University of Technology, Auckland, New Zealand. He has a Master of Commerce degree with first class honours and a PhD in Marketing from the University of Auckland. In 2006, Mark won the Emerald/EFMD best thesis award for outstanding doctoral research in Marketing Strategy. Prior to his academic career, Mark had fifteen years business experience in brand management. His research experience is in the areas of branding, relationship marketing, business-to-business marketing and private label branding. Mark has published in the *Australasian Marketing Journal, Industrial Marketing Management, International Journal of Retail & Distribution Management, Journal of Product and Brand Management, Journal of Business & Industrial Marketing*, as well as *Marketing Theory*. Mark is also co-editor of *Business-to-Business Brand Management: Theory, Research and Executive Case Study Exercises* which is Volume 15 of the Advances in Business Marketing and Purchasing Series.

Contact: Mark S Glynn, Faculty of Business and Law, Auckland University of Technology, Private Bag 92006, Auckland 1142, New Zealand; E mark.glynn@aut.ac.nz.

Chapter 11

Legal aspects of brand management

Andrew Terry

Abstract

The law plays a central role in branding. The utility, and the value, of brands is built on their legal recognition and protection. The registered trademark regime under the *Trade Marks Act 1995* (Cth) is the primary instrument for brand protection through the monopoly it confers on the proprietors of distinctive names and logos. In Australia there are almost half a million registered trademarks (and closer to three quarters of a million if registrations in multiple classes are counted). This protection is supplemented by the common law passing off action and by the prohibition of misleading conduct under the *Trade Practices Act 1974* (Cth) – both of which provide important residual protection for unregistered marks and for elements of the brand beyond the reach of the *Trade Marks Act*.

This chapter outlines the legal protection for brands. It addresses the extension of the scope of protection under the *Trade Marks Act* from traditional notions of trademarks to aspects of packaging, shape, colour, sound and scent, and to the development of passing off and misleading conduct into versatile actions offering brand protection beyond the scope of registered trademark protection. The challenge of protecting brands in a global business environment is also considered.

Keywords

trademarks; registered trademarks; unregistered trademarks; passing off; misleading conduct; proprietary rights; intangible assets

Introduction

> *The protection of trade marks is the law's recognition of the psychological function of symbols. If it is true that we live by symbols, it is no less true that we purchase goods by them. A trademark is a merchandising short cut which induces a purchaser to select what he wants, or what he has been led to believe he wants. The owner of a mark exploits this human propensity by making every effort to impregnate the atmosphere of the market with the drawing power of a congenial symbol. Whatever the means employed, the aim is the same – to convey through the mark, in the minds of potential customers, the desirability of the commodity upon which it appears. Once this is attained, the trademark owner has something of value. If another poaches upon the commercial magnetism of the symbol he has created, the owner can obtain legal redress.*
>
> Frankfurter J in *Mishawaka Rubber & Woollen Mfg. Co v S.S. Kresge Co*
> 316 US 203 at 205 (1942)

The value of brands is built on their legal recognition and protection. The law does not create brands, but it sustains them and thereby supports the massive branding industry which is an entrenched feature of contemporary commerce. Their value is built on a complex legal regime – primarily legislative but supplemented by the common law – which has evolved to recognise and protect brands. The legal aspects of branding are a non-negotiable reality of branding. Without legal protection, a brand may emerge but cannot survive.

The law does not recognise or protect 'brands' as such. It recognises and protects trademarks which are the primary legal expression of the marketing concept of brand and the oldest form of intellectual property right in the world. IP Australia – the Australian Government agency responsible for administering patents, trademarks, designs and plant breeders' rights – records that protection of the public against wrongly marked goods can be traced back to early Roman times, and comments that: 'Our punishment today for infringing a trademark is not as exemplary as that of the Elector Palantine, in the 14th century, who took so grave a view of an innkeeper who had passed off a rather low grade wine for a superior variety known as 'Rudesheimer' that he had him hanged'.

Australia's regulatory regime for protecting brands is relatively complex. Regulatory regimes for 'company names', 'business names', and 'domain names' are all part of the rich tapestry. As noted by the Australian Government's Advisory Committee on Intellectual Property (ACIP):

> *Trade marks and business, company and domain names are four distinct identifiers that serve different purposes in the market place. The registration of a trade mark provides exclusive rights to the use of that mark, whereas the registration of a domain name provides a license to use that internet address, and the registration of business and company names are essentially legal obligations on the part of those intending to conduct business.*
>
> ACIP 2006, p. 4.2

The *Corporations Act 2001* (Cth) requires a registered company to have a company name unless its ACN is used as its 'name' (s117(2)(b)). Except in the case of an ACN name which is unique if not inspiring, a company name is *not* a unique identifier and 'company names that are confusingly similar (but not identical) to registered business names can be registered and traded under, creating potential conflicts' (ACIP 2006, p. 4.2)

The Business Names legislation of each state and territory requires a business to register its trading name if the business is not being carried on under its own name. ACIP notes that although an application for a business name which is identical to an existing company name will not be registered and that a name that is identical to an existing business name in that state is unlikely to be registered, the test for pre-existing business names are very literal. Although, for example, an application for registration of a business name *Fred's Pie* in NSW is unlikely to succeed if there is already such a business name in NSW, a variation to *Fred's Hot Pies* may be accepted' (ACIP 2004, p. 3).

Domain name registration is administered, for Australian domain names, by .au Domain Administration Ltd, an industry self regulatory body. Registration is on a 'first come, first served' basis subject to eligibility rules, but no checks are made to see whether the domain name is identical to or similar to a registered company name, a business name or a trademark registered by another person. ACIP has noted that it is a public misconception that domain name registrars check for existing prior rights such as a registered trademarks when registering a domain name (ACIP 2006, p.5).

The business, company and domain name regimes exist to provide quasi-unique identifiers but do not confer proprietary rights. ACIP has noted that confusion exists in the business community as to the nature of the rights, if any, associated with each identifier: 'Not only is it often mistakenly believed that business and company names grant *proprietary rights* analogous to those conferred by trade mark registration, it is at times thought that business, company, and domain names offer a form of *immunity* from infringement of a registered trade mark' (ACIP 2006, p. 4.2). In its earlier *Issues Paper*, ACIP noted that: 'The registration of a domain name does not of itself confer proprietary rights in the use of that name' (ACIP 2006, p. 3). This is the role of the *Trade Marks Act 1995* (Cth) – the only regulatory regime which confers proprietary rights through which value is accumulated and protected. The focus of this chapter is on trademarks which the law recognises and protects either as *registered* trademarks under the *Trade Marks Act* and which may identified by the universal symbol ®, or as *unregistered* trademarks which may be identified by the symbol ™, and which – although not established and protected by the *Trade Marks Act* – may be protected by the common law under the tort of passing off or by the statutory action for misleading or deceptive conduct under s52 of the *Trade Practices Act 1974* (Cth).

Unregistered trademarks

The opening paragraph of this chapter suggested that, although the law does not create brands, it provides the legal infrastructure to support and sustain them. It is nevertheless interesting, if not important, to record that the law is entitled to some credit for the development of branding. Under the ancient Assize of Bread and Ale, enacted in the mid thirteenth century and the first law in British history to regulate the production and sale of food, medieval traders were required to distinguish their goods by marks to enable the identification of manufacturers of adulterated goods. The unintended consequence was the promotion of branding. Customers began to select particular bakers and brewers whose product they enjoyed on the basis of the distinguishing mark, which in turn led to unethical traders applying a competitor's mark to their own less attractive product, which in turn demanded a legal response. Centuries before the enactment of trademarks legislation[28], the common law extended its protection to the trader's goodwill in his or her mark through an action which became known as 'passing off'. By the early twentieth century, the tort was capable of protecting goodwill in a range of circumstances. Equity freed the action from any requirement of deceit[29] and established that the basis of the action was to protect the trader's property in 'the business or goodwill likely to be injured by misrepresentation rather than the narrower protection of right of property in a mark, name, or get-up' (*Spalding v Gamage* (1916) 32 RPC 273 at 284). Today there are three elements, often referred to as the 'classical trinity', which must be fulfilled – goodwill owned by a trader, misrepresentation, and damage to goodwill[30]. In practice, the plaintiff must:

(i) establish a goodwill or reputation attached to the goods or services;

(ii) demonstrate a misrepresentation by the defendant to the public (whether or not intentional) leading or likely to lead the public to believe that the goods or services offered by him are the goods or services of the plaintiff; and

(iii) demonstrate that the misrepresentation has caused or threatened damage to the plaintiff's reputation or goodwill.

In *Reckitt & Colman Ltd v Borden Inc* (1990) 17 IPR 1, 7 Lord Oliver commented that the law of passing off can be summarised in one short general proposition: 'No man may pass of his goods as those of another'.

A much more recent addition to the brand proprietor's armoury has been s52 of the *Trade Practices Act 1974* (Cth) which provides that:

---

28 The *Merchandise Marks Act 1862* (UK) introduced a criminal code relating to false marking but a register of trade marks did not emerge until the *Trade Marks Registration Act 1875* (UK). Australia's first Federal legislation was the *Trade Marks Act 1905* (Cth) although prior to federation each of the colonies had their own trade marks legislation and had established trade mark registers.

29 *Singer Manufacturing Co v Wilson* (1887) 3 App Cas 376 (House of Lords).

30 *Erwen Warnick BV v Townend & Sons (Hull) Ltd* [1979] AC 731 (House of Lords); *ConAgra Inc v McCain Foods (Aust) Pty Ltd* (1992) 33 FLR 302 (Full Federal Court).

> *A corporation shall not, in trade or commerce, engage in conduct that is misleading or deceptive or is likely to mislead or deceive.*

Section 52 has been described as a 'comprehensive provision of wide impact' (per Fox J in *Brown v Jam Factory Pty Ltd* (1981) ATPR 40-213 at 42,928). At the time of the introduction of the *Trade Practices Act*, the proposition that s52 would become one of the most important and most litigated provisions in the entire statute book would have been greeted with some scepticism. It is located in Part V, Division 1 under the heading 'Consumer protection – unfair practices', and it was intended as a residual consumer protection provision to catch conduct falling outside the specific prohibitions which follow it. Its metamorphosis from its intended consumer protection role to a versatile and significant action for purely *inter partes* and essentially commercial litigation is without precedent in Australian jurisprudence. Section 52, in conjunction with a range of flexible civil remedies, acts as a broad-spectrum antidote to a wide range of conduct falling short of the norm that it establishes. It does not simply add to the general law, but in some circumstances totally embraces common law actions. In the branding space, the common law passing off action and the statutory misleading conduct action overlap. In *Hornsby Building Information Centre Pty Ltd v Sydney Building Information Centre Ltd* (1978) ATPR 40-067 at 17,693, Murphy J observed that 'passing off is a classical example of misleading or deceptive conduct'. Although the doctrinal bases of the common law and the statutory actions are different – the tort of passing off is designed to protect the plaintiff's property in the business or goodwill likely to be injured by the misrepresentation, whereas s52 is designed to protect consumers from misleading or deceptive conduct – both actions are activated by a misrepresentation and the overlap is well established. As Mason J explained in *Parkdale Custom Built Furniture Pty Ltd v Puxu Pty Ltd* (1982) ATPR 40-307 (at 43,785):

> *The remedy to prevent deception of the public often has the incidental effect of protecting a competing trader's goodwill which would also be injured by that description.*

In cases where trademarks are unregistered, the tort of passing off and s52 provide significant protection in circumstances where a competitor's use of another trader's mark or name or other indicator constitutes a misrepresentation. In branding cases, the actions are virtually indistinguishable and invariably operate in tandem as alternative actions. But despite the undoubted efficacy of passing off and s52 in relation to unregistered marks, the protection is nevertheless limited. While the *Trade Marks Act* provides a monopoly in relation to the trademark in relation to the particular goods or services distinguished by the trademark, the protection of passing off and s52 is only as wide as the reputation of the brand for which protection is sought. The actions are activated by a misrepresentation. This can be made out only if the plaintiff has an established reputation in relation to which the respondent's conduct can be characterised as a misrepresentation. A plaintiff with a reputation in a name or brand in a particular geographic area may succeed in restraining a competitor from carrying on business using that name in that area, but will not succeed in restraining the defendant from using that name in areas where the plaintiff has no prior reputation.

For example, in *Targetts Pty Ltd v Target Australia Pty* [1993] FCA 191 the respondent, which at the time of the litigation had 82 discount department stores throughout mainland Australia, was restrained from using its name in connection with any business of retail sale of clothing, footwear or manchester products within 30 kilometres of the intersection of Charles and Brisbane streets in Launceston Tasmania. In this area, the reputation in the substantially identical name 'Targetts' resided with a local department store. The respondent's use of its name in this geographic area was held to be likely to mislead or deceive members of the public in Launceston and also constituted passing off. Heerey J stated that:

> The existence of the reputation of Targetts in Launceston and the likelihood of deception amongst its customers and potential customers by the use of a deceptively similar name and logo by Target persuade me to the conclusion that such conduct by Target would constitute the tort of passing off, actionable at the suit of Targetts.

In *Taco Co. of Australia Inc. v Taco Bell Pty Ltd* (1982) 42 ALR 177, the Full Federal Court held that a substantial and long-established US franchised system which operated in the US under the name 'Taco Bell' could not restrain a Sydney restaurant from carrying on business under that name. The Sydney company had used the name for four years before the US company commenced operations in Sydney. It was held that the Sydney restaurant's use of the name was not misleading or deceptive. The US company's reputation did not extend to Australia and the reputation in the name 'Taco Bell' in Sydney resided in the local company. It was the US company which had engaged in misleading or deceptive conduct and passing off by using a name that was associated locally with that used by the Sydney restaurant. The *Taco Bell* case has been criticised for its hard-line approach in requiring business activity within the jurisdiction, even though that activity could be slight and need not require an actual place of business in the jurisdiction. A more liberal test was laid down a decade later by the Full Federal Court in *ConAgra Inc v McCain Foods (Aust) Pty Ltd* (1992) 33 FCR 302. The court distinguished use in the jurisdiction from reputation in the jurisdiction, holding that it was not necessary for a trader to have a place of business in Australia or even sell its goods in Australia to be successful in maintaining a passing off action. The restatement of the passing off requirement from 'goodwill attached to a business' to 'reputation in the jurisdiction' has facilitated the protection of business reputation in Australia, but the actual decision in *ConAgra* nevertheless indicates the difficulty in establishing the requisite 'sufficient reputation' (Terry & Forrest 2008, p. 194).

> In the absence of a misrepresentation there is no remedy. Passing off and s52 cannot restrain 'misappropriation' – 'reaping without sowing' – if appropriate disclaimers preclude any possibility of misrepresentation (Terry 1988, p. 296); (Terry 1989, p. 204). In the 'Duff Beer' case (Twentieth Century Fox Film Group v The South Australia Brewing Co Ltd 1996) ATPR 41-483) Tamberlin J accepted that "An express disclaimer can, if sufficiently prominent, destroy

any suggestion of association between a character and the product under consideration".

It was nevertheless held in relation to 'Duff' beer that a disclaimer of an association with the television series 'The Simpsons' would not be effective as, rather than indicating a dissociation, the disclaimer would reinforce the conclusion that the beer was intended to be marketed with a keen awareness of the existence of 'The Simpsons' programme and with the force of 'The Simpsons association'.

In one respect, however, the protection is wider than the *Trade Marks Act*. Although the origins of passing off lie in the common law's recognition of a trader's right to protect its mark, the tort has developed into a versatile action protecting promotional as well as trading goodwill in a range of circumstances which makes it an important weapon in the branding armoury. In *Cadbury Schweppes Pty Ltd v Pub Squash Co Pty Ltd* (1981) 55 ALJR 333 at 336, Lord Scarman held that:

> *[Passing off] is wide enough to encompass other descriptive material, such as slogans or visual images, which radio, television or newspaper advertising campaigns can lead the market to associate with a plaintiff's product, provided always that such descriptive material has become part of the goodwill of the product.*

Section 52 similarly provides a broad spectrum antidote to misleading conduct in a range of branding scenarios beyond the trademark itself. The passing off and statutory actions are not specific in their application and provide a remedy in a variety of cases of commercial misrepresentation, whether in relation to names, get-up and trade dress, advertising or other indicators constituting a misrepresentation of association, sponsorship, approval, endorsement or some other commercial connection.

The *Red Bull* litigation[31] provides an example. The facts, as outlined in a later case[32], were that two competing energy drink products – 'Red Bull' and 'LiveWire' – were packaged in cans of similar size and colour. The cans each had a 'strong diagonal thrust' in their design. There were significant differences, including the brand names and the forms of writing on the cans. There was emphasis, by an expert witness at trial, on what was described as the 'gestalt' of the brand, in the sense of '[a]*n integrated perceptual structure or unity conceived, as functionally more than the sum of its parts',* which was said to be *'almost identical'*. The Full Court held that, where the purchaser may have in mind the connotations of the name rather than the name itself, such connotations may tend to undermine what might otherwise be a basis for clear distinction. Similar colour combinations and the diagonal thrust of designs, notwithstanding the fact that other minor players in the market traded under similar colours, affected the Court's conclusion that there was a capacity to deceive. The Federal Court held that this postulation of *gestalt* – 'the overall identity

---

31   *Red Bull Australia Pty Ltd v Sydneywide Distributors Pty Ltd* [2001] FCA 1228 (Federal Court), upheld on appeal *Sydneywide Distributors Pty Ltd v Red Bull Australia Pty Ltd* [2002] FCAFC 157 (Full Court).

32   *Natural Waters of Viti Ltd v Dayals (Fiji) Artesian Waters Ltd* [2007] FCA 200 per Bennett J.

of a brand as it relates to consumers', being the identity which included 'not only the name, colour, physical properties and packing, but also associations with the brand and branding defects used to create associations, including its advertising and the 'channels' through which it is sold' – did not extend beyond the permissible limits of the traditional concept of 'get-up' as understood and referred to in the authorities. The 'total image' and 'brand associations' of *Red Bull*, as established by extensive advertising and promotion, were such that passing off and s52 actions were successful.

Registered trademarks

The primary machinery for the protection of brands is the registered trademark system. The tort of passing off and s52 provide versatile residual protection in cases of unauthorised use of unregistered marks, but proprietary rights are available only if a trademark is registered under the *Trade Marks Act 1995* (Cth). The *Act* grants a national monopoly in the brand in relation to the goods or services[33] for which it is registered, and avoids the 'difficult and expensive litigation' (*Re 'Holly Hobbie' trade mark* (1984) 1 IPR 486 at 488) which invariably accompanies passing off and s52 actions. Currently, over 60,000 applications for registration are lodged each year in Australia with over 45,000 trademarks registered annually

For 2007-2008, 61,690 applications were lodged, although when applications for the same mark in multiple classes are included the number is 112,045. In 2007-2008, 46,305 trademarks were registered (83,447 multiple classes). In 2007-2008, the leading applicants for registration were:

Table 11.1 Leading applicants for registration

Applicant Name	Country Code	Total Applications 2007
Glaxo Group Limited	GB	111
ALDI Foods Pty Ltd	AU	98
Societe Des Produits Nestle SA	CH	94
Johnson & Johnson	US	87
Telstra Corporation Limited	AU	82
Aristocrat Technologies Australia Pty Ltd	AU	80
Mars Australia Pty Ltd	AU	80
Woolworths Limited	AU	75
Australian Football League	AU	71
Novartis AG	CH	67
Source: IP Australia		

[33] Originally registration was available only in respect of goods, but amendments to the *Trade Marks Act 1955* (Cth) allowed registration in relation to services from 1 February 1980.

The current regime is enshrined in the *Trade Marks Act 1995* which extends the availability of statutory registration beyond that available under the former *Trade Marks Act 1955* which was limited to 'a device, brand, heading, label, ticket, name, signature, work, letter or numeral, or any combination thereof' which indicated a 'connection in the course of trade'. The *1995 Act* significantly broadens the concept of a registrable trademark. 'Trade mark' is defined in s17 as:

> *a sign used, or intended to be used, to distinguish goods or services dealt with or provided in the course of trade by a person from goods or services so dealt with or provided by any other person.*

'Sign' is defined in s6 as:

> *[including] the following or any combination of the following, namely any letter, word, name, signature, numeral, device, brand, heading, label, ticket, aspect of packaging, shape, colour, sound or scent.*

The availability of protection for aspects of packaging, shape, colour, sound or scent is particularly significant and extends considerably the scope of a registrable brand.

There are nevertheless – but not surprisingly – relatively few registrations for the new intangible marks. There are three major registration requirements. Any 'trade mark' can be registered if it is used or intended to be used, is capable of being represented graphically, and distinguishes the applicant's goods or services. The graphical representation requirement poses challenges particularly for sounds and scents. The *Trade Mark Regulations* (reg 4.3(7)) provide that, if registration is sought in respect of a colour, shape, scent, sound or aspect of packing, the application for registration must include a 'concise and accurate description of the trade mark'. Scents and sounds themselves cannot be registered, but their graphical representation can. The distinctiveness requirement is a significant threshold which all trademark applicants must meet, and which is nevertheless particularly challenging for applicants for intangible marks. Section 41(2) of the *Trade Marks Act 1995* (Cth) requires that the trademark be capable of distinguishing the goods or services of the applicant from the goods or services of other traders. In making this determination, the Registrar must have regard to the extent to which the trademark is 'inherently adapted to distinguish the designated goods or services from the goods or services of other persons'.

Table 11.2 Colour, shape, scent and sound trademarks 1996-2008

	Filed	Registered	Rejected	Pending
Colour	866	206	579	81
Shape	1975	659	1130	186
Scent	8	0	7	1
Sound	72	40	30	2
Source IP Australia				

In *BP plc v Woolworths Ltd* (2004) FCA 1362, Finkelstein J referred to US authorities in relation to the categories of 'distinctiveness':

> *The categories are: (1) generic; (2) descriptive; (3) suggestive; and (4) arbitrary or fanciful. Generic terms can never be trade marks. Descriptive terms can, but only if they have acquired a secondary meaning. Suggestive, arbitrary or fanciful terms are inherently distinctive.*

The reference to 'secondary meaning' is a reference to distinctiveness which is not inherent but which is acquired from the effect of the owner's efforts in the marketplace. If the Registrar finds that the trademark is not 'inherently adapted to distinguish' the applicant's goods or services, the trademark may nevertheless be registered if the applicant has sufficient evidence of use of the trademark prior to filing the trademark application to establish that the mark does in face 'distinguish the designated goods or services as being those of the application' (s41(6)).

Satisfying distinctiveness is a particular challenge in relation to sound and scent marks. Finkelstein J in *BP plc* explained the challenge in relation to colour in these terms:

> *Most objects have to be of some colour. So merely applying a colour to a product will not act as an identifier for that product. In deciding whether colour functions as a trade mark it is necessary to determine whether the trader has used the colour in a way that informs the public that the product emanates from a particular source. Put another way, colour must be used to distinguish products and not as mere ornamentation or decoration.*

In *BP plc* – an appeal from a decision of the Registrar of Trade Marks which refused BP's application to register the colour green in relation to fuel products and services – Finkelstein J held that the colour green in the particular shade in the application was not inherently distinctive of BP's goods and services – it was a colour used quite innocently by other owners and operators of service stations and is simply descriptive. The colour green could only be distinctive if it had acquired a 'secondary meaning':

> *Accordingly, for BP to succeed in its appeals it must establish two things: first, that it has used the particular shade of green as a trade mark and, second, that in the minds of the public the primary significance of that shade of green, when sued in connection with the supply of petroleum products or the provision of petroleum services, identifies the source of those goods or the provider of those services as originating from a particular trader, though not necessarily from an identified trader.*

Although the Full Court did not disagree with this reasoning, it allowed Woolworth's appeal from the decision of the Federal Court allowing registration. Although green was the prominent colour used by BP, it was not the exclusive colour. The Full Court was 'unable to conclude that any trade mark was of colour by BP ... has been other than green as the dominant colour in conjunction with yellow as the subsidiary colour'. The mere fact that consumers associated green with BP did not satisfy the test of distinctiveness: 'Evidence of promotion and use does not, without more, demonstrate distinctiveness'. Survey evidence establishing that consumer's associated green with BP service stations was not convincing:

> The trade mark applications are not for the colour green alone. They are not of the colour green alone as a trade mark, as the predominant colour of the service station. They are for the use of the colour green as the predominant colour of the trade mark that is to be applied to the fascias of buildings, petrol pumps etc. This calls for, or implies within the available scope of the trade mark, the use of another (unspecified) colour or colours. On the other hand, the stimulus was ... for the colour green alone ... although it was only the predominant colour over the service station. This stimulus posits a different trade mark than claimed in the application.[34]

The *Trade Marks Act* adopts international practice (*Nice Agreement* 1957) in establishing 45 trademark classes – 34 of goods and 11 for services[35]. Registration can be obtained in more than one class, but registration is granted only for the goods or services in each particular class in respect of which the registration requirements – essentially 'distinctiveness' – have been satisfied.

In addition to registration to protect a trademark which distinguishes the applicant's goods or services from those of other traders, there is provision in the Act for three other forms of registration in respect of: defensive trademarks; certification trademarks; and collective trademarks. *Defensive trademarks* are trademarks that are so well known that their use by another person in respect of other goods or services will be taken to indicate that there is a connection between those other goods or services and the registered owner of the trademark and can be registered even through the 'used or intended to be used' requirement cannot be statistical (s185). *Certification trademarks* are signs certified by the owner or a person approved by the owner in relation to quality accuracy or some other characteristic (including, in the case of goods, original material or mode of manufacture) and which distinguish the goods or services from other goods or services (s169). *Collective trademarks* are signs used which distinguish the goods or services 'dealt with or provided in the course of trade by members of an association' from goods or services of persons who are not members of the association (s162).

Registration is granted not to a trademark in isolation but in relation to particular goods or services distinguished by the trademark. The owner of a registered trademark has the exclusive rights to use the mark in relation to the goods and/or services in respect of which it is registered, to authorise others to use the mark in relation to the goods and/or services in respect of which it is registered, and to obtain relief in the event of infringement (s20). A registered trademark is infringed if another person uses a mark in relation to goods or services in respect of which the trademark is registered (s20(1)), or when a substantially identical or deceptively similar mark is used on goods or services similar to those covered by a registered trademark (s102 (2)).

---

[34] *Woolworths Limited v BP plc* [2006] FCAFC 132.
[35] The trade mark classes are set out in Schedule 1 of the *Trade Mark Regulations*.

The tests for determining whether another person has used a sign 'substantially identical' or 'deceptively similar' to the registered trademark are well established. In the case of 'substantial identity', the signs are compared side by side and similarities to or differences from the essential features, as identified by the judgment of the court and the evidence, are assessed. If they differ only in inessential respects, they are 'substantially identical'. In the case of 'deceptive similarity', the courts are guided by s10 which provides that a 'trade mark is taken to be deceptively similar to another trade mark if it so closely resembles that other mark that it is likely to deceive or cause confusion'.

In the latter case, the alleged infringer is given a defence if it is established that the use of the mark 'is not likely to deceive or cause confusion' (s120 (2)). There is a third category of infringement which relates to 'well-known' marks which can be infringed by the use of substantially identical or deceptively similar marks in relation to unrelated goods or services where the plaintiff's mark is so 'well known in Australia ... the sign would be likely to be taken as indicating a connection between the unrelated goods or services and the registered owner of the trade mark' such that the owner's interests 'are likely to be adversely affected' (120(3).

Registration is initially for a period of 10 years (s72) and thereafter it can be reviewed indefinitely at 10-yearly intervals. A registered mark can be removed from the Register if it was improperly obtained (s88) or for non-use (Part 9). A registered trademark can also be removed from the Register, and the exclusivity conferred on the owner lost, if the registered trademark 'consists of a sign that, after ... registration ... becomes generally accepted within the relevant trade as the sign that describes or is the name of an article, substance or service' (s27, s87); i.e. if the trademark loses its distinctiveness and becomes a generic term identifying a product group rather than the branded product. There is irony in that the success of a trademark has the potential to threaten its validity – as the original proprietors of registered trademarks such as 'kerosene', 'escalator' and 'cellophane', which are now in the public domain, have found to their cost.

Colleen Segall suggests the following rules be applied to protect a trademark from becoming generic:

1. Distinguish a trademark from surrounding text by adopting a fanciful typeface, capitalisation, initial caps in quotes, bold rather than plain lettering, or a different colour.

2. Use a trademark as a proper adjective, not as a common descriptive adjective, followed by the common descriptive name (noun) of the product. The correct use is: 'VASELINE petroleum jelly' and this should be done at least the first time the trademark appears in any printed material. The incorrect use is: "You can apply the VASELINE'.

3. A trademark should not be used as a verb, such as 'XEROX the report'. The correct usage is: 'Copy the report on the XEROX copier'.

4. A trademark should not be used in a plural form, such as 'Use our HYPERFLOs'. The correct usage is: 'Use our HYPERFLO filters'.

5. A trademark should not be used in a possessive form, such as 'KODAK's versatility'. The correct usage is: 'A KODAK camera is versatile'.

6. Identify the trademark by using, adjacent to the trademark, the ® symbol of a registered trademark, and, if the mark is not yet registered, the ™ symbol. Alternatively, use an asterisk adjacent to the trademark to refer to a footnote which states: 'A (registered) trade mark of X company'.

The use of a footnote is also a convenient way of linking the trademark with the owner or licensee by stating 'A trade mark of X company' (Segall 1990, pp. 52-3).

The greatest, albeit inevitable, limitation on the registered trademark system is of course 'territoriality'. Trademarks are registered, and protected, under national regimes. Although under the influence of the WTO its 150 members have a non-negotiable obligation under the TRIPS agreement which mandates minimum trademark protection, 'the territorial nature of trademark law and the lack of a single universal registration system present challenges to franchisors and other brand proprietors expanding operations beyond the home market in which intellectual property rights have been secured' (Terry 2008).

A trademark registered in Australia confers protection only in Australia. Conversely, a trademark registered overseas confers no rights in Australia. The first user of a trademark with respect to particular goods or services is entitled to registration. In the absence of fraud, it is not unlawful for an Australian trader to become the registered proprietor of a mark which has been used extensively by another trader overseas, provided that there has been no use of the foreign mark in Australia at the time of application for registration. The mark need be neither novel or invented:

> [t]he fact that another's idea, word or design has been taken does not preclude an application: the objection that 'I thought of it first' has not of itself been a ground for opposition. A claim to proprietorship is precluded by a better claim, but only in respect of the same or a 'substantially identical' mark.

McKeough, Stewart & Griffith 2004, p. 508

Australian courts are nevertheless prepared in 'passive name' piracy cases to hold that prior use, however slight, by an overseas enterprise will defeat the claims of a local applicant even though the mark enjoys no general market reputation in Australia. In *Moorgate Tobacco Co Ltd v Philip Morris Ltd [No.2]* [36], Justice Deane of the High Court stated that:

> It is not necessary that there be an actual dealing in goods bearing the trade mark before there can be a local use of the mark as a trade mark. It may suffice that imported goods which have not actually reached Australia have been offered for sale in Australia under the mark …. In such cases, however, it is possible to identify an actual trade or offer to trade in the goods bearing the mark or an existing intention to offer or supply goods bearing the mark in trade.

---

[36] (1984) 156 CLR 415 at 433.

While simply holding discussions or negotiations about whether a trademark will be used in Australia is not sufficient to amount to use, the establishment of a trading channel may be considered use of the mark, even prior to sale of goods bearing the mark (Terry & Forrest 2008).

The limitations of territoriality have led to international cooperation to facilitate international registration. The 1981 *Madrid Agreement Concerning International Registration of Marks* was the first international instrument designed to simplify the administrative procedures of trademark registration in multiple jurisdictions. It, nevertheless, proved unwieldy, and therefore lacked the critical mass hoped for when key jurisdictions such as the US and the UK, amongst others, did not accede to it. Many of the objections to the Madrid Agreement were specifically addressed in the widely accepted Madrid Protocol established in 1989. Under the *Madrid Protocol*, which is administered by the World Intellectual Property Organisation, only one application need be filed. An international registration is equivalent to an application or a registration of the same mark made directly in each of the countries designated, and offers significant advantages for enterprises of member countries with international aspirations (Terry & Forrest 2008).

Conclusion

The significance of branding has not always been apparent to the judiciary, despite the role of the law in its development. In 1885, Chitty J commented that:

> *The English trader is generally too much occupied with his business to devote much time to the invention of new or fancy words, and he is not always gifted with that degree of fancy which is capable of coining new words. Besides the English public is not so ready, apparently, to buy articles passing under an entirely new name, which may give rise to a suspicion of adulteration.*

> Re Trade Mark 'Alpine' (1885) 29 Ch D 877 at 880

Developments over the last century – driven initially by the mass marketing of consumer products and more recently by the extension of the branding concept to services – have dramatically revised this paradigm. These developments have been accompanied by increased legal protection, which has enabled brand owners to 'build up in a brand a set of values, both tangible and intangible, which are appropriate and attractive to consumers and conducive to the development of customer loyalty' (Clarke & Peroff 1987, chpt 4). In the words of Graham and Perott:

> *In the broad area of marketing, nowhere else do the marketing man and the lawyer come closer together than in the area of branding. And nowhere else does the law afford those involved in marketing such powerful rights in the defence of valuable assets. Curiously, however, the relationship between marketing people, on the one hand, and trade mark lawyers, on the other, is frequently tenuous or even hostile. It would pay each side to understand and communicate with the other, for by doing so both they and their companies stand to gain the considerable advantages afforded under trade mark law (Clarke & Peroff 1987, chpt 4).*

References

ACIP (Advisory Committee on Intellectual Property) 2004, A *review of the relationship between trade marks and business names, company names and domain names, Issues Paper,* January.

ACIP (Advisory Committee on Intellectual Property) 2006, *A review of the relationship between trade marks and business names, company names and domain names,* March.

Clarke G & Peroff M 1987, 'The Legal Side of Branding', in J Murphy (ed) *Branding. A key Marketing Tool,* Macmillan Press, UK.

McKeough J, Stewart A & Griffith P 2004, *Intellectual Property in Australia,* 3rd edn, LexisNexis Butterworths, Sydney.

Segall, C 1990, 'Aspects of trade mark usage', *Law Society Journal,* October.

Terry A 1988, 'Unfair competition and the misappropriation of a competitor's trade values', *Modern Law Review,* 51.

Terry A 1989, 'Exploiting Celebrity: Character Merchandising and Unfair Trading', UNSWLJ, 12.

Terry A & Forrest H 2008, 'Where's the Beef? Why Burger King is Hungry Jack's in Australia and Other Complications in Building a Global Franchise Brand', *Journal of International Law and Business,* 171.

IP Australia is the Australian Government agency responsible for administering, inter alia, Australia's registered trademark system. Its website, www.ipaustralia.gov.au, is a valuable resource.

Author biography

Andrew Terry has recently been appointed Professor of Business Regulation in the Faculty of Economics and Business at the University of Sydney after a long career at the University of New South Wales, with the last fifteen as Head of the School of Business Law and Taxation in the Australian School of Business. Andrew's primary research interest is franchising—a sector in which the significance of branding is enshrined in the definition of franchising in the *Franchising Code of Conduct* which requires the operation of a business 'substantially or materially associated with a trade mark, advertising or commercial symbol' of the franchisor. Andrew has researched and published extensively on franchising in Australia and overseas, and is the Honorary Dean of Beijing Normal University's Franchise Management School. He has been inducted into the Australian Franchising Hall of Fame.

Contact: Professor Andrew Terry, Discipline of Business Law, Faculty of Economics and Business, Economics and Business Building (H69), The University of Sydney, NSW 2006; P +61-2-9114-0619; F +61-2-9351-7473; E andrew.terry@sydney.edu.au.

Chapter 12

Brand evolution and demise

COLIN JEVONS

ABSTRACT

Contrary to uninformed opinion, death is inevitable for most brands. Responsible brand management requires an understanding and acceptance of this inevitability, which must be planned for. Evolution – either gradual or sudden – is a consequence of a competitive marketplace and, while incompetence can speed the process of demise, it will happen anyway, as with living organisms. Managerial resources should be allocated with an understanding of this inevitability.

KEYWORDS

brand evolution; brand demise; brand life cycle

Introduction

Can a brand last forever? This question is not an irrelevant philosophical topic; it is very important for both managers and researchers. Managers need to understand the practical issues affecting brand longevity, and this fundamental issue must be well understood by researchers if their work is to be authoritative. In a dynamic and competitive marketplace, brands are continually evolving; growing, changing and dying. It has been shown that incompetent management can speed the process, but this chapter focuses not on managerial action to protect and grow the brand but instead arguing for the strategic view that all brands will eventually die no matter how competent their management. If it is impossible for the vast majority of brands to live forever, it makes no sense to plan and manage as if they were immortal. If death is inevitable, it is important to accept and plan for this.

Techniques and theories about how to keep brands viable for as long as possible have been well researched (e.g. Keller 1999; Thomas & Kohli 2009), but their validity should not be over-estimated. For example, in response to the failings of inappropriate interpretations of the product life cycle, it was claimed that 'only…poorly managed brands have a finite life cycle. …if a brand turns out to have a finite life cycle, it is not the brand that failed but the people who managed it' (Plummer 1990, p. 26). The implication here, that brands should be immortal and that it is only managerial incompetence that results in brand death, is not actually true in most cases. In another example, Paddy Barwise, in endorsing Lehu's (2006) book, asserts that 'Unlike people, brands can live and even thrive indefinitely'. For many brands and their managers, this is a dangerous proposition. The death of most brands is inevitable, as will be proven later in this chapter, and should be planned for.

(A separate chapter in this book, on brand icons, looks at a few remarkable and very high-profile exceptions.)

Species fail and become extinct, brands fail, companies fail, financial systems fail, people fail. The mathematical relationship that underpins the link between the frequency and size of the extinction of companies is virtually identical to that which describes the extinction of biological species in the fossil record; only the time scales differ (Ormerod 2005). Those biological species that have become extinct were, of course, not masters of their own destinies and did not even know about their impending demise, let alone try to avoid it. Managers quite rightly try to prolong the life of a brand as much as possible, just as medical experts try to prolong individual human lives as much as possible. Yet, although we are well aware that doctors cannot postpone the inevitable for ever, we treat business death as something to be avoided at all costs.

The knowledge and fear of death can potentially be crippling to human existence; understanding our mortality 'might dominate the human will and rob it of its freedom…an agonizing accompaniment of man's [sic] divine gift of reason' (Noyes 1973, p. 227). But back in the first century AD, the Roman Stoic philosopher Seneca argued that it was vital to conquer fear and anticipate the inevitability of death, and indeed that learning to die was the best way to manage one's life. We plan our lives as humans knowing that they are finite; if we thought we were immortal we would manage, plan and invest differently. From the point of view of consumer behaviour, it has recently been shown that materialistic individuals form strong connections with brands at least partly because of the fear of their own death (Rindfleisch *et al.* 2008) – perhaps because a luxury object gives some sense of immortality resulting from the relief of some existential anxieties through cultural acceptance (Arndt *et al.* 2004), or perhaps association with a luxury brand is an escape from the brutal reality of self-awareness (Mandel & Smeesters 2008). From the point of view of brand managers, who are supposed to act in a dispassionate manner for the objective benefit of their employer, this chapter argues that they should learn to live with and profit from the eventual death of brands rather than waste resources in vain attempts to set up brands as immortal. (For a more academic treatment of this argument, see Jevons, Ewing & Khalil 2007 and Ewing, Jevons & Khalil 2009). After all, since even children as young as the age of four understand animal and human death (Barrett & Behne 2005), surely highly trained and rewarded adults should be able to understand and incorporate that concept in their professional lives and to avoid the poor allocation of business resources that can arise from not accepting the inevitable death of brands.

The product life cycle

The product life cycle is well known. It starts with a period of investment, where resources are devoted to developing a product before any revenue is generated. On introduction to the market, a product's revenue stream starts and profits move from negative to positive and start to increase, an increase that steepens through a growth phase. Sooner or later profit and then revenue growth slow. They change to a gradual reduction during maturity and, in the final decline stage, both revenue and profit reductions accelerate and get worse until the product no longer makes a positive contribution. At this stage, alert management cuts its losses and withdraws the product from the market using a form of commercial euthanasia.

This popular model has provided useful guidance for managers in allocating marketing resources, although some writers have objected to its use (for example, Plummer 1990.) It has also clearly been misused, notably in its use as a predictive tool (Dhalla & Yuspeh 1976). This misuse may be a case of the metaphor being taken too seriously; the idea of the product as a living being might, in the case of this erroneous application, result in a product being written off earlier than it should. It can be clear that a living being is in a state of terminal decline; plant and animal health specialists are trained in recognising the symptoms and taking appropriate action such as euthanasing an aged and suffering animal, or cutting down a dangerous old tree. Interestingly, life scientists have not yet discovered the fundamental biological cause of the inevitable decline and death of all living organisms – although our fragile global ecology would rapidly collapse were this not to be the case. Be that as it may, as is shown in other chapters in this book, this process of decline is not necessarily terminal in the case of a brand, and there are many techniques available to a manager to extend its healthy life. So just as it is socially unacceptable in the vast majority of cases to euthanase human beings, so too should managers not prematurely kill off a product or a brand.

Figure 12.1 Stage of the product life cycle

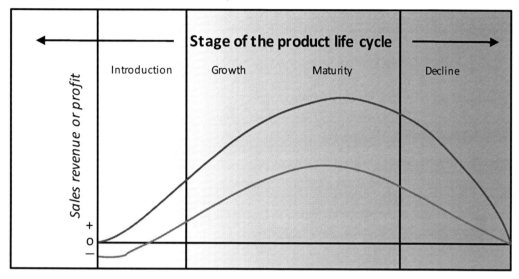

Evolution is inevitable

Schumpeter (1943) described gales of creative destruction that tore down tired old industries and replaced them with radically new and innovative ones – an excellent example of how difficult times – such as the world war that was raging when he published his theory, or climate change, or to a lesser extent the global economic problems that currently beset us – can provide the conditions for radical renewal. It does not, though, help us understand the life cycle of existing brands. Richard Dawkins' (1976) idea of the selfish gene, where living organisms were conceptualised simply as vehicles for the propagation of their genetic material rather than as having any other intrinsic value, is also superficially attractive to brand researchers who observe that a brand can live through a variety of different product forms. Examples of this include: IBM, which started life as a typewriter manufacturer, moved into computers, and is now a leading consulting firm; GE, which began as a business that offered general electrical products and is now a major player in financial markets; and Nokia, which began in the Finnish forest products industry and transformed itself into a world leader in the mobile telecommunications industry. Such brand transformations are extreme examples of Blumenthal's (2002) consistency-relevancy paradox by remaining relevant to consumers (or becoming relevant to a different population of consumers) through a series of changes, as opposed to remaining strictly consistent to their origins. They have prospered through success in the market-based rather than the product-based quadrants of Ansoff's growth matrix. In contrast, Keller (1999) provides the examples of Budweiser, Coca-Cola and Hershey as brands that have maintained consistency in long-term brand imagery as the cause of their continued success. He also makes the appropriate generalisation that it is the underlying principle of fierce defence of a competitive position that results in continued success, as in the case of Procter and Gamble.

These cases of brands that have radically transformed their product offerings while maintaining unchanged names are a nice analogy to Dawkins' selfish genes. One might think that this was an example of the inheritance of acquired characteristics, which has been suggested in biology with varying degrees of credibility as a factor supplementary to the normal inheritance of characteristics through genetic material but is now generally accepted as only possibly applying to the very simplest of organisms, if at all. A brand that remains true to its origins remains, in biological terms, true to its genes or genotype; a brand that changes product or product class is undergoing a change of what biologists would call its phenotype, or the way in which its existence is physically expressed. Indeed, Dawkins (1976) coined the term 'meme' to describe an idea that behaved rather like a gene, which has some similarities with the concept of a brand. It does provide some hints to the argument developed in this chapter, but must be treated with care because it again emphasises the corporate issues of managerial action and innovation, and not market conditions.

Incompetence

Of course, managerial incompetence can easily result in brand or product failure. Lack of vision in an industry can lead to a sales curve that unnecessarily replicates a truncated product life cycle. For example, there are excellent examples of incompetent management in the transportation industry over the years. Car manufacturing boomed for most of the second half of the twentieth century but is now in serious trouble in most of its major markets, at least partly as a result of failure to anticipate the effects of climate change and peak oil as well as shorter-term but also predictable factors like global recession. However, in the US – its first major market – the rise of the car industry had a clear mirror image in the decline of the American railroads (a phenomenon that was later replicated in many other countries as they developed economically). The managers of the railroads failed to understand that their customers were buying a transportation service rather than the clever engineering used in a railroad; and, infrastructure developed to support road rather than rail transportation in response to consumer demand for more convenience. The railroads themselves had superseded individual transport by horse and carts – to the distress of the manufacturers of buggy-whips who in turn had failed to realise that they, too, were in the transportation business. The need for transportation has grown extraordinarily since the days of the horse and cart, but three industries in succession have got themselves into serious trouble through myopic approaches to serving their customer needs (Levitt 1960).

Similarly, and more remarkably from a branding point of view, the former management of Kodak abjectly failed to recognise the meaning of their own brand messages, which had focused on the recording of images from the inception of the business when George Eastman first introduced the Kodak camera in 1888 with the message 'You press the button, we do the rest', progressing to the iconic 'Kodak moment' of more recent memory. The operational complexities of manufacturing and distributing light-sensitive film with valuable silver ingredients blinded later Kodak executives to the reality that their customers were buying an image recording service – entirely in accordance with the brand message – and not the complicated product that Kodak executives were so focused on producing. Customers understood the Kodak brand better than Kodak did, and the firm rapidly lost market share, profitability and stock market grace as digital photography rapidly overtook film.

These are examples of a corporate issue – managerial incompetence. However, while we could speculate on why the leaders of some of the biggest and most powerful industries tend to focus myopically on engineering and operational issues rather than on customer needs, this is not the point of this chapter. Most product classes have life cycles that are too long for easy model development, and it is difficult in any case to predict incompetence (on other than a personal, individual level!). Of course, just as incompetence can happen, managers can also show remarkably strong competence. Indeed, those of us who work in business schools would like to think that we are helping reduce the amount of mismanagement and increasing the chances of managers working very well indeed. There are excellent anecdotal reports of such branding successes and failures (for example, Haig 2003; Groucutt 2006), but it is impossible to develop an overarching conceptual model to predict these remarkable stories of strength or weakness. They tend to be characterised by particular market conditions and extraordinary human judgement or misjudgement. They are amusing, and can be instructive, but we cannot reliably generalise from them.

Corporate vs market issues

It is important to understand the difference between production-driven and market-driven phenomena. The biological world, from which the life cycle metaphor is taken, has a number of production-based models that are superficially attractive to those seeking to develop useful theories of brand demise.

Brands certainly show many characteristics of a life cycle. Of course, they are born – often with major development and promotional expenditure if the financial backing is big enough. They grow – especially if supported and fortified well. Along the way, they can lose control of themselves. In employer branding, where a company sells the employment experience to current and potential staff, it has been argued that organisations focus too strongly on branding for entry-level employees and less so on attracting mid-career staff who are required as the business changes, leading to potential misunderstandings and a dilution of employer brand equity (Moroko & Uncles 2009). They cross-fertilise with other brands that have some similarities with them (Aaker & Joachimsthaler 1999). They can reproduce themselves through brand extension (Aaker 1990; Hem, de Chernatony & Iversen 2003), which is analogous to the asexual reproduction of simple organisms. They of course have relationships between themselves and their stakeholders (Fournier 1998), including top-down repositioning by management (Ewing *et al.* 1995) and repositioning by consumers (Beverland & Ewing 2005). They grow, change, and purposefully improve (Merrilees 2005). They exist in communities for mutual benefit (McWilliam 2000; Muniz & O'Guinn 2001; Algesheimer *et al.* 2005). They change through acquisition by purchase and through renaming (de Chernatony 2006) just as many humans change their names during a symbolic 'purchase' procedure involving considerations like dowries or jewellery in wedding rituals. They can become independent of parents through choice or necessity (Jevons 2005). And, although the thought is unpleasant, most will inevitably die in the long run (Ewing, Jevons & Khalil 2009).

Competition stimulates most innovations (very few innovations are 'new-to-the-world' offerings), and this same competition drives the way in which products gain and lose popularity in the marketplace. Even where new and improved technology replaces perfectly functional products, rather than the old product becoming dysfunctional through the wear and tear of old age, this simply compresses the life cycle process into a product replacement cycle (Norton & Bass 1987, 1992; Sheth & Sisodia 1999). While individual products do, in general, follow the product life cycle model, it would be a mistake to assume that industries, product classes or individual brands would follow the same sequence. The brand life cycle (Simon 1979) was identified as a different concept to the product life cycle to explain evidence that price elasticity varied during a brand's life.

Market drivers of change

Market conditions themselves can drive brand offerings. For example, Golder and Tellis (1993) showed in some extracts from Financial World magazine that demand for a particular type of offering can extend beyond the life of a brand that might currently be delivering it: '… world's biggest chain of highway restaurants…', '…pioneer in restaurant franchising…' and '…most fabulous success story in restaurant chains…', and point out that the statements were not describing McDonald's – as a modern reader might think – but were actually written in the 1960s and were describing Howard Johnson's restaurants. This business – and the brand – is now virtually dead, although brand resurrection attempts are rumoured from time to time. The 'highway restaurant' concept, of course, remains powerful to consumers, although it is delivered through different brands and products. The biological analogy would be that different genotypes were resulting in similar phenotypes.

The difference between the product life cycle model and the brand cycle model is significant. Keeping with the biological metaphor, it is similar to the difference between the biological model of evolution described above and the way in which individual organisms develop, grow, decline and die. Just as living organisms cannot choose whether or not to age (human disguises such as hair dye, Botox and the like notwithstanding!), so too can most brands not postpone the inevitable, despite attempts to change superficial appearance. The life of a brand involves not just management wishes and action, but also matters over which management has little control, such as the actions and beliefs of consumers and the reference groups the consumer admires. The brand is subject to market forces that are considerably more powerful than its management, who can only pretend to control its long-term destiny. So, for example, the sociological phenomenon of 'proletarian drift', first used to describe the way in which high-prestige items are gradually adopted by lower and lower status consumers (Fussell 1983), is a societal phenomenon and as such is out of the control of a mere brand manager. Interestingly, this proletarian drift can also be reversed when working class imagery becomes fashionable amongst the middle classes – for example in the desire for brand authenticity, or even with brands as cultural resources (Holt 2002). The life of the brand is dependent on the dynamics of the marketplace, and not on production.

Death is inevitable

Golder (2000) analysed the urban myth that 19 out of 25 market leading brands had maintained their leadership for at least 60 years, and discovered that the 25 leaders had actually been carefully selected for their longevity from a group that was four times larger. The 25-brand sample was highly biased in a way that is sadly common in journalism, where accuracy often suffers at the expense of deadlines and the saleability of ideas. For example, many ill-conceived 'business person of the year' awards have been given to people who were subsequently disgraced, and Time magazine now emphasises that its ' Man [now Person] of the Year' award, notably given to Adolf Hitler in 1938 and Joseph Stalin in 1939 and 1942, is given to the person considered most *influential* in that year and not the most *praiseworthy* – which remains at odds with public perception of this apparent honour.

Analysing the past is, of course, much easier than predicting the future, and the general business press is replete with stories of people who have become successful and rich and not with the multitude of poor people with potential for future success, or who have tried and failed to succeed. This is a common problem of ex-post-rationalisation and an over-emphasis of success. So, although it is of course very important to understand the strategic factors that underpin brands that have remained successful for many years, it is more important to acknowledge the truth that more leading brands fail than survive in both the medium and the long term. Why is it more important? Because brands that fail are in the vast majority, and management resources and rewards should be allocated accordingly. There is no point in wasting resources on flogging a dead – or dying – horse in a vain attempt to improve its performance. Returning to the human analogy, while medical ethics have not yet come to terms with this, we can soon expect some thoroughly unpleasant resource allocation discussions about the appropriateness of making huge investments in extending human lives that are already in terminal decline at the expense of younger, healthier people with more future potential to contribute to society but perhaps with less current wealth.

Just as with people, the danger, of course, is in prematurely writing a brand off. Just as the product life cycle should not be used as a predictive tool, so too should the inevitability of brand death not be prematurely anticipated; for example, Lego, which was suffering from an over-extended brand in 2004 and making large losses, was able to return to increased sales and healthy profitability in 2008, mainly by consolidating its brand offerings. Unprofitable brand extensions such as a line targeted at girls were killed off; areas outside their management expertise but still attractive, such as Lego theme parks, were partly sold but the brand identity maintained.

Conclusion

Failure and death is inevitable. Depressing though the thought may be, some organisations can and do plan well for this unpleasantness. Ben and Jerry's, for example, have a 'flavor graveyard' on their website where discontinued flavours are commemorated in a quirky Halloween style. This action, of course, helps to preserve the parent brand – and the business.

Brand managers have the responsibility of maintaining a brand's profitability and efficiency for as long as possible for the benefit of the ultimate owners of that brand. While there is potential for continued profitability, a manager should use the various techniques and theories available to maximise the benefits – and certainly avoid premature brand euthanasia – because premature euthanasia is murder. Evolution, on the other hand, is a good thing, and the rise of new and better beings will inevitably result in the demise of older, relatively weaker ones. On occasion, incompetent management can result in the premature death or suicide of brands, but we like to think that market issues are more likely to drive changes. Once the brand seems to be approaching its inevitable end, the attitude that 'while there's life, there's hope' can be damaging, and a fruitless struggle to preserve something that is in terminal decline is not just undignified, it can waste resources that could be better directed.

Perhaps I could misquote the poet Arthur Hugh Clough to conclude. His intention was to criticise the attitude he describes, but he is himself dead now so can't complain about me taking his words at face value.

'Thou shalt not kill, but needs not strive officiously to keep alive' (Mulhauser 1974).

References

Aaker, DA 1990, 'Brand Extensions: the good, the bad and the ugly', *Sloan Management Review*, pp. 47-56, Summer.

Aaker, DA & Joachimsthaler, E 2000, 'The Brand Relationship Spectrum', *California Management Review*, Vol. 42, no. 4, pp. 8-23.

Algesheimer, R Dholakia, U & Herrmann, A 2005, 'The Social influence of Brand Community: Evidence from European Car Clubs', *Journal of Marketing*, Vol. 69, July, pp. 19-34.

Arndt, J Solomon, S Kasser, T & Sheldon, K 2004, 'The Urge to Splurge: a terror management theory account of materialism and consumer behaviour', *Journal of Consumer Psychology*, Vol. 14, no. 3, pp. 198-212.

Barrett HC & Behne T 2005 'Children's understanding of death as the cessation of agency: a test using sleep versus death'. *Cognition* Vol. 96, no. 2, pp. 93-108.

Beverland M & Ewing M 2005, 'Slowing the adoption and diffusion process to enhance brand repositioning: the consumer driven repositioning of Dunlop Volley', *Business Horizons*, Vol. 48, pp. 385-391.

Blumenthal, D 2002, 'Beyond ' form versus content' : Simmelian theory as a framework for adaptive brand strategy', *Journal of Brand Management*, Vol. 10, no. 1, pp. 9-18.

Ewing, MT Fowlds, DA & Shepherd, IRB 1995, 'Renaissance: a case study in brand revitalization and strategic realignment', *Journal of Product and Brand Management*, Vol. 4, no. 3, pp. 19-26.

Ewing, MT Jevons, C & Khalil, E 2009, 'Brand Death: A Developmental Model of Senescence' , *Journal of Business Research*, Vol. 62, no. 3, pp. 332-338.

Fournier, S 1998, 'Consumers and Their Brands, Developing Relationship Theory in Consumer Research', *Journal of Consumer Research*, Vol. 24, (March), pp. 343-372.

Fussell, P 1983, *Class, a guide through the American Status System* New York: Ballantine.

Golder, PN 2000, 'Historical Method in Marketing Research with New Evidence on Long-Term Market Share Stability', *Journal of Market Research*, Vol. 37, May, pp. 156-172.

Golder, PN & Tellis, GJ 1993, 'Pioneer Advantage: Marketing Logic or Marketing Legend?', *Journal of Marketing Research*, Vol. 30, May, pp. 158-70.

Groucutt, J 2006, The life, death and resuscitation of brands. *Handbook of Business Strategy 2006*, pp. 101-106.

Haig, M 2003, *Brand failures: the truth about the 100 biggest branding mistakes of all time*, Kogan Page, London.

Hem, L de Chernatony, L & Iversen, N 2003, 'Factors Influencing Successful Brand extensions', *Journal of Marketing Management*, Vol. 19, pp. 781-806.

Holt, D 2002, 'Why do Brands Cause Trouble? A Dialectical Theory of Consumer Culture and Branding', *Journal of Consumer Research*, Vol. 29, June.

Holt, D 2004, *How Brands Become Icons*, Harvard Business School Press.

Jevons C, Ewing, M & Khalil, E 2007, 'Managing brand demise', *Journal of General Management*, Vol. 32, no. 4, pp. 73-81.

Jevons, C 2005, 'The return of the prodigal brand', *12th Conference on Historical Analysis & Research in Marketing (CHARM)*, Long Beach, California, April.

Jevons, C Gabbott, M & de Chernatony, L 2005, 'Customer and brand manager perspectives on brand relationships: a conceptual framework', *Journal of Product and Brand Management*, Vol. 14, no.5, pp. 300-309.

Keller, KL 1999, 'Managing Brands for the Long Run: brand reinforcement and revitalization strategies', *California Management Review*, Vol. 41, no. 3, Spring, pp. 102-124.

Lehu, J-M. 2006, *Brand rejuvenation, how to protect, strengthen and add value to your brand to prevent it from ageing*, London, Kogan Page.

Mandel, N & Smeesters, D 2008, 'The Sweet Escape: The Effect of Mortality Salience on Consumption Quantities for High and Low Self-Esteem Consumers', *Journal of Consumer Research*, 35 (August), pp. 309-323.

McWilliam, G 2000, 'Building stronger brands through online communities', *Sloan Management Review*, Spring, pp. 43-54.

Merrilees, W 2005, 'Radical brand evolution: a case-based framework', *Journal of Advertising Research*, June, pp. 201-210.

Moroko, L & Uncles, M 2009, 'Business Insight: Employer Branding', *The Wall Street Journal*, 23 March.

Mulhauser, FL 1974, *The Poems of Arthur Hugh Clough*, Oxford University Press.

Muniz, AM & O'Guinn, TC 2001, 'Brand Community', *Journal of Consumer Research*, Vol. 27, March, pp. 412-432.

Norton, JA & Bass, FM 1987, 'A Diffusion Theory Model of Adoption and Substitution for Successive Generations of High Technology Products', *Management Science*, Vol. 33, pp. 1069-1086.

Norton, JA & Bass, FM 1992, 'Evolution of Technological Generations: The Law of Capture', *Sloan Management Review*, Vol. 33, no. 2, pp. 66-77.

Ormerod, P 2005, *Why Most Things Fail*, London, Faber and Faber.

Plummer, JT 1990, 'Outliving the Myths', *Journal of Advertising Research*, pp. 26-28, Feb/Mar.

Schumpeter, J 1943, *Capitalism, Socialism and Democracy*, Harper Perennial.

Rindfleisch, A Burroughs, J & Wong, N 2008, 'The Safety of Objects: Materialism, Existential Insecurity, and Brand Connection', *Journal of Consumer Research*, Vol. 36, June, pp. 1-15.

Sheth, J & Sisodia, RS 1999, 'Revisiting Marketing's Lawlike Generalizations', *Journal of the Academy of Marketing Science*, Vol. 27, no.1, pp. 71-87.

Simon, H 1979, 'Dynamics of Price Elasticity and Brand Life Cycles: an empirical study', *Journal of Marketing Research*, Vol. 16, November, pp. 439-52.

Tellis, G & Crawford, CM 1981, 'An Evolutionary Approach to Product Growth Theory', *Journal of Marketing*, Vol. 45, Fall, pp. 125-132.

Thomas, S & Kohli, C 2009, 'A brand is forever! A framework for revitalizing declining and dead brands', *Business Horizons*, Vol. 52, no. 4 (July-August), pp. 377-386.

Author biography

Colin Jevons is currently senior lecturer in marketing at Monash University, with a Ph.D. in brand management, his main area of research and teaching interest. He is on the editorial boards of three international journals and highlights of his over 50 refereed publications include articles in *Journal of Business Research*, *Journal of Advertising* and *Journal of Product and Brand Management* as well as best paper awards at conferences in both the UK and USA. He has edited special issues of *Journal of Business Research* on thought leadership in brand management and has served on the organising committees of many UK and European conferences in brand management.

Contact: Dr Colin Jevons, Department of Marketing, Monash University, Caulfield campus, 26 Sir John Monash Drive (P O Box 197), Caulfield East Vic 3145, Australia; P +61-3-9903-2304; E Colin.Jevons@BusEco.monash.edu.au.

Part III: Brand Futures

Part III is future-oriented. Attention is focused on emerging challenges and opportunities for brand management.

Arguably the future of brand management isn't being played out in New York, London, Sydney or Auckland, but is happening on the streets of Beijing, Shanghai, Chongqing and Xi'an, or even Qiqihar and Hotan. The emergence (and re-emergence) of brands in China is reviewed, both from consumer and management perspectives (Chapter 13). Identified is a shift from 'Made in China' to 'Sold in China' to 'Brand China', reflecting the self-assurance of Chinese manufacturers and the growing self-confidence of Chinese consumers. Implicit in this discussion is the view that to understand brand futures we should be looking at emergent trends in countries as diverse as China, India, Brazil, Indonesia, Chile and Ghana.

There is renewed interest in the theme of consumers' relationships with their brands (Chapter 14). The metaphor of inter-personal relationships is applied to consumer-brand relationships, in that we can talk of marriage and commitment, and casual acquaintances and flings, and divorce and separation. Relationships take many forms. These varied relationships provide meanings to the persons who engage, in terms of personal relevance (e.g. self-connection) and cultural relevance (e.g. community). Over a series of interactions, and in response to contextual change, relationships change and evolve.

The brand 'as an experience' is attracting more attention, partly because of the growth of service economies and virtual communities where the emphasis is on the lived experience, not tangible product attributes in the traditional sense of product branding (Chapter 15). Examples include retail brand experiences (the 'theatre' of shopping and dining), theme parks and expos (from Seaworld to Expo 2010 Shanghai), and museums and factory tours (like the Hershey Museum and Guinness Storehouse tours). These examples highlight concepts such as interaction, engagement, potency, activity and authenticity.

Authenticity reappears as a theme in the next contribution (Chapter 16). Brands such as Chateau Margaux, Lonely Planet and Dyson gain authenticity through honest story-telling; in so doing, they communicate a genuine love of craft which resonates with consumers. Through their actions, authentic brands display quality leadership, heritage and sincerity. Brands that truly nurture authenticity become 'living heritage'. But, to return to a theme addressed much earlier (Chapter 1), of the brands routinely bought by consumers, how many are seen as authentic? What is the role of authenticity, interaction, engagement, potency and so forth in driving sales? Can we measure and account for these facets of brands, or is that to tread a path that leads to the inauthentic?

The final contribution examines shifting brands (Chapter 17). For those who have a strictly business interest in brand management, this is an uncomfortable ending. Where there is positive word-of-mouth, there is also negative. Where there are brand relationships, there is also disillusionment, boredom, divorce, remorse and hatred. Where there are brand communities, there are also anti-brand communities. Understandably, marketers dwell on the positives, but they ignore the dark-side at their peril. And, maybe, there is a silver-lining. Many well-known brands today started life as upstarts and challengers, and often they were anti-establishment. Anyone under the age of twenty-five might find this hard to believe of Virgin, Body Shop and Benetton, but that is how these brands were originally positioned. As dramatically shown in the film *Social Network*, misfit FaceMash morphed into mainstream Facebook in half-a-dozen years. Non-brands have become brands in their own right – think only of the transformation of cheap, discounted private labels into heavily-bought, highly-regarded retail brands like Tesco's portfolio. As the future unfolds, it will be a continuing story of brand reception, possible resistance and, almost certainly, revision and reinvention.

Chapter 13

Emerging brands: The case of China

MICHAEL EWING, LYDIA WINDISCH & JOHN ZEIGLER

ABSTRACT

Dynamic market conditions and seemingly insatiable demand have created a complex and exciting environment for the development of both domestic and international brands in the Peoples' Republic of China. Inside China, there are ever increasing numbers of consumers with ever increasing discretionary income. Globally, the perceptions of the 'Made in China' label and increased market shares by Chinese manufacturers in many foreign markets have implications for the management and performance of Chinese brands. The challenges and opportunities for Chinese domestic, international and transnational brands are considered in this chapter.

KEYWORDS

China; domestic; international; transnational brands

Introduction – why China?

China may have been the first society to demonstrate the use of metaphors to add intangible value to products and to thus create 'brands'. Eckhardt and Bengtsson (2007) have found preliminary evidence of branding (White Rabbit brand on a packet of sewing needles) dating back to the Song Dynasty (960 to 1127 CE), long before the concept of 'brands' became prominent in the West.

Twenty-first century China is a geographically and economically diverse country. In a very short time period it has grown into a commercial powerhouse, producing over half of the world's growth through unprecedented economic, social and market development (Peng 2005). China will soon be home to the world's fourth-largest population of wealthy households[37]. There are 650 million mobile phone users in China, with six million new subscribers added every month. There are more than 340 million internet users in China[38]. In January 2009, the Chinese Government increased its estimate of how much the economy grew during 2007. The revision meant China's economy overtook Germany's to become the world's third largest in 2007. In fact, China's economy has grown tenfold in the past 30 years[39]. Tim Condon, head of Asia research at ING Group NV in Singapore, said: 'If China continues to grow at its average rate in the past 20 years and if the US does the same, it will overtake the US. There's no doubt that that will happen - it's just a matter of time.'[40]

Economic activity in China dictates much of what occurs in the global financial markets of the world. Assumptions that the rules of business in China are the same as anywhere else in the world are quite erroneous. As James McGregor, former Wall Street Journal China Bureau Chief, has stated: 'Nothing is as it seems and nothing about business in China is easy.' For example, there are more than 135,000 advertising agencies in China, but it's believed not all of them win business on the basis of merit. Recently, a renowned global agency presented its credentials in a new business pitch, to discover that the prospective client had invited their local agency to watch from behind mirrored glass.

However you look at it, emerging markets are where some of the most exciting developments in branding are taking place (and this will be true in the future). In response, this chapter will explore branding in China from three perspectives: the consumer's, management's, and through the developing phenomenon of Chinese brands abroad. For consumers in China, one of the most pressing issues is around the differing brand experiences across the 'tiers' of Chinese cities. Additionally, the competition between domestic brands and incoming international foreign brands is an issue. And, Chinese brand managers are faced with multiple market fronts, including China, the Asia-Pacific region, and further afield in the US and Europe.

---

[37] Mckinsey Quarterly
[38] Internet World Stats, May 2009
[39] BBC New, 19 January: China's Economy Leapfrogs Germany's
[40] Bloomberg, January 19: China Passes Germany to Become Third-Biggest Economy (Update3)

Management of Chinese brands in each of these markets requires differing approaches and differing strategies to anticipate and successfully cope with a myriad of economic, political and social factors.

This chapter is set out as follows. First, we explore branding in China and how the differing social and economic 'tiers' of cities affect the performance of domestic and international brands. Second, we examine consumers' responses to domestic and international brands with particular reference to the brands that have performed well. Third, brand management within China is discussed, including the development of transnational brands in the East-Asian region. Fourth, we show how Chinese brands are performing internally, and how these brands can be affected by various country-of-origin effects such as the 'Made in China' factor. This chapter then concludes with some thoughts on how brands in China, and Chinese brands abroad, may develop in the future.

Branding in China

While China is highly regionalised, delineation can be drawn between the predominantly coastal 'Tier 1' cities, and the 'Tiers 2 and 3' inland cities (Sinha 2007). This separation of development did not occur naturally – during the 1980s, the Chinese government began to allow investment by foreign firms into China under a specific strategy of opening up only seaboard ports (useful for import and export) (Zhao 1999). Tier 1 cities (such as Beijing, Shanghai and Gungzhou) are large, predominantly eastern seaboard cities (see Figure 13.1) They are considered more cosmopolitan, and people from these cities generally have had more exposure to foreign cultural experiences and influences – having interacted with foreigners in their own cities or while abroad. Consequently, consumers in these cities have had greater exposure to foreign brands, and international brands do better in these cities than in regional areas.

Regional cities (Tiers 2 and 3, but predominantly Tier 2), such as Chengdu, Hangzhou and Xian (see Sinha 2007 for a listing of Chinese cities by 'tiers'), have smaller populations but are more numerous than Tier 1 cities. Regional cities are more inland and tend to have populations who have travelled less outside of China and have had less exposure to foreign influences and foreign brands. Consumers in these areas are considered much more traditional in their outlook than consumers in the Tier 1 cities, and international brands have traditionally not performed as well in these areas (for a number of reasons that will be explored later in this chapter). Domestic brands (and regional brands specific to the area) have tended to perform much better.

As Tier 1 cities are increasingly becoming up-market, cosmopolitan metropolises, the production costs for manufacturers in these cities have also increased. As a consequence, manufacturers and firms are now looking to place production and office facilities in relatively cheaper Tiers 2 and 3 areas. With these increased investments from China's ever-growing industrialisation, standards of living are improving in the inland regions, resulting in a commensurately ever-growing middle class that has increasing amounts of discretionary income. Nineteen per cent of China's total GDP in 2004 originated from the Tier 2 regional cities (National Bureau of Statistics 2004). With a high disposable income relative to the rest of the country (RMB30,000 per annum, or approximately US$4,000) and with a curiosity to try particularly Western brands and products, China's new middle class will, it is believed, soon make up the majority of Chinese consumers. In 2015, China's middle class is expected to constitute around 80 million households[41].

Figure 13.1 GDP per capita by provinces in mainland China, 2004
(South China Sea Islands not shown)

Source: WikiProject China Provinces, 2006.

According to *The People's Daily Online* (July 2009), China has overtaken the US to become the world's second largest luxury market (Japan being the first). It claimed that China's 'super rich' bought a quarter of the world's luxury goods in 2008, at an estimated US$8.6 billion[42]. The world's largest multinationals have been quick to take advantage of the growth potential in China. With a mix of savvy marketing and smart adaptation to Chinese culture, major global brands are increasingly becoming household names.

---

41 McKinsey Quarterly, The value of China's middle class, June 2006
42 World Luxury Association

Consumption and purchasing behaviours by Chinese consumers mirror the transitional nature of the Chinese economy. Work by Uncles (Uncles & Kwok 2008a; Uncles & Kwok 2008b) has reported that Chinese consumers are beginning to embrace more 'Westernised' purchasing venues such as supermarkets and hypermarkets, but still retain a connection to more traditional store types such as grocery stores and free/wet markets (a form of traditional neighbourhood open food market).

Gao *et al.* (2006) point out that foreign brands appear to have the advantage in transitional economies such as China, as these brands are already stronger and can draw on a greater store of resources (both financial and human) to support the brand. Yet, Gao *et al.* (2006) also argue that domestic brands will have an advantage within the marketplace, as they are closer to consumers, supported by local governments, and have access to domestic market information. Given these various advantages and disadvantages, estimating the success of both domestic and foreign/international brands within the Chinese context is difficult and complex. There are no broad generalisations when it comes to describing the success, or lack thereof, of brands within China. Rather, a myriad of factors play into consumers' responses to domestic, international and transnational brands.

Figure 13.2 Advertising in China

Consumer perspectives

Chinese consumers' responses to domestic brands

Although becoming increasingly sophisticated (Cheng-Lu *et al.* 2004), Chinese consumers – especially in the inner Tiers 2 and 3 cities – still demonstrate ethnocentrism in their purchasing behaviours (Hsu & Nien 2008). Two-thirds of the respondents in the *Real China Revealed* study by Ogilvy Discovery and Mindshare Insights (2006) indicated that they would not pay more for well-known international brands, but that they would pay more if a product demonstrates good value for money. Not surprisingly, domestic Chinese brands (such as Legend, Fenghua & Slek to name a few) have enjoyed something of a rise in popularity (Ewing *et al.* 2002).

The performance of domestic brands in China needs to be understood in the context of the central government's 'tiered' development strategy. China is big. Moving products through the country is difficult and expensive. China is also very regionalised. Regional infrastructure makes the movement of goods even more problematic. For example, regional governments have been known to impose taxes on products that are not produced in that region (Zeng & Williamson 2003). Thus, transporting products from elsewhere (whether international or domestic products from other regions) into inland regional areas is more expensive. So, there is a preference by consumers for regional domestic brands.

Chinese consumers' responses to international brands

International companies looking to enter into the Chinese market often face a number of cultural and regulatory hurdles, including brand name translation and consumer sentiment towards foreign brands.

Brand name translation

A significant issue for international brands entering the Chinese market is brand name translations, and the meanings that are derived from translating brand names. Coca-Cola's success in China is an example of combining astute business strategies with a meaningful translation of the brand name. The translation of Coke-Cola ('kekoukele') gives a literal translation of 'Can-Be-Tasty-Can-Be-Happy' (Li & Shooshtari 2003) and a concept translation of 'tastes good and makes you happy' (Dong & Helms 2001) – an exceptionally salient and meaningful translation in terms of the Coca-Cola product. Conversely, product confusion can arise with some brand names – Maxwell House coffee was initially translated as 'mai-shai' – indicating that it was the Mai family brand, or that it was 'related to wheat' (Dong & Helms 2001). For a coffee-based product, this was an obvious problem. The script in which the brand is written (logographic, syllabic and alphabetic) may also affect the ability of Chinese consumers to relate meanings to the brand name (Pan & Schmitt 1996).

Foreign brands in China are associated with high quality, and Chinese consumers have high expectations of these brands (Tai 2008). Certain product categories in China are disproportionately affected by cultural and generational factors. For example, in the clothing and apparel markets, the vast majority of Chinese consumers have small and undifferentiated wardrobes (Wai-Chan, Cheung & Tse 2007). The attraction towards a clothing item, especially for foreign brands, is not dictated by the associated brand name. However, younger Chinese consumers are beginning to develop more 'Westernised' approaches to brands – demonstrating increased consumer involvement with clothing brands and an increased perception of premium brands as status brands (O'Cass & Choy 2008). Accordingly, companies looking to enter China, or to increase an already existing market share in China, will need to be mindful of this 'youthful' aspect of the Chinese market. Already, international brands have had varying degrees of success in China due to a variety of factors, including variable consumer-acceptance/resistance, joint-venture successes/failures, and local competitive responses. The following are some examples of successful international brands in China, and some of the strategies that may have produced these favourable outcomes.

International brands

Nokia currently controls the mobile handset market with more than 35 per cent market share in China. It has been Nokia's largest single market since 2005. Central to Nokia's success has been its efforts to decentralise and its ability to talk to the many target audiences which exist in China. For example, since 2003 Nokia has expanded from having three sales offices in China to having 70. Rather than eight national distributors, it now has 50 provincial distributors. In addition, Nokia continues to develop products designed specifically for Chinese consumers in lower-tier cities and rural areas. Understanding that most of the population in less developed areas could not relate to the romanised version of Chinese characters, Nokia created simpler phones which allow users to write characters with a stylus.

Budweiser has undoubtedly become a symbol of national teamwork and cooperation. And although it only accounts for 2 per cent of the Chinese beer market, Budweiser controls more than 40 per cent of the premium beer market. The brand plans to distribute its product to more than 200 cities, up from 100, over the next five years.

In China, McDonald's boasts over 1,000 outlets and continually drives marketing innovations, including home delivery and a considerable online focus. Despite a slowing of the global economy, McDonald's continues to thrive – with expansion plans for another 150 stores in 2009.

Another example is Proctor & Gamble's skincare brand, Olay. It is China's largest advertiser with a budget of more than RMB1 billion (approximately US$150 million). In contrast to its message in more developed countries, Olay is considered an aspirational brand in China, with the brand promise of finding you a husband. Its unique positioning has led to phenomenal success in comparison to local, more established Chinese brands.

Counterfeiting

The production and distribution of counterfeits of major luxury brands in China is a significant issue (Bian & Velouotsou 2007; Phau & Teah 2009). Research from the Asia Pacific region has indicated that, when luxury brands are subject to counterfeiting activities, consumers of the genuine brand feel a loss of exclusivity and resort to consuming the luxury brands in less conspicuous manners – or even abandoning the genuine brand altogether (Commuri 2009). However, consumers in Shanghai appeared to make little differentiation between genuine and counterfeit productions of luxury brands, even on fundamental aspects of quality, reliability and functionality (Pahu & Teah 2009). Such challenges to the authenticity of brand in China are a key consideration when examining the behaviour of the brands.

Management perspectives

Ewing *et al.* (2008) conducted a study of the brand orientation of senior managers at 69 Chinese companies in 2007. Results indicated that the profitability and organisational performance of companies could be differentiated on the basis of brand orientation – in particular, whether brands excel at delivering the benefits customers truly desire, whether the brand is properly positioned, whether the brand is consistent, whether the brand portfolio and hierarchy make sense, and whether the brand managers understand what the brand means to customers. Put simply, companies that scored higher in terms of these brand orientations were the more successful firms in the sample. In a follow-up, the authors also conducted qualitative interviews with senior managers at ten major Chinese companies. Results from these interviews showed that over the past 10 years there has been an evolution in terms of companies' brand strategies and orientations, particularly around 2004–05 (a notable period in China when the central government began implementing policies argued to have a 'consumption-boosting' effect on the spending behaviours of Chinese consumers). In particular, many companies noted that they began to develop more sophisticated and proactive brand strategies (possibly also as a response to the growing sophistication and brand awareness of Chinese consumers).

The strategic brand development of these companies included multiple brand approaches to respond to a growing segmentation in the Chinese market, and also the development of umbrella brands to house several brand lines when there was too much disparity between the brand lines. The brand managers at these Chinese companies demonstrated that they were responsive and willing to invest in the development of their companies' brand identities, and cognisant of a range of leveraging strategies (such as using corporate social responsibility) in order to build brand equity.

In addition to the development of local brands internally, there is an increasing push across Asia, and with some Chinese firms, to develop Asian transnational brands – brands that are positioned as 'Asian' brands rather than as 'Chinese', 'Malaysian' or 'Taiwanese' brands (Cayla & Eckhardt 2008) – thereby shifting the brand away from nationalistic affiliations towards regionalism. Cayla and Eckhardt's (2008) extensive case studies of firms across the East Asian region showed that the benefits of strategically positioning a brand as 'Asian' are seen as an increased association with the idea of East Asia (cosmopolitan, youthful, urban and modern) and less association with nationalism images that may not accord with the product or brand (i.e. Singapore and beer).

Branding from China

Chinese brands abroad

In March 2001, Jiang Zemin announced a 'going aboard policy' for China, an encouragement for Chinese companies to start broadening their investments beyond China's borders. This announcement came as the Chinese government's investments in the research and design of government laboratories, biotechnology companies, and technology start-up groups that began in the 1990s came to maturation. In response to the announcement, many leading Chinese companies are prioritising globalisation and multinational investment as a key business strategy (Dietz, Orr & Xing 2008). In particular, the Chinese government has urged some of the largest Chinese companies to expand through selling branded products abroad (Kotler, Pfoertsch & Michi 2006). While large multinationals have penetrated China's market, a number of Chinese brands have started looking for new foreign market opportunities. Infiltrating new markets has been swift, as many Chinese companies already have experience selling internationally. However, Chinese products are facing major quality issues which still need to be addressed in the short term. With recent recalls across various product categories, China has a considerable hurdle to overcome in convincing consumers that 'Made in China' products are of a high quality. A generation ago, many Japanese and Korean brands were in a similar position. To counteract the negative perception, corporations such as Sony and Samsung built global markets by concentrating on product innovation and technological ingenuity - continuously reinforcing reliability and quality.

While many Chinese companies may be thinking in terms of financial strategies for international development and investment, Brouthers and Xu (2002) found that some Chinese companies were indeed shifting to a branding strategy as a way to increase market share. One of China's leading companies, Haeir, implemented a deliberate strategy to improve both domestic and international market shares (see Liu & Li 2002), which cemented it as a major player in the international market. Haier group, located in the Qingdao (an eastern seaport city in Shandong province), reportedly cornered almost half the US market for small refrigerators in 2002, and over 60% of the US market for wine coolers (Zeng & Williamson 2003). Importantly, this market share increase was achieved under the Haier brand name, not as a supplier under another US or European name. Additionally, these overseas successes were gained while Haier maintained a leading brand preference amongst consumers on the domestic front in China (Ogilvy Discovery and Mindshare Insights 2006).

China brands

Tsingtao is a brand closely associated with China and is growing in popularity overseas. According to Interbrand[43] it is China's best brand ambassador.

Lenovo, formerly known as Legend, bought the IBM notebook brand for US$1.25 billion in 2005. Lenovo is the number one PC maker in China, and is one of the best known Chinese brands overseas, according to Interbrand. However, despite its success, Lenovo continues to struggle with establishing brand preference overseas, with foreign consumers still demanding IBM.

Haier, a household appliance company, has established itself overseas as a brand that represents cheap but reliable refrigerators and washing machines. Haier generates USD 2.6 billion revenue a year with 25 per cent derived from foreign markets, and is considered the leader of all established Chinese brands overseas. Haier spends around four per cent of its revenue on research and development, and has established local product development teams in Tokyo and the US to develop more high-end products and to expand its customer base.

Huawei Technologies makes telecommunications equipment and generates US$8.2 billion in revenue per annum, 65 per cent of which comes from overseas markets. Huawei invests more than USD800 million on research and development every year and is already competing successfully with the likes of US-brand Cisco for telecom network equipment. Huawei is now moving into the consumer space, making handsets and set-top boxes for televisions.

Established in 1999, Chery is the fastest growing and fourth largest car brand in China. It is also China's biggest car exporter, selling over 50,000 cars in 30 developing countries in 2008. Most significant was Chery's export deal in July 2007 with Chrysler. The first Chinese-made cars are scheduled to be shipped to the US and Europe in 2010.

However, there have also been some notable failures, such as TCL computers. In 2002 TCL was China's largest corporation. It tried to buy brand reputation by buying in French TV maker Thomson. But five years later, the company is in extreme financial strife.

---

[43] (Made in China report 2007)

Country of origin effects – an evolution towards 'Brand China'?

Brands originating from China have previously been viewed by the international consumer market as an indication of cheapness and as having a commensurate lack of quality (Ewing, Napoli & Pitt 2001; Loo & Davies 2006; Fombrun & Pan 2006 for a more detailed analysis of these effects). However, the 'Made in China' label is becoming more powerful in its own right, synonymous with cheap but acceptable products (especially for cheaper scale products such as pens and Christmas decorations (Zeng & Willliamson 2003)). At the other end of the product spectrum, Chinese companies are increasingly demonstrating that they can produce competitively-priced and high-quality goods in product areas such as whitegoods and motorcycles (Gao, Woetzel & Wu 2003). As Loo and Davies (2006) point out, *Brand China* – an image that encapsulates both traditional values and elements of progressive modernity – could be a superbrand in the making. However, this kind of evolution takes time, as the case study below illustrates.

Odes motorbikes

Located in Shandong province (eastern seaboard province), Odes Limited is an example of a Chinese company utilising a globalised and diverse range of production and management experience, including a German director, an Australian designer, and European (Italian) manufacturers for parts – 95% of which have ISO9000 certification. They produce motorbikes, ATV, go-karts and other sports vehicles. With their mid-range entry dirt bike, the MCF450, they have taken a deliberate strategy of producing a bike that is not intended to rise in price, even during an economic downturn. A similar strategy was employed by Pearl River Pianos, which deliberately produced a high-quality, inexpensive entry-level piano, thus increasing its market share in the US from 5% to 10% in one year (Zeng & Williamson 2003).

Australasian Dirt Bike, a leading magazine for off-road motorcycling in Australia and New Zealand, took the somewhat bold step of both reviewing and carrying as the cover article in the June 2009 edition the Odes' MCF450. While the reviewer's final comment was that he would not personally purchase the motorcycle, he nonetheless admitted that he was 'surprised at how good the Odes actually was' and concluded 'A Chinese revolution? Not yet, but I hear a rumbling in the distance' (p. 58). Naturally, the traditional dominators of this product category were quick to disparage the Odes MCF450 in the July 2009 issue of *Australasian Dirt Bike*, with the general manager of motorcycles for Honda Australia sending a letter to the editor of *ADB* loaded with phrases such as '...reworked copies of established manufacturers at around half the price of the genuine product' and 'to be bought by riders who are content to put up with the not-quite-right syndrome' (p. 40). However, the August 2009 issue brought further comment from a reader, applauding the magazine for testing the Odes' MCF450 and also commenting that 'I think we all have to concede that that Chinese bikes will be serious competitors at some stage not too far down the track' (p. 40). The final instalment in this dirt bike soap opera in the September issue brought a further twist. The Swedish manufacturers of Öhlins motorbike suspensions wrote to *Australasian Dirt Bike* that, following a careful examination of the images in the original June article, the Odes bike did not appear to have genuine Öhlins suspension as claimed by Odes, adding that 'not even the stickers are genuine Öhlins!' (Ohlsson 2009, p. 45). Furthermore, the Swedish company had no record of any contact with Odes Limited, and would be considering legal action if the company continued to claim to be producing bikes fitted with Öhlins components. An editorial note attached to this letter indicated that the editor of *Australasian Dirt Bike* had contacted Odes Limited, who stated that they believed they had been dealing with the Taiwan office of Öhlins but were now looking into the matter.

This Odes case demonstrates many of the issues that abound in the brand space that is China, including the struggle to overcome the negative connotations of 'Made in China', and allegations of counterfeiting and knock-off products.

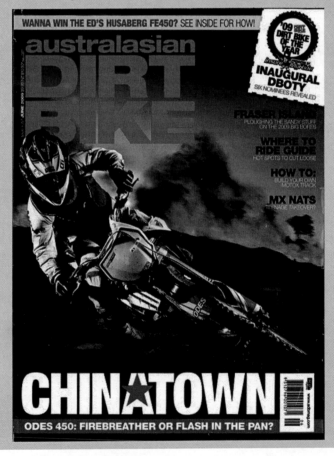

China tomorrow

While it would be tempting to examine the economic and market development of China through the lens of the western model, doing so would produce a faulty and flawed picture. Anna Tsui (2004, 2007) has argued in a number of papers for research to undertake an *emic* approach – that is, collect data and derive theories from within the culture to enhance the relevance of the findings and to be culturally specific – as opposed to an *etic* approach – that is, apply a seemingly 'culture-neutral' framework to the findings from any given context. Tsui's (2007) argument is that there is a tendency, especially in the management literature, to homogenise research under the same theoretical banner. Instead, she argues that an indigenous approach should be taken to any research conducted in other cultural contexts, especially in contexts such as China. For brands, taking such an approach is of special importance. There are many China-specific and Asia-specific brand phenomena that do not necessarily have parallels with US or European experiences of brands. Some of these issues – such as transnationalism, Made in China, and authenticity – have been covered in this chapter. However, as has been demonstrated by other authors, with Chinese consumers having access to increased amounts of disposable income, similarities to Western brand patterns have become apparent (Uncles, Wang & Kwok 2010). A valid and reliable knowledge of how Chinese consumers respond to brands provides the foundations for brand managers to be able to successfully address these challenges in the Chinese market. In particular, Cayla and Arnould (2008) call for both branding researchers and managers to develop marketing reflexivity to question and adapt the basic assumptions and premises that have been developed in one context before applying them in a different context. Over the next ten years, it seems China will change from an investment-led economy to a consumption-led economy, evolving from 'Made in China' to 'Sold in China'. Keeping pace with these changes will require responsive and accurate brand management practices.

References

Atsmon, Y., & Dixit, V. 2009, 'Understanding China's wealthy'. *The McKinsey Quarterly*, July.

Berthon, P., Ewing, M. T., & Napoli, J. 2008, 'Brand management in small to medium-sized enterprises'. *Journal of Small Business Management*, 46(1), 27-45.

Bian, X & Veloutsou, C. 2007, 'Consumers; attitudes regarding non-deceptive counterfeit brands in the UK and China'. *Brand Management*, 14(3), 211-222.

Broomfield, P. 2009, 'Attitude adjustment'. *Australasian Dirt Bike*, 50-58.

Brouthers, L. E., & Xu, K. 2002, 'Product stereotypes, strategy and performance satisfaction: The case of Chinese exporters'. *Journal of International Business Studies*, 33(4), 657-677.

Cayla, J. & Arnould, E.J. 2008, 'A cultural approach to branding in the global marketplace'. *Journal of International Marketing*, 16(4), 86-112.

Cayla, J. & Eckhardt, G.M. 2008, 'Asian brands and the shaping of a transnational imagined community'. *Journal of Consumer Research*, 35, 216-230

Chan, W.-C., Cheung, R. C., & Tse, A. 2007, 'China: Small budgets, small wardrobes'. *McKinsey Quarterly*(4), 70-73.

Cheng-Lu, W., Siu, N. Y. M., & Hui, A. S. Y. 2004, 'Consumer decision-making styles on domestic and imported brand clothing'. *European Journal of Marketing*, 38(1/2), 239-252.

Commuri, S. 2009, 'The impact of counterfeiting on genuine-item consumers' brand relationships'. *Journal of Marketing*, 73, 86-98.

Dietz, M. C., Orr, G., & Xing, J. 2008, 'How Chinese companies can succeed abroad'. *McKinsey Quarterly*, pp. 22-31, from http://ezproxy.lib.monash.edu.au/login?url=http://search.ebscohost.com/login.aspx?direct=true&db=buh&AN=33291062&site=ehost-live&scope=site

Dong, L. C., & Helms, M. M. 2001, 'Brand name translation model: A case analysis of US brands in China'. *Journal of Brand Management*, 9(2), 99.

Eckhardt, G., & Bengtsson, A. 2007, 'Pulling with white rabbit out of the hat: Consuming brands in Imperial China'. Paper presented at the Association for Consumer Research, European Conference.

Ewing, M., Napoli, J., & Pitt, L. 2001, 'Managing Southeast Asian Brands in the Global Economy'. *Business Horizons*, 44(3), 52.

Ewing, M. T., Napoli, J., Pitt, L. F., & Watts, A. 2002, 'On the renaissance of Chinese brands'. *International Journal of Advertising*, 21(2), 197-216.

Fengru, L., & Shooshtari, N. H. 2003, 'Brand naming in China: Sociolinguistic implications'. *Multinational Business Review*, 11(3), 3-21.

Fombrun, C. J., & Pan, M. 2006, 'Corporate reputations in China: How do consumers feel about companies?', *Corporate Reputation Review*, 9(3), 165-170.

Gao, G. Y., Yigang, P., Tse, D. K., & Yim, C. K. 2006, 'Market share performance of foreign and domestic brands in China'. *Journal of International Marketing*, 14(2), 32-51.

Gao, P., Woetzel, J. R., & Wu, Y. 2003, 'Can Chinese brands make it abroad?', *McKinsey Quarterly*(4), 54-65.

Henderson, J. 2009, 'Letters: Chinadown?', *Australasian Dirt Bike*, 40.

Hinton, T. 2009,'Letters: Honda on Odes', *Australasian Dirt Bike*, 40.

Kotler, P., Pfoertsch, W., & Michi, I. 2006, *B2B Brand Management*. Berlin: Springer.

Liu, H., & Li, K. 2002, 'Strategic implications of emerging Chinese multinationals:: The Haier case study'. *European Management Journal*, 20(6), 699.

Loo, T., & Davies, G. 2006, 'Branding China: The ultimate challenge in reputation management?', *Corporate Reputation Review*, 9(3), 198-210.

Lu Hsu, J., & Han-Peng, N. 2008, 'Who are ethnocentric? Examining consumer ethnocentrism in Chinese societies', *Journal of Consumer Behaviour*, 7(6), 436-447.

National Bureau of Statistics of China 2004, from http://www.stats.gov.cn/enGliSH/

O'Cass, A., & Choy, E. 2008, 'Studying Chinese generation Y consumers' involvement in fashion clothing and perceived brand status'. *Journal of Product & Brand Management*, 17(5), 341-352.

Ohlsson, B. 2009, 'Letter: Öhlins or not?', *Australasian Dirt Bike*, 41.

Pan, Y., & Schmitt, B. 1996, 'Language and brand attitudes: Impact of script and sound matching in Chinese and English'. *Journal of Consumer Psychology*, 5(3), 263-277.

Peng, M. 2005, 'Perspectives: From China strategy to global strategy'. *Asia Pacific Journal of Management*, 22(2), 123-141.

Phau, I. & Teah, M. 2009, 'Devil wear (counterfeit) Prada: a study of antecedents and outcome of attitudes towards counterfeits of luxury brands'. *Journal of Consumer Marketing*, 26(1), 15-27.

Sinha, K. 2007, 'The challenge for brands in the other China'. *China Business Review*, 34(5), 28-62.

Sinha, K., & Zhao, I. 2006, 'Consumers in the real Chin'. *Discovery, Ogilvy and National Insights*, MindShare China.

Tai, S. H. C. (2008). 'Beauty and the beast:: The brand crisis of SK-II cosmetics in China'. *Asian Case Research Journal*, 12(1), 57-71.

Tsui, A. 2004, 'Contributing to global management knowledge: A case for high quality indigenous research'. *Asia Pacific Journal of Management*, 21(4), 491-513.

Tsui, A. S. 2007, 'From homogenization to pluralism: International management research in the academy and beyond'. *Academy of Management Journal*, 50(6), 1353-1364.

Uncles, M. & Kwok, S. 2008, 'Generalizing patterns of store-type patronage: an analysis across major Chinese cities. International Review of Retail', *Distribution & Consumer Research*, 18(5), 473-493.

Uncles, M. D., & Kwok, S. 2009, 'Patterns of store patronage in urban China'. *Journal of Business Research*, 62(1), 68-81.

Uncles, M. D., Wang, C & Kwok, S. 2010, 'A temporal analysis of behavioural brand loyalty among urban Chinese consumers'. *Journal of Marketing Management*, forthcoming.

Zeng, M., & Williamson, P. 2004, 'HBR Spotlight: China tomorrow, the great transition, the hidden dragons', *Harvard Business Review*, 82, 119-119.

Zhao, L. 1999, 'Strategic options for building the Chinese NGO sector in an open world'. *The International Journal of Not-For-Profit Law*, 2(2), 15-20.

Author biographies

Prior to becoming a full-time academic, **Professor Mike Ewing** was Marketing Research Manager for Ford Motor Company's South African subsidiary. Over the past fifteen years, he has taught in Australia, Austria, Brunei, China, the Czech Republic, England, Finland, Hong Kong, Malaysia, the Netherlands, Singapore, South Africa, Sweden and the Philippines. In 2004, Mike won Monash University's inaugural Faculty of Business and Economics Dean's Teaching Award, and in 2007 he received the inaugural Dean's Research Award. Mike conducts research in the area of marketing communications (advertising effects, brand management, health promotion and the technology–communications interface), marketing strategy, services marketing and social marketing. As well as publishing more than 85 articles in refereed international journals, Mike is an active member of a number of professional associations, and serves on the editorial boards of eight international journals.

Contact: Michael.Ewing@buseco.monash.edu.au.

Lydia Windisch is completing her doctoral thesis in psychology and is currently employed as a Research Assistant within the Department of Marketing. Lydia's research background is in the areas of cross-cultural and indigenous psychologies, with an emphasis on social and health policy development. During 2008, Lydia worked on a wide range of marketing research projects including branding, consumer behaviour, corporate reputation, health marketing and corporate social responsibility, some of which were in collaboration with commercial partners. She has published in the *Journal of Early Childhood*, the *International Journal of Advertising*, and *Industrial Marketing Management*.

Contact: Lydia.Windisch@buseco.monash.edu.au.

A staunch advocate of marketing effectiveness, **John Zeigler** launched the world's first integrated agency in 1986. Having lived and worked in three continents, John is a great believer in reinvention and what that implies for brands in this global 'think local' market. He is adamant that the development of creative work and its evolution and management should be most highly valued; and, that clients should be involved in all these processes. John considers himself a creative marketer who believes in harnessing the potential of others. As the leading voice, chairman and CEO of DDB Group, Asia Pacific, Japan & India, John's responsibilities span 21 agencies in 16 countries and more than 2,500 employees. John graduated from Monash University with a Bachelor of Business – Marketing and a Masters Degree (MBM), and is past president of the Monash Marketing Alumni.

Contact: John.Zeigler@apac.ddb.com.

Chapter 14

Consumer's relationships with brands

Susan Fournier

Abstract

This chapter presents a brand management paradigm based on the foundational principles of relationships: (1) Brand relationships are a means to an end: brand relationship managers must consider the whole person and understand how the brand adds meaning into people's lives. (2) Brand relationships are diverse and multi-faceted: relationship management requires sensitivity to the operative contract and relationship form. (3) Brand relationships are process phenomena: savvy relationship strategies consider the dimensions on which relationships develop and address the causes that drive evolution and change over time. Our perspective enlightens current customer relationship management (CRM) practice by providing a deeper appreciation of the 'R' in CRM.

Keywords

consumer-brand relationships; brand meaning; relationship diversity; relationship processes; dynamic relationships.

Introduction

Every discipline needs an organising concept—a central idea that defines the essence of what the field is all about. Starting in the late 1990s, the marketing paradigm shifted from transactions to relationships, fundamentally changing the art and practice of brand management at its core (Deighton 1995; Peppers & Rogers 1993; Webster 1992). The paradigm shift was spurred by a climate acutely attuned to the economics of retaining versus attracting customers (Reichheld & Sasser 1990; Vavra 1992). It was empowered by relationship-enabling technologies in manufacturing, communications, and distribution that allowed addressable communications, the customisation of products and messages to individual consumer tastes, and the tracking of individual purchase histories over time (Blattberg & Deighton 1991; Blattberg, Glazer & Little 1994).

Relationship ideas first developed a stronghold in business-to-business and service environments where understanding long-term engagements with channel partners and clients was paramount (Berry 1983; Dwyer, Schurr & Oh 1987). The development of relationship notions in the consumer products realm was slower to catch on, perhaps due to an implied scepticism of the relevance and applicability of relationship principles in a world of inanimate packaged goods, durables, and brands. Still, the idea that 'relationships' existed between consumers and products/brands has always had a place in brand marketing (e.g. in the notion of loyal brand relations or lapsed brand relationships) and anecdotal evidence such as consumers' outraged reactions to the New Coke reformulation provided proof of the lived validity of the idea. Sparked by an empirical piece demonstrating the legitimacy and power of consumers' relationships with their brands (Fournier 1998, see also Fournier & Yao 1997), much research has now been conducted under the brand relationship umbrella. A lot has been learned about the nature and functions of consumers' brand relationships, and the processes whereby brand relationships develop at the hands of consumers, cultures, and marketers.

Branded businesses have now lived through a decade of investment in customer relationship management (CRM): the systems, programs and processes that identify prospects, create customer knowledge and build brand relationships (Boulding *et al.* 2005). Sales of sophisticated CRM software designed to collect and analyse the purchase histories of individual customers reached US$9 billion in 2008 (Mertz 2009). Today's data mining systems generate a staggering array of CRM outreach programs, sending customers targeted, personalised and carefully-timed communications to spark purchases, thank people for their patronage, and offer recognition through special offers, customised products and invitations to the company's inner circle of friends. Despite economic hard times, or perhaps because of them, 75% of managers in a recent Gartner study indicated that they would make significant relationship investments via CRM in light of expected increases in profitability (Mertz 2009).

At this point, relationship management via CRM has become a hard science. Using sophisticated econometrics and data mining software to segment customers into platinum, gold, silver, and lead levels within the profitability pyramid, and optimisation programs to calculate the most efficient interaction plans, CRM helps firms focus scarce marketing resources on profitable customers with high revenues and low costs-to-serve (Zeithaml, Rust & Lemon 2001). Firing or otherwise alienating customers with negative contribution margins, once unheard of in a 'customer is king' world, has taken hold as a cornerstone CRM strategy (Mittal, Sarkees & Murshed 2008). Mittal and colleagues (2008) found that 85% of executives surveyed had undertaken customer divestment actions. In our own recent survey we conducted of 900 consumers, 30% claim to know someone who has been fired by a firm. In the context of estimates that as many as 30% of customers destroy firm value (Haenlein, Kaplan & Beeser 2007), disciplinary actions against bottom-tier customers are compelling. The practice fits well within the contemporary culture of accountability for marketing spend (Ambler 2003).

Despite positive effects on company bottom lines, we charge that managers have failed to maximise brand relationships through their CRM investments. Although CRM stands as an effective *customer management* tool, its value as a *relationship development* tool is less obvious. CRM systems help quantify customer equity—the lifetime economic value of the customer to the firm (CLV)—but they remain silent on the psycho-social relationship equities that CRM was originally conceived to provide. Although managers embrace the idea of building relationships through CRM, their systems remain agnostic on the types of relationships consumers form with brands and companies, and the processes by which these relationships progress and deepen over time.

When we asked how a company knows if it has a relationship with a customer, marketing managers at Fortune 500 firms had this to say: 'There's a relationship if the customer has repeat purchases or has been with us for more than one year'; 'They have a relationship when they use two or three of the firm's products'; 'We give them membership cards so we know who has a relationship.' The problems are obvious. Repeat purchase is a limited, and misleading, indicator of a customer relationship. So-called loyalty programs may build purchase frequencies, shorten inter-purchase intervals or encourage cross-purchasing, but positive effects on emotional attachment, commitment and trust are rarely attained. Some loyalty programs constitute outright entrapment, with lock-in contracts that prevent people from leaving rather than encouraging them to stay. Other programs qualify legitimately as outright bribes and shams. The bottom line is this: the one-sided marketing optimisation programs that dominate CRM are not *relationship* programs, and yet our CRM systems fail to help managers appreciate these different ideas.

Ten years ago, consumer researchers charged that brand relationship marketing was 'powerful in theory, but troubled in practice' because marketers did not fundamentally understand what relationships with customers were all about or how they should be built and maintained (Fournier, Dobscha & Mick 1998). It is our opinion that this state of affairs has not improved. In this chapter we refocus managerial attention back on the key word in the CRM acronym: *relationship*. If firms are to create and capture all the value that brand relationship marketing has to offer, it's time to put relationships back into CRM.

This chapter draws from research and practice concerning consumers' relationships with brands to inform a paradigm for brand management grounded squarely in relationship principles.[44] To manage brands by managing brand relationships, managers need to appreciate and deliver against three relationship realities. First, managers need to understand the relationship, and to do that, they have to understand the people and the functions their brand relationships serve. Second, brand relationship management must adapt to the particular type of relationship being engaged; there is no one size fits all relationship management approach. And lastly, brand relationship management requires sensitivity to process: brand relationships are reciprocating phenomena that constantly evolve and change. Brand managers must acknowledge that everything the brand does affects the relationship, for the good or for the bad.

Principle 1: Know your customers as people and understand the role the brand plays in their lives

You can know a purchaser by collecting purchase and demographic data, but to have a relationship you really need to understand what the person's life is all about.

If managers are to manage consumer-brand relationships, they have to understand their purpose: relationships, brand-specific or otherwise, are meaning-laden resources engaged to help people live their lives. According to this tenet, the relationships formed between brand and consumer can be understood only by looking to the broader context of the person's life to see exactly what is serviced by engagement with the brand. It is important not to reify brand relationships – relationships are facilitators, not ends in and of themselves. A strong relationship develops not by driving brand involvement, but by supporting people with meanings that can help them live their lives.

Nowhere is this disconnect greater than within our current CRM systems. Contemporary CRM operates on an understanding of people as 'consumers', capturing data that taps purchase histories and calculates costs-to-serve. Although metrics like acquisition and retention costs, cross-selling potential, behavioural loyalty and customer lifetime value advance the company agenda, they decidedly leave the person out. There is a big difference between a CRM system attuned to consumer behaviour and one that considers the whole person. You can *know* your customer by collecting purchase and demographic data, but to have a relationship

---

44 This chapter derives in part from the author's previous work, published as S. Fournier (2009) 'Lessons Learned about Consumers' Relationships with their Brands', in J. Priester, D. MacInnis & M.E. Sharp (eds) *Handbook of Brand Relationships*, N.Y. Society for Consumer Psychology and M.E. Sharp and also S. Fournier and J. Avery (2011, forthcoming), 'Putting the 'R' Back in CRM', *Sloan Management Review*.

you really need to *understand* what that person is feeling and what his/her life is all about.

Knowing and understanding are two very different things. At issue is a distinction between collecting information and constructing meaning. Information involves the disintegration and reduction of the complex into small, manageable bites. Today's CRM systems, the brainchildren of information technology professionals, are optimised for information management. Meaning, on the other hand, is the larger sense made out of many small units; it involves the assembly of information bites into larger, more complex and abstract wholes. Information and meaning work at cross purposes: in the search for meaning, context is everything; in the search for information, context is noise. Without context you cannot understand the individual, and without contextual understanding a relationship cannot be forged.

For illustration, let's take a look inside Peapod's CRM system to consider Brenda, a 50-year old Gold-level customer with an average purchase of $124 and a tightening inter-purchase cycle that has reduced from 15.1 to 9.7 days. Brenda's shopping basket includes staples as well as fresh meats and vegetables. She has stopped using grocery stores entirely. Brenda never complains and serves as an advocate attracting others. Peapod reasons that they can get Brenda to platinum level if they can fix just one thing. Brenda uses the 'pick-up at the supermarket' option instead of having her groceries delivered, and Peapod incurs incremental operating costs maintaining both distribution systems. Peapod intends to migrate Brenda from the less popular pick-up alternative so that they can decrease Brenda's cost-to-serve.

Careful listening during Brenda's service interactions provides deeper insight into the person and her relationship with the brand. We talked to Brenda the week after she signed on to the Peapod service. Brenda described herself as 'out of control' when 'Peapod came on her radar screen'. Her life was 'hectic and stressful times four'. In addition to a full-time job managing the tutoring centre at a local college, Brenda was completing coursework for an undergraduate psychology degree. She was also dealing with the pressures of becoming a mom again in mid-life: Brenda adopted the son of her recently deceased daughter—a challenge intensified by the serious health problems her grandson confronts. Brenda 'did not hesitate one second' to 'do the right thing' by her grandson. She is a strong believer in what she calls 'stewardship': 'you make sacrifices, you care for others who need it, you take responsibility...you do what you have to do'. Brenda 'always acts in good faith' and 'takes the good faith of others for granted'. Brenda believes in 'playing by the rules'. According to Brenda, 'the rules are unambiguous no matter what culture or religion you come from. There are right things and wrong things. Ways to treat people. Things you just do and do not do.'

Brenda deliberated for a week or so before signing up with Peapod. The service was, after all, 'a bit of a luxury expense for a non-luxury type person'. But Peapod's promise to make her life more manageable eventually won out. 'I couldn't deny the benefits. It was like a balancing act,' she said. 'I know I shouldn't have those feelings about a product but I did. I felt, they are going to help me! Peapod is going to help me get through all this! It's like a contract of help and it's like a balancing act and if all goes well I will get from here to there with food in the fridge and nothing tipping over.' By the end of three months, Brenda admits she was 'addicted': 'I don't know what I ever did without Peapod. They created a monster. I place the order and arrange a time for my husband to pick it up in Swampscott. It works perfectly for us and fits with his schedule at the firehouse. I won't go back into a grocery store again!'

Fast forward six months after signing on with Peapod. Brenda graduates *summa cum laude*. Despite a difficult winter, her grandson is now healthy again. Although Brenda's life is 'still characteristically out of control', she reports having placed her last order with Peapod upon learning about the pick-up policy change. Brenda explains:

> I went to put in my order around 1 a.m. I thought something must be wrong with my computer when it would not accept my request for a pickup time in Swampscott. I tried for an hour, and it kept coming back 'Pick up in Medford,' which is a half hour away. The next day I called. The representative just said 'Oh yeah, I see that change here.' Well, it wasn't that simple! 'I see that change?' Weren't they listening? Didn't they understand?... This is the computer age and don't tell me, if they know who is clicking and putting in an order to a store that they are no longer using there's no reason for them to not call you and try to explain. That's just common courtesy.... They should have cared about all of us, each and every one...I mean, she's got the screen in front of her. If you can read, it's all there. They have my name, my address, my phone number. I pay them with a check. They have everything they need to know me. They've got practically the fingerprints of my firstborn. They should have known....They betrayed me. I don't want to sound like my whole life revolved around Peapod, but it was a form of betrayal like you have this agreement with them, they are going to be there and then they aren't there. It's like the companies you see in the news that close their doors, and when the workers show up there's no jobs for them. It was the same kind of feeling.

Peapod knew what Brenda purchased, but they were clueless about the kind of person their gold customer was. Had Peapod understood Brenda—her life constraints, her family challenges, her husband's schedule, the degree to which the family was dependent on the Swampscott pickup routine to keep their life in balance—they might have anticipated what their operational change would mean. Had Peapod understood the responsibilities Brenda guaranteed in her own personal relationships—stewardship, caring for others, commitment, sticking to the rules, and above all doing what needs to be done—they might have handled their news event differently. Brenda took it for granted that Peapod would act in good faith, and Peapod let her down. Peapod did not simply change a delivery policy; they violated a strong relationship contract at its core.

Ironically, Peapod had access to all the right data through their many interactions with Brenda. But they failed to recognise these signals as information, let alone convert the data into the deeper meanings that could keep their customer close. Adding insult to injury, the company tried to lure Brenda back with cash incentives after she defected. 'Don't throw money at me', Brenda advises. 'I'm worth more than $25 bucks to you. Show me that I matter. Admit that you screwed up.'

Understanding the role of the brand relationship implies more flexible thinking about what a 'meaningful relationship' might be all about. Academics and managers alike fall into the trap of assuming that strong brand relationships have to be about deep identity expression: that the driving need behind people's brand relationships has to do with trying on the identities that the brand enables, or otherwise gaining status through display of the brand. The danger with this logic is that it limits the relationship phenomenon: the perspective becomes meaningful only in high visibility/high involvement categories where identity risks apply. Brand relationships can serve higher-order identity goals, addressing deeply-rooted identity themes and enabling centrally-held life projects and tasks. But they can also address functions lower on the need hierarchy by delivering against very pragmatic current concerns. Karen, our struggling single mother from the original research (Fournier 1998) bought Tide, All and Cheer (laundry detergents) because one of these reliable mass brands was guaranteed to be on sale when she needed it. Karen's brand portfolio was filled with habitual purchases of otherwise 'invisible brands' (Coupland 2005). These relationships allowed Karen to extend her scarce resources and to develop the skills and solutions she needed to make it through her day. Karen's commercial exchanges can still be understood as brand relationships. Less emotional, surely, and less salient, perhaps; but brand relationships they remain.

The status of the brand relationship as a means versus an end is particularly clear within the context of relationships forged at the brand community level. Brand community research has taught us that people are often more interested in the social links that come from brand relationships than they are in the brands that allow those links to form (Cova & Cova 2002). People often develop brand relationships to gain new social connections or to level out their connections in some significant way. Brand relationships can also provide venues wherein emotional support, advice, companionship and camaraderie are provided. As research into so-called 'third place' brands (Rosenbaum *et al.* 2007) has pointed out, these strong brand relationships are a consequence not a cause; they result from the social connections engendered through the brand relationship. Researchers must take care not to prioritise identity needs over those that are more functional, nor should they focus disproportionately on personal relationships versus collective relationships supporting the brand.

In the end, robust brand relationships are built not on the backs of brands but on a nuanced understanding of people and their needs, both practical and emotional. The reality is that people have many relational needs in their lives, and effective brand relationships cast a wide net of support. Brand relationships might serve to: 'raise the quality of my interactions', 'help me pursue luxuries guilt-free', 'sustain my passions', 'explore different parts of my identity', 'express my devotion', 'deepen bonds through shared ownership', 'distance me from an unwanted self', 'provide comfort through routines and rituals', 'stay adventurous', and so forth.

Brand relationship efforts that comprehensively recognise and fulfil the needs of real people – individually and collectively – are those that deliver results.

There is a risk in relationship management of runaway applications: what is needed is a way to identify the legitimacy or relationship potential of a given brand. Category involvement once served this purpose, but the concept is not consumer-sensitive. Others have considered brand anthropomorphism, but this factor is a red herring or moot point in the simplest case. We do not need to qualify the 'human' quality of the brand character as a means of identifying the brand's relationship potential: all brands – anthropomorphised or not – 'act' through the device of marketing mix decisions, which allow relationship inferences to form (Aaker, Fournier & Brasel 2004; Aggarwal 2004). More useful are screening criteria that build not from product categories and brand characteristics but from the contexts of people's lives. One such approach develops from the insight that consumers play active roles as meaning makers in their brand relationships (Allen, Fournier & Miller 2008), mutating and adapting the marketers' brand meanings to fit their life projects, concerns and tasks. The key is to understand how meanings attain significance in the context of the person's lifeworld. We have come to understand this question as a search for 'meanings that matter', the answer to which lies in the construct of brand meaning resonance (Fournier, Solomon & Englis 2008). Figure 14.1 provides a multifaceted model for thinking about the resonance construct and its role as a relationship strength mediator. Resonance forces a shift in thinking from firm- and competition-centric criteria such as the salience, uniqueness, favourability and dominance of brand meanings to the reverberation and significance of those meanings in the personal and sociocultural world. Resonance focuses not on what brands mean, but rather on how they come to mean something to the people who use them. Resonance highlights the developmental mechanisms driving the initiation and maintenance of consumers' relationships with brands.

Figure 14.1 Resonance: How meanings matter

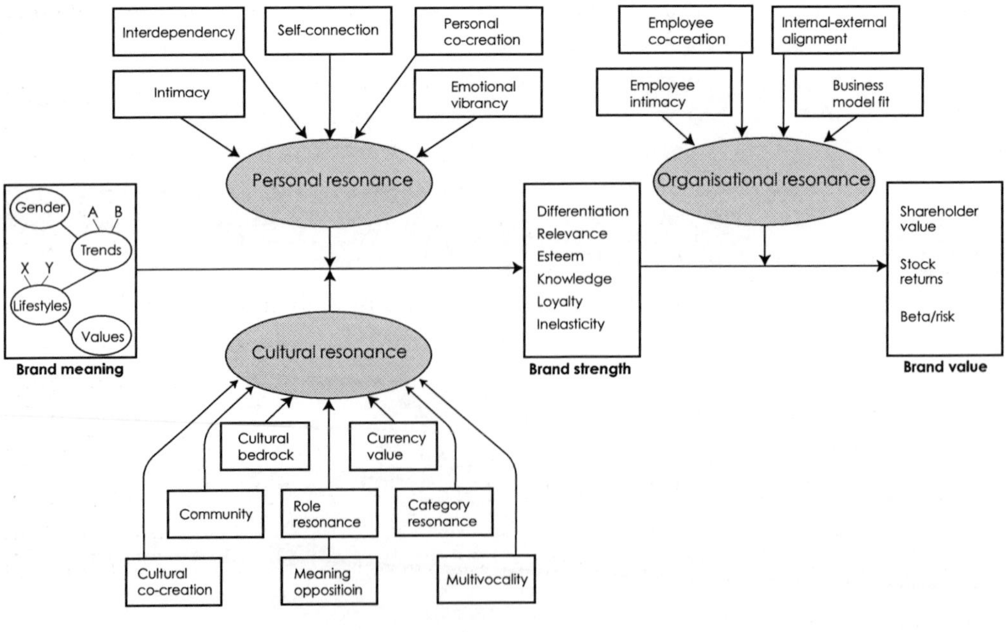

Source: Fournier, S, Solomon, M & Englis B 2009, 'When Brands Resonate', in *Handbook of Brand and Experience Management*, B H Schmitt (ed.), Boston, MA, Elgar Publishing.

Holt (2004), Schroeder & Salzer-Mörling (2005) and Thompson, Rindfleisch & Arsel (2006), to name but a few, have contributed greatly to our understanding of the cultural processes that enable brand resonance. This research serves a critical perspective-gaining function by shifting attention from consumers' relationships with brands to brands' relationships with cultures. We have also seen that predictable psycho-social factors can trigger relational activity by precipitating a search for resonant brand meanings (Fournier 1998). Events such as coming of age, the transition to parenthood or a change in marital status serve as self-defining moments wherein identity planes experience tectonic shifts. Companies that anticipate these shifts with meaningful brand bridges add much-needed semantic continuity to consumers' lives; this is rewarded with strong brand relationship activity. Brand research can greatly inform these fertile periods wherein the individual's hunger for meanings is exacerbated, and explicate the processes involved in the birth of a person's relationship with a brand.

The notion of resonance and the meaning-based tenet on which it is built have implications for how we think about the strength of a given brand relationship. Relationships that resonate have a specific focal goal: they make people's lives somehow better or happier. The construct of subjective well-being within the domain of positive psychology (Diener, Kesebir & Lucas 2008) has much to offer in understanding whether our brand relationships are valuable to people in ways that matter: by improving and enriching their lives.

Principle 2: Appreciate relationship diversity and adapt brand management to the relationship form

Managers love to focus on loyal brand relationships. But what about all the other important brand relationship forms?

The second relationship principle calls attention to the reality of relationship diversity: brand relationships come in many different types and forms. Marketers have always been interested in strong versus weak relationships, and extensive learning has been generated under the brand loyalty rubric. Today's CRM systems also operate on the observation that not all customer relationship are created equal. But, in segmenting customers based on costs and lifetime values, the customer pyramid misses the insight that the profitability of any given customer is actually an outcome of the relationship, not the basis on which that relationship is defined.

Past research has shown that people form many different types of relationships with brands and companies (Fournier 1998). Some are deep and long-lasting; others are superficial and fleeting over time. Some relationships service emotional and social needs; others are utilitarian at their core. Some relationships are positive while others are negative. Our research has identified 52 different dimensions on which people's relationships with brands vary (see Figure 14.2). Although relationship strength may reign supreme for practical reasons, this is but one of many important dimensions along which brand relationships can be defined.

Figure 14.2 A compendium of relationship dimensions

Emotionally close/ Emotionally distant	Frequent/ Not frequent
Intimate/ Not intimate	Helps express who I am/ Does not
Deep/ Superficial	Intense feelings/ Superficial feelings
Based on mutual liking/ Not	Emotional/ Not emotional
High sharing of information/ Limited	Hierarchical/ Not hierarchical
Long term/ Short term	Formal/ Informal
Regular/ Irregular	Fair/ Unfair
Stable/ Fleeting	Secret/ Out in the open
One-sided/ Mutual	Hidden/ Known to others
Active/ Inactive	Friendly/ hostile
Intense interaction/ Superficial interaction	Compatible goals and desires/ incompatible
Interdependent/ Independent	Productive/ Destructive
Democratic/ Autocratic	Relaxed/ Tense
Important to both individuals involved/ More important for one that the other	Flexible/ rigid Difficult to break off/ Easy
Equal in power/ Unequal in power	Interesting/ Dull
Reciprocating/ Non-reciprocating	Reliable/ Not reliable
Harmonious/ Clashing	Positive feelings/ Negative feelings
Conflict-laden/ Conflict-free	Easy to resolve conflicts/ Difficult
High costs and responsibilities/ Low	Altruistic/ Selfish
Warm/ Cold	Solicited/ Unsolicited
Trustworthy/ Not trustworthy	Imposed/ Voluntary
Sincere/ Insincere	Cooperative/ Competitive
Supportive/ Not supportive	Much at risk/ Little at risk
Committed/ Non-committed	Choice-driven/ Chance-driven
Driven by attraction to other/ Repulsion-driven	Easy to enter/ Difficult to start
Utilitarian and task-orientated/ Emotional	Temporary/ Permanent

Survey research using mapping techniques (Fournier 2009) provides a structure for understanding people's brand relationships (See Figure 14.3). In this pilot study, 225 MBA students rated normative relationships with 35 strong national and regional brands on the 52 relationship facets using seven-point semantic differential scales. Another 150 MBA students rated eleven prototypical human relations along these same dimensions. Multidimensional scaling using INDSCALE identified seven dimensions accounting for 78% of the variance in brand relationship ratings: cooperative and harmonious versus competitive and hostile; emotional and identity-vested versus functionally oriented; strong and deep versus weak and superficial; equal and balanced versus one-sided and hierarchical; long term and enduring versus short term; interactive/interdependent versus independent; and flexible/voluntary versus constrained/imposed. The first four of these dimensions emerged cleanly in the rating of human relations as well, accounting for 58% of the variance. The map in Figure 14.3 depicts the brands and human relations plotted on dimensions of strength and type of reward.

Figure 14.3 Brand relationship map

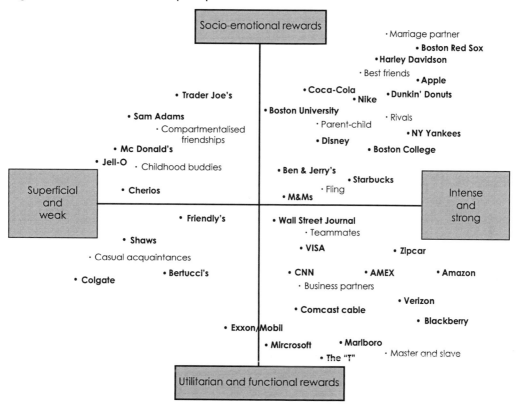

In ten years of application and research we have progressed little in our understanding of this complex brand-relationship space. Consumer research typically demarcates exchange relationships from communal relationships and provides one important step in the right direction (Aggarwal 2004). But, the exchange/communal paradigm (Clark & Mills 1979) taps but the tip of the iceberg of relationship variability, especially when one considers that exchanges are relegated to 'non-relational status' in this research. Select forms of commercial relationships have received research attention: for example, friendships (Price & Arnould 1999), secret relationships (Goodwin 1992), flings (Alvarez & Fournier,

2011) and the abusive partner (Hill 1994; Hill & Kozup 2007). Still, managerially-focused relationship research tends to focus on positive and strong brand relationships, or those that can readily be improved to be so. Our analysis reinforces the prominence of negative brand relationships; a fully-enabled perspective on consumer-brand relationship behaviour must lose its false optimism and incorporate dysfunctional relationship forms. Recent empirical work by Miller, Fournier & Allen (2011, forthcoming) probes the resonance of eight prominent brand relationship types across several of these dimensions: abusive, adversarial (enmities), communal, committed partnerships, dependencies, exchange, master-slave relationships, and secret affairs. Still, relationship-inspired theory concerning these and other brand relationship forms is deficient. The status of consumer-brand relationship mapping stands much like that observed for business-to-business relationships more than twenty years ago: 'Much remains to be done in distinguishing commercial, work, and romantic relationships. Also, the model is presented abstractly. It lacks conceptual detail and obvious ways to operationalise key variables' (Dwyer, Schurr & Oh 1987, p. 20).

The point remains that managers need to be more open-minded when it comes to the brand relationships on their radar. Managers remain fixated on one type of relationship: the loyal relationship, where, as in marriage, the consumer plays the role of committed and passionate spouse. Marital relationships are not inherently more valuable than other relationships: all relationships are meaningful to the people for whom they are engaged. Importantly, lots of different relationships can be profitable—*provided they are managed right*. If we are to capture all the value that brand relationship marketing has to offer, managers must learn to negotiate a more varied relationship space. The trick is to know what kind of relationships customers have established so that each can be optimised in its own right.

Contract theory can be particularly useful for developing managerial insight into specific brand relationships. Relationships are intrinsically contractual: they are created when two parties come together with the intention of forming a collective understanding of what each party will provide and receive over time (MacNeil 1980). The relationship contract is comprised of rules and norms that guide perceptions, attributions, inferences, judgments and actions within that particular relationship (MacNeil 1985; Rousseau 1989; Rousseau & Parks 1992). Relationship rules are statements that prescribe, proscribe or permit particular types of behaviours; they provide standards of conduct that guide partners' behaviours and inform interpretations of the same (Metts 1994). Relationship rules shared within a social group are referred to as norms. The operation of relational norms in the consumer setting has been empirically supported (Aggarwal 2004; Aggarwal & Law 2005; Aggarwal & Zhang 2006): consumers import norms from human relationships into the brand relationships that they form.

Relationship contracts also specify the fundamental 'gives' and 'gets' of the relationship: promises to do something (or to refrain from doing something) in return for a payment-in-kind (Rousseau & Parks 1992). Contracts also include operative relationship development goals and primary resource exchanges (Fitzsimons & Bargh 2003; Kayser, Schwinger & Cohen 1984), benchmarks for assessing satisfaction (Baucom *et al.* 1996), prototypical beliefs about relational successes and failures (Baucom *et al.* 1989), expected risks and rewards (Sabatelli & Pearce 1986), transgression tolerance zones (Rusbult *et al.* 1991), trust forms and bases (Rousseau *et al.* 1998), and appropriate assuagement devices in the face of broken rules (Metts 1994). Relationship templates can be usefully thought of as scripts or schemata (Andersen 1993; Baldwin 1992) that offer the person workable relationship theories-in-use.

According to this perspective, each relationship is governed by a different psychological contract, or set of guiding norms and rules (Baldwin 1992; Rousseau 1989; Rousseau & Parks 1992). Our research explores the contract terms for a several popular commercial relationships (Fournier, Avery & Wojnicki 2004). A brand partnership, for example, prioritises the mutual helping norm. Partners give without getting, display flexibility in company dealings, and accommodate problems with a 'let's work together' approach. Best customers are governed by norms of privilege. They expect special treatment that sets them apart. Best customers overvalue how much they put into the relationship and undervalue how much they take out. In flings, what matters most is keeping the emotional rewards ratio high. Consumers who view themselves as masters in a master-slave engagement expect distanced but unquestioning service. Companies in these relationships are expected to anticipate needs, to be seen but not heard, to stick to the rules, and to speak (with great formality) only when spoken to. The company slave in this relationship is never intimate, and the boss is always right. Opportunism – 'self-interest seeking with guile' – is the global norm governing commercial exchange relations (Williamson 1975). Research in psychology supports unique rule sets for particular types of communal relationships: for example, rules of compartmentalised friendship, marriage, kinship, workplace, and marketplace relations (Argyle & Henderson 1984; Davis & Todd 1982; Kayser, Schwinger & Cohen 1984; O'Connell 1984). Relationship contracts are important because they determine the terms governing the potential profitability of a given relationship. Contracts outline the actions firms must take and avoid taking in order to keep the relationship sound.

Harley-Davidson found much value in research identifying the Best Friendship as the dominant relationship template for their brand. Harley had long operated on the assumption that the company was in the business of engaging committed partnerships by building dedicated loyalty to the brand. Although friendships and marriages occupy the same ideal space of deep, emotionally-rewarding engagements, the contractual differences between these relationships matter significantly. A marriage is a socially-supported contract to stay together despite circumstances, foreseen and unforeseen. Core drivers of marital bonds are commitment and love. Best friendship, in contrast, is a totally voluntary interdependence between parties intended to facilitate socio-emotional goals. The dimension most characteristic of friendship is reciprocity: friends willingly give each other the shirts off their backs, for example, and are there whenever needs arise. Friendships are also fundamentally about intimacy—recall the old adage that friends know more about you than your spouse does—and the vulnerability that heightened intimacy entails. The do's and don'ts of these different relationships contrast sharply and sometimes conflict in fundamental ways. Marriage partners erect barriers to exit and freely try to change the other, for example, while such actions violate best friendships at the core. Buddies are friends too, but their drivers involve interdependence, not intimacy levels. To manage properly, you have to know what type of relationships consumers have engaged (see Figure 14.4).

The Director of Harley Owners Group (H.O.G.) took this insight to heart when managing his operations. In his wallet, he kept an index card titled 'The Things My Successor Needs to Know', which summarised implications derived from managing HOG customer relationships as best friendships. By articulating the rules of friendship, HOG management could successfully negotiate and manage their customer relationships, and affect corrections when their actions went off course.

Current CRM systems offer limited guidance for maximising value creation across different relationships: monies are simply directed toward more profitable relationships and away from those generating less revenue or incurring higher costs-to-serve. By considering which relationship templates are operative, managers can identify their most common or strategic relationships, and allocate resources appropriate to their maintenance and growth.

Figure 14.4 Playing by the rules: Marriage versus friendships

	MARRIAGE PARTNERS	BEST FRIENDS	BUDDIES
DO	• formalise the union • negotiate the contract • verbalise the need for change • strive to meet all needs • add surprises/spark • erect barriers to exit	• encourage other friendships • self disclose • listen • ask and reciprocate • be reliable, predictable	• compartmentalise per activities • show only part of the self • sustain interaction • make entry/exit easy
DON'T	• breach fidelity pledge • forget intimate details	• leak secrets • discuss implicit contract • try to change the other • impose external pressures • erect barriers to exit	• establish intimacy, deep or broad • encourage emotional involvement • make demands or add repsonsibility • drop by uninvited • use things without permission

Principle 3: Relationships are dynamic phenomena that require active management over time

Relationship management is process management: you have to understand how relationships evolve and why they change.

The third principle emphasises the dynamic and interdependent nature of consumer-brand relationships. At a basic level, relationships unfold through a series of temporal stages including initiation, growth, maintenance and decline. Different relationships manifest characteristic development trajectories such as the biological life cycle model, the spiked passing fad, cyclical resurgence, or the fluctuating highs and lows of approach-avoidance, love-and-hate. Changes in or actions on the part of the person, brand and environment trigger the relationship evolution process; entropy and stress factors precipitate relationship decline. Relationships are dynamic, temporal phenomena: they require active management over time.

Despite the inherent dynamism of brand relationships, few developmental models for managing relationship processes exist. Although we have spent decades designing programs to instil customer loyalty, we have captured few mechanisms beyond commitment through which consumers advance their relationships with brands.

A useful approach to process specification is to identify the primary currency driving a given brand relationship, and expose the milestones and mechanisms that represent progress along this path. Research conducted for Harley-Davidson, for example, illuminated the journey of 'becoming a rider' through a progressive accumulation of status-granting cultural capital of various kinds – knowledge, skills, experiences and social connections as well as dispositions concerning what is authentic within the group (see Figure 14.5). Models developed for members of the Harley Owner's Group focused on the accumulation of power and influence in the system, and pivotal experiences providing status credentials in this regard. Zildjian, a manufacturer of drum cymbals, manages its relationships by managing the process whereby a person 'becomes a drummer' and merges his/her identity with the drummer identity. The New York Philharmonic might manage the process of 'becoming a donor': establishing deeper and deeper emotional bonds to the point where the person feels responsible for the continued future of the orchestral music. The point of these examples is that relationship development is not always best understood as a process of increasingly deepening relationship commitment; rather, relationships 'develop' along foundations that critically define the type of engagement at hand.

The relationship contracts perspective also provides a valuable lens on the developmental mechanisms shaping brand relationships. Relationship interrupts that render the operative contract salient, most notably in the form of transgressions, critically affect the relationship trajectory and course. By studying the relationship in its point of crisis, managers can reverse-engineer what makes the relationship thrive. But everything the brand 'does' affects the relationship – from the personality-suggestive colours and fonts of the company website to the tonality of communications from the brand (Aaker *et al.* 2004). Research suggests that consumers make inferences from meaning-laden brand behavioural 'signals', so as to interpret and reinterpret the type of relationship contract in play.

Figure 14.5 Cultural capital model for the development of relationships with the Harley-Davidson brand

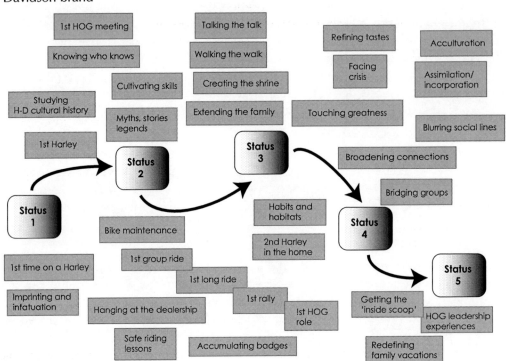

Relationship development can also be understood as a contract signalling process wherein rules and terms evolve (Fournier, Avery & Wojnicki 2004). Figure 14.6 presents a working model for the various mechanisms involved in the contracting process. Two subprocesses are particularly interesting for their ability to inform longstanding problems in branding. Supra-contracting (Narayandas & Rangan 2004) involves extra-role behaviours beyond contract requirements that are engaged voluntarily and purposively on the part of the consumer (or brand) in order to signal a desire to transition the relationship to a new, deeper level. Supra-contracting is observed in the form of word-of-mouth advocacy, active customer recruitment, brand citizenship behaviours, and employee gifting. Loyalty, as we have come to understand it, can be seen as mutually reinforcing supra-contracting on the part of consumers and brands. A second process, contract misalignment, highlights the risks exposed in the inherently interdependent relationship setting. Psychological contracts, though individually interpreted, are assumed to be shared by both parties, who act *as if* their individual contract is aligned with the psychological contract of the relationship other; the concept of the normative contract has been developed to capture this idea (Rousseau 1989). Our research (Fournier, Avery & Wojnicki 2004) exposes the frequent presence and consequence of misaligned consumer-firm contracts, particularly in circumstances where the person has been led to believe s/he is a best customer of the firm.

Figure 144.6 A blueprint for relationship-sensitive brand management

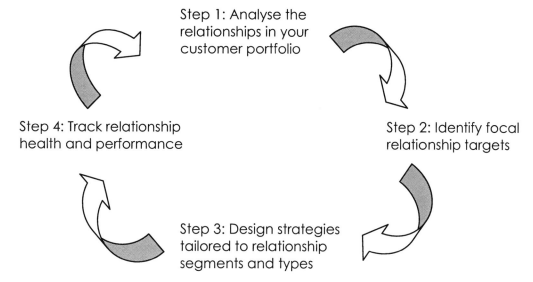

Step 1: Analyse the relationships in your customer portfolio

Step 2: Identify focal relationship targets

Step 3: Design strategies tailored to relationship segments and types

Step 4: Track relationship health and performance

Applying the principles: A relationship management framework for the brand

Figure 14.7 offers a four-step blueprint for a brand management protocol that is sensitive to relationship fundamentals and thereby capable of maximising the value created and captured through consumer relationships with the brand.

Figure 14.7 Relationship contracting process mechanisms

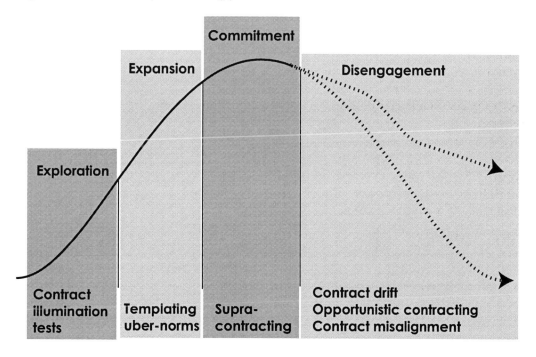

Exploration

Expansion

Commitment

Disengagement

Contract illumination tests

Templating uber-norms

Supra-contracting

Contract drift
Opportunistic contracting
Contract misalignment

Source: Fournier, S, Avery, J & Wojnicki, A 2004, 'Contracting for Relationships', presentation at *Association for Consumer Research Conference*, Portland, Oregon.

Step 1: Analyse the relationships in your customer portfolio

Effective brand relationship management begins with a deep and nuanced understanding of the different types of relationships that firms and their customers co-create. As Davenport and his colleagues have emphasised, developing an understanding involves first scanning for, listening to, and interpreting the signals that customers send during transactions (Davenport, Harris & Kohli 2001). Operatives at L.L. Bean and American Express are trained to capture notes about customer transactions, and convert that information into a contextual understanding of the customer in a broader sense. An L.L. Bean representative can recommend against a particular purchase, for example, knowing that since a given customer's son is really rough on his shoes, footwear with bungie cord ties will likely not stand up. Marriott International's Ritz-Carlton operates a system called 'Mystique' that shares more discreet staff observations about guests, from a log of the kinds of fruit left on room-service plates to notes of a guest's and oncoming cold (Johnson 2006). By adding contextual data obtained when talking with customers, and by shadowing purchasers through service interactions and store visits, insightful companies can develop leadership in customer knowledge management that informs the brand relationship activities of the firm.

But true understanding probes even deeper: it goes beyond insights specific to purchase and consumption to develop empathy concerning the individual's broader emotional life. Smart companies transcend the firm's perspective to consider what the experience feels like through the customers' eyes and why it makes a difference. Obtaining such data is not easy. Harley-Davidson retains ethnographers who live the Harley lifestyle; they require executives to spend time in the field such that empathic insights are brought back inside (Fournier & Lee 2008). Procter & Gamble leverages ZMET, a technology for mapping the deeper metaphoric meanings that people evoke in a given conceptual domain (Christensen & Olsen 2002). Web 3.0 offers tantalising possibilities for decoding people's experiences. Semantic applications use intelligent agent software to scrape through reams of information and intuit the meanings they contain. Arguably, managers need to shift their analytic focus from specific brands to broader consumption categories and life paths if they are to become listening and learning organisations with a window into people's lives. Savvy relationship managers adopt a broad definition of relevant data and invest in intelligence systems that can remake fragmented consumers into meaningful wholes.

With meanings in hand, managers turn to specifying their operative relationship spaces and profiling the relationships people engage with their brands. Depth interviewing can help companies uncover the explicit and implicit rules governing customer interaction; critical incident interviews can uncover the rules of engagement that are broken in times of relationship termination, stress or strain. Surveys in which people rate brands in terms of relationship needs and motives (e.g. establish roots, sustain passions, obtain support), relationship dimensions (e.g.

strong/weak, formal/informal, positive/negative), strength of the relationship (e.g. levels of commitment, passion, intimacy, and trust), or more general profile types (e.g. partnership, fling, best friendship) can be applied to generate relationship maps and structures. Companies can use perceptual mapping software to determine the actual space for their brands or to identify ideal spaces that consider strengths, opportunities, and weaknesses. Companies can also segment their customers based on the types of relationships they form. Lastly, field experiments can be conducted in which company relationship actions vary according to different hypothesised relationships. By determining whether company actions produce expected behaviours or generate negative responses, a company can interpolate the types of brand relationships that have formed.

Step 2: Identify focal relationship targets

In the second stage of informed brand relationship management, the firm identifies which relationships to target so as to maximise value creation. A firm may focus on relationships that are prevalent or dominant, or cultivate those that are somehow strategic to the firm. Firms can focus on emblematic relationships: the type of relationship that best characterises the category or the brand. Alternately, firms can map all of the relationships held by their brands versus competition to uncover strategic gaps that can be targeted with new or repositioned brands. A fourth option is to focus on optimising all the different relationship types revealed in the relationship segmentation. Firms can strengthen positive relationships, encourage growth within fleeting or weaker relationships, or shift negative relationships to more positive and profitable terms. Lastly, firms can strategically align their relationship practices to enable an ideal relationship type that somehow embodies the firm's mission, business model, or culture, or expresses the core values of the brand. The options are many; the choice is the company's to make.

Step 3: Design strategies tailored to relationship segments and types

In the third step, managers design strategies tailored to the focal relationship types and segments identified for their brands. Informed brand relationship management embraces relationship variability, and develops plans that manage relationships according to their operative rules. As with Harley-Davidson, firms should build a hierarchy of rules and follow it: what are the inviolate rules of each type of relationship that must never be broken; which rules are nice-to-have but less important to the health of the relationship at hand. Critical is an understanding of how profitability is related to the relational rules undergirding each relationship. Which rules are most costly? Which rules drive retention or revenues? Can planning prioritise rules that are beneficial to both consumers and the firm? To develop strategic ideas, managers can reverse engineer their most well-functioning relationships to understand the actions that built them, and apply these same tactics with new or dysfunctional relationships to encourage development along similar lines.

Step 4: Track relationship health and performance

The final step in informed brand relationship management involves relationship-inspired tracking and performance evaluation. Relationship metrics must go beyond traditional awareness, liking, and purchase measures to include indicators of relationship strength, health, and quality if they are to inform present or future strategies and plans. Fournier's brand relationship quality index (Fournier 1998, 2000), Thomson et al.'s measure of brand-self attachment (Thomson, MacInnis & Park 2005) and Escalas' self-brand connection (Escalas 2004) are useful in this regard. Customised item batteries tapping relationship benefits, motives, and rules, as developed during the stage 1 exploratory, can also be incorporated into tracking studies to monitor and evaluate segments and their profitability or size. Metrics sensitive to specific relationships have yet to be validated. This is an important shortcoming in best practice since you cannot measure relationship strength or vitality independent of the relationship form.

Attachment theory and its secure, anxious/ambivalent and avoidant relationship styles can also be measured to indicate person moderators of relationship activity (Paulssen & Fournier 2008), as can relationship styles (independent, discerning, and acquisitive, Matthews 1986), orientations (power versus intimacy, McAdams 1984) and drives (McAdams 1988).

Concluding thoughts

Brand relationships, done right, are powerful tools for creating value. But our systems need to move beyond a decades-long fixation on profitability as a driving design criterion if this value is to be captured by the firm. Businesses must deliver profits, but businesses that decide to pursue relationships must be held to the higher standards that the psycho-social relationship strategy implies. As relationship providers, marketers must establish a clear understanding of what their relationships mean to consumers and how they add value to or detract value from people's lives. Relationship marketers must accept that with relationships come costs and responsibilities, not just financial gains and rewards. When brand managers stop managing and start relating, more informed practice will come.

References

Aaker, J, Fournier, S & Brasel, A 2004, 'When Good Brands Do Bad', *Journal of Consumer Research*, 31 (June), 1–25.

Aggarwal, P 2004, 'The Effects of Brand Relationship Norms on Consumer Attitudes and Behavior', *Journal of Consumer Research*, 31 (1), 87–101.

Aggarwal, P & Law, S 2005, 'Role of Relationship Norms in Processing Brand Information', *Journal of Consumer Research*, 32 (3), 453–464.

Aggarwal, P & Zhang, M 2006, 'The Moderating Effect of Relationship Norm Salience on Consumers' Loss Aversion', *Journal of Consumer Research*, 33 (3), 413–419.

Allen, C, Fournier, S & Miller, F 2008, 'Brands and their Meaning Makers', in *Handbook of Consumer Psychology,* eds. Haugtvedt, C, Herr, P & Kardes, F. Mahwah, NJ: Lawrence Erlbaum Associates, 781–822.

Alvarez, C & Fournier S 2011 (forthcoming), 'Brand Flings: When Great Brand Relationships are Not Built to Last', to appear in *Consumer-Brand Relationships: Theory and Practice,* eds. Fetscherin, M, Fournier, S, Breazeale, M, & Melewar TC. London: Routledge.

Ambler, T 2003, Marketing and the Bottom Line (2nd Edition). London: FT Press.

Andersen, PA 1993, 'Cognitive Schemata in Personal Relationships', in *Individuals in Relationships (Understanding Relationship Processes,* Volume 1), ed. Duck, S. Newbury Park, CA: Sage Publications, 1–29.

Argyle, M & Henderson, M 1984, 'The Rules of Friendship', *Journal of Social and Personal Relationships,* 1, 211–237.

Baldwin, MW 1992, 'Relational Schemas and the Processing of Social Information', *Psychological Bulletin,* 112 (3), 461–84.

Baucom, DH, Epstein, N, Rankin, LA & Burnett, CK 1996, 'Assessing Relationship Standards: The Inventory of Specific Relationship Standards', *Journal of Family Psychology,* 10 (1), 72–88.

Baucom, DH, Epstein, N, Sayers, S & Sher, TG 1989, 'The Role of Cognitions in Marital Relationships: Definitional, Methodological, and Conceptual Issues', *Journal of Consulting and Clinical Psychology,* 57 (1), 31–38.

Berry, LL 1983, 'Relationship Marketing', in *Emerging Perspectives on Services Marketing,* eds. Berry, LL, Shostack, GL, and Upah, G. Chicago, IL: American Marketing Association, 25-34.

Blattberg, RC & Deighton, J 1991, 'Interactive Marketing: Exploiting the Age of Addressability,' *Sloan Management Review* (Fall), 5-14.

Blattberg, RC, Glazer R & Little, JDC 1994, *The Marketing Information Revolution,* Boston, MA: Harvard Business School Press.

Boulding, W, Staelin, R, Ehret, M & Johnston, WJ 2005, 'A Customer Relationship Management Roadmap: What is Known, Potential Pitfalls, and Where to Go', *Journal of Marketing,* 69 (4), 155–661.

Christensen, GL & Olsen, JC 2002, 'Mapping Consumers' Mental Models with ZMET', *Psychology and Marketing,* 19 (June), 477-501.

Clark, MS & Mills, J 1979, 'Interpersonal Attraction in Exchange and Communal Relationships', *Journal of Personality and Social Psychology,* 37 (1), 12–24.

Coupland, JC 2005, 'Invisible Brands: An Ethnography of Households and the Brands in their Kitchen Pantries', *Journal of Consumer Research,* 32 (1), 106–118.

Cova, B & Cova, V 2002, 'Tribal Marketing: The Tribalisation of Society and its Impact on the Conduct of Marketing', *European Journal of Marketing,* 36 (5/6), 595-620.

Davenport, TH, Harris, JG & Kohli, AK 2001, 'How Do They Know Their Customers So Well?' *MIT Sloan Management Review* (Winter), 63-73.

Davis, KE & Todd, MJ 1982, 'Friendship and Love Relationships', *Advances in Descriptive Psychology,* 2, 79–122.

Deighton, J 1995, 'A New Marketing Paradigm?' presentation at the Harvard Business School conference on *The Future of Marketing,* Boston: MA.

Diener, E, Kesebir, P & Lucas, R 2008, 'Benefits of Accounts of Well-Being: For Societies and for Psychological Science', *Applied Psychology,* 57 (July), 37–53.

Dwyer, FR, Schurr, PH & Oh, S 1987, 'Developing Buyer-Seller Relationships', *Journal of Marketing,* 51 (2), 11–26.

Escalas, JE 2004, 'Narrative Processing: Building Consumer Connections to Brands', *Journal of Consumer Psychology,* 14 (1&2), 168-180.

Fitzsimons, GM & Bargh, JA 2003, 'Thinking of You: Non-conscious Pursuit of Interpersonal Goals Associated with Relationship Partners', *Journal of Personality and Social Psychology,* 84 (1), 148–64.

Fournier, S 1998, 'Consumers and their Brands: Developing Relationship Theory in Consumer Research', *Journal of Consumer Research,* 24 (March), 343–373.

Fournier, S 2000, 'Dimensionalizing Brand Relationships through Brand Relationship Strength', Presentation at Association for Consumer Research Conference, Salt Lake City, Utah.

Fournier, S 2009, 'Lessons Learned about Consumers' Relationships with their Brands', in *Handbook of Brand Relationships,* eds. Priester, J MacInnis, D & Park, CW., N.Y. Society for Consumer Psychology and M.E. Sharp, 5-23.

Fournier, S & Avery, J 2011(forthcoming), 'Putting the 'R' Back in CRM', *Sloan Management Review.*

Fournier, S & Lee L 2008, 'Getting Brand Community Right', *Harvard Business Review* (April), 105-111.

Fournier, S & Yao, JL 1997, 'Reviving Brand Loyalty: A Reconceptualization with the Framework of Consumer-Brand Relationships', *International Journal of Research in Marketing,* 14 (5), 451-472.

Fournier, S, Avery, J & Wojnicki, A 2004, 'Contracting for Relationships', Presentation at Association for Consumer Research Conference, Portland, Oregon, October 8.

Fournier, S, Dobscha, S & Mick, D 1998, 'Preventing the Premature Death of Relationship Marketing', *Harvard Business Review,* 76 (January), 42–51.

Fournier, S, Solomon, M & Englis, B 2008, 'When Brands Resonate', in *Handbook of Brand and Experience Management,* eds. Schmitt, BH & Rogers, DL, Northampton, MA: Edward Elgar, 35-57.

Goodwin, C 1992, 'A Conceptualization of Motives to Seek Privacy for Nondeviant Consumption', *Journal of Consumer Psychology,* 1 (3), 261–284.

Haenlein, M, Kaplan, AM & Beeser, AJ 2007, 'A Model to Determine Customer Lifetime Value in a Retail Banking Context', *European Management Journal,* 25 (June), 221-234.

Hill, RP 1994, 'Bill Collectors and Consumers: A Troublesome Exchange Relationship', *Journal of Public Policy & Marketing,* 13 (1), 20–35.

Hill, RP & Kozup, J 2007, 'Consumer Experiences with Predatory Lending Practices', *Journal of Consumer Affairs,* 41 (1), 29–46.

Holt, DB 2004, *How Brands Become Icons: The Principles of Cultural Branding.* Boston: Harvard Business School Press.

Johnson, A 2006, 'Hotels Take 'Know Your Customer' to a New Level', *Wall Street Journal*, (February 7), D1.

Kayser, E, Schwinger, T & Cohen, RL 1984, 'Laypersons' Conceptions of Social Relationships: A Test of Contract Theory', *Journal of Social and Personal Relationships*, 1, 433–58.

MacNeil, IR 1980, *The New Social Contract*, New Haven, CT: Yale University Press.

MacNeil, IR 1985, 'Relational Contracts: What We Do and Do Not Know', *Wisconsin Law Review*, 483–525.

Matthews, S 1986, *Friendships through the Life Course: Oral Biographies in Old Age*, vol. 161. Beverly Hills, CA: Sage Library of Social Research.

McAdams, DP 1984, 'Human Motives and Personal Relationships', in *Communication, Intimacy, and Close Relationships*, ed. V. Derlega. New York, NY: Academic Press, 41–70.

McAdams, DP 1988, 'Personal Needs and Personal Relationships', in *Handbook of Personal Relationships: Theory, Research, Interventions*, ed. S. Duck. New York, NY: Wiley, 7–22.

Mertz, SA 2009, 'Dataquest Insight: CRM Software Market Share Analysis, Worldwide, 2008', Gartner Inc., (July 6).

Metts, S 1994, 'Relational Transgressions', in *The Dark Side of Interpersonal Communication*, eds. Cupach, W & Spitzberg, B. Hillsdale, NJ: Lawrence Erlbaum, 217–239.

Miller, F, Fournier, S & Allen C 2011 (forthcoming), 'Exploring Relationship Analogues in the Brand Space', to appear in *Consumer-Brand Relationships: Theory and Practice*, eds. Fetscherin, M, Fournier, S, Breazeale, M, & Melewar TC. London: Routledge.

Mittal, V, Sarkees, M & Murshed, F 2008, 'The Right Way to Manage Unprofitable Customers', *Harvard Business Review* (April), 94-102.

Narayandas, D & Rangan, VK 2004, 'Building and Sustaining Buyer-Seller Relationships in Mature Industrial Markets', *Journal of Marketing*, 68 (July), 63–77.

O'Connell, L 1984, 'An Exploration of Exchange in Three Social Relationships: Kinship, Friendship, and the Marketplace', *Journal of Social and Personal Relationships*, 1, 333–45.

Paulssen, M & Fournier, S 2008, 'Attachment Security and the Strength of Commercial Relationships', Working paper, Boston University.

Peppers, D & Rogers, M 1993, *The One to One Future*, New York, NY: Doubleday.

Price, LL & Arnould, EJ 1999, 'Commercial Friendships: Service Provider-Client Relationships in Context', *Journal of Marketing*, 63 (4), 38–56.

Reichheld, F & Sasser Jr., WE 1990, 'Zero Defections: Quality Comes to Services', *Harvard Business Review* (September-October), 105-111.

Rosenbaum, MS, Ward, J, Walker, BA & Ostom, AL 2007, 'A Cup of Coffee with a Dash of Love: An Investigation of Commercial Social Support and Third-Place Attachment', *Journal of Service Research*, 10 (1), 43–59.

Rousseau, DM 1989, 'Psychological and Implied Contracts in Organizations', *Employee Responsibilities and Rights Journal*, 2 (2), 121–39.

Rousseau, DM & Parks, JM 1992, 'The Contracts of Individuals and Organizations', *Research in Organizational Behaviour,* Vol. 15, 1–43.

Rousseau, DM, Sitkin, SB, Burt, RS & Camerer, C 1998, 'Not So Different After All: A Cross-Discipline View of Trust', *Academy of Management Review,* 23 (3), 393–404.

Rusbult, CE, Verette, J, Whitney, GA, Slovik, LF & Lipkus, I 1991, 'Accommodation Processes in Close Relationships: Theory and Preliminary Empirical Evidence', *Journal of Personality and Social Psychology,* 60 (1), 53–78.

Sabatelli, RM & Pearce, J 1986, 'Exploring Marital Expectations', *Journal of Social and Personal Relationships,* 3, 307–321.

Schroeder, J & Salzer-Mörling, M 2005, *Brand Culture,* London: Routledge.

Schwinger, T 1980, 'Just Allocations of Goods: Decisions among Three Principles', in *Justice and Social Interaction,* ed. G. Mikula. New York, NY: Springer-Verlag, 95–125.

Thompson, C J, Rindfleisch, A & Arsel, Z 2006, 'Emotional Branding and the Strategic Value of Doppelganger Brand Image', *Journal of Marketing,* 70 (January), 50–64.

Thomson, M, MacInnis, D & Park, CW 2005, 'The Ties that Bind: Measuring the Strength of Consumer's Emotional Attachments to Brands', *Journal of Consumer Psychology,* 15 (1), 77–91.

Vavra, TG 1992, *After-Marketing: How to Keep Customers for Life through Relationship Marketing,* Burr Ridge, IL: Irwin Professional Publishing.

Webster, FE 1992, 'The Changing Role of Marketing in the Corporation,' *Journal of Marketing* 56 (October), 1-17.

Williamson, OE 1975, *Markets and Hierarchies,* New York, NY: The Free Press.

Zeithaml, VA, Rust, RT & Lemon, KN 2001, 'The Customer Pyramid: Creating and Serving Profitable Customers', California Management Review, 43 (4), 118-142

Author biography

Susan Fournier is Associate Professor and Dean's Research Fellow, Marketing, at Boston University School of Management. Susan is an active researcher and consultant in the areas of branding and relationship marketing. Current projects explore the creation of shareholder value through branding, cultural paradigms for brand management, the development of person-brands, and dynamic processes of consumer-brand relationship evolution. She has received best article awards for work published in *Journal of Consumer Research, Journal of Marketing, Harvard Business Review* and *Journal of the Academy of Marketing Science,* and is the author of many best-selling Harvard Business School cases.

Contact: Professor Susan Fournier, Boston University School of Management, 595 Commonwealth Avenue, Boston MA 02215; P 617 353 2773; F 617 353 4098; E fournism@bu.edu.

Chapter 15

Experiential branding

BILL MERRILEES & DALE MILLER

ABSTRACT

An exciting aspect of branding is the emergence of research which starts to address the challenge of branding experiences. In practice, various attempts have been made to embed experience in some brands, and yet researching and managing 'the total brand experience' while having much potential seem to have been neglected until now. This chapter addresses that gap by critically examining the nature of brand experience and the current state of knowledge. We then discuss and reflect on some current applications of brand experiences. Some of the brand experience areas we explore are: retail brand experiences, city branding experiences, show branding experiences, and museum branding experiences. These diverse areas indicate the potential scope of experiential branding. Finally, we explore different methods of managing branding experiences which, if done successfully, can ensure a sustainable competitive advantage. Overall, the chapter invites you, the reader, to embark on a thought-provoking journey towards experiential branding.

KEYWORDS

brand experiences; experiential branding; managing experiences; services branding; retailing; museums

Introduction

Brand experience is an exciting and dynamic aspect of branding. The idea is inter-mingled in much of the branding literature. Usually, brand experience is assumed, without any clear delineation of exactly what is entailed by the concept or its scope. Indeed, although the idea of experiential branding is appealing and logical, experiential branding as a term appears infrequently in the literature. The discussion here uses the terms 'brand experience' and 'experiential branding' interchangeably. The aim of this chapter is to clarify the nature of brand experience, to draw out its significance, and to explore how to manage it. Specifically, the chapter explores experiential branding in a range of contexts.

We especially acknowledge two seminal papers on the nature of the brand experience (Tybout & Carpenter 2001; Brakus, Schmitt & Zarantonello 2009). Additionally, Tynan and McKechnie (2009) present a very useful state-of-the-art literature review on consumer experiences. Further, several special journal issues on experiences have been useful (Dennis & King 2007; Grewal, Levy & Kumar 2009). Significantly, some of these landmark papers are 2009 publications, indicating the recent surge in interest about consumer and brand experiences, and reinforcing the relevance of discussing brand experience.

Although our focus is explicitly on brand experiences, we find it prudent and useful to include leading articles that are framed more around related themes, namely customer experiences and shopping experiences. The different experiences are of course different phenomena, but there is considerable overlap. Any insight from better understanding customer or shopping experiences will be very useful for understanding brand experiences. In this regard, especially useful are the papers or special journal issues by Tynan and McKechnie (2009), Dennis and King (2007), and Grewal *et al.* (2009).

The first part of the chapter debates and discusses the nature of brand experiences. In part, the debate is conceptual, although we draw on as many empirical papers as appropriate. Special use is made of the two seminal papers (Tybout & Carpenter 2001; Brakus *et al.* 2009). Given their major contributions to the literature, each of these papers is featured as a section in its own right. Additionally, we provide a critique of each paper, recognising the merit of each paper but also indicating some limitations. A further section reinforces the Tybout and Carpenter (2001) approach, namely the service-dominant logic approach, especially through the lens of Tynan and McKechnie (2009).

The second part of the chapter discusses select applications of the brand experience topic, with a view to analysing how the brand experience concept operates in different contexts. Examining alternative contexts pushes the test for robustness, and offers the possibility of adding more insight about the concept. Applications considered include retail brand experiences, web-shopping brand experiences, city branding experiences, community fair or show branding experiences, and museum brand experiences.

The third part of the chapter moves from the *concept* of brand experience to different methods of *managing* brand experience, starting again with Tybout and Carpenter (2001). One challenge raised by Tybout and Carpenter (2001) goes to the heart of the problem of managing brand experiences. That is, how can you possibly brand something that is so erratic and variable, when the essence of branding is about 'burning' an unalterable impression or identity; and delivering it in a tight, consistent way? From the Tybout and Carpenter (2001) benchmark approach to managing brand experiences, we move to managing experiential brands of greater complexity, namely community fairs. Tseng, Qinhai and Su (1999) provide a further application of a management technique for managing customer experiences. Finally, in this third part, we discuss the very important contribution coming from a special issue of the *Journal of Retailing* on customer experience management (Grewal *et al.* 2009).

Nature of brand experience

Tybout & Carpenter: The conceptualisation of brand experience

Tybout and Carpenter (2001), in a benchmark article on brand experience, contrast functional brands, image brands and experiential brands.

Functional brands

Functional brands are basically bought by consumers to satisfy functional needs – to wash clothes, to clean teeth, or to commute to school by bus. Companies with brands that are essentially functional (such as Gillette) often emphasise improvements to product specification through research and development. Tybout and Carpenter (2001) give an interesting example where IBM's competitors offered faster computers (better product specification) but neglected service. Consequently, customers of these rival computer firms 'experienced considerable downtime' (Tybout & Carpenter 2001, p. 81). IBM responded with better customer service – another component of performance. In general, functional brands tend to emphasise either superior performance or superior economy.

Image brands

A second category of brands discussed by Tybout and Carpenter (2001) are what they call image brands. Image brands create value principally by projecting an image. The images define the brand's uniqueness, create symbols valued by consumers, and represent more emotional-laden connections. Design or product features are important for consumer durables such as cars and electrical appliances, and for deluxe items like Waterman pens. User imagery is also important in brands like Nike.

Experiential brands

The third Tybout and Carpenter (2001) category of brand is experiential brands. Rather than a product emphasis, experiential brands focus on how consumers feel when interacting with the brand. Brand experience is co-created by the brand and the consumer at the time of consumption, and consequently is unique and highly personal. Based on the interaction aspect, it would seem that there is a sense in which all service brands have an experiential component. That is, all service brands have a need for a unique and engaging experience. Disney and Starbucks are given as prime examples of experiential brands.

Of special significance is the attention to multiple stimuli that create the brand experience, not just the core product, but any add-on service as well as the physical environment encasing the service encounter. Thus, they note that:

> ... If a product is part of an experiential brand, ownership of it may never be transferred to the consumer. Instead, **products**, **environments** and **services** are combined to create temporary multisensory encounters with the brand. ... Consequently, the 'place' and 'people' components of service delivery are particularly important in creating strong experiential brands.
>
> (Tybout & Carpenter 2001, p. 90; **emphasis added**)

Adding more detail to the brand nature, Tybout & Carpenter note three dimensions for experiential brands, namely:

- valence,
- potency, and
- activity.

Valence can be either positive or negative; potency can be mild or intense; and activity can be passive or active. The three dimensions are useful for classifying different experiential brands. Thinking of a roller coaster in a theme park would elicit the description of negative (scary), intense, and active for the three dimensions respectively. In contrast, watching a dolphin show at, say, Seaworld on the Gold Coast or at Dolphin Lagoon on Sentosa Island (Singapore) would give dimensions of positive, mild, and passive.

Tybout and Carpenter (2001) discuss the notion of functional or image brands transforming into experience brands. They give the example of Green Mountain Energy Resources, which offers green electricity for a premium price and sponsors musical festivals that educate consumers to learn more about protecting the environment <http://www.greenmountainenergy.com/>. Another example given is Nike building the very energetic multi-media Nike Town stores.

A critique of Tybout & Carpenter (2001)

The three-part brand classification of Tybout and Carpenter (2001) is extremely useful. Contrasting functional, image and experiential brands is an excellent starting position. Their finale that considers the possibility of functional or image brands transforming into experiential brands is informative. It also paves the way to discuss contemporary developments such as social network brands.

There are some limitations in their work, linked in particular to their rigid approach to functional and image brands. Consider first their view about functional brands. The quotation above regarding IBM, their competitors and the problems *experienced* by the users of particular brands indicates to us that *brand experiences* apply as much to functional brands as to any brand, even though Tybout and Carpenter (2001) classify experiential brands as a separate one of three categories. The expanded interpretation that we give to functional brands should not be surprising because functional brands are about functional uses of brands – *'uses'* implies *'experiences'*. One presumes that functional brands that do not work well when used by the consumer will be quickly penalised in the market place. The customer service response by IBM indicates the relevance of service to functional brands, again reinforcing the scope of the brand experience for functional brands.

Other literature is consistent with our view that functional brands can be associated with brand experiences. Morrison and Crane (2007) focus on how emotions influence service brand evaluation, especially services with a high functional element such as dentists. To clarify further, Morrison and Crane (2007) distinguish between *technical quality* (what the service delivers) and *functional quality* (how the service is delivered). Interestingly, they argue that it is the *functional* aspect of service where emotions might play an important role. In terms of hotel services, it is suggested that staff relational service will influence guest emotions more than the physical environment (décor). Mowle and Merrilees (2005) demonstrate how wineries can leverage the functional qualities of product quality into emotional values. In some cases, the cellar door experience and selective restaurant experience are used to develop the symbolic properties of the brand image. For the first time, that study suggested interdependency between the functional and symbolic properties of branding.

Similarly, reconsider Tybout and Carpenter (2001) in their interpretation of image brands. As per our extended note regarding functional brands, it is also clear that *brand experiences* apply to image brands. Prestige car image brands, based on product features, have various brand experiences associated with them: the look of the car, the sound of the car, and the sensation of the car when driving. User aspects of image brands like Nike especially suggest user related *brand experiences*. Thus, brand experiences are relevant to all three types of brands; indeed, they are inalienable and inseparable from the brand.

In summary, Tybout and Carpenter (2001) provide a major contribution in defining the nature of experiential brands and hence the obvious benchmark in the brand experience literature. Before examining further literature that reinforces the Tybout and Carpenter approach, it must be recalled that their classification of brand-types is too restrictive.

Reinforcement of the Tybout & Carpenter approach

The service-dominant logic paradigm shift (Vargo and Lusch 2004) highlights two of the central constructs in the Tybout and Carpenter (2001) approach, namely value in use (rather than value in exchange) and co-creation of value (where both consumers and the firm create value).

Tynan and McKechnie (2009) consolidate and extend the nature of the service-dominant logic framed experience marketing. Their complex network of experience interactions includes the focal customer, other customers, opinion leaders, the brand, the firm and employees. These interactions could theoretically be re-framed as brand experiences.

Brakus, Schmitt & Zarantonello (2009): A new paradigm

The major contribution of Brakus *et al.* (2009) is a conceptual model of brand experience that develops scales for the dimensions of brand experience. Focus groups and prior literature contribute to the development of items for four dimensions of brand experience:

- sensory,
- affective,
- intellectual, and
- behavioural.

Multiple studies demonstrate the robustness of the four, multi-item dimensions, providing a major breakthrough for brand experience research.

Brakus *et al.* (2009) use their measure of brand experience to predict consumer behaviour. In their model results, satisfaction is the main determinant of loyalty, with direct support from brand experience and brand personality. Satisfaction is mainly determined by brand personality and to a much lesser extent brand experience. Finally, brand personality greatly influences brand personality. In broad terms, the model demonstrates predictive validity in that brand experiences has several consequences – including brand personality especially, but also satisfaction and loyalty.

A critique of Brakus, Schmitt & Zarantonello (2009)

Before we are too critical, it is important to recognise the critical contribution of Brakus *et al.* (2009). This major study in a leading journal articulates relevant constructs that were previously lacking in the brand experience literature.

One might question the generalisability of some of the scales and their items. In particular, the behavioural dimension includes:

- I engage in physical actions and behaviours when I use this brand.
- This brand results in bodily experiences.
- This brand is not action orientated.

(Brakus *et al.* 2009, p. 58)

If we compare a chess tournament event brand with a tennis tournament event brand, these three scale items would rate tennis as much more action-oriented (which it is), but is it more behavioural? We are not sure, but it has nothing to do with the speed of the match! Is a slow-food restaurant brand *automatically* less behavioural than a normal restaurant – let alone a fast food restaurant? We totally disagree with this suggestion, yet that is what the behavioural scale implies.

Another source of disquiet, and perhaps more conjectural, are the brand experience measures for about thirty brands, ranging from LEGO at the high brand experience extreme to La Prairie (premium skincare) at the low experience. There seem to be some very experiential brands – like Harley-Davidson – which attract a relatively low overall score (4.41 in the case of Harley-Davidson). Does it pass the face validity test to say that Harley-Davidson is only marginally rated as an experiential brand (for a contrary view, see Schouten and McAlexander 1995; Schembri 2009)? Similarly, there are several highly interactive brands, such as Blackberry, that score *below* the 4.0 threshold for an experiential brand. This evaluation does not make sense. At a more detailed level, why does Disney only score 3.84 on the behavioural dimension? The Disney experience may be ultimately about imagination, but it is behavioural-driven (foot power) and very tiring for most families at the end of the day!

The biggest criticism of the Brakus *et al.* (2009) approach is exemplified in their predictive model. Unfortunately, what is missing from the model is the actual product or service. Most models of satisfaction do show loyalty as a consequence. However, satisfaction is usually determined by *product quality* or *service quality* (and may include both core and peripheral service components) which is missing in the model presented. In one sense it does not matter, for predictive validity purposes, that there is a missing link in the model. A simple correlation with one or more consequential variables (even just brand personality) is sufficient to demonstrate predictive validity.

However, the missing core service component is indicative of the nature of the Brakus *et al.* (2009) brand experience concept. We can contrast their concept with Tybout and Carpenter (2001) who consider the role of products, environment and services as multiple stimuli creating multisensory experiences. Essentially, Brakus *et al.* (2009) focus on the environment aspect and the multisensory consequences, but they do not consider the contribution to brand experience from the product and service.

Expressed differently, they describe the brand experience, but abstract from the brand itself. The core activity of the brand experience (drinking a cup of coffee, for example) greatly influences the brand experience, and therefore needs to be added to the Brakus *et al.* (2009) model. Thus, the four dimensions of brand experience developed by Brakus *et al.* (2009) help *augment* the brand experience generated by the core and peripheral activities of the brand experience. However, their four-dimensional brand experience model is only a *partial* representation of brand experience because it omits the *core brand experience activities* associated with the core product (service) brand activities. The predictive power of the four-dimension model will certainly be reduced after service quality is included in the model, but this matter requires further research.

Having discussed alternative approaches to conceptualising the nature of brand experiences, we now turn to examining the application of the brand experience concept in specific contexts.

Applications of the brand experience concept

Retail brand experiences

The notion by Tybout and Carpenter (2001) that products, environments and service combine to create a multisensory encounter with the brand has resonance with other works. For example, Merrilees and Miller (1996) coined the expression 'total shopping experience', referring to the totality of the experience created by the core merchandise combined with physical ambience combined with the (inter-personal) service. Interestingly, the same three stimuli proposed by Tybout and Carpenter (2001), namely: product, place and service are involved as a combination to create a multisensory encounter. We invoke the expression 'total brand experience', which is slowly finding its way into the literature, although the understanding is still embryonic (e.g. Haeckel, Carbone & Berry 2003) (Box 1). We argue that all brands create a total brand experience, although we note that Tybout and Carpenter (2001) are adamant that only a few functional and image brands can be termed experiential brands.

Box 1

A definition of total brand experience

Combining the ideas of Tybout and Carpenter (2001) with Merrilees and Miller (1996) suggests the following definition of total brand experience:

Total brand experience occurs when multiple stimuli (core product, environment and peripheral service) combine to create temporary multisensory encounters with the brand.

Recent shopping experience research adds to our understanding of brand experiences, keeping in mind the different context: shopping experiences are consumer-focused, not necessarily brand-focused. The two contexts fuse when shopping experiences are analysed in a specific retailer situation. In their preamble to a special issue on experiential retailing, Dennis and King (2007) note a long lineage of scholars studying the role of experience and enjoyment in shopping. In particular, they conclude that the great majority of these studies demonstrate a strong link between retail atmospherics and sales.

In a different retail context, retail banking, the O'Loughlin, Szmigin and Turnbull (2004) study discusses brand experiences in the context of 'representing corporate values and brand images of financial service providers' (p. 529), which is ostensibly what would be expected. However, they found surprisingly that there were paradoxical brand experiences combining '..."very strong negative feelings" towards the bank on one hand and "long-term loyalty" on the other' (p. 529). These contradictory brand experiences present a significant challenge for managing experiential branding. Furthermore, they identify the importance of people (employees) 'neutralising or compensating for ...negative corporate perceptions' (p. 529). The usual roles ascribed to senior managers are first to achieve employees' brand buy-in, and consequently to establish those employees as brand representatives, brand ambassadors or brand champions. The idea of local employees creating a local positive brand experience, when the overarching brand experience is negative, is a little understood but potentially critical area.

Floor (2006) explores the potential for experience brands in the retailing domain, and identifies six types of experience brands (entertainment, expertise, design, hedonism, lifestyle and bargain brands). He argues that offline ('bricks and mortar') retailers can create multisensory experiences, and that the role of retailing is far greater than just selling. His criteria for experience brands are:

- authenticity,

- product related, and

- consumer involvement,

supported by frequent innovations. Moreover, 'stores can learn from theatres', and 'experience brands ... will have to captivate their customers every time' (Floor 2006, pp. 198-199), a position which accords with calls for brand consistency. Finally Floor (2006, p. 199) emphasises that operational support for the experience brand is necessary, as is the balance 'between emotional and functional benefits'.

Web brand experiences

E-retail brand experiences are especially interesting because the experience is compacted through a computer screen. When the internet first appeared, many of the web brand experiences were negative with security and privacy issues, and because of sites with poor navigation. To some extent, these experiential problems have been mitigated. A useful introduction to the link between interactive electronic marketing and brand management is the special issue in the *Journal of Brand Management* (Uncles 2001). The articles in the special issue span many topics, including the role of e-logos, positioning on the web, transferring brand equity from offline to online, and the overall impact of the internet on brands. Recent work highlights the role of web atmosphere and excitement in creating web experiences (Jayawardhena & Wright 2009; Manganari, Siomkos & Vrechopoulos 2009).

In terms of actually understanding how brand experiences work over the internet, focus should move to e-interactivity. E-interactivity includes:

- the two-way interaction between the viewer and the e-brand;

- the ability to personalise the situation for the individual;

- the ability of the individual to control the communication and learn; and

- the ability to get feedback.

(Merrilees & Fry 2002)

In the context of a pure online CD retailer, CD Now, Merrilees and Fry (2002) indicate that brand attitudes to the online retailer are greatly influenced by the online brand experience. In particular, interactivity (essentially representing the combined equivalent of offline staff service and store design) is the most influential determinant of online brand attitudes. Another aspect of the online brand experience, navigability, is also very influential on online brand attitudes. Interactivity itself is influenced by online enjoyment and navigability.

Importantly, Merrilees and Fry (2002), one of the first empirical studies of online brand attitudes, show that online brand experiences matter. That is, *online brand experiences* (interactivity and navigability) affect *brand evaluative performance*, in the form of brand attitudes.

City branding

A particularly interesting application of the brand experience concept is 'city branding'. City branding is a relatively recent foray of brand research (see Hankinson 2004; Virgo & de Chernatony 2006). A recent contribution is Merrilees, Miller and Herington (2009), who model city brand attitudes as a function of numerous city brand attributes to ascertain the meaning of the city brand from the residents' perspective. What is especially interesting about city brand experiences is the complexity and variety of activities that depict them. For example, Merrilees *et al.* (2009) provide evidence that the following activities form the city brand experience: job and business opportunities, nature assets, social bonding (friends and family), safety, a clean environment, transport options, shopping facilities, leisure activities (indoor and outdoor including markets and festivals), and education and health facilities. In this sense, city brand experience is perhaps the ultimate brand experience because of the sheer complexity and everyday importance of the experience.

Lorentzen (2009) takes the city brand experience notion further and addresses the opportunities of cities in the experience economy. The experience economy includes not only entertainment and culture, but also services and places. City-based experiences co-locate consumption experiences and their co-production. Lorentzen (2009) observes that art and culture cluster in big cities, while small cities embark on experience-based strategies such as those related to events and branding.

Fairs, festivals, theme parks and show brand experience

Fairs and theme parks are an interesting case of experiential brands. The early forms were strongly place branded – such as Steeplechase Park and Luna Park in Coney Island – and they promised a myriad of experiences, including: rides, shows, many forms of entertainment, special foods such as candyfloss, displays, animals, and much more (Lukas 2008). These early formats had superseded the place-based great world exhibitions such as the 1851 Crystal Palace Exhibition in London, the 1893 The World's Columbian Exhibition in Chicago, and the 1900 Paris World Fair. Even today, World Expos continue to be specifically place based (2010 Shanghai; 2012 Yeosu, South Korea; 2015 Milan).

Fairs and shows of varying scales have a long-standing history in many countries. For example, the Sydney Royal Easter Show had its beginnings in 1822, and in 1891 Queen Victoria gave permission for the addition of 'Royal' to the name of the show. Its early days were focused on agricultural aspects with an emphasis on experience, and it gathered momentum when fireworks displays were added in 1884, sideshows in 1888, showbags in 1900, and mechanical rides in 1901 (<http:// www.rasnsw. com.au/ timeline.htm>).

Our continuing research, especially in Australia and Canada, indicates that people have very powerful memories of their previous visits to the community fair or show, regardless of how long ago it was. These findings are consistent with portrayals in the media at the time of such events. People have their favourite attractions that they interact more with, as well as one or two components that they avoid for various reasons. Usually visits occupy about 3-5 hours, so there is a major mental commitment to the brand experience.

Lukas (2008) gives the Pirates of the Caribbean ride as an example of the principle of the theme park as a brand, in the sense that the attraction connects patrons. Partly using the Roberts (2004) 'lovemarks' concepts, Lukas explains that the Pirates ride achieves the following:

- conveys a story or dream, perhaps a mystery;

- sensuality; the senses are used to connect people with the concept; and

- intimacy; people are attached to the brand through commitment.

(Lukas 2008, p. 183)

These principles also resonate with fairs and shows, and indeed with markets. For example, markets such as some farmers' markets with a long history – like the Hamilton Farmers' Market in Ontario Canada, dating from 1837, or the more recent resurgence of markets emphasising fresh locally produced organic foods in countries such as Australia and the United Kingdom (e.g. the award winning Brigg Farmers' Market established in 2001; < http://www.farmersmarkets.net/>).

Museum brand experiences

Popular cultural tourism generally and museum visitation specifically is essentially 'experiential' cultural tourism, the accumulation of experiences rather than bodies of more schematic knowledge (Prentice 2001). Museum offerings invoke authentic experiences through associations and imaginings, as well as by means of immediate sensation (Prentice 2001).

A special case is the branded museum – such as the Coca-Cola Museum, the Hershey Museum and the Heineken Museum – emphasising the history of the particular brand. The Hollenbeck, Peters and Zinkhan (2008) research, based on the Coca-Cola Museum in Atlanta, found that the museum experience is a reminder of the brand's role in consumers' lives. A brand museum socialises the brand by connecting visitors to other brand enthusiasts, and contextualises the brand by illustrating the brand's achievements and innovation, as well as localising the brand to a particular city (Hollenbeck *et al.* 2008).

Importantly and similarly to a themed flagship store like Nike Town, a brand museum 'theatricises' the brand by staging a retail spectacle (Hollenbeck *et al.* 2008), an idea consistent with Floor's (2006) position on experience brands in retail stores. The spectacle entails an engaging, interactive and participatory experience. Participating in a multisensory, interactive experience draws patrons to the brand. Entertainment (using the environment elements of colours, lights and sounds) enhances the search for brand essence. For example, Hollenbeck *et al.* (2008) note that a second-floor display of a drink dispenser representing eight of Coke's products captivated many visitors for more than an hour.

Having discussed alternative approaches to conceptualising the nature of brand experiences and the application of the brand experience concept in specific contexts, we now turn to examining issues arising in the management of brand experience.

Managing brand experience

Tybout & Carpenter (2001) as a starting point

Building functional brands focuses resources on either the product (for superior performance) or the place and price elements of the marketing mix (for superior economy). In general, the emphasis is on increasing the functionality of the brand. Image brands are built through stronger emotional connections to consumers. The relevant image might be self-image or image in relation to a social group.

In terms of experiential brands, Tybout and Carpenter (2001) note two major challenges. The first is the ability to create the brand experience consistently. Virgin Airlines manages this aspect through very tight recruitment and selection of staff procedures to minimise employee variability of service. Similarly, Virgin follows up their selection of staff with careful training and development, further reinforced with everyone, including Richard Branson, as brand role models.

The second challenge to experiential brands is the potential for satiation to occur. Tybout and Carpenter (2001) ask whether the third trip to Disney World can possibly match the first one. They suggest a strategy of continuously expanding and enhancing the experience, though this is difficult to achieve in practice without creating unrealistic expectations. This concern is consistent with Floor's (2006) notion about the need to captivate the customer every time in retail experiential brands, and about frequent innovations. Tybout and Carpenter (2001) suggest an interesting alternative strategy, namely creating multiple, differentiated experiential brands within the one category. They gave the example of Lettuce Entertain You Enterprises which has more than 30 restaurants in the Chicago area, with Italian (Lettuce's Scoozi), Chinese (Lettuce's Ben Pao), French (Lettuce's Mon Ami Gabi), and other variants. In each case, the experience is authentic, unique and memorable because the décor, menu and staff embody the particular theme. There is also scope to extend the experiential brand through tangible reminders of the consumption experience (as in the case of Disney). Experiential brands can benefit from using the internet to extend and enrich the consumption experience – for example, enriching the Star Trek experience among the show's fans. Interactive chat rooms to discuss television show episodes become a means of integrating the show into their everyday lives (Tybout and Carpenter 2001).

Community fairs and shows

Part of the problem with fairs is the multiple objectives they have had over the years:

- entertainment for city and rural residents;
- education of the city residents about the role and nature of agriculture; and
- displaying agriculture through showcasing the best produce or livestock as well as displaying other new products.

Further, fairs are a complex form of experiential brand. Essentially they represent a collage of multiple events, with each event – such as ringside or the flower display – a unique experience in its own right. If managing a single event is difficult, managing multiple events contemporaneously is exponentially more complex. Moreover, the transitions between events have to be managed in some sense. In short, it is necessary to conceive of a special type of business model to manage the fair experience brand. Special attention has to be given to the fair manager in co-ordinating the total fair experience. To an extent, there is the direct management of operations. However, some events are not directly controlled by the fair manager, and so indirect means are necessary to control the brand. Adding to the complications, it is also necessary to design crowd involvement into the fair brand, because the brand experience is co-created by the patrons of the fair. Crowd involvement comes through participation in the event itself, but also through the transitions from one event to another. Pathways and signage contribute to the brand experience.

Tseng, Qinhai and Su (1999) adapt the Bateson (1995) servuction model to map the service experience of customers. Essentially, a three-step procedure is proposed:

Step 1:   Recognise and map the customer's service experience.

Step 2:   Discover potential problems and opportunities based on examining the actual customer experience at each point in the process.

Step 3:   Take action to improve service operations.

(Tseng *et al.* 1999, p. 55)

The three steps potentially lead to the goal of improving the customer's perception of value. The approach is conceptual and is similar to many service blueprinting models. Both service and retailing examples are given, but the model is not tested.

Volume 85 (1) (2009) of the *Journal of Retailing* provides a very useful set of seven papers on customer experience management in retailing. Summarising the issue, Grewal, Levy and Kumar (2009) note that customer experience management represents a business strategy designed to manage the customer experience, which includes all points of contact at which the customer interacts with the business. The management control variables are based on managing the promotion experience, the pricing experience, the merchandise and product brand experience, the supply chain management experience, and the location experience. Each of these component experiences are analysed by dozens of articles, so there is no simple set of propositions to tie them together.

Essentially the papers are consistent with Tybout and Carpenter (2001) and Merrilees and Miller (1996) where the total brand experience is based on *multi-stimuli* (especially product, environment and service) creating multisensory outcomes. In Grewal *et al.* (2009) the emphasis is on the *multi-stimuli* (promotions, merchandise) front end, as one would expect in a customer-experience *management* emphasis. One limitation is that they pay insufficient attention to the multi-sensory outcomes, because the articles are focused more on the managerial inputs (the stimuli).

In one sense, most of the special issue articles derive customer experience propositions from previous research articles that do not take a customer experience lens, which may confound their approach. However, a more reflective reading of Grewal *et al.* (2009) shows that different consumers can experience different promotions differently. Loss leaders can be interpreted by some consumers as a short-term windfall, but more cynically by other consumers. Moreover, it becomes a complex task how the retailer should manage the plethora of promotions across multiple media and stimuli. Few studies integrate the multi-media projection of promotion stimuli, let alone across all of the retail mix.

Conclusions

The Tybout and Carpenter (2001) paper provides a useful start to our journey to understand the brand experience concept. Their emphasis on multiple stimuli creating multisensory encounters helps us to define the total brand experience (Box 1). Adding reinforcement articles and further applications gives us a better understanding of what is quite a complex concept. City brand experiences and community fair brand experiences are, by their nature, at the more complex end of brand experiences. In contrast, web-brand experiences are relatively simpler and more compact.

Brakus, Schmitt and Zarantonello (2009) make a major conceptual advance through articulating a four-dimension representation of the brand experience concept. Conceptualising brand experience in this way should facilitate future quantitative studies of brand experience. The chapter challenges the adequacy of the Brakus *et al*

(2009) approach, arguing that it omits the vital core product component of the brand experience. We prefer to position the Brakus *et al.* (2009) approach as a partial representation of brand experience, very useful but requiring extension to capture the core product component of the brand experience.

Managing brand experiences is very difficult because of the volatile nature of the brand experience. The series of alternative approaches studied here indicates how to manage brand experiences successfully.

The chapter progresses the understanding of experiential branding in various ways:

- synthesising the existing brand experience literature,

- cross-pollinating from related consumer and shopping experience literature,

- re-interpreting the literature, and

- adding new perspectives (for example our re-interpretation of Tybout and Carpenter, 2001; and our re-interpretation of Brakus *et al.* 2009).

Notwithstanding, much more research is needed, especially when compared to other strands of branding research.

This chapter has advanced the understanding of experiential brands and how to manage them. The next major challenge for researchers, working in collaboration with practitioners, is to devise an effective means of creating experiential brands.

References

Bateson, J 1995, *Managing Service Marketing*, The Dryden Press, Hinsdale Il.

Brakus, J, Schmitt, B & Zarantonello, L 2009, 'Brand experience: what is it? How is it measured? Does it affect loyalty?' *Journal of Marketing*, 73 (May), pp. 52-68.

Dennis, C & King, T 2007, 'Special issue on social and experiential retailing: Guest editorial', *International Journal of Retail & Distribution Management*, 35 (6).

Floor, K 2006, *Branding a Store*, Kogan Page, London.

Grewal, D, Levy, M & Kumar, V 2009, 'Customer experience management in retailing: an organizing framework', *Journal of Retailing*, 85 (1), pp. 1-14.

Haeckel, S, Carbone, L & Berry, L 2003, 'How to lead the customer experience: to create a total brand experience finds must provide the right directions', *Marketing Management*, 12 (1), pp. 18-23.

Hankinson, G 2004, 'The brand images of tourism destinations: a study of the saliency of organic images', *Journal of Product & Brand Management*, 13 (1), pp. 6-14.

Hollenbeck, C, Peters, C & Zinkhan, G 2008, 'Retail spectacles and brand meaning: insights from a brand museum case study', *Journal of Retailing*, 84 (3), pp. 334-353.

Jayawardhena, C & Wright, L 2009, 'An empirical investigation into e-shopping excitement: antecedents and effects', *European Journal of Marketing*, 43 (9 & 10), pp. 1171-1187.

Lorentzen, A 2009, 'Cities in the experience economy', *European Planning Studies*, 17 (6), pp. 829-845.

Lukas, S 2008, *Theme Park*, Reaktion Books, London.

Manganari, E, Siomkos, G & Vrechopoulos, A 2009, 'Store atmosphere in web retailing', *European Journal of Marketing*, 43 (9 & 10), pp. 1140-1153.

Merrilees, B & Fry M-L 2002, 'Corporate branding: a framework for e-retailers', *Corporate Reputation Review*, 5 (2-3), pp. 213-225.

Merrilees, B & Miller, D 1996, *Retail Management in Australia: A Best Practice Approach*, RMIT Press, Melbourne.

Merrilees, B, Miller, D & Herington, C 2009, 'Antecedents of residents' city brand attitudes', *Journal of Business Research*, 62 (3), pp. 362-367.

Morrison, S & Crane, F 2007, 'Building the service brand by creating and managing emotional brand experience', *Journal of Brand Management*, 14 (5), pp. 410-421.

Mowle, J & Merrilees, B 2005, 'A functional and symbolic perspective to branding Australian SME wineries', *Journal of Product & Brand Management*, 14 (4), pp. 220-227.

O'Loughlin, D, Szmigin, I & Turnbull, P 2004, 'From relationships to experiences in retail financial services', *The International Journal of Bank Marketing*, 22 (7), pp. 522-539.

Prentice, R 2001, 'Experiential cultural tourism: museums & the marketing of the new romanticism of evoked authenticity', *Museum Management and Curatorship*, 19 (1), pp. 5-26.

Roberts, K 2004, *Lovemarks: the future beyond brands*, Powerhouse Books, New York.

Schembri, S 2009, 'Reframing brand experience: the experiential meaning of Harley-Davidson', *Journal of Business Research*, 62 (12), pp. 1299-1310.

Schouten, J & McAlexander, J 1995, 'Subcultures of consumption: an ethnography of the new bikers', *Journal of Consumer Research*, 22 (1), pp. 43-61.

Tseng, M, Qinhai, M & Su, C-J 1999, 'Mapping customers' service experience for operations improvement', *Business Process Management*, 5 (1), pp. 50-64.

Tybout, A & Carpenter, G 2001, 'Creating and managing brands', in D. Iacobucci (ed), *Kellogg on Marketing*, John Wiley, New York, Chapter 4.

Tynan, C & McKechnie, S 2009, 'Experience marketing: a review and reassessment', *Journal of Marketing Management*, 25 (5-6), pp. 501-517.

Uncles, M 2001, 'Editorial: Interactive electronic marketing and brand management', *Journal of Brand Management*, 8 (4/5), pp. 245-254.

Vargo, S & Lusch, R 2004, 'Evolving to a new dominant logic for marketing', *Journal of Marketing*, 68 (1), pp. 1-17.

Virgo, B & de Chernatony, L 2006, 'Delphic brand visioning to align stakeholder buy-in to the City of Birmingham brand', *Journal of Brand Management*, 13 (6), pp. 379-392.

Author biographies

Bill Merrilees' research interests encompass branding (including corporate branding and brand morphing) and innovation in a variety of contexts including firms, cities, communities, retailing, and franchising. His research has been published internationally in the *European Journal of Marketing*, the *Journal of Business Research*, *Industrial Marketing Management* and the *Journal of Strategic Marketing*. His publications extend to books (including *e-Retailing*, Routledge) and books chapters; also, he is a recent joint Guest Editor (with Dr Charles Dennis) of a Special Issue of the *European Journal of Marketing*. Based in Griffith University Queensland, Bill is also Visiting Professor at the DeGroote School of Business, McMaster University (Canada), and invited Guest Speaker at the University of Guelph (Canada), Brunel University (England), and Glasgow Caledonian University (Scotland).

Contact: bill.merrilees@griffth.edu.au.

Dale Miller's research spans branding in various domains including cities, communities, retailing, corporate branding, corporate rebranding and not for profit branding, as well as retail innovation and sustainable business. She has published widely, including in the *Journal of Business Research,* the *European Journal of Marketing, Long Range Planning,* the *International Journal of Retail and Distribution Management,* and the *Journal of Retailing and Consumer Services.* Her publications also include book chapters and the book, *Retail Marketing: a Branding and Innovation Approach* (TUP). Based in Griffith University Queensland, she is also a Visiting Researcher at the University of Western Ontario. Dale also lectures in Hong Kong.

Contact: d.miller@griffth.edu.au.

Chapter 16

Brand authenticity

MICHAEL BEVERLAND

ABSTRACT

In an age of increasing consumer cynicism towards brands, marketers are being urged to become more authentic. Yet, how can brands project authenticity when many people believe commercial objects are, by definition, fake? This chapter identifies how marketers can create brands that reflect consumers' desired identity or authentic self. Rather that overtly stating that your brand is 'authentic' or 'real', brands gain authenticity through warts'n'all storytelling, a living heritage, a genuine love of craft, and sincere commitments to action. Based on extensive research with consumers and brand managers, this chapter offers seven guiding principles for developing authentic brand stories: be at one with community, iconoclastic leaders, fight the system, stick to your roots, love of craft, artisanal amateurs, and the results of intuitive genius. It draws on case studies of brands that have achieved sustained success but are rarely featured in business branding books. Examples include: Chateau Margaux, Bruichladdich and the Morgan Motor Company as well as more traditional examples such as Apple, Dyson and Virgin.

KEYWORDS

authenticity; consumer culture; brand management; storytelling

Introduction

Under the stewardship of Quaker Oats, Snapple shouldn't have failed—not if you believe in branding and marketing. Quaker's strategy was simple—take a brand, built by amateurs, to the next level through the application of marketing's famous four Ps. The Quaker team did a superb job of developing market-driven innovations, accessing mass retailers, and investing in advertising campaigns. How could it be, then, that four years after buying Snapple for US$1.7 billion, Quaker was forced to sell it for the markdown price of US$300 million (and some thought this was too much)? Simply, the Quaker team forgot that consumers drank Snapple because of its quirks—consumption of this drink was a reaction to impersonal mass production and mass marketing. Drinking Snapple was a powerful cultural display in an age of conformity and artificiality (Deighton 2003). The very marketing amateurism evident in the pre-Quaker days gave the brand authenticity—the central driver of its equity.

Contrast Quaker's approach with Australian-based Pacific brands' revival of the iconic Dunlop Volley shoe. After starving the brand of marketing investment (in innovation, channel support and ad spend) for years, Pacific Brands decided to reposition the shoe as an entry-level quality brand that people were not ashamed to own. These seemingly modest expectations belied the extent of the challenge facing the marketing team at Pacific Brands. Although the shoe had once been the only choice for Australian consumers and sports people, Nike and other global competitors had outflanked functional Dunlop by focusing on quality and fashion, dramatically shifting consumer expectations of athletic footwear. From the number one seller in the early 1970s, by the 1990s the Volley was viewed internally as a commodity, by low-priced retailers as a loss leader, by specialist sports retailers as an anachronism, and by consumers as something the 'old man wore when mowing the lawns'. In short, the brand was a cash cow fast turning into a dog. The Pacific Brands team aimed to turn this around; although never in their wildest dreams could they have planned for what happened next.

During the late 1990s, Australian teens 'borrowed' their fathers' worn out Volleys from the garden shed and proudly began wearing them. Innovative teens were wearing this shoe as a semi-political statement—a rejection of Nike's and Adidas' big budgets, high prices, and large sponsorship deals. The Dunlop team started to receive requests from editors of street magazines run by and for innovative teens for advertising and for free shoes. Suddenly, the Volley was the hottest item on the street and in dance clubs. Dunlop could've exploited the shoe's sudden 'cool' status with a retro-inspired mass-marketing campaign. Such a campaign would have had short-term benefits (the shoe would become the latest fad), but no lasting effect.

Instead, Dunlop listened to members of the rave culture and decided not to exploit these teens. Rather, they provided free shoes to street artists for sculptures, giveaways at raves, and unique shoes designed by up-and-coming teen designers. Eventually the in-crowd moved on. But the effect was obvious—the brand was seen as a re-born local icon, an authentic object reflective of the Australian way of doing better with less. The authentic response of the Dunlop team to teens resulted in increased brand equity at low cost (Beverland & Ewing 2005).

The contrast between these two brands sets the scene for this chapter. Why did the lack of marketing at Dunlop work, whereas Quaker's heavy marketing investment failed? I maintain that certain brands are imbued with authenticity, and that such brands require a different marketing management approach than those positioned solely around functional, emotional or experiential benefits. However, building brand authenticity is not easy. After all, the two examples above identify that, on the face of it, authenticity is something given to a brand by consumers not something that marketers can create and manage. Closer examination of other brands reveals a more complex picture, with marketers playing an important role in feeding the cultures surrounding these brands.

The rest of this chapter examines how and why marketers ought to focus on building brand authenticity. Before we do so, it is important to identify the nature of authenticity, why authenticity matters to consumers and marketers, and why building authenticity is challenging.

The centrality of authenticity to post-modern brand consumption

Consumers determine a brand's authenticity

What do we mean by the term 'authenticity'? Historically, when marketers talked of authenticity they meant 'the genuine article' as opposed to counterfeits (Beverland 2005). Thus, marketers effectively conferred authenticity to the product – usually through branding, trademark protections, legal force, and recently through DNA markers. However, in today's market the consumer primarily determines what is authentic. Therefore, authenticity is perceptual—that is, what is real or genuine is in the mind of the consumer. The following example – taken from an interview with Charles Morgan, the current owner and managing director of the Morgan Motor Company – illustrates this change in how authenticity is determined.

> *Rather than a brand I think it's more an attempt to interest the cult and keep the cult going. We like providing stories that people can tell in the pub and feel that that makes them part of the family. And so our brand is made up around a series of myths, some of which are true, some of which are owned. The one about the wooden chassis in France, we have tried and tried to get rid of that, but it is still persists. And I think eventually we're going to have to say ok yeah yeah yeah it's true. (Charles Morgan, Morgan Motor Company)*

Charles' quotation identifies the subjective nature of brand authenticity. Morgan hand builds traditional English sports cars. Part of the body is made of wood, although the chassis certainly is not. Despite this, French fans of the brand continue to believe the chassis is made of wood, a point Morgan no longer see any reason in denying. As Charles notes, central to Morgan's brand story are myths—some that are true, and others that are created and owned by consumers. The French consumers' view is an example of a story that is not true, but provides an element of mystique that is alluring. Critically, Morgan has given up trying to tell these consumers what is authentic; rather, they are happy to allow consumers to create stories that work for them precisely because they help the brand (we'll return to Morgan later).

Recent research has suggested three attributes of a brand are critical to consumer judgments of authenticity (Napoli, Dickinson, Beverland & Farrelly forthcoming). These are:

1. **Quality leadership.** Quality leadership is the belief that behind the brand are passionate artisans using the finest quality materials and meeting exacting standards to continually push the barriers of product excellence. Examples include: Apple, Chanel, Dyson, and New Zealand's Weta Works (producer of *Lord of the Rings*, *Chronicles of Narnia* and *King Kong*).

2. **Heritage.** Heritage is the belief that the brand is connected to time, place, and culture. The brand exudes commitments to traditions, reminds consumers of a golden age, and is based on timeless designs. Examples include: the Morgan Motor Company, Chateau Margaux, Louis Vuitton, and In-N-Out Burger.

3. **Sincerity.** Sincerity is the belief that the brand lives up to its espoused values and commitments. Examples include: the Body Shop, Lonely Planet, Untouched World, and Champagne Bollinger.

On the face of it, the three characteristics of consumer-based brand authenticity seem no different to traditional brand positioning models. After all, brands often position themselves around functional performance, heritage, values and beliefs. However, brand authenticity is something that is demonstrated in practice rather than stated in marketing communications (Beverland & Luxton 2005). Also, consumers desire rich combinations of all three characteristics when assessing a brand's authenticity. Finally, it is consumers that determine what quality is, what and how heritage matters, and whether brands are sincere. Brand managers, like the CEO of the Morgan Motor Company, can feed the market with stories, but consumers ultimately determine authenticity. In contrast, traditional brand models with their emphasis on 'staying on message' represent a top-down, marketer driven model of meaning creation whereby consumers are seen as passive recipients of brand communications (Holt 2004). As such, traditional approaches to brand management need revision when trying to project authenticity.

Why does brand authenticity matter?

Why does brand authenticity matter? First, consumers desire it. Second, research indicates authenticity increases brand equity. Consumers view authentic brands more favourably. Authentic brands have a higher status among consumers, thus resulting in greater loyalty and price premiums. Dyson's cyclone vacuum cleaner provides a great example. Dramatically more expensive than its rivals, the Dyson is viewed as an object of real beauty in that most boring of categories—home appliances. So loved are these machines that Japanese housewives proudly display them in their homes rather than storing them out of sight (Dyson 2002). Also, consumers form greater bonds with authentic brands than other brands. This results in greater loyalty, word-of-mouth support, the formation of brand communities, and tolerance of one-off failures.

Because consumers' brand choices are an extension of their desired self (Belk, Wallendorf & Sherry 1989), they use certain brands to achieve self-authentication (or confirm their desired identity). Brands are chosen because traditional markers of identity such as race, religion, community, and culture are breaking down due to increased globalisation, decreased barriers between states, and the increasing ubiquity of branded spaces (including schools, churches, political parties, universities) (Arnould & Price 2000). Because consumers' still desire communal connections, brands that enable them to connect to people, time, place and culture are viewed as genuine partners, resulting in increased emotional bonds between customer and brand. Since research identifies a link between a desire to connect and brand authenticity, authentic brands are critical to the identity of the postmodern consumer (Beverland & Farrelly 2010).

Brand managers also benefit from building authenticity. First, research reveals that brand authenticity is a better predictor of purchase intentions than brand love, trust or credibility (Napoli *et al.* forthcoming). Such results have led many marketers to invest in 'authentic branding strategies'. Second, recent surveys indicate that brand authenticity increases brand equity. For example, authentic brands are more likely to attract a higher share of big spending consumers and more word-of-mouth support (Principals-Synovate 2008).

New Zealand produced 42 Below Vodka provides a classic example. In a crowded category where vodka equals Russian-Made, 42 Below offered a very high priced, award-winning product backed with a range of in-your-face viral adverts reflecting the no-nonsense attitude of New Zealanders. The tongue-in-cheek adverts drew directly on cultural myths and stereotypes, and breached virtually every New Zealand advertising standard. But, the product out-pointed famous vodka brands in international competitions. And, the ads were extremely funny, resulting in substantial word-of-mouth support. Authentic brands attract wealthy and aspirational consumers prepared to pay higher margins – and they refer the brand to friends. The result: higher margins at lower cost.

Authentic brands are also remarkably robust. Many of the brands examined in this chapter are decades old – or more. Iconic Bordeaux winery Chateau Margaux has a brand history stretching back over 600 years. In 2009, the Morgan Motor Company will celebrate its 100th birthday—at a time when large car companies such as Chrysler, Ford and General Motors require government handouts to survive. Authentic brands can stumble and even go bankrupt. However, such brands also attract consumers dedicated to their survival. Throughout the Steve Jobs-free period at Apple, consumers continued to rally around the troubled brand out of a desire to retain the creative spirit it epitomised (Belk & Tumbat 2005). Following the

Jobs-led return to its roots, Apple has increased its market capitalisation and its market share with the iMac, the iPod, the MacBook Air and the iPhone.

Finally, as the rest of this chapter will demonstrate, authenticity is not something that can be faked or copied. In contrast to functional performance, lifestyle claims and experiential marketing strategies, the authenticity of a brand's story is something that provides an ongoing point of difference *vis-à-vis* competitors. Authentic stories have other benefits too. Such is the interest in authentic brands that they often garner more press attention than their size merits, and therefore can increase their awareness at little expense. For example, despite the performance superiority of Toyota's beautiful Lexus cars, high profile programs such as the BBC's *Top Gear* prefer to cover smaller brands such as Aston Martin, Ferrari and BMW because they 'have soul'. Although Lexus is viewed as technically excellent, it is also seen as boring and must rely on marketing spend to build awareness. The great wine estates of the world enjoy similar benefits, garnering most of the news coverage while accounting for less than one per cent of global wine sales.

Can marketers manufacture authenticity?

Although brand authenticity is critical, building it is not easy. In fact, authenticity is often seen as the polar opposite of mass marketing, advertising and brand building (Beverland, Lindgreen & Vink 2008), and has become such an overused term that firms must work harder than ever to prove they are authentic (Mack 2009, p.10). Authenticity is believed to be natural, unforced and un-staged, free from self-interest and commercial considerations. Naomi Klein's *No Logo* (2000) and anti-brand organisation Adbusters attack brands for their very inauthenticity, while John Seabrook (2000) and Daniel Harris (2003) characterise commercial culture as superficial and meaningless. Big brands such as Starbucks may also be attacked for shutting down small neighbourhood coffee shops that promote a more authentic atmosphere and genuine dedication to producing quality coffee, despite the fact that historical analysis reveals authenticity is often manufactured by small manufacturers as a competitive response to mass-producers (Beverland 2005; Thompson, Rindfleisch & Arsel 2006).

Part of the problem relates to how marketers promote authenticity. Research reveals that explicit statements such as Wrangler's 2003 billboard advertising campaign ('Born Authentic') actually diminishes authenticity. Furthermore, marketing *per se* is not the problem; rather, consumer research suggests that the appearance of commercial motivation is the issue (Beverland 2006). For example, self-taught artist the Reverend Howard Finster lost authenticity when he adopted 1-800 telephone numbers, explicitly targeted artworks to customer segments, and produced branded lines of paintings to expand his market (Fine 2004). Brands judged insincere may also struggle to gain authenticity. For example, US beer brand Coors struggled to gain traction with the North American gay community because its owners sponsored anti-gay causes. The brand was viewed as attempting to exploit the gay community while at the same time undermining the rights of community members (Kates 2004).

Marketers can, therefore, play a role in the creation of brand authenticity despite the aforementioned difficulties. Perhaps it is because of these difficulties that so few brands are considered in the same vein as great artists and given iconic status. The next section identifies how these few brands have created an aura of authenticity.

Building authenticity through storytelling

Stories are particularly powerful. They make an impression because they bring people together. The nature and structure of storytelling is remarkably similar across different cultures and periods in history (Booker 2004). Authentic brands tell a particular type of story, as demonstrated in Figure 16.1. The most effective stories involve conflict — whether with nature (*Moby Dick* or *The Perfect Storm*), other people or beings (*The Fountainhead* or *Alien*), or self (*Lord of the Rings* or *A Perfect Mind*). The right amount of conflict is critical in the context of branding. Too much and the brand is an advocate, such as People for the Ethical Treatment for Animals (PETA) that ends up preaching to the converted and alienating the rest of us. Functional brands have too little conflict at the heart of their story — while fighting germs may be an important benefit for Ajax, it hardly engenders intense emotion among consumers. Put simply, no conflict makes for boring stories:

> *Imagine Jaws without a hungry white shark, Superman without kryptonite, or the tale of Red Riding Hood without a ferocious wolf: the teenagers would have had a great summer at the beach, Superman would not have a worry in the world, and Little Red Riding Hood would visit her grandmother and then go home. Boring and predictable springs to mind! Movie director Nils Malmros once said, 'Paradise on a Sunday afternoon…. Sounds great, but it sure is boring on film.' In other words, too much harmony and not enough conflict makes for a story that is about as exciting as watching paint dry. (Fog, Budtz & Yakaboylu 2005, pp. 32-33)*

The stories of authentic brands include conflict that involves sustained effort. Richard Branson often uses a David and Goliath story when entering a new category. The message is simple — offering better service for less won't be easy when we're up against large, entrenched, protected and arrogant competitors, but if we all pull together we'll win. Likewise, James Dyson recounts how company after company turned down his cyclone vacuum cleaner, so he bet the house and started his own firm (and won). Central to the authenticity of the *Lord of the Rings* franchise is Peter Jackson's struggles to remain true to Tolkien's vision and produce three films rather than try to condense the story into one film because studios believed movie-goers desired instant gratification.

Figure 16.1 Brand stories and conflict

Source: Fog, Budtz & Yakaboylu 2005, p. 84.

The seven stories behind authentic brands

Brand authenticity involves (at least) one of two core stories:

1. the brand hero triumphs against incredible odds, and

2. the brand hero must overcome a dilemma without an apparent solution.

Supporting these larger stories are seven smaller ones. These are identified in Figure 16.2.

Figure 16.2 Building brand authenticity

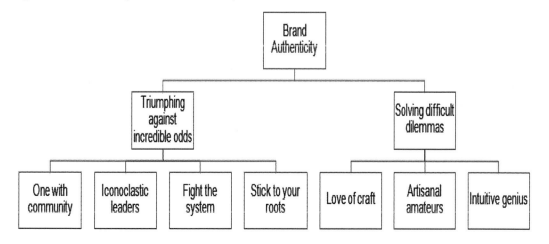

Triumphing against incredible odds

Authentic brands communicate their ability to triumph against the odds in four ways.

First, they locate themselves within communities and play a key role in fighting for their community's interests. This engenders incredible loyalty, awareness and free press, providing the basis for competitive advantage.

Second, the leaders that started or run authentic brands never settle for second best. As such they are intolerant of poor performance and lazy thinking, but create an environment in which the best flourish.

Third, the people behind authentic brands are on a mission to change the system. Authentic brands triumph against great odds because they refuse to be bound by conventions. In contrast, the vast majority of brands play by the rules and, as such, achieve little that is interesting.

Finally, authentic brands triumph against great odds because they are stubborn — that is, they stick to their roots and keep the faith when others have given up.

Story one: One with community

When bands such as the Rolling Stones visit Auckland in New Zealand, they all pay a visit to Real Groovy Records — the iconic Upper Queen Street store with its famous neon sign. Real Groovy stocks a vast range of new and used LPs, cassettes, CDs, DVDs and music memorabilia (among many other things). No history of the local music scene could be written without mentioning this brand. Part of the authenticity of this brand is that it sides with musicians and lovers of music, whereas other stores report to shareholders. The team behind the store has made many decisions that seemed to defy commercial sense while reinforcing their role in the music community.

For example, when New Zealand music was struggling for radio play in the early 1980s, Real Groovy decided to sell LPs by local artists at cost. This resulted in improved chart performance for New Zealand musicians, forcing radio to play local music in order to remain relevant to their listeners. It's difficult to imagine how artists such as Crowded House would have achieved the success they have without this initial support. Real Groovy again demonstrated their commitment to community when they bailed out cash-strapped BFM — the University of Auckland's student-run station. When the student union was looking to cut costs, Real Groovy stepped in with advertising support, thereby keeping alive an important independent voice on the radio scene. Again, many local musicians gained their first airplay on BFM because mainstream radio rejected more alternative acts.

Such immersion in the local music community has several benefits. First, consumers remain loyal to the brand even though prices may be higher. Real Groovy has higher costs than mainstream retailers because of its generous loyalty scheme and its second-hand trade policy that allows consumers to trade in old music for store credit. The store's owners are also reluctant to engage in widespread discounting because they believe it insults artists. Real Groovy has seen off many larger competitors and maintained sales even in the face of competition from large discount category killers such as *The Warehouse*. Being part of the community has one further benefit—community members rally around the brand in times of trouble. In 2008, Real Groovy was forced into receivership because several partners retired and removed their capital. Just over a month later, new partners – many of who were leading members of the local recording industry and had grown up with the brand – recapitalised the business. Their reasons were simple—it was impossible to imagine the New Zealand music scene without Real Groovy.

Authentic brands assimilate into the psyche of nations and subcultures. Can we imagine an Australia without Vegemite, France without Champagne, America without Harley Davidson, or Britain with Harrods? Importantly, if we turn the relationship around—Vegemite without Australia, Champagne without France—we also get a sense that something is wrong. After all, champagne-styled wines made outside of France are now simply called by their functional name 'sparking wines'. When brands become part of a community, purchasing them becomes an act of loyalty and identity. Other brands may enter the market with better performance (a Harley is by no means the best performing motorcycle on the market), better pricing or more marketing, but they lack the necessary authenticity to compete against entrenched locals (witness the failure of Starbuck's in Australia and eBay in New Zealand [where local provider Trademe rules]).

The loyalty shown to local brands is driven by the belief that these brands are in the community for the long term. Bigger flashier rivals may stay in the community while times are good, but are likely to close stores, lay staff off and move production when times get tough. While authentic brands stand up for the community, other brands seek to exploit subcultures when market conditions are right or when it is safe to do. For example, Coors attempted to target the gay community when homosexuality was seen as acceptable, whereas Levi's had stood by and supported the community when it was socially unacceptable to do so (Kates 2004). The snowboard brand Burton is held in high esteem because of its role in developing the sport. Burton continued to make snowboard gear and to support and publicise the sport, even though many ski runs initially banned snowboarders. Subsequently, ski brands such as Rossignol have struggled to enter the snowboard market. In making the cult movie *Dogtown and Z-Boys*, Vans focused on producing a movie about the joys of skateboarding, but did not engage in any product placement – fully aware that their core fan base would whiff the 'stink of commercialism'. Instead, viewers responded to a company implicitly giving back to the community that had adopted them.

Story two: Leader as iconoclast

Leaders that challenge convention often found authentic brands—be it Muccia Prada, James Dyson, Richard Branson, Steve Jobs, Coco Chanel, Peter Jackson, Gordon Ramsay or Ralph Lauren. In each case, these individuals have gone against commonly accepted wisdom and won. Branson is a regular late entrant into concentrated mature markets such as airlines, banking, rail and mobile phones. Every time he does so, experts predict failure. And Virgin has failed, but we continue to love Branson because of his entrepreneurial spirit that seeks to shake up convention and 'stick it to the fat cats'. Branson takes on entrenched competitors and, in many cases, not only wins but also forces market leaders to offer better deals to their customers. As a result, formerly mature categories start to grow, often increasing returns for everyone.

James Dyson was angered by the fact that the basic technology behind vacuum cleaners had not changed since the first vacuum was invented. Modern vacuum cleaners therefore continued to lose suction after a few uses, resulting in poor cleaning performance. What angered Dyson more was (like Branson) that the consumer was being exploited by large lazy corporations who, instead of investing in innovation, focused on superficial style changes and marketing campaigns. Every major vacuum cleaner manufacturer who saw no potential in his cyclone design turned Dyson away. To see his vision come to life, Dyson took on considerable debt and founded his own firm. So successful has he been that a new generation of consumers no longer uses the word 'Hoover' to refer to vacuum cleaners (Dyson 2002).

Coco Chanel had a similar effect on women's fashion. Prior to World War I, European women dressed in complex clothes that restricted movement and took hours to get on. Dresses at the time were impractical, precisely because they were made to reflect the dominant (and male) view that women should be covered from head to toe. In contrast, Chanel's were elegant, simple, androgynous, and left ankles and arms uncovered. Chanel-designed clothes could also be changed in minutes. Predictably, Chanel's designs outraged moral conservatives and the fashion world of the time. Her influence, however, was immediate—women's fashion in 1918 was a world-away from 1914, and by the 1920s Chanel reined supreme (Charles-Roux 1995).

To their critics, people such as Chanel, Ralph Lauren, Gordon Ramsay, James Dyson, and Steve Jobs are seen as overbearing, intolerant individuals who treat their staff with contempt (and take all the credit for success). Many hate Gordon Ramsay because he swears, shouts, insults, manhandles and fires staff on a whim. Such behaviour runs counter to modern human resource practice and beliefs in fairness. Critics and consumers educated in a politically correct, self-esteem focused education system revile Ramsay and other tough bosses. Why then has Ramsay retained 80 per cent of his staff over the past ten years? And why did most of his staff follow him (and give up jobs at London's top restaurant) when he started his first business? Research reveals that staff love leaders like Ramsay because they push them to achieve their best and because they get rid of poor performers (Smith 2008). In contrast, inauthentic leaders fail to quickly address the issue of underperformance, and thereby the entire team suffers, with the resulting loss of talent.

Iconoclastic leaders lend brands authenticity precisely because they represent the desire in all of us to change things for the better, or rebel against convention. They are also loved because of their obvious passion for their craft—say what you like about Ramsay, but no one can deny his passion for fine cuisine and the customer experience (nor his love of talent). Rebel leaders also have one other brand benefit—they attract and retain the best talent, often at lower salaries. When Apple opened its first Australian flagship store, they received thousands of applications from Apple enthusiasts keen to take massive salary cuts to work for the company. As well, despite their flaws, staff go the extra mile for these leaders when deadlines approach (staff at Ralph Lauren often work late nights as deadlines approach because of a desire to 'do it for Ralph'). Consumers see their own enthusiasm reflected in that of staff and respond accordingly.

Story three: Fight the system

Being authentic has long been associated with going against convention. The Romantic Movement in the 19th century desired an authentic life by rejecting the rational order of the day (associated with industrialisation and the triumph of reason over emotion). Authenticity for the Romantics was to be found in nature, craft traditions and emotion. Punk and new wave artists were similarly inspired, rejecting the over blown music of the early 1970s in favour of a return to simple song structures laced with raw emotion. Although they rejected the dominant norms of the day, these artists created a body of work that endures and continues to inspire new generations. This spirit is embodied in authentic brands. Harley Davidson represents the rejection of conformity and rules in favour of hitting the road and experiencing the freedom of the outlaw. The Morgan Motor Company embodies a similar desire with its tagline 'driven at heart' and its reference to safety regulators as the 'fun police'.

Apple's playful advertisements challenge people to 'think different' while their stores feature images of rebels such as Gandhi, John Lennon and Martin Luther King. Apple's famous 1984 advertisement played during the super bowl captured this rebellious attitude, attacking the conformity and sterility of life under IBM. The flying of the skull and crossbones flag over their headquarters further enforced this position. Apple's cofounder Steve Jobs continues to embody the 60s spirit of 'fighting the man' by taking on big music and movie companies with iTunes, which pays higher royalties to artists and allows new artists to find a market without label backing. Despite the success and growth of Apple, the brand continues to present itself as a more humanistic, creative and playful entity in contrast to the 'system' as represented by Microsoft, Dell and IBM.

As part of a new breed of entrepreneurial environmental marketers, Brigid Hardy aims to change how we think about green products and household cleaners. Her label Beauty Engineered Forever (or B_E_E) aims to dominate supermarket shelves at the expense of Proctor and Gamble. After rejecting the globe trotting lifestyle of McKinsey, Hardy took up the challenge (given to her by a local entrepreneur) of making high performing environmentally friendly cleaners. Failing to see why consumers should have to trade off performance and beauty to be sustainable ('I hate the whining approach to green issues—buy me because you should even though we're not as good'), B_E_E products meet the highest possible performance standards so consumers can use less to gain better results. Rejecting the 'hair shirt' mentality that goes with many green products, advertising labelling for B_E_E is strong on design, erotica and playfulness—including 'I'll be your sensitive brute' (laundry concentrate), 'I triumph over grime and evil' (laundry powder), and 'I promise I'll be gentle' (fabric softener). Consumers have responded too, making B_E_E one of the fastest growing companies in New Zealand.

Many of France's food and beverage producers position themselves as purveyors of tradition in order to contrast themselves with global competitors focused on standardisation, sterility and conformity. Chateau Margaux is just one of many authentic brands that reject the conformity of taste being wrought by New World wine producers armed with scientific techniques and simple varietal labelling. These wines are seen as clean but bland. Chateau Margaux, in contrast, embodies the reaction to this trend, stressing the role of nature, place and culture in producing wine. In contrast to New World wines that offer immediate gratification, Chateau Margaux's wines are 'complex' and must be appreciated over time. Rather than iron out vintage variation, such differences from one year to next are celebrated because they reflect the natural order of things. While Australian winemakers suffer a downturn in sales and margins, Margaux continues to be lauded as one of the world's great estates.

Authentic brands embody the contrarian spirit of great artists. Since the choice of brand often reflects our desired self, authentic brands capture the rebellious spirit that all of us have but often feel we can't act on. Typical of many of them is the desire to retain important traditions and operate on old world business models that produce great products - rather than support poor ones with marketing (e.g. Microsoft's approach to Vista [so playfully pilloried by Apple]) - and capture the rebellious spirit. Importantly, they often refuse to accept tradeoffs—for example, between performance and design (Apple), performance and sustainability (B_E_E), service and low price (Virgin), and innovation and tradition (Morgan and Chateau Margaux). In doing so, these brands often approach things differently at a time when others converge around accepted practices, thus reinforcing a sense of sameness and me too-ness in the mind of the consumer.

Story four: Stick to your roots

Authentic brands seem stubborn when viewed through the lens of 'the customer is always right'. While marketing theory suggests the need to adapt to customer needs, changing societal standards and competitor tactics, the brands covered so far often reject new trends, new technologies and new ways of doing things in favour of sticking to their roots. The people behind authentic brands stick to their roots because they believe they are right—which is also why they rate highly on sincerity. There are also good reasons for doing so—failing to appreciate your roots can get you into serious trouble. For example, when skateboard shoemaker Vans decided to extend into other sports, skaters abandoned them in droves. Following a brush with bankruptcy, the brand returned to its core market and continues to be successful. Australian surf brands such as Ripcurl and Billabong are suffering similar problems as they move into fashion markets and staff their stores with people who know little about surfing.

Australia's greatest wine, Penfolds Grange, provides a sobering lesson for marketers keen to mess with a brand's roots. Grange is truly regarded as one of the world's iconic wines. The story of Grange is one of a passionate craftsman battling against the odds to produce something truly unique. Max Schubert (then Penfolds chief winemaker) desired to produce a wine that expressed the uniqueness of Australia. Critically, he desired to produce a wine that would rightfully take its place among the great wines of the world. At the time, local wines were pale imitations of European products (often labelled as 'Burgundy' or 'Hermitage' even though they bore no relation to these wines). Schubert laboured to produce Grange, a dry wine style that blended the best red grapes from Penfolds vineyard holdings in South Australia. Initial results were so discouraging that Penfolds board ordered Schubert to cease his experiments. Undeterred, Schubert continued on in secret.

Entered in a local wine show under a nondescript code, the wines won several awards (Grange simply takes time to mature in the bottle to be at its best). Feeling vindicated, Schubert continued to produce Grange in good years, ultimately producing Australia's greatest red wine. Emboldened by this, the Penfolds team under new owners Southcorp decided it was time to exploit the franchise. Suddenly Grange was released every year, and a new wine—white Grange (or Yattarna) was released. In 2001, Grange was being discounted in bottle shops and critics were voicing concern that the wine was no longer as good as it should be. White Grange also received unfavourable reviews and was often passed in at auction.

Grange was in trouble because the marketing and winemaking teams had turned their back on its roots. Schubert desired to produce a world-class wine that was a unique expression of Australia at its best. He was not motivated by high prices or record auction prices. In contrast, the motivation behind the extension to White Grange was profit. Far from being a unique wine, White Grange was simply another expensive chardonnay. As well, changes to Grange had been made to appeal to the American market, thus alienating traditional fans. Now under new stewardship (Fosters), the brand is attempting to return to its roots with a new marketing campaign featuring a contemplative Max Schubert and his initial experimental bottles with the tagline: 'To the Renegades: Max Schubert, winemaking legend and creator of Penfolds Grange. To those who do thing for love not money.'

The history surrounding brands is critical to its authenticity. As identified earlier, heritage, sincerity and love of production are central to consumer judgments of authenticity. Mess with a brand's roots and consumers are likely to leave in droves. By extending into mass fashion, surf brands such as Ripcurl run the risk of alienating their core constituency because surfers don't like seeing non-surfers wear 'their gear' (Beverland, Farrelly & Quester 2010). Remaining true to one's roots does not mean simply repeating pass practices because this results in products that quickly become obsolete. What is crucial is to retain the original spirit of the brand.

Although Morgan rejected advice to adopt mass production techniques, outsource production of core parts and use modern materials, they have adopted Japanese quality methods, invested in safety and emissions standards, and built new models such as the Aero, Aeromax and hydrogen powered Lifecar. Likewise, every new product released by Apple reinforces its original mission of creating insanely great, user friendly products.

Solving difficult dilemmas

The second conflict-ridden story involves solving difficult problems where no obvious solution is apparent (see Figure 16.1). Authentic brands solve these problems in three ways.

First, they profess to love their craft and therefore spend significant time perfecting their skills and products/services. Thus, difficult problems are solved because the people behind authentic brands love what they do and are always seeking perfection.

Second, they play up their creative genius. By engaging in breakthrough innovations, the people behind authentic brands constantly amaze with their genius and expertise. This story is all the more effective when these people play up their intuition and gut feel, and downplay training and the role of market research.

Third, authentic brands emphasise their essential amateurish motivations—the people behind the brands do what they do because they want to. They are not bound by the restrictions of normal corporations, nor restricted by formal training. Thus, the heroes behind the brand solve difficult problems because they think differently and are open to different solutions.

Story five: Love of craft

Ayn Rand's classic 1943 novel *The Fountainhead* involves two characters of relevance to our discussion on authentic branding. The first, Peter Keating, loves the fame and trappings that come with architecture and therefore gives up everything he loves in order to make buildings people want. Peter is not a very good architect but he is an excellent impression manager, being whatever people want him to be. At the end of the novel he is a man destroyed—a soulless individual who realises how meaningless all the temporary trappings of fame are.

His opposite, Howard Roark (the hero and Peter's friend), drops out of architecture school when it no longer has anything to teach him, works for a fading architecture practice run by iconoclast Henry Cameron, and survives on small commissions given to him by individuals who want something different. Eventually, Roark's radical architectural vision (the character is based on Frank Lloyd Wright) gains acceptance and ends the novel a successful architect and husband. In a critical passage of the novel, Howard tells Peter that to achieve true happiness in work one must 'love the doing' rather than the fame and the wealth. The people behind authentic brands embody this spirit.

Authentic brands are staffed with people passionate for the product/service and run by leaders heavily involved in all aspects of production. Charles Morgan (of the Morgan Motor Company) continues to race Morgans at Le Mans and other events. The firm is staffed with classic motoring enthusiasts, many of whom restore and race their own cars. Real Groovy is run by, and for, music lovers. It is not uncommon for staff to spend a third of their pay at the store on music and movies. Richard Branson requires all management staff to front airline check-in counters every month to keep in touch with the main job at hand. Ralph Lauren is known for walking the floors of Bloomingdales to ensure his clothes are presented just right. Steve Jobs gets involved in all aspects of production at Apple, often overruling designers or delaying product releases until they meet his exacting standards. Steven Levy (2000, p. 139) recalls Steve Jobs's reasons for rejecting the first Macintosh circuit board on aesthetic grounds:

> When you're a carpenter making a beautiful chest of drawers, you're not going to use a piece of plywood on the back, even though it faces the wall and nobody will ever see it. You'll know it's there, so you're going to use a beautiful piece of wood on the back. For you to sleep well at night, the aesthetic, the quality, has to be carried all the way through.

The man behind New Zealand's Weta Works studio, Peter Jackson, loves the art of film making so much so that no detail is too small. For example, in the opening battle scene of the *Fellowship of the Ring*, an alliance of dwarves, elves and humans desperately fight the armies of darkness. The scene is set thousands of years before the formation of the Fellowship. Weta staff were aware that, over time, technologies would change and evil creatures such as orcs and goblins would also evolve. As such, there are subtle differences in the features and technology (such as weapons and armour) of the different races (Sibley 2006). Many filmmakers would have re-used the same props to save on time and budget. They would have rationalised that most people wouldn't know. Not Jackson. Like Steve Jobs quoted above, he would know – as would fans.

Love of production is central to consumer-based brand authenticity. Authentic brands sit in contrast with the majority of brands on the market. Just as we switch companies and jobs for better pay and conditions, few brands inspire employees to turn down a better offer. Most employees view their current firm as a means to an end. We usually try and make it through the week so that we can engage our passions at the weekend. As such, few brands staffed by such employees inspire consumer loyalty. Just like Peter Keating, many of us have been told to get a practical job instead of following our passions. Just as we secretly admire artists for having the courage to do what they love, so we admire brands that are run and staffed by true enthusiasts—people that will do whatever it takes to ensure the survival of the brand. As a result, such dedication results in innovative products that become part of history—such as the Apple Macintosh, Sony Walkman, Chanel's little black dress, Dyson cyclone vacuum, Hermès Birkin bags, Louis Roederer Cristal, Manolo Blahnik shoes, and the Aston Martin DB5.

Story six: Artisanal amateurs

Marketers love to revel in their cleverness and professionalism. They love recalling successful efforts at targeting consumers, extending brands, responding to customer needs, benchmarking against competitors, and adopting scientific methods of analysis. They make no secret of their motivations either — they are there to make money and crush the competition. And, they usually do so by trying to sell more stuff most of us don't really need. In contrast, authentic brands seem to be run by amateurs that reject customer research and marketing in favour of gut feel, intuition and craft techniques. And yet, amateurs have some redeeming features:

1. They are unpaid. Because of this, they usually do things because they want to.

2. They often think differently because of their lack of training.

3. They are unencumbered with concerns of fame, paying bills, and meeting next quarter's targets.

As such, amateurs are often remarkably grounded, humble and playful.

A great example is Altoids — the popular mints originally made in Wales (but now produced in the US). In a remarkable article, Claudia Kotchka (VP of Design at Proctor and Gamble) identified why Proctor and Gamble (P&G) couldn't produce brands with the authenticity of Altoids. Recalling Snapple, Kotchka (2006) noted how Altoids brand authenticity would be destroyed by the 'P&G effect'. First to go would be the Altoids tin. Tin is more expensive than plastic, is heavier (thereby increasing shipping costs), is old fashioned, and the unique moulded design is difficult and expensive to change in response to changing trends. Second to go would be the high quality paper inside the tin that protects the mints from breaking. Again, too many parts, too much expense, and paper would be unnecessary in a newly designed plastic container.

Third to go would be the wacky flavours — after all no market test would highlight mass interest in liquorice mints, ginger mints, and cinnamon mints. Fourth to go would be the strength of the mints themselves, as this puts many people off. Finally, the shape and size of the mints would be standardised with new production processes because focus groups disliked their rough, seemingly hand-cut shape. Kotchka concluded that the result of this attempt to 'smooth out the edges' of Altoids would be to destroy the product's value in the eyes of its customers — many of whom collect Altoids tins and advertising. P&G would have turned an authentic brand into a me-too one.

In-N-Out Burger provides another example of amateurism. This cult hamburger chain from Southern California charges low prices, offers few items, produces everything fresh to order (and still hand cuts fries), pays the highest wages in the fast food sector, and enjoys cult-like devotion among consumers. Despite having relatively few stores, high costs, and strong competition, In-N-Out Burger has some of the highest returns in the industry. Also, as a fast food provider its burgers do not suffer the same poor quality associations endured by other brands. And, in an industry were staff turnover is rampant, In-N-Out enjoys extremely high levels of loyalty (Moon 2003). How has this seemingly old-time burger chain outperformed its larger, smarter and more customer focused rivals? Simple—because it emphasises old-fashioned things like quality, care for product and staff, friendly service, and community. In-N-Out is not successful in spite of its lack of professionalism; rather, its very amateurism gives the brand its charm as well as a focus on what really matters—taste and service.

Although these brands seem amateurish, don't take this as evidence that the people running them have no commercial understanding. Many of the managers of these brands have MBAs and are interested in commercial success. Nothing captures this more effectively than Steve Jobs's quip that 'real artists ship' in relation to getting the original Apple Macintosh to the market on time. Take a tour of one of the great wine houses of Bordeaux such as Château Margaux and you'll come away thinking that the wine is produced by intuitive artists with ancient hand-made equipment, and recipes passed down through generations. This, however, is just part of the story. Behind closed doors these wineries use state-of-the-art technology, and have a detailed scientific understanding of raw materials and technological processes.

Story seven: The intuitive genius

Behind every authentic brand is a creative genius, whether it is James Dyson, Steve Jobs, Steve Wozniak and Jonathan Ive, John Galliano, Marc Jacobs, Peter Jackson, Muccia Prada, Coco Chanel, and so on. These geniuses regularly solve problems that mere mortals cannot, and they usually do so in innovative ways. These designers and leaders embody a paradox. They regularly produce products that people love, yet reject marketing, consumer research and consumer-espoused needs. They heretically believe that customers rarely know what they want. Worse than that (for marketing academics anyway), they blame customer research for their failures.

In his book *The Pursuit of WOW!* (1994, p. 108), Tom Peters discusses how Muccia Prada's one flirtation with conventional customer-driven market research resulted in clothes that Prada was ashamed of, that critics savaged and that customers ignored. As Peters states: 'The clothes were over-designed, and it seemed that commercial considerations and self-consciousness were leading her.' Prada now immerses herself in the market, constantly on the look-out for emerging trends, small details and global styles. This information adds to Prada's already famed memory and provides an ongoing source of creative ideas as new knowledge is combined with old for each new season's line. Hardly the stuff of market orientation!

Bought a bottle of Château Margaux lately? Lucky you! It costs around US$500 per bottle in a good year and is nearly unobtainable – as it has been for the past 300 years. Such desirability must be driven by constant customer-driven innovations and changes, right? Wrong. Estate Manager Paul Pontallier has little time for segmentation, targeting and positioning. His *raison d'être* is simply to offer the best possible expression of the estate given the seasonal conditions. He is adamant that he doesn't make wine for a consumer, nor adapt anything he does for segments. His main concern is living up to the esteemed heritage of the brand (sentiments echoed by business-savvy owner Corinne Mentzelopoulos).

Marketers are taught that brands should be developed to meet customer needs and adjusted in line with customer insights from brand-tracking studies. Firms are encouraged to alter structures and systems to ensure they are at one with the all-powerful customer. Yet, authentic brands openly reject the slavish worship of customers, and treat conventional marketing tools – such as segmentation, targeting and positioning – with a degree of contempt (in fact some such as Morgan go so far as to state that 'the customer is often wrong'). However, taking such statements at face value would be dangerous. Many authentic brands suffered in the past when they traded on their status instead of offering market leadership.

So how do they maintain market relevance? The staff behind authentic brands are totally immersed in their markets and are avid collectors of general information. But market immersion is different from being market driven. Indeed, Tom Peters (1994) contrasts being 'of the market' (market driven) with being 'in the market' (market immersion). Market *immersion* involves key employees being active members in the marketplace as a way of sourcing valuable insights and trends. Fashion designers provide great examples. LVMH's Bernard Arnault encourages his designers to travel widely, not because he wants them to adopt the looks of a particular subgroup within a culture, but because the smallest details provide designers with inspiration. Quiksilver takes a different approach, ensuring staff engage in the sport (surfing, skating and snowboarding) and all that the lifestyle has to offer. They are also expected to use multiple brands *in situ* to gain insights on emerging technologies as well as fashion trends, to 'see and be seen', to observe, to chat with consumers, and to report any insights to the organisation's marketing team.

Such activities are vital for three reasons:

1. Immersion provides marketers of authentic brands with a vital source of new performance standards and stylistic trends. The information collected is often qualitative, experiential and diverse, in contrast to what many of the more conventional brands gather.

2. This information can be filtered into product styling or brand marketing to ensure ongoing relevance without diluting the brand.

3. This information enables designers such as John Galliano (of Louis Vuitton) and Jonathan Ive (VP of Industrial Design for Apple), or other product developers (from brew masters to car designers), to swear that their products are derived from personal inspiration – or the indefinable (and seductive) creative spirit – rather than from 'formal' market research.

What should brand managers do?

Based on an analysis of a broad range of authentic brands, I now provide eight do's and don'ts for brand managers who aim to build authentic brands. Collectively they may require a change in the ways things are done, but they also transform the quality of a company's brand strategy and its ability to deliver exceptional results over the long term.

Don't just say it, show it!

Consumer research reveals that overt claims of authenticity are viewed as marketing hype. Worse, such claims may render genuinely authentic brands fake (Beverland *et al.* 2008) – e.g. Wrangler jeans' 2004-5 billboard campaign featured two denim-clad models under the tag line 'Born Authentic'. Just as consumers may wonder whether something is wrong when brands talk constantly about quality, saying that you are authentic may raise concerns in the minds of consumers. Like quality, authenticity must be shown and not stated. To project authenticity, brands can draw on a number of attributes including: historical associations, relationship to place or subcultural space, non-commercial values, and the creative process. The Penfolds campaign to return the brand to its roots provides a good example of this approach.

Embrace the tension at the heart of authentic brands

The mantra of modern brand management has always been consistency of message. Yet the brands above are laden with contradictions—they are old and forever relevant, up-to-date but timeless, they are commercially successful yet deny their commercial prowess and motives. The managers of authentic brands need to become experts at managing these tensions. Instead of masking inconsistency, they must deal with the many paradoxes associated with authentic brands and effectively operate two parallel systems—one focused externally on communicating a sincere story about the brand, and one focused behind the scenes on counter-balancing relevancy with timelessness.

Appear forever timeless while offering product leadership

Authenticity is neither fashion, retro nor nostalgia. Consistent with Ralph Lauren's statement: 'I offer style, not fashion', managers of authentic brands continually update their products without sacrificing the brand's roots. They perceive their brand to be a 'living document' which evolves with the times, adopting new cultural icons and associations while never forgetting the past. Authentic brands are like onions: you can peel them to get to deeper layers of meaning; although, as you do so another layer emerges. Authentic brands must always be relevant, often representing the pinnacle of quality in their respective product class. Managers of authentic brands deliver functional excellence—by demonstration rather than by marketing hype.

Immerse yourself in the marketplace and wider culture

The owners and managers of authentic brands collect vast amounts of diverse information and filter this down to employees. While not all firms reject formal market research techniques, they do not give precedence to this form of information; small details or one-off experiences are often accorded equal or greater value than brand-tracking research or focus groups. For example, Quiksilver management routinely asks their staff (and staff ask their children) what they think about the latest surf fashion lines, as their decision to buy (or not to) is considered a crucial litmus test. Marketers of authentic brands need to encourage direct observation gained during staff travel, and information gained via personal experience with the products; they place great weight on the much-maligned 'gut feel'. Importantly, they need to seek information gained via immersion in the market or through membership of a subculture rather than through formalised research with specific demographics. Ideas that inform the practices of such brands should come from *in situ* experiences, tangential sources (viewing other cultures), and involvement in industry-specific forums.

Avoid the temptation to exploit your brand for commercial gain

Being authentic places limitations on how far a brand can be stretched. The jury is out on Ralph Lauren Paint, Prada Socket Sets, or Piper Heidsieck's Baby Piper. These extensions may reinforce the brand (e.g., paint can be positioned as part of the Ralph Lauren's lifestyle image, socket sets reinforce the audacity of Prada), or be seen as trying to milk a brand for commercial gain. The consumers we spoke to were often ambivalent about extensions. Some thought that surf brands extending into other sports diluted the brand's authenticity, while others were happy as long as the brand continued to maintain product leadership in surfing. Likewise, second and third tier quality labels of fine wines often reinforced the brand's position because they represented even greater selectivity in raw material. What marketers of authentic brands must remember is that any extension must appear non-commercially driven and must reinforce, rather than dilute, the authenticity of the original brand.

Employ a brand historian

The brands mentioned above drew directly on their histories as a form of competitive advantage. Too few companies retain records of their past. The author of this chapter has been contacted by firms wanting to reclaim their history only to find that too many past employees have moved on, or passed away, and that too few records were kept. These brand managers often have tantalising evidence to suggest that they are the oldest brand in their class or country, or that they were the first brand of their type, only to see such claims usurped by others with the evidence to back up their claims. Likewise, many brands have colourful characters or associations in their past, and yet too little information exists to build a rich, multifaceted story around them. Brand managers should view their brands as historical documents and retain every record and every press clipping (good or bad); and they should regularly engage writers to provide a historical record (if only for internal training purposes). Vespa has developed a Piaggio Historical Archive which contains more than 150,000 documents from the company's past. VW and Jack Daniel's have done likewise.

Don't be afraid of letting consumers in

Although the owners of authentic brands may not worship the customers' viewpoint when developing new innovations, they do welcome customers into the cult. And, they respect customer concerns about their brand. On the outside, In-N-Out appears unchanged since founding, avoiding demand for chicken and vegetarian burgers as well as salads and larger burgers. However, In-N-Out also has a *secret* menu. After customers started asking for Neapolitan milkshakes (a mix of chocolate, strawberry and vanilla) and burgers with three patties or above, the owners re-keyed all the firm's cash machines in order to allow for the sale of these innovations. And, although no four-four burger is offered on the menu (four patties and four slices of cheese—the record is 24-24), in-the-know customers can ask for it, and service staff can process such requests without problems (Moon 2003). (In-N-Out's secret menu is now a 'not-so-secret menu' as it is advertised on their webpage.) The lesson is clear: the brand is partly owned by the consumers, and so you must respect their views even if you disagree with them.

Make the most of lucky breaks

The Pacific Brand's marketing team got lucky when teens started wearing the Volley. They were even luckier because their inexperience with this market made them cautious in responding to the Volley's sudden change of status. Authentic brands make the most of these lucky breaks. The marketing team behind Isla-based whiskey brand Bruichladdich are master storytellers. Their famous WMD whiskey arose from a misunderstanding due to CIA paranoia. Fans of the whiskey can watch the manufacturing process live online. The CIA (unbeknownst to Bruichladdich staff) contacted the distillery when one camera went down, inquiring when it would be back up. On inquiring whether the 'customer' was a single malt fan, Bruichladdich received the following reply: 'No, we are not single malt fans, we are the CIA and believe you are making weapons of mass destruction.' Bruichladdich used this story as a motivation for a new product—WMD—that stands for 'whiskey of mass distinction' and features a yellow submarine on the label.

Conclusion

The search for authenticity is an enduring theme in Western thought. The desire for authenticity has now crossed into the brand arena as many consumers look for alternatives to mass-marketed, overly-commercialised and meaningless brands. Authentic brands may stumble, but our fascination with them remains unabated. Even when abused and devalued, their latent equity continues to appeal to investors. Despite appearances, their owners manage these brands very carefully, but often not in accordance with the traditional marketing dictum. Creating an authentic brand represents a challenge to modern marketers and to brand managers who revel in their marketing skills, constant updating, customer service and scientific understanding of the marketplace.

To commercialise, authentic brands must develop open-ended and rich stories rather than just develop mere positioning statements. They must espouse enduring values, become part of the cultural landscape, emphasise their love for the product/service, and develop a powerful organisational memory that acts as a repository for their enduring brand story. Being authentic also requires managing the tension between commercial imperatives and the espoused values of the brand. Authentic brands solve this tension by building powerful images of authenticity, while immersing themselves in the marketplace to gain inspiration for innovations. The brands presented here are brands that have lasted the test of time (some trace their lineage back 600 years). By adopting the principles identified here, brand managers can tap into a universal and human yearning for authenticity and, potentially, also assist their brands to endure for hundreds of years.

References

Arnould, EJ & Price LL 2000, 'Authenticating acts and authoritative performances: questing for self and community', In *The Why of Consumption: Contemporary Perspectives on Consumer Motives, Goals, and Desires*, ed. S Ratneshwar, DG Mick & C Huffman, London: Routledge, 140-163.

Belk, RW, Wallendorf M & Sherry JF Jr. 1989, 'The Sacred and the Profane in Consumer Behavior: Theodicy on the Odyssey', *Journal of Consumer Research*, 16(June), 1-38.

Belk, RW & Tumbat G 2005, 'The Cult of Macintosh', *Consumption, Markets & Culture*, 8(3), 205-217.

Beverland, MB 2005, 'Crafting brand authenticity: the case of luxury wine', *Journal of Management Studies*, Vol. 42 No. 5, pp. 1003-1029.

Beverland, MB 2006, 'The '"Real Thing": Branding Authenticity in the Luxury Wine Trade', *Journal of Business Research*, 59 (Feb), 251-258.

Beverland, MB 2009, *Building Brand Authenticity: 7 Habits of Iconic Brands*. Palgrave Macmillan: Basingstoke.

Beverland, MB & Ewing MT 2005, 'Slowing the Adoption and Diffusion Process to Enhance Brand Repositioning: The Consumer Driven Repositioning of Dunlop Volley'. *Business Horizons*, 48 (October), 385-392.

Beverland, MB & Farrelly FJ 2010, 'The Quest For Authenticity In Consumption: Consumers' Purposive Choice Of Authentic Cues To Shape Experienced Outcomes'. *Journal of Consumer Research* in press.

Beverland, MB, Lindgreen A & Vink MW 2008, 'Projecting Authenticity through Advertising: Consumer Judgments of Advertisers' Claims'. *Journal of Advertising*, 37 (1), 5-16.

Beverland, MB & Luxton, S 2005, 'The projection of authenticity: managing integrated marketing communications (IMC) through strategic decoupling', *Journal of Advertising*, Vol. 34 No. 4, pp. 103-116.

Beverland, MB, Farrelly FJ & Quester P 2010, 'Authentic subcultural membership: antecedents and consequences of authenticating acts and authoritative performances', *Psychology & Marketing* in press.

Booker, C 2004, *The Seven Basic Plots: Why We Tell Stories*. Continuum: London.

Edmonde, C-R 1995, *Chanel*. Harvill Press: London.

Deighton, J 2003, Snapple, Harvard Business School Case 9-599-126.

Dyson, J 2002, *Against the Odds*. Orion: New York.

Fine, GA 2004, *Everyday Genius: Self-Taught Art and the Culture of Authenticity*. Chicago, University of Chicago Press.

Fog, K, Budtz C & Yakaboylu B 2005, *Storytelling: Branding in Practice*. Springer, Copenhagen.

Harris, D 2003, *Cute, Quaint, Hungry and Romantic: The Aesthetics of Consumerism*. Da Capo Press.

Holt, DB 2004, *How Brands Become Icons*, Cambridge, MA: Harvard Business School Press.

Kates, SM 2004, 'The Dynamics of Brand Legitimacy: An Interpretive Study in the Gay Men's Community', *Journal of Consumer Research,* 31 (Sept), 455-464.

Klein, N 2000, *No Logo: Taking Aim at Brand Bullies*. Picador: New York.

Kotchka, C 2006, 'The Design Imperative in Consumer Goods', *Design Management Review,* 17(1), 10-14.

Levy, S 2000, *Insanely Great: the Life and Times of Macintosh, the Computer that Changed Everything*. New York: Penguin Books.

Mack, A 2009, 'Betting on the Uncertain'. *Brandweek* Jan 5, 10.

McDowell, C 2003, *Manolo Blahnik*. Cassell & Co: London.

Moon, Y 2003, *In-N-Out Burger*, Harvard Business School Case 9-503-096.

Napoli, J, Dickinson SJ, Beverland MB & Farrelly FJ 'Keeping it Real: Measuring Consumer-Based Brand Authenticity', *Journal of Consumer Psychology* in review.

Peters, T 1994, *The Pursuit of WOW! Every Person's Guide to Topsy-Turvy Times*. New York: Random House.

Principals-Synovate 2008, *2008 Authentic Brand Index Study*. Melbourne, Australia.

Rand, A 1943, *The Fountainhead*, Bobbs-Merrill: New York.

Rose, RL & Wood SL 2005, 'Paradox and the Consumption of Authenticity through Reality Television', *Journal of Consumer Research,* 32 (Sept), 284-296.

Seabrook, J 2000, *Nobrow: The Culture of Marketing + The Marketing of Culture*. New York: Random House.

Sibley, B 2006, *Peter Jackson: A Film-Maker's Journey*. HarperCollins: Auckland.

Smith, C 2008, 'Real Leaders'. *Idealog,* 17 (Sept-Oct), 133.

Thompson, CJ, Rindfleisch A & Arsel Z 2006, 'Emotional Branding and the Strategic Value of the Doppelganger Brand Image', *Journal of Marketing,* 70 (1), 50-64.

Author biography

Michael Beverland is Professor of Marketing in the School of Management, University of Bath. He is also a visiting professor at RMIT University, School of Economics, Finance and Marketing, Australia. Michael is a recognised academic authority on the production and consumption of authenticity with highly cited publications appearing in prestigious journals such as the *Journal of the Academy of Marketing Science,* the *Journal of Advertising,* the *Journal of Consumer Research,* the *Journal of Management Studies,* the *Journal of Product Innovation Management, Psychology and Marketing,* and the *European Journal of Marketing*. He has also received several large competitive research grants (DP0985178, DP0664943) from the Australian Research Council to examine aspects of branding and consumption. Beverland has spoken widely on authenticity on radio and been quoted regularly in the press. As well, he works with research agencies advising brands on delivering authentic experiences.

Contact: Michael Beverland, School of Management, University of Bath, The Avenue, Claverton Down, Bath, Avon, BA2 7AY, United Kingdom; P + 44 (0) 1225 386742; F + 44 (0) 1225 386473; E M.Beverland@Bath.ac.uk.

Chapter 17

Shifting brands: Reception, resistance and revision

ROBERT AITKEN

ABSTRACT

This chapter presents a consumer-centric and co-creational view of how our understanding and experience of brands has shifted over time. In particular, it plots the move from a firm-centric and managerially focussed position to a consumer-centric and experientially motivated one where consumers enjoy increasing influence over the relationship between them, the firm and the brand. This is represented not only by the ways in which people construct their own sense of brands and by their appropriation of them, but also by the ways in which people connect and relate to each other and to the wider world. The ownership, management and control of brands that were once presumed the prerogative of the firm are now contested by consumers whose individual experience and collective action are the ultimate arbiters of value and the consummate co-creators of meaning. Given the complex and dynamic relationship between value and meaning, a brand becomes a site for social, political and cultural engagement that has as much to do with individual and collective identity as it has to do with economic utility. The shifting sands of brand experience outlined in this chapter reflect the different roles that brands play in people's lives and the contrasting responses that these engender.

KEYWORDS

brands; branding; brand communities; brand tribes; anti-branding; co-creation; social construction

Introduction

Branding plays a central role in marketing and is the subject of an extensive body of work by both practitioners and academics. This work encompasses the psychological, social, cultural, experiential and symbolic aspects of branding in addition to its functional importance as the central pillar around which a company or organisation develops its communication strategy. At a practical level, for example, brands have conventionally been assumed to engender loyalty, enhance premium pricing, ensure quality and inhibit risk. At a theoretical level, brands connect the conscious needs and not-so-conscious desires and aspirations of consumers to the deliberate and manufactured offerings of producers. In this way, brands have been seen as mediators of consumer experience where the emphasis is on matching a firm's output to a consumer's input.

A brand is an organisation's loudest and most public statement of its promise to provide the consumer with what he or she wants. As such, it is the company's most powerful asset and its most valuable resource. A brand is a powerful asset because its primary function is to establish a position in the marketplace in such a way that it differentiates itself enough from its competitors to capture a significant number of consumers. Conventionally, this differentiation is based on particular product attributes or benefits (such as fuel efficiency) and/or on the emotional, psychological, cultural and symbolic nature of the brand appeal (for example, Apple users are cool).

However, there is a certain irony in the fact that a brand – as an organisation's greatest public asset and its most persuasive symbolic offering – is largely intangible (Levy 1999). You cannot pick a brand up, hold one in your hands, or pop one in your pocket. Brands exist as ideas or emotions, or as collections of perceptions (Fournier 1998), and are as much about self-expression and identity as they are about acquisition and ownership. Yet a brand's equity – its commercial value, the aggregated worth ascribed to it and for which its success is measured and traded in the marketplace – is starkly tangible.

This separation between arbitrary brand perception and predictive brand performance is at the heart of recent, and continuing, critiques of branding. In addition, challenges to modernist conceptions of consumers, changing patterns of reception, resistance to brand hegemony, consolidation of brand communities, burgeoning interactivity and the co-creation of meaning and experience are changing how we understand the role that branding plays in society.

The way we were

Conventionally, branding has been seen as firm-centric, managerially focussed and transactionally orientated (Ballantyne & Aitken 2007). Brands are 'owned' by firms and organisations and are managed strategically to achieve such aims as increased awareness, strengthened brand identity or deepened market penetration. Brand messages are fashioned under the auspices of brand managers and 'delivered' to consumers through integrated marketing communications campaigns. The emphasis, in this process-orientated procedure, is on achieving coherence and consistency of message and transportability of appeal to homogenised markets comprising consumers whose consumption patterns are predictable. As an industrial production model more concerned with market monopoly and global penetration, this system has many advantages for the firm but increasingly less appeal for the consumer. While acquisition procedures may secure cheap resources, labour policies may limit wages, economies of scale may ensure low prices, and corporate communications may guarantee uniform messages, they are increasingly out of step with an informed, interactive and socially-concerned public.

Reading brands

One of the catalysts for a re-appraisal of how brands work in relation to consumer experience was the articulation of how consumers respond to brand communications. In particular, research into reception theory, derived largely from structuralism and semiotics and exploring the individually-orientated relativism of post-structuralism, emphasises the active and integrative process of constructing meaning at the point of engagement with a message such as a brand advertisement (Scott 1994). That is, meaning is not seen as pre-determined and predictable and embedded in the brand message, as in conventional firm-centric communications; rather, it is constructed by the consumer as he or she interacts with it. A reader-response approach suggests how a consumer's knowledge, experience, expectations, beliefs, values and motives, for example, operate on a brand communication to produce a meaning or an interpretation that may be quite different from the one intended by the producer of the message (Aitken, Lawson & Gray 2008).

In contrast to conventional approaches to brand message comprehension, there is no 'correct' reading of a brand text in reader-response theory. Cognitive and rationalist responses to brand messages centre on the notion that consumers process and interpret messages according to a dominant paradigm of reading. This dominant paradigm privileges conventional strategies of message construction and assumes that, if the strategies are employed accurately, they will be read appropriately. The belief that a desired or preferred reading is possible as long as the message or executional strategies are used accurately has led, in branding and advertising effects research, to an over-emphasis on message construction and an under-estimation of the dynamic role of the reader.

The major implication of this for research into and attitudes towards branding, indeed advertising and promotion in general, is the recognition that the act of responding to brand communication is a complex, dynamic and potentially arbitrary process. The potential for oppositional readings and the opportunity for alternative responses are also central to the social construction of meaning that is characteristic of brand communities and brand tribes. Further support for such alternative ways of responding to brands was provided by developments in uses and gratifications research. This work extended the initial emphasis on psychological aspects of uses and gratifications to include more social and cultural responses to brands, and acknowledged how consumers appropriate brands and brand messages to suit their own and collective purposes (Aitken, Lawson & Gray 2008; O'Donohue 2001; Ritson & Elliot 1999). This more fractured and arbitrary approach to understanding how consumers respond to brands and brand messages and to how they objectify their experiences provides a conceptual framework that helps to explain the development of major challenges to branding orthodoxy.

Consuming resistance

One of the major challenges to branding hegemony has been the rise and rise of consumer activism and resistance. While there is a long history of consumer resistance to marketing in general and to brands in particular (McLibel, Starbucked, etc.), and of popular awareness of its effects (see, for example, Adbusters), Naomi Klein's bestselling *No Logo - Brands, Globalization & Resistance* (2000) and the subsequent DVD and YouTube video is a unifying moment of such defiance. Aimed squarely at multinational companies and the anti-social effect of their branded worlds, Klein provides a compelling account of how mega brands (such as Nike, McDonalds, Disney, Gap, WalMart and Starbucks) have eschewed the promises of the information age – namely choice, interactivity and increased freedom – and instead packaged these promises as commercial products that can be bought over the counter. Ignoring the irony of *No Logo* itself becoming a brand of sorts, Klein admonished corporate brands for their substitution of human ideals, aspirations and values with surrogate slogans and seductive simulacrums. Citing the absence of genuine opportunities for self-fulfilment and proposing clear evidence of duplicity, Klein's treatise presented a coherent explanation of the exploitative potential of brands that meshed effectively with growing resistance to world trade initiatives in general and to disillusionment with corporate power in particular. Such resistance reinforces the cultural and socio-political nature of consumption and highlights the central role that brands can play as mediators of meaning in the social-construction of reality.

Brand communities

However, closely related to the active and explicit resistance to branding emanating from Klein's *No Logo* is the exponential growth witnessed by brand communities. While these previously *ad hoc* groups have existed since the advent of brands, their geographical dislocation has more recently been mitigated by the interconnectivity afforded by web-based communications. This has enabled them to cohere into virtual communities, united by a common interest in or a collective resistance to particular brands. Brand communities are consumer collectives formed around brands through social relationships based on identity and affinity (Muniz & O'Guinn 2001). Characterised by consciousness of kind, by evidence of rituals and traditions, and by a common sense of moral obligation, these post-modern communities are opposed to modernist managerial and social institutions and are united in their sharing of particularised brand values, meanings and experiences. Such sharing and belonging creates a sense of place and purpose for people, and –

in a post-modern world where identity is fragmented and purpose is unclear – brands offer the potential for the self to be re-constructed and for the community to be re-connected.

Indeed, the aggregation of people around a brand appeals to the construction of the self both individually and collectively. The post-modernist self requires recognition by others, which enhances identity and creates bonds and relationships. The strength of these bonds and the sense of belonging to a group, called the 'consciousness of a kind' by Muniz and O'Guinn (2001), are powerful progenitors of ownership and possession, and represent a shift in the locus of control from the company to the consumer or to the brand community. Interesting examples of such communal appropriation of brands and re-mediation of meanings can be found in the highly involved and fiercely loyal communities of Star Trek (Cova, Pace & Park 2007; Kozinets 2001), and the Apple Newton community (Muniz & Schau 2005).

One of the classic examples of this type of brand community is that represented by Harley-Davidson (Schouten & McAlexander 1995; McAlexander, Schouten & Koenig 2002). The Harley-Davidson brand community is well recognised as a case of how a community organically evolves around a brand. Membership of this community occurs via ownership of a Harley Davidson motorcycle, and newcomers automatically become members of the Harley Owners Group (HOG) when they purchase their bikes. The HOG is an international organisation, sponsored by Harley-Davidson and positioned exclusively for Harley bike owners.

A strong image about Harley bikes and the Harley experience is nurtured from a set of core values that not only create a stereotype of the bikers (clothes and personal appearance), but also defines a lifestyle (behaviour and attitudes). There is a dominant ethos amongst the bikers that embodies underlying cultural values, principles and needs (Schouten & McAlexander 1995). There are also a number of sub-groups organised around more specific (or specialised) levels of identification within HOG that testify to the brand community's inclusivity and the brand's elasticity. Interestingly, regardless of the level or intensity or interest, all groups adopt the same core values and adapt the bikers' ethos to their own beliefs, behaviours and lifestyles.

Rallies and 'brandfests' provide opportunities to experience the meanings assumed by the brand values, and these are reinforced by the participatory and collective adoption of rituals and traditions. Indeed, these values represent a Harley ideology intrinsically linked to wider and more symbolic American ideals of freedom and rebellion and to the social construction of masculinity.

In contrast to the explicit brand focus on Harley Davidson is the Burning Man phenomenon analysed by Kozinets (2002). This is an example of a counter-culture that shares many of the characteristics of brand communities but, in this case, united in their opposition to market-led and brand dominated commercial environments. Burning Man is a one-week, anti-market event where consumers practice alternative forms of exchange, experience life in a communal environment, and position consumption as self-expressive art. This re-constructed community occurs annually in the Black Rock Desert of Nevada (in the US) with the core purpose of creating 'an experience of caring human contact' in a society where marketing forces are seen as intrusions (or corruptions) of the integrity of cultural processes (Kozinets 2002). The festival, a brandfest in reverse, is an event to protest against traditional marketing practices and to celebrate experience as an alternative type of consumption distanced from traditional marketing logics.

The event is based on 'radical self-expression' through any kind of art, and follows ten basic principles:

1. **Radical inclusion.** Anyone is welcome and there are no prerequisites for participation in the community.

2. **Gifting.** Burning Man is devoted to acts of gift giving, with unconditional gift value, and this practice does not contemplate a return or an exchange for something of equal value.

3. **Decommodification.** The community seeks to create social environments that are unmediated by commercial sponsorships, transactions or advertising.

4. **Radical self-reliance.** The event encourages the individual to discover, exercise and rely on his or her inner resources.

5. **Radical self-expression.** It arises from the unique gifts of the individual. No one other than the individual or a collaborating group can determine its content. It is offered as a gift to others. In this spirit, the giver should respect the rights and liberties of the recipient.

6. **Communal effort.** Communal effort includes the shared values of creative cooperation and collaboration. The community strives to produce, promote and protect social networks, public spaces, works of art, and methods of communication that support such interaction.

7. **Civic responsibility.** Community members who organise events should assume responsibility for public welfare and endeavour to communicate civic responsibilities to participants.

8. **Leaving no trace.** This includes respecting the environment and a commitment to leaving no physical trace.

9. **Participation.** Burning Man is committed to a radically participatory ethic. There is a belief that transformative change, whether in the individual or in society, can occur only through the medium of deeply personal participation.

10. **Immediacy.** Immediate experience is, in many ways, the most important touchstone of value in this culture. No idea can substitute for this experience. The experience concludes with the symbolic burning of the giant man, the 'apogee and central metaphor of the festival' (Kozinets 2002), representing a passage of purification and freedom from oppressive capitalist practices.

McAlexander *et al.* (2002) adopted a similar customer-centric perspective to analyse brand communities, and emphasised the meanings and the experience of these communities as essential and intrinsic parts of the customer experience. Closely observing the experiences of customers at a Jeep jamboree, the authors point to the support and endorsement provided by Jeep's manufacturer, DaimlerChrysler, and to the extent that these brand communities are valued – both by the company and by the participants.

Hosted by brand and marketing managers, these events are designed to bring together potential and actual customers to share the experience of ownership from a more integrative and socially-orientated standpoint (McAlexander *et al.* 2002). Brand managers incentivise these events and encourage participants to share their stories and experiences and to exchange information around the brand. Indeed, proactively linking consumers with Jeep engineers to engage in discussion about new product development is central to the co-creation of brands – the ultimate phase of brand development.

The role of brand communities in the continuous negotiation of the social construction of brands and brand meanings is perhaps best exemplified in the case of Hummer (Hummer is a trademark of General Motors Corporation (GM), which produces Hummer, Hummer H1 and Hummer H2). The original multi-purpose military vehicle was adapted and redesigned as a sports utility vehicle, and has inspired unprecedented amounts of both admiration and opposition among the North American public.

According to Luedicke (2006), Hummer demonstrates the potential of a brand to generate intense controversy and polarisation, and presents the alternate Hummer brand communities as groups of 'shared ideological distinctions' that include: 'off-road capability versus environmental irresponsibility, positive attention versus selfish vanity, and social superiority versus excessive overconsumption-combined' (p. 491). These distinctions raise a large number of issues and meanings around which consumers are able to identify and interact. At the core of these issues and meanings lies the fate of the brand.

Anti-branding

Anti-brand communities are the antithesis of brand communities, and while both are organised around certain brands – usually with a strong global presence such as Microsoft, Dell or Nike – the motivation to participate in these communities derives from consumers' explicit opposition to them. As Szmigin and Carrigan (2003) suggest, some groups have developed alternative models of consumption and different modes of exchange. They represent this as 'a continuum of progress from the dominant branding position through the resistance of boycotting and anti-branding, producing a re-enabling of consumers in some form of community mode' (p.5).

Considered as a new form of consumer activism (Hollenbeck & Zinkhan 2006), the explicit purpose of these anti-brand communities is to create a reaction to the notion of mass marketing and to question traditional marketing as represented by large corporations and brands.

The research conducted by Hollenbeck and Zinkhan (2006) identified some of the key aspects that encourage the formation of and support for the formation of those groups. These are:

- **Common moral obligations.** Participants share the same sense of social and moral obligations, and they feel a common call to articulate and participate in collective actions.

- **Support networks.** Participants nurture social interactions via the internet, provide a support group to achieve common goals, and support reciprocal exchange of ideas and advices.

- **Workplace challenge.** Particularly for ex-employees, the web community provides a social structure offering individual self-assurance and support for participants experiencing negative interactions with the company they oppose.

- **Resource hub.** Participants share information and resources in order to maintain the community and to increase involvement.

In these cases, communities reinvent or reconceptualise dominant modes of exchange and are characterised by an obligation to social, cultural and political change. For these communities, the level of a brand's commitment to concepts such as human rights, to issues such as environmental sustainability, and to practices such as recycling, fair-trade, organics and sustainability determines the extent of their support for or the strength of their opposition to that brand. Even though some of these practices have started to be assimilated into mainstream corporate practice, the authors suggest that the proliferation of these communities 'reveals the shifting balances in power between the consumer and supplier' (Hollenbeck & Zinkhan 2006).

Hollenbeck and Zinkhan (2006) developed a research agenda to explore and understand the characteristics and the formation of these types of community. They began by examining three anti-brand websites: anti-Wal-Mart, anti-McDonald's, and anti-Starbucks. Their initial conclusions suggested that the formation of anti-brand communities provided an effective medium for consumers to consolidate and express their dissatisfactions with brands, corporations and marketing practices. Indeed, these brand communities also drive the process of identification – individually and collectively – by fostering a sense of belonging to a cause and by the sharing of meanings. In this case, the construction of self-identity and the celebration of a collective identity occur not as an attachment to or identification with a certain brand, but via a shared opposition to it.

Further, their location in cyberspace, not only provides virtually free and unlimited access for their participants, but, more importantly, enables them to share their concerns, rally support and organise collective resistance to broken brand promises, or what they see as brand mal-practice, instantaneously. Examples of uncovering such brand duplicity as Walmart's secret sponsorship of a road trip across America disingenuously promoting the brand's social commitments, Dell's oblivious community monitored telephone refusals to accept responsibility for faulty products and Apple's failure to recall defective batteries despite internal advice to the contrary, represents the scale of the challenge to brands at the hands of informed, active and concerned global communities.

Brands and tribes

The idea of consumer tribes – closely related to brand and especially anti-brand communities but enjoying wider and more freely associative relationships – is related to the idea of social re-composition in a fragmented, post-modern society (Cova & Cova 2002). This re-composition is based on free arrangements through personal and individual preferences and on social, cultural and political ideologies. What binds the tribe together, in addition to a common passion, is a shared belief in a particular discourse of consumption (Cova & Pace 2006).

The notion of a tribe, therefore, goes beyond mere purchase and consumption activity to become a multi-originator of relationships that creates new services, acts as innovator and entrepreneur, and generates and develops participatory culture (Cova, Kozinets & Shankar 2007). In this context, consumers are creators, producers, suppliers, consumers and – most importantly – arbiters of value in exchange and value in use. The peer-to-peer sharing of music, the production and circulation of individualised versions of Star Wars movies, and the often hilarious mash-ups of music videos on YouTube are testament to a brand environment where ownership and copyright are eschewed and appropriation, creativity, interactivity and community are celebrated.

In such contexts, brand meaning is determined by the co-creation and sharing of experience and by the socially-constructed and community mediated value of exchange. In a world where people make sense of life and express their identities through experiences of consumption, particularly the consumption of brands, these exercises in reciprocal and communal meaning construction define lifestyles, delineate discourses and inform the collective conscience.

Consumer empowerment through the interchange of information naturally provides the context for co-creation of brand uses and meanings. The experience of 'My Nutella, The Community', a community-oriented website creating a network of Nutella users and fans, 'has been producing sub-cultural components capable of sustaining its cult and forcing Ferrero (the producer) to re-shape the meaning of the brand' (Cova & Pace 2006). For some, these tribes represent the future of consumption, given their collective experience of brands and their common commitment to co-creation (Cova *et al.* 2007).

Brand tribes and communities and anti-branding communities illustrate the dichotomy between the branded world criticised by Klein and the empowered, appropriated and mediated paradigms of alternative branding. Within these communities it is possible to see how traditionally-orientated brand owners can, through ceding power, enhance their brands, or how resistance to the consumer co-option and co-creation of brands might meet with active resistance.

The butterfly effect

At the start of 2009, a story entitled 'Virgin: The World's Best Passenger Complaint Letter', appeared in the online version of the popular newspaper, The Daily Telegraph. The letter, amusingly complaining about the quality of food on a Virgin Airways flight, started out as a viral internet phenomenon before being picked up by the mainstream media and then reverberating between the world of the blogosphere and the traditional media. At the time of writing, this letter had been the most read article in the Telegraph. The author's description of his awful experience was read by millions of individuals, and it is only possible to guess at how this might negatively impact upon the carefully cultivated Virgin brand that promises excitement, freedom and fun. The company quite simply broke its promise and failed to deliver, and that failure was broadcast around the world.

This, and similar examples, represents a profound change and a shift in the power between consumers and brand owners. Previously, the complaint about Virgin might have influenced some friends, family and localised networks. In this case, the complaint has impacted upon the minds of millions of consumers. Under such circumstances, ideas that a brand and its managerially-preferred meaning is a unidirectional communication are contested. In these circumstances it becomes apparent that the brand is not in the hands of the marketing department alone, or in the hands of the whole company, but crucially in the hands of all of those who encounter and experience the brand. Ownership of the brand thus becomes the prerogative of all those who experience it.

The question that arises from this shift in ownership is to ask how companies and brand managers might adapt to the changing brandscape, and how they might seek to operate and develop strong brands in such an environment. A first step in understanding this challenge is to recognise that the consumer is not a passive recipient of company derived brand messages and images, but is increasingly an active participant in the formation of the brand itself; the consumer is no longer just an end-user, but the co-creator of the brand.

Understanding what a brand actually is and who owns it has long been contested within marketing. Taking a simplified view, there are those who see the brand as something that is owned and managed by a firm – that is, as an asset with the value of the asset carefully measured on the company balance sheet. On the other hand, there are theorists such as Nicholas Ind (2004) who proposes that the brand is the firm and all of the activities of the firm as perceived by individuals. With such a view it would be impossible to isolate the value of the brand as an entry on a balance sheet, just as it is impossible to separate the brand from the company; the brand becomes the enactments of the company interpreted by each individual. Between these two perspectives of brands, it is possible to detect not only a commonality but also a considerable difference. The commonality is that both perspectives propose that the firm influences the perception of the brand, but the difference is the matter of degree of influence and the way in which the firm controls the brand.

Another important step is to understand the nature of what has actually provided this dramatic shift in the nature of branding, and that means understanding the way in which Web 2.0 operates. It is a change that is not commensurate with those who seek to retain control of the brand within the company through traditional methods of advertising and promotion. This might be described as a process-driven, controlled system in which brand and advertising managers identify a brand position, formulate a strategy, and transmit that strategy to receptive consumers.

Instead of such a strategy, brand managers are confronted with the chaotic and uncontrolled environment of Web 2.0. Within this disordered environment, their brand becomes subject to the potential of chaos – or as it is popularly known, the Butterfly Effect (Williams 1997). This effect is the potential of a butterfly flapping its wings in one place to cause a hurricane to appear in another. If the example of the Virgin story is examined, a single individual posted a complaint letter to the world of Web 2.0 (the butterfly) and the effects have multiplied to a crisis in the offices of Virgin Airlines (the hurricane).

However, whilst such an individual story might have an immediate crisis effect, Web 2.0 has even greater potential to shape a brand through the mosaic of individual and collective experiences manifest in consumer review sites such as Epinions, or in collaborative networks such as MySpace, Bebo and Facebook, or in the multitude of blogs and twittering that are shared in cyberspace. Once again, a challenge is presented to the orthodoxy of the firm-centric brand – a challenge to the idea that the brand resides in the marketing department. Instead, reflecting Ind's view of the brand, each individual in the firm has a role to play in delivering the implicit promise that the consumer perceives from the brand. After all, any action of the firm, or the action of any employee, might represent the potential for a reshaping of the perception of the brand. In the world of Web 2.0, a single incident or a single bad experience from an individual consumer has the potential to shape the brand perception of a wide audience.

Sometimes deliberatively, often intensely and always cumulatively, these brand communications provide a dynamic and entirely interactive reminder that the fate of a brand rests with the experience of the consumer.

The brand paradox

The meaning of a brand is the result of a consumer's cumulative experience and perceptions that reveal and influence the construction of identities both collectively and individually (Fournier 1998; Askegaard 2006). As an identifier, the brand is linked to issues of ownership; as a differentiator, the brand becomes a signifier of meanings and values (Ballantyne & Aitken 2007). Acting as a differentiator and an identifier, and through an aggregation of meanings and symbols, a brand is a powerful influence on consumer behaviour and thinking (Heilbrunn 2006), and impacts culture by infusing or reinforcing meanings into people's lives (Schroeder & Salzer-Morling 2006).

The interaction between brands and consumers goes beyond conventional relationships where companies 'talk' to consumers through their brands. Even more than such two-way dialogue, brands and consumers are influenced by the environment (Bergvall 2006) and by culture (Schroeder & Salzer-Morling 2006). This interaction brings multiple perspectives and participants to the process of creating, replicating and re-creating meanings and has enormous managerial implications.

Interacting with the culture and the environment, a brand engages in an expanded 'multilogue' (Berthon, Holbrook, Hulbert & Pitt 2007) with a variety of stakeholders. These interactions affect the construction of identities for consumers (Bergvall 2006) and brands, influence the production of brand meanings often constrained by cultural codes (Schroeder & Salzer-Morling 2006), and impact the dissemination of values in society. The control of brand meanings, therefore, can be seen as the prerogative of the consumer who adds to it or not, reinforcing or changing the brand message through their use and experience of the brand.

This process is clearly evident in the complex and dynamic nature of the multifaceted and intricate relationships that characterise consumer experiences of the American Girl brand (Diamond, Sherry, Muniz, McGrath, Kozinets & Borghini 2009). These authors provide a comprehensive and convincing explanation of the ways in which a brand can be seen as a cultural gestalt, a brand meaning that is infinitely greater than the sum of its component parts. Brands comprise a myriad of individual and collective perceptions and experiences that resonate powerfully with underlying individual, social, cultural and political values. The 'cynosure' presented by this iconic American brand is thus a site where issues of identity and questions of values and belief are contested in the continual negotiation of cultural meaning (Diamond *et al.* 2009).

The co-creation of brand meanings by consumers shifts brand ownership from the managerialist and legalist sphere of intellectual property rights and trademarks (Schultz & Schultz 2004) to consumers and brand users. This consumer empowerment (Kozinets & Handelman, 2004; Pongsakornrungsilp, Bradshaw & Schroeder 2008) is developed through word of mouth (WOM), through the consumers' brand associations, and through the consciousness of consumer rights. These practices are able to destroy brand value and affect brand equity (Ballantyne & Aitken 2007), forcing companies to re-adjust performances, re-position products, and re-align promises.

When consumers are involved in the process of creating value for brands and thus affecting brand equity, they are also able to create threats and opportunities for firms (Pongsakornrungsilp *et al.* 2008). This co-creation changes the control and ownership of the brand from firm- to consumer-centred. Indeed, consumers are moving to own the brand in a very tangible and immediate sense. The relationship between brand advocates and brand adversaries and the challenge it represents to conventional notions of brand ownership is, therefore, central to understanding the ways in which consumers mediate their lives. Brand meanings are constantly co-created and re-presented by the community, reflecting, as they do, the everyday experience of its constituents. The resulting brand essence is dynamic, authentic and – most importantly – collective.

So, the meaning of a brand is the result of a consumer's cumulative experience, and those experiences are developed with each contact with the brand. The promise that is implicit in the brand creates an expectation from consumers, and that expectation is evaluated with each brand experience. In the world of Web 2.0, in which disparate interests can so readily be formed into new networks, new tribes and new communities, the control over the meaning of a brand is slipping further away from traditional brand owners. It is a world in which an individual consumer might have his or her voice amplified, and one in which the collective voice of a community plays a major role in shaping wider perceptions of brands. In all cases, the power to control the brand is diminishing. This might be a hard concept for brand owners to accept, but Web 2.0 has created ever greater opportunities for the consumer to appropriate brand meanings.

Such appropriation by both brand and anti-brand communities, and the alternative approach to branding that this implies, represents a considerable challenge to firms: how to manage the unmanageable? There is an inherent contradiction in the idea of managing the unmanageable, but that is the task that is confronted by those companies who see themselves as brand owners. In the present environment, however, the term brand owner becomes contradictory, perhaps even redundant. It is unrealistic to assume that it is possible to own the individual or collective experiences and perceptions of a brand.

Consumers have indeed hijacked the brand. A refusal to engage with these brand hijackers, a refusal to engage with these co-owners, is to risk losing any control over the brand. Instead, engagement with individuals, with brand communities and with the fragmentary tribes offers a way of enlisting the support and energies of these co-owners in a process of co-creation. At the heart of alternative branding, then, is the paradox that a brand belongs to those who perceive it and not to those who produce it.

Acknowledgements

The author would like to express his sincere gratitude and many thanks to Adriana Campelo and Mark Avis for their intelligent, insightful and practical contributions to this chapter.

References

Aitken, R; Lawson, R & Gray, B 2008, 'Advertising effectiveness from a consumer perspective', *International Journal of Advertising*. 27(2), pp. 279-299.

Ballantyne, D & Aitken, R 2007, 'Branding in B2B markets: Insights from the Service-Dominant logic of marketing'. *Journal of Business and Industrial Marketing*. 22 (6), pp. 363-371.

Bergvall, S 2006, 'Brand Ecosystems' in J Schroeder & M Salzer-Morling (eds), *Brand Culture*, Routledge, London and New York.

Berthon, P; Holbrook, M; Hulbert, J & Pitt, L 2007, 'Viewing Brands in Multiple Dimensions', *MIT Sloan Management Review,* 48 (2), pp. 37-43.

Cova, B & Cova, V 2002, 'Tribal Marketing: The Tribalisation of Society and Its Impact on the Conduct of Marketing', *European Journal of Marketing,* 36 (5/6), pp. 595-620.

Cova, B; Kozinets, R V & Shankar, A 2007, *Consumer Tribes,* Elsevier, Oxford.

Cova, B & Pace, S 2006, 'Brand Community of Convenience Products: New Forms of Customer Empowerment - the Case "My Nutella the Community', *European Journal of Marketing,* 40 (9/10), pp. 1087-1105.

Cova, B; Pace, S & Park, D J 2007, 'Global Brand Communities across Borders: The Warhammer Case', *International Marketing Review,* 24 (3), pp. 313-329.

Diamond, Nina; Sherry, John F; Muniz Jr, Albert M, McGrath, Mary Ann, Kozinets, Robert V, & Borghini, Stefania 2009, 'American Girl and the Brand Gestalt: Closing the Loop on Sociocultural Branding Research', *Journal of Marketing,* 73 (3), pp. 118-134.

Fournier, Susan 1998, 'Consumers and Their Brands: Developing Relationship Theory in Consumer Research', *Journal of Consumer Research,* 24, pp. 343-373.

Hollenbeck, CR & Zinkhan, GM 2006, 'Consumer Activism on the Internet: The Role of Anti-Brand Communities', *Advances in Consumer Research,* 33, pp. 479-85.

Ind, N 2004, *Living the Brand: How to Transform Every Member of Your Organization Into a Brand Champion,* Kogan Page, London.

Kozinets, R V 2001, 'Utopian Enterprise: Articulating the Meanings of Star Trek's Culture of Consumption', *Journal of Consumer Research,* 28, pp. 67-88.

Kozinets, RV 2002, Can Consumers Escape the Market? Emancipatory Illuminations from Burning Man', *The Journal of Consumer Research,* 29, pp. 20-38.

Levy, S J 1999, *Brands, Consumers, Symbols, and Research: Sydney J. Levy on Marketing,* Sage Publications, Thousand Oaks, CA.

Luedicke, MK 2006, 'Brand Community under Fire: The Role of Social Environments for the Hummer Brand Community', *Advances in Consumer Research,* 33, pp. 486-93.

Luedicke, M K & Giesler, M 2007, 'Brand Communities and Their Social Antagonists: Insights from the Hummer Case' in B Cova; RV Kozinets, & A Shankar (eds), *Consumer Tribes,* Elsevier, Oxford.

McAlexander, J.H; Schouten, J W & Koenig, HF 2002, 'Building Brand Community', *The Journal of Marketing,* 66, pp. 38-54.

Muniz, Albert M Jr. & O'Guinn, T C 2001, 'Brand Community', *The Journal of Consumer Research,* 27, pp. 412-32.

Muniz, Albert M Jr & Schau, HJ2005, 'Religiosity in the Abandoned Apple Newton Brand Community', *Journal of Consumer Research,* 31, pp. 737-47.

O'Donohoe, Stephanie 2001, 'Living with ambivalence: Attitudes to advertising in postmodern times', *Marketing Theory Articles,* 1 (1), pp.91-108.

Pongsakornrungsilp, S; Bradshaw, A & Schroeder, JE 2008, 'Brand community as co-creation value in the service-dominant logic of marketing', Customer Research Academy Workshop (CRAWS), University of Manchester, 2-4 April 2008.

Ritson, M & Elliot, R 1999, 'The Social Uses of Advertising: An Ethnographic Study of Adolescent Advertising Audiences', *Journal of Consumer Research,* 26, pp.260-277.

Schouten, JW & McAlexander, JH 1995, 'Subcultures of Consumption: An Ethnography of the New Bikers', *The Journal of Consumer Research,* 22, pp. 43-61.

Szmigin, I & Carrigan, M 2003, 'New Consumption Communities: Resisting the Hegemony of the Marketing Process', Lancaster University, URL (consulted September 2007): http://www.mngt.waikato.ac.nz/ejrot/cmsconference/2003/proceedings/criticalmarketing/Szmigin.pdf.

'Virgin: the world's best passenger complaint letter?' 2009, in Telegraph, London, 20 Mar 2009 retrieved on 8 April 2009 from http://www.telegraph.co.uk/travel/travelnews/4344890/Virgin-the-worlds-best-passenger-complaint-letter.html.

Williams, GP 1997, *Chaos theory tamed,* National Academy Press, Washington DC.

http://www.naomiklein.org/no-logo

http://www.adbusters.org/ (1989)

http://antiadvertisingagency.com/tag/consumer-resistance

Author biography

Robert Aitken is a Senior lecturer in the Department of Marketing at the University of Otago. His academic and research interests include advertising, branding, co-creation, consumer behaviour, service-dominant logic, ethics, communications and the media. He is a constructivist who is interested in how people make sense of the world and an idealist in wanting to know how they propose to make it a better place.

Contact: Department of Marketing, University of Otago, PO Box 56, Dunedin, New Zealand; P 64 3 479 5497; F 64 3 4798172; E rob.aitken@otago.ac.nz.

Discussion questions

To stimulate thoughtful reflection authors have provided the following questions:

Chapter 1 - Perspectives and paradigms in brand management

1. What lies at the heart of brand management – as practiced and as researched?

2. Discuss the extent to which brand management is characterised by irreconcilable paradigms.

3. To which disciplines should a manager turn when engaged in brand management? This question is best considered by placing yourself in the position of a manager who is in the process of developing and launching a new brand, an iPad for instance.

4. Why is it important for any brand manager to understand consumer heterogeneity? In what ways are consumers heterogeneous with respect to the brands they buy and use?

Chapter 2 - Brand equity: Linking financial and customer perspectives

1. For a particular brand, consider the FBBE perspective. How much are the brand assets worth? Should the assets be liquidated? What is the exchange price of the asset?

2. Thinking from the CBBE perspective, how might marketers have an impact on the mental state of consumers to generate market place behaviour such as purchase and brand endorsement?

3. Review how CBBE and FBBE could be linked to gain a better understanding of the brand equity of an established consumer brand.

4. In an acquisitions situation how would an appreciation of CBBE and FBBE be more helpful than relying solely on FBBE metrics?

Chapter 3 - Brand manifold: Managing the temporal and socio-cultural dimensions of brands

1. Drawing on your own experience, discuss ways in which corporations have attempted to control their brand image. How have these attempts at control been successful/unsuccessful? Do you believe the balance of brand control lies more with the corporation or the consumer?

2. Using Popper's 'Three World Trichotomy', can you think of a brand where the product manifest (world one) does not match the abstract perception of the brand (worlds two and three). What are the implications for the brand where the abstract and the concrete do not match?

3. Using the brand manifold analyse and chart Ford as a brand from its creation to today.

4. How have corporations encouraged/discouraged consumers to help create brands?

Chapter 4 – Brand positioning

1. Look up the 'Priceless' campaign on MasterCard's website. Reverse engineer and then write out its apparent T-C-B macro-positioning strategy, explaining your nominations of T, C, and B. Advanced question: Do the same for Visa.

2. Look up the websites for five or six major brands of laundry detergent in your country and identify each brand's key-benefit claim. Which brands are apparently pursuing a 'central' meso-positioning strategy and which brands a 'differentiated' strategy? Advanced question: Fit the brands' benefit claims into an I-D-U matrix (see the Rossiter and Percy or Rossiter and Bellman textbook for how to do this).

3. Take your university, or a local one, as the 'brand' and, using the a-b-e micro-model of positioning, construct for possible use in its advertising:

   an a → b strategy,

   an e⁻ → b strategy, and

   a b → e⁺ strategy.

   Explain your rationale in each case. Advanced question: Generate a good key-benefit claim (a headline for a print ad or brochure) for each strategy.

4. Consult any marketing or advertising textbook (other than mine) and criticise its theory of, or approach to, 'brand positioning' in light of what you have learned from this chapter.

Chapter 5 – Understanding brand performance measures

1. Consider why it is important for managers like Jill Klein to focus their attention on measures of brand performance, especially behavioural (revealed-preference) measures.

2. Look at the tables in this chapter and describe any patterns that you see in the data.

3. List some of the wider implications that Jill might draw from analysing the behavioural data presented in this chapter. For example, can we say something about the brand loyalty of consumers and the partitioning of markets?

4. Encouraged by the analysis of UK data in this chapter, comment on how Jill might go about investigating brand performance in urban China – in say the cities of Nanjin, Tianjin, Shanghai and Guangzhou.

Chapter 6 – Predictable patterns in buyer behaviour and brand metrics: Implications for brand managers

1. The distribution of purchase frequencies for brands invariably follows an NBD distribution. What does this say about the role of marketing mix inputs such as price and advertising?

2. Many authors and commentators are enthusiastic about focusing on existing customers and building customer loyalty. Do the results here suggest a focus on loyalty is unimportant?

3. The chapter suggests that *achieving true points of difference seems elusive*. On what basis is this conclusion made?

4. The idea of emotional bonds and commitment to brands is popular in marketing. Can consumers be deeply committed to brands if they don't pay much attention to the ones they use?

Chapter 7 – A model of brand salience

1. Undertake a brand recall exercise. Recall brands from a particular category (e.g., shampoo). Analyse the first three brands that you have recalled. What made you recall these brands first? Are these brands market leaders? Have you purchased one of these brands recently?

2. For the first three brands recalled in question one, undertake a brand association exercise. Think of the words that you associate with the brand (e.g., Coca Cola is black, fizzy, fun, summer, and cold). Allow yourself one minute per brand. Think about the brand associations that you have recalled for each brand. Are the brand associations positive or negative? Are they different for each brand? How do these associations relate to what you think about the brand?

3. Analyse a brand from your own organisation. Think about the elements that are involved in communicating this brand's position to the public. How does your organisation develop brand knowledge and brand awareness? How might this be improved?

4. What actions could your organisation take to increase the salience of its brands?

Chapter 8 - Co-branding: When mixing images and metaphors can deliver better results

1. What does co-branding mean? What are its advantages and potential dangers?

2. Provide some examples of congruent and incongruent co-branding strategies? Articulate what makes two or more brands 'fit' together and how this can be leveraged effectively.

3. Discuss how sponsorship can involve co-branding. Describe examples from a recent global event.

4. Reflect on how co-branding may also harm brand equity. What risk management strategy can be put in place to mitigate such risks?

Chapter 9 - Employer brands

1. Consider how teams from human resources management and brand management might work together to support a brand.

2. From your own experience, identify a firm that fits into the accurate-attractive cell of Figure 9.4. Discuss how this firm might sustain its employer brand.

3. Now consider a firm that fits into the aspirational-unattractive cell of Figure 9.4. Discuss what might be done to improve the firm's employer brand.

4. Examine the relationship between employer brands and corporate brands. In what ways do the two concepts of brands overlap and differ?

Chapter 10 - Business-to-Business brand management

1. Is the marketing expenditure on branding by B2B marketers justified? Give your reasons.

2. Why are B2C perspectives of brands not always relevant in business to business brand marketing?

3. What can we learn from academic research about building a B2B brand?

4. How do B2B brands help build long term buyer seller relationships?

Chapter 11 - Legal aspects of brand management

1. *The first use in a market of a particular get-up in a market does not confer monopoly or proprietary rights so long as any subsequent use by another trader is not likely to deceive the ordinary reasonable consumer into mistaking that trader's good for the goods of another.*

    The authorities establish that a trader is entitled to adopt the features of competitors' products, providing the result is not likely to deceive or mislead the reasonable consumer into mistaking the trader's goods for the goods of competitors.

    Kenny J in *Nutrientwater Pty Ltd v Baco Pty Ltd* [2010] FCA 2 at 9, 104.

    Consider the implications of these propositions for the brand manager.

2. *In that sense, Mars is a victim of its own success.*

    This comment was made by the trial judge in *Mars Australia Pty Ltd* v *Sweet Rewards Pty Ltd* [2009] FCA 605 in the context of an unsuccessful passing off and misleading conduct action which Mars, the manufacturer of the well-known bite size confectionary known as the Malteser, brought against Sweet Rewards who distributed a similar bite-sized confectionary known as a Malt Ball using packaging which was claimed to be so similar that it was apt to confuse consumers into thinking that Malt Balls were associated with Maltesers or tasted like them. The decision was upheld on appeal by the Full Federal Court ([2009] FCAFC 174). The Court noted that the evidence established that:

    -   *confectionary is commonly packaged in primary colours and that red, in various shades, is a predominant and common, even ubiquitous, colour;*

    -   *confectionary packaging commonly displays a picture or representation of the product, frequently showing a cross-section or 'cut through' of the product;*

    -   *it is not unusual for the name of the product to be written on a diagonal, from bottom left to top right;*

    -   *it is common for packaging to include all of the above features.*

    Consider the extent to which a market leader can protect itself against competitors whose product get-up is a derivative of that of the market leader.

3. When will a company be able to obtain trademark protection for a particular colour which it intends to use in a rebranding of its national network of retail outlets? Will passing off and misleading conduct operate to protect the company from 'copycats' in these circumstances?

4. Trademark rights are granted and protected by domestic law. What complications does this cause for companies in international markets, and what can such companies do to protect their names, marks and brands.

Chapter 12 - Brand evolution and demise

1. Put yourself in the position of brand manager for an iconic brand, such as Ivory Soap in the USA, which has been a market leader for many decades. Market share has dipped slightly in recent months. What would you do?

2. What events would trigger a decision to kill a brand?

3. Under what circumstances would it be possible to revive a brand that has died?

4. How would you go about the process of killing a brand while retaining as much corporate profitability and brand equity as possible?

Chapter 13 - Emerging brands: The case of China

1. As a marketing manager of a Western multinational (MNC), what are the key brand management challenges you would expect to face in China?

2. As the marketing manager of a wholly-owned Chinese firm, what brand management challenges would you expect to face: (a) in the domestic market, and (b) in the export market?

3. To what extent do you expect China brands to evolve and be received in the West? Do you think they will follow a similar or different pattern to Japanese brands in the 1970s–1980s and/or Korean brands in the 1990s?

4. As a brand consultant, would you advise Chinese managers to pursue a monolithic (e.g. Virgin, Yamaha, Mitsubishi, Sony) or a branded (e.g. P&G, Unilever, GM) approach?

Chapter 14 - Consumers' relationships with brands

1. What consumer-brand relationships are you able to identify in your own life?

2. Thinking of these relationships as multiplex phenomena, what key dimensions are there for the brands you buy?

3. Describe the evolution of relationships with the brands that you buy, taking into account your interactions and contextual change.

4. Considering your previous answers, think about how this information might be used by brand managers?

Chapter 15 - Experiential branding

1. Using the Brakus *et al.* (2009) four dimensions of experiential brands, discuss how you could manage the experience of strong experiential brands like Disney and Starbucks through managing each of the four dimensions?

2. Using the Brakus *et al.* (2009) four dimensions of experiential brands, discuss how you could elevate the experience of marginal experiential brands like Harley-Davidson and Blackberry. Discuss both online and offline strategies that you could employ, highlighting which dimensions you are targeting.

3. Explain why it is so challenging to manage an experiential brand. What do you see as the best ways of doing it?

4. If someone approached you for help in designing an experiential brand, what advice would you give? What if it was the Prime Minister, a fundraiser for a local charity or the manager of the local surfing championships?

Chapter 16 - Brand authenticity

1. Why are brands increasingly being seen as authentic?

2. Examine two brands—one you think is authentic and one that is not. What explains the difference?

3. How would you make the fake brand discussed in question 2 above authentic?

4. Are their brands that are mixed? Do you feel some brands may be authentic sometimes but not others? Do you disagree with some the status of some of the brands included here? If so, explain why? In doing so, think of issues such as your personal goals, situation differences, and even demographic factors.

Chapter 17 - Shifting brands: Reception, resistance and revision

1. The question of who 'owns' a brand used to be simple and straightforward-it was the firm. What has happened to our understanding of brands and branding to change this view?

2. In what ways is it possible for consumers to use brands to influence how companies do business?

3. What role do brands play in how people and communities define their identity?

4. What is meant by a brand promise?